THE STATE AND ECONOMIC LIFE

EDITORS: Mel Watkins, University of Toronto; Leo Panitch, York University

5 JAMES P. BICKERTON

Nova Scotia, Ottawa, and the Politics of Regional Development

For at least sixty years the Atlantic provinces have been recognized as a depressed region of Canada. Yet little remedial action of any consequence was taken by the Canadian government until the 1960s. Despite the avowed political commitment to reducing regional disparity, the position of Atlantic Canada in general and Nova Scotia in particular has remained substantially unchanged.

James Bickerton approaches the politics of regional development by focusing on the historical periphery-centre relationship between Nova Scotia and Ottawa. Political, ideological, and organizational factors for many years blocked the development of any concerted regional policy at the centre, to the detriment of the periphery.

Eventually conditions favoured a shift in the attitude of the federal government toward the region and its economic problems. But the resulting policies were shaped by political forces largely beyond the control of periphery élites. The compromises, half-measures, sporadic attention, and numerous policy shifts that characterized 'regional development' over the past twenty-five years have left basic regional inequalities intact.

Still, the author concludes, even these inadequate activities provided Nova Scotia and the whole Atlantic region with at least a vacillating flow of resources for discretionary economic development spending, and these would not have been otherwise available.

JAMES BICKERTON is Assistant Professor in the Department of Political Science, St. Francis Xavier University.

Nova Scotia, Ottawa, and the Politics of Regional Development

JAMES P. BICKERTON

UNIVERSITY OF TORONTO PRESS
Toronto Buffalo London

© University of Toronto Press 1990
Toronto Buffalo London
Printed in Canada

ISBN 0-8020-2711-3 (cloth)
ISBN 0-8020-6745-X (paper)

Printed on acid-free paper

Canadian Cataloguing in Publication Data

Bickerton, James
  Nova Scotia, Ottawa, and the politics of regional development

  Includes bibliographical references.
  ISBN 0-8020-2711-3 (bound) ISBN 0-8020-6745-X (pbk.)

  1. Nova Scotia – Economic conditions – 1867–1918.*
  2. Nova Scotia – Economic conditions – 1918–1945.*
  3. Nova Scotia – Economic conditions – 1945–   .*
  4. Regional planning – Canada.   5. Canada – Economic policy.   6. Federal-
  provincial relations – Nova Scotia.*   I. Title.

  HC117.N68B52 1990   338.9716   C90-093528-6

Contents

Preface

I came by my interest in the subject-matter of this book quite naturally. Growing up in industrial Cape Breton provided an almost visceral experience of the meaning of regional disparities and the large role assumed by government in what could euphemistically be described as 'a declining region.' The grand illusion in capitalist societies of the separation of the public and private sectors, of 'politics' and 'economy,' always flimsy at best on Cape Breton Island, disappeared entirely with the DOSCO crisis and regional-development programs of the 1960s. At a time of national economic prosperity and an expanding public sector, hope for economic salvation and renewal through concerted government intervention did not seem unfounded. Subsequent events made a mockery of those original hopes. What went wrong? What was the true nature of the relationship between 'politics' and 'economy' as it pertained to the plight of a community, indeed a whole region, relegated to the margins of the Canadian economy and polity? The answer to this question, of course, turned out to be more complex and the obstacles to any fundamental change in the lot of the periphery more imposing, than my original assumptions would have led me to believe.

During the researching and writing of this work, a number of people provided me with support, encouragement, and guidance. Professors Leo Panitch, Jane Jenson, and Maureen Molot were important to this undertaking, and played a crucial role as sources of insight, support, and encouragement, not only in the writing of the original thesis, but during the whole period of my graduate work at Carleton University. A close friend and colleague, Alain Gagnon, provided me with an example of diligence as well as a constant and much-appreciated gentle prodding throughout the life of the project. Other companions and colleagues at

Carleton, now widely dispersed, were also helpful and supportive. At St Francis Xavier University, Bernie Liengme proved exceedingly generous with his time and assistance in the last-minute rush to move words from disc to print. My deepest gratitude is reserved for my wife, Theresa MacNeil, who lived with this manuscript as long as I did, and saw me through to the end.

I should also like to express my gratitude to the Social Sciences and Humanities Research Council of Canada, which provided me with a Doctoral Fellowship between 1981 and 1984.

This book has been published with the help of a grant from the Social Science Federation of Canada, using funds provided by the Social Sciences and Humanities Research Council of Canada.

J.P.B.

Abbreviations

ADA	Area Development Agency
ADB	Atlantic Development Board
AIB	Anti-Inflation Board
APEC	Atlantic Provinces Economic Council
APPDA	Atlantic Provinces Power Development Act
ARDA	Agricultural and Rural Development Agency
BEDM	Board of Economic Development Ministers
BESCO	British Empire Steel and Coal Corporation
CBLP	Cape Breton Labour Party
CBRT	Canadian Brotherhood of Railway, Transport and General Workers Union
CCF	Co-operative Commonwealth Federation
CCL	Canadian Congress of Labour
CFFU	Canadian Fishermen and Fish Handlers Union
CFU	Canadian Fishermen's Union
CSU	Canadian Seaman's Union
DCL	Deuterium of Canada Ltd.
DEVCO	Cape Breton Development Corporation
DOSCO	Dominion Steel and Coal Corporation
DREE	Department of Regional Economic Expansion
DRIE	Department of Regional Industrial Expansion
ECC	Economic Council of Canada
EFF	Eastern Fishermen's Federation
ERDA	Economic and Regional Development Agreement
FRED	Fund for Rural Economic Development
GDA	General Development Agreement
ICR	Intercolonial Railway

ICTIP	Interdepartmental Committee on Trade and Industrial Policy
IEL	Industrial Estates Limited
ITC	Department of Industry Trade and Commerce
JLMSC	Joint Labour-Management Study Committee
MBTTC	Maritime Board of Trade Transportation Committee
MCPAA	Maritime Coal Production Assistance Act
MFRA	Maritime Freight Rates Act
MFU	Maritime Fishermen's Union
MMRA	Maritime Marshlands Rehabilitation Act
MSED	Ministry of State for Economic Development
MSERD	Ministry of State for Economic and Regional Development
Nat Sea	National Sea Products
NDP	New Democratic Party
NEP	National Energy Program
NFFAWU	Newfoundland Fish, Food, and Allied Workers Union
NIRD	National Industrial and Regional Development
NSFL	Nova Scotia Federation of Labour
NSPC	Nova Scotia Power Corporation
OBU	One Big Union Movement
OTA	Occupational Training Act
PCO	Privy Council Office
PIC	Prices and Incomes Commission
PIP	Petroleum Incentives Program
PMO	Prime Minister's Office
PRA	Nova Scotia Petroleum Resources Act
QWU	Nova Scotia Quarry Workers Union
RDIA	Regional Development Incentives Act
SIU	Seaman's International Union
SPS	Special Planning Secretariat
SYSCO	Sydney Steel Corporation
TAC	Total Allowable Catch
TLC	Trades and Labor Congress
TQM	Trans-Quebec Maritimes Pipeline
TVTA	Technical and Vocational Training Act
UFAWU	United Fishermen and Allied Workers Union
UI	Unemployment Insurance Program
UMF	United Maritime Fishermen
UMW	United Mine Workers
VEPB	Voluntary Economic Planning Board

Royal Commissions and Task Forces

1917   Royal Commission to Inquire into Railways and
        Transportation (Drayton-Ackworth Commission)
1925–6 Royal Commission on the Coal Mining Industry in Nova
        Scotia (Duncan Commission)
1926   Royal Commission on Maritime Claims (Duncan
        Commission)
1927   Royal Commission on the Fisheries (MacLean Commission)
1934   Royal Commission of Provincial Economic Inquiry (Jones
        Commission)
1935   Royal Commission on Financial Arrangements Between the
        Dominion and the Maritime Provinces (White Commission)
1937–40 Royal Commission on Dominion-Provincial Relations
        (Rowell-Sirois Commission)
1944   Royal Commission on Provincial Development and
        Rehabilitation (Dawson Commission)
1946   Royal Commission on Coal (Carroll Commission)
1949   Royal Commission on Transportation (Turgeon
        Commission)
1957   Royal Commission on Canada's Economic Prospects
        (Gordon Commission)
1960   Royal Commission on Coal (Rand Commission)
1960   Royal Commission on Transportation (MacPherson
        Commission)
1962   Provincial Fact-Finding Body on Labour Legislation
        (Mackinnon Task Force)
1966   Royal Commission on the Nova Scotia Coal Industry
        (Donald Commission)

1969 Royal Commission on Industrial Relations in the Construction Industry (Woods Commission)

1974 Royal Commission on Education, Public Services, and Provincial-Municipal Relations (Graham Commission)

1979 Nova Scotia Department of Development Task Force on SYSCO

1981 Task Force on Major Projects (Blair-Carr Task Force)

1982 Task Force on Atlantic Fisheries (Kirby Task Force)

Nova Scotia, Ottawa, and the Politics of Regional Development

Introduction

Though the ultimate stakes in politics reflect the conflict between capital and labour, politics mediates that conflict in a thousand different ways that, between them, turn domination into hegemony.[1]

The Maritimes has been recognized as a depressed region of Canada for at least the past sixty years. The first major government inquiry into the region's depressed economic state was undertaken in 1926.[2] While Newfoundland fared even worse after its entry into Confederation in 1949, there was little remedial action of any consequence taken by the Canadian state to address this problem until the 1960s. Even then, despite a significant advance in the standard of living within the region, and the avowed political commitment to reducing regional disparities embodied in the creation and thirteen-year history of the Department of Regional Economic Expansion (DREE), the position of Atlantic Canada within Confederation remained substantially unchanged; indeed, it is arguable that in some respects it has worsened.[3] For example, earned-income shares per capita by region have changed only marginally since 1926; worse, in the 1980s unemployment levels in the four Atlantic provinces have been at their highest since the 1930s.

This book will explore the changing role of politics and the state in centre-periphery relations in Canada through an examination of the politics of regional development. While excellent work on the underdevelopment of the Maritime provinces has been done of late, and some consensus exists on the general historical pattern of industrialization, deindustrialization, and marginality of the region within Confederation, disagreement and debate persist over the exact causes of regional underdevelopment, the meaning of contemporary problems and developments within the region, and the historical role of politics and the state in Maritime underdevelopment.[4] Much of this disagreement is rooted in divergent theoretical understandings of the nature and dynamics of the development process in capitalist democracies. Such understandings have informed and directed analyses of the problem, creating certain biases towards the discovery of particular causes for observed effects, and leading from there, in (sometimes) logical progression, to the suggestion of potential or probable solutions.

The position will be taken here that in order to understand the role of the state in the process of capitalist development, the state should be conceptualized as *a field of political struggle for socio-political forces*, and that, as such, it is simultaneously a *product* and a *determinant* of this process. This position demands an analysis of the relationship between politics, the state, and the development process on the periphery. Under certain conditions politics in capitalist democracies reinforces the subordinate status of underdeveloped peripheries. But in other circumstances it can ameliorate, 'cushion,' or compensate for this political and economic subordination. In the case of Canada, the mechanisms that underlie the historical domination of the centre over the Atlantic-Canadian periphery need to be explored, as do the attempts by social classes and socio-political forces on the periphery in general to utilize the channels available to them to make gains and secure concessions from the centre. Of course, it must be understood that 'gains' and 'concessions' may be either narrowly restricted to certain groups in the region or widely shared. To this extent the concept of 'region' must not be permitted to obscure the social and political divisions, conflicts, and diversity of interests that go to make up the region, and the ongoing political struggle to have *particular* interests defined as 'the regional interest.'

To begin, how is one to understand the process of *development* and the uneven benefits and costs it appears to bestow upon different regions? Development is an ambiguous and amorphous concept that is commonly used to denote both a perceived societal state or *condition* (e.g., 'developed' states versus 'less-developed' or 'underdeveloped' states) and a dynamic *process*. Unlike 'growth,' which refers to the simple quantitative expansion of the production of goods and services within a given economic structure, development generally requires expansion along with diversification and structural change. A developed economy can be expected to have the capacity to produce an expanding quantity of goods and services as well as expanded opportunities for the realization of human capacities and potentials in an environment conducive to a high quality of life. The process of development must therefore be considered as a dynamic one, with a qualitative dimension. Schumpeter has characterized it as 'creative destruction,' embodying growth, innovation, and change. This emphasis on 'process,' however, is often accompanied by implicit notions of purpose or outcome, such as the free and full realization of human potentials, both individual and collective. Thus, the Atlantic Provinces Economic Council (APEC) has defined 'development' as the process by which all members of society gain access to an expanding number of opportunities for personal and collective growth.[5]

Underdevelopment is a concept that has meaning only in relation to development and, like the latter, is often used to denote a condition and/or a process. In some formulations, the use of the term 'underdeveloped' can be understood to mean the simple absence of both the condition and the process of development. (Alternatively, the absence of the condition but the presence of the process earns the designation 'developing.') However, 'underdevelopment' has also been used to denote an ongoing process that, in its effects, is the mirror image of development. This formulation is most commonly associated with those dependency theorists who argue that, under capitalism, the development of some societies and regions (those at the centre) is predicated upon the active underdevelopment of others (on the periphery). The accumulation process produces expanding wealth at one pole and increasing impoverishment at the other.

Accumulation is a more precise term than economic growth for capturing what goes on when economic growth occurs in a capitalist economy.

In the capitalist marketplace, firms do not simply become larger and more profitable, thereby adding to aggregate economic activity, or conversely, smaller or bankrupt, thereby subtracting from the aggregate. Rather, when looked at collectively, all this frantic activity tends toward the transformation of the process of production itself. This occurs because the competitive units must 'accumulate' in order to survive. That is, they are forced to reinvest a substantial portion of the economic surplus produced by their workers in order to keep up with the new efficiencies and technological breakthroughs being made by other firms in the world economy. Thus, the accumulation process denotes qualitative as well as simply quantitative change.[6]

Though essential to a process of capitalist development, 'accumulation' is not coterminous with 'development.' However, the accumulation process, continually spurred on by the demands of capitalist competition and the logic of capital accumulation, does hold the key to understanding the basic underlying dynamic of regionally circumscribed processes of development/underdevelopment. Within the confines of a capitalistically structured world economy, no occupation, skill, industry, or region is insulated from the dynamics of the process of ever-expanding accumulation: forced participation and competition become the rule. The populations of regions either compete – in some way become more integrated, profit-yielding, and productive in their economic activities – or leave themselves open to a process of external domination and long-term degeneration into marginality and underdevelopment.

In capitalist societies most of the power to effect the transformation of regional economies remains under the control and within the realm of private capital, and over time such power and control have tended to become more concentrated and centralized. In the case of Canada, the central government's historic relationship with capital and labour, and the 'Americanization' of key sectors of the Canadian economy, limited the ability of the state to influence capital's strategies and decisions in such a way as to simultaneously maximize benefits for the national economy, for peripheral regional economies, and for subaltern classes within the Canadian social formation. While the subordinate integration of Canadian productive capacity into the North American economy as a mainly branch-plant operation and storehouse of natural resources inhibited the potential for diversified growth and development in all of Canada's regions, in the Maritimes the 'space' for a viable regional manufacturing capacity was increasingly constricted as control over investment, technology, and markets was alienated from the periphery and devolved to national or international firms in the larger centres.

Within the context of this oligopolistic, externally controlled structure, with its disadvantageous patterns of investment and production for peripheral regions, the attempt to advance the development process within the Maritimes, even 'staving off' further erosion of its already vulnerable position, becomes a formidable challenge. *Politics* can and does exert important effects upon the pattern and course of capital accumulation. There are a number of ways to define politics, largely dependent upon the particular model or paradigm that is used to interpret what is 'political' and what is not. Most contemporary definitions place the authoritative allocation of scarce values at the centre of what is considered 'political' in society, in other words, the state. But while *the state* – defined by Macridis and Brown as 'all the structures and organizations that make decisions and resolve conflicts with the expectation that their decisions will be obeyed: the civil service, the legislature, the executive, the judiciary, the host of public or semi-public corporations and organizations that are called upon to resolve differences and to make decisions'[7] – is at the core of any definition of it, politics should not be understood to be limited simply to the actions and deliberations of the state proper. Politics is also about the ways and means by which some people or groups acquire and maintain influence or control over this process, that is, with *relations of political power* in society.

However, although the political realm remains *potentially* responsive to the demands of subordinate classes and regions, and therefore useful as a means of combating marginality and underdevelopment within particular social formations, it does not follow that politics will *necessarily* perform this role. Neither does it follow that *limitations* may exist on the use of politics for this purpose. In their attempt to combat the consequences of their own marginality the Maritime provinces since the 1920s have attempted to alter the attitude of the national political élites and the policies of the central government with regard to the plight of disadvantaged regions. This course was adopted because within the political and economic context of Confederation purely local social and political movements could not hope to secure successfully the necessary structural changes that would improve regional economic conditions. Yet the strategy of utilizing established political channels to influence national policies proved to be of dubious merit as the interests of a small peripheral region such as the Maritimes were often neglected or sacrificed to brokerage politics within the national parties, or to the demands of intergovernmental bargaining in a federal system, or to entrenched ideological and policy orientations reflecting the established balance of power within Canadian society and within the state itself.

Despite numerous set-backs for Maritimers in their quest to involve the central authorities more intimately in the resolution of their economic problems, in more recent times the Canadian state has played an ever-increasing role in encouraging and advancing a process of economic change within the region. Yet any preconceptions or expectations that the developmental tendency of such a modernization process inevitably would be one of a spatially homogeneous, integrated capitalism have been shown to be sadly mistaken. An even regional dispersion of the factors and conditions of 'development' does not appear to be in any way spontaneous, inevitable, inherent, or natural, and contradictions, counter-tendencies, and blockages of various sorts have been strewn in the path of any linear development process. With industrial bases that are underdeveloped relative to their service and public sectors, with chronically low labour-force participation rates and high unemployment rates, and with evidence of a continuous increase in the degree of dependence on federal transfer payments,[8] the Atlantic provinces, despite a quarter-century of varying levels of state attention to the matter, demonstrably have not been pulled out of the whirlpool of regional economic decline, though the situation has been made more palatable. A revivification of private-capital accumulation in the region through state subsidization has failed to produce the surge of self-perpetuating private investment and diversity of economic activity that was anticipated. The level of per capita private investment remains well below the Canadian average,[9] and now the rising social expenses that accompany poor economic performance are increasingly under attack for their contribution to bloated government deficits, while a return to the discipline of market forces is advocated as an alternative.

Given the current situation, how are we to understand the history of state involvement in regional development, and the apparent failure of state policies? The origins, objectives, and rationale of a range of policies and programs that can be loosely categorized under the heading 'for the purpose of regional development' can be best explained through reference to the social and political forces attempting to exert influence over state actions in this area. The interests, class basis, ideological disposition, and political motivations of the actors involved have been varied, as has been reflected in the hodgepodge of state actions (and non-actions) in the field of regional development. Tom Kent, former deputy minister for the Department of Regional Economic Expansion (DREE), and past president of both the Cape Breton Development Corporation (DEVCO) and the Sydney Steel Corporation (SYSCO), in lamenting the brief rise and early decline of regional-development policy in Canada, has argued that 'regional development' in Canada suffered as the result of an *intellectual failure*. 'The failure [of regional development] was not star-dictated. It was intellectual. The sad fact is that, despite the obvious strength of regional concerns in a country as large and thinly populated and diverse as Canada, regional policies have been allowed to be the most unclear of public issues.'[10]

According to Kent, this lack of clarification of the problem and the issues involved hindered not only the design of appropriate policies, but also the generation of a high level of public awareness, knowledge, sensitivity, and debate on the relevant issues, a necessary prerequisite for the long-term political commitment and public effort needed to adequately address the problem. Of course, the fact of the matter is, this 'intellectual failure' had a *social* and *political* causation. It was rooted in the contending interests and forces that promoted and defined the issue, determined its meaning, and shaped policy content. Depending upon *which* forces were predominant or uppermost in influencing and shaping *particular* state initiatives, 'regional development' – as an *issue* and a *policy field* – took on a different hue. Moreover, this policy process took place within parameters of political struggle that were determined by historical conditions and circumstances that worked to expand or constrict the 'margin of manoeuvre' available to regional political forces on the periphery to win gains or concessions from the centre.

In this context a number of questions can be posed. How has the issue of *regional development* been 'constructed' in Canadian politics and promoted to the state agenda? How has it been related, if at all, to other major issues, such as intergovernmental fiscal relations, social policy, economic policy, and ethno-national relations? How has it been fitted into partisan political strategies and what has been the influence of party competition and shifting political alignments on the receptivity of parties to the issue? How has the problem been understood by regional representatives and state functionaries, federal and provincial? And how have the 'politics' of regional development been transformed into 'policies' put forward as solutions? Finally, what are the conditions – economic, ideological, political – that govern the extent of influence regional political forces are likely to wield over national policies? That is, *when can significant concessions be won for the periphery, in what circumstances, and with what types of arguments*?

The purpose of this book is to inquire into the political economy of centre-periphery relations through a historical analysis of regional development as a *political issue* and as a *policy field*. Its focus is the emergence and construction of the issue of disparities in regional development, the timing and mode of state intervention into this field, the factors shaping the government's program of action and the general principles of legislation subsequently enacted, and finally the broad effects of state policy in this area. The approach can be characterized as a form of class analysis that draws upon various Marxist theories of politics and the state, but also upon the writings of non-Marxist political theorists, particularly Sidney Tarrow's, on centre-periphery relations. Data have been drawn from numerous primary and secondary sources: books and articles published on various aspects of Canadian government and politics and regional-development policies in Canada; the documents and reports of a number of governmental and non-governmental departments, agencies, and commissions; newspaper reports and accounts; archival papers; and personal interviews.

1 Development and Underdevelopment on the Periphery: Competing Perspectives

This chapter argues that in capitalist democracies the process of development cannot be understood independently of the sphere of politics and the state. Yet, as will be shown, this sphere has been either ignored or simplistically interpreted in the various analyses that have been undertaken on the question of the underdevelopment of Canada's Maritime provinces. This exclusion or reduction of the 'political' has stemmed from the theoretical deficiencies or biases of the analysts, a shortcoming that has led to an incomplete or distorted view of centre-periphery relations in Canada and the process of capitalist development on the periphery.

It should not be assumed that the capitalist state is neutral in the reproduction of regional inequalities, but neither can it be asserted that the actions of that same state are necessarily and everywhere contributory to the reproduction of uneven regional development. Marxist analyses in particular have often proceeded directly from the imputed needs of capital to the actions of the state. A review and critique of some of the relevant literature follows.

Mainstream Perspectives on Regional Development

Numerous studies have attempted to explain the underdevelopment of the Maritime provinces within Confederation but, until recently, scholarly historical research into Maritime politics, economy, and society dealt mainly with the pre-Confederation period, and somewhat less so with Confederation itself.[1] This preoccupation with the formative years of the region, preceding and leading up to its union with the Canadas, reflects the attraction for historians that has been held by the region's role in the imperial rivalries of the eighteenth century, as well as its role in the constitutional development of British North America.

According to noted regional historian E.R. Forbes, the negligible role accorded the Maritimes by the dominant school of historians in Canada is indicative of the strong influence exercised by Frederick Jackson Turner's frontier thesis. In 1893 Turner published his famous essay setting out the hypothesis of the westward-moving American frontier acting as a ' "crucible" in which "immigrants were Americanized, liberated, and fused into a mixed race," ' in the process sloughing off their ideas of social stratification with other cultural baggage. The thesis, which argued that the frontier was the source of America's dynamism, could be readily applied to Canada, and Forbes finds ample evidence of the pervasive influence of this thesis in the writings of many Canadian historians. One of the implications of this was to cast the long-settled Maritimes – 'that part of the country furthest removed from the frontier stage' – in a negative light. Simple logic suggested that the attributes of the people of this region would be in direct contrast to those of the dynamic frontier. Not only did this mode of analysis divert attention away from the Maritimes, it contributed to an image of the region as 'conservative, socially stratified, and unprogressive.'[2]

The Staples Thesis

Work done on the economic development of the region in the post-Confederation period did nothing to alter this impression of the Maritimes, and indeed formed the perfect complement to the social and cultural implications of the frontier approach. What was to become the dominant explanation for the decline of the Maritimes – from prosperous colonies in 1860 to one of the depressed backwaters of the Canadian economy by 1930 – painted a rather dismal and uneventful picture, one that would certainly discourage further critical inquiry into the region's fate.[3] The 'orthodox point of view' on the decline of the Maritimes was the staples argument of Fay and Innis[4] and S.A. Saunders.[5] This approach, first elaborated by Canadian economic historians H.A. Innis[6] and W.A. Mackintosh,[7] cites Canada's exploitation of its resource endowment for external markets as the motive force in its historical development. Growth and change in the Canadian economy and society were dependent upon external demand for resources in which Canada possessed a comparative advantage. Changes in technology affected both the type of resources in demand and the mode of exploitation.

The application of the staples model to the case of the Maritimes led to the widely accepted thesis that the economic stagnation of the region within Confederation was the outcome of inexorable technological changes that left its resource endowment marginal to the pattern of growth in twentieth-century North America. Saunders argued that neither the Reciprocity Treaty (1854) nor Confederation was 'fundamental in determining economic trends in the Maritimes' during the 1850–80 period, which marked the high point and decline of the traditional staples-based economy. He put the emphasis instead on the failure of overseas markets, the passing of wood-and-wind ship technology, and the failure to adapt to the new continentally oriented Canadian economy.[8] The rapid disappearance of Maritime manufacturing after 1919 was seen in terms of 'readjustments,' Maritime industry being simply too weak to be competitive.[9]

The proponents of the staples approach typically placed a heavy emphasis on geographic and technological factors in the process of development. But its founders disagreed over its eventual impact on the pattern of development in Canada, with Mackintosh seeing the staples trade as providing the basis for a stage theory of growth and Innis more pessimistic about breaking out of the staples role of 'hewers of wood and drawers of water.' He warned of the potential implications of being trapped in the role of staples producer for more highly industrialized and diversified economies – a role he clearly foresaw Canada falling into when he posited its progression in the twentieth century 'from colony to nation to colony.' Yet, neither Mackintosh nor Innis claimed that this reliance on the exploitation and export of some natural resource, or combination thereof, was *necessarily* a permanent condition for new settler societies or more mature staples producers on the periphery.

In this sense the continued reference to a staples-based conception of regional economic development in the contemporary context can be accused, in the context of a mature industrial society such as Canada's, of distorting the staples thesis and offering a narrowly restricted view of economic development, one that grossly exaggerates the potential of natural-resource exploitation to provide the basis for an advanced industrial economy. In effect, it amounts to a thinly veiled justification for the historic overreliance on resources that has characterized the Canadian economy, especially in so-called hinterland regions such as the Maritimes. The staples approach has also been criticized for its tendency to 'dehumanize' historical social processes. Thus, the state has received relatively little attention in staples analysis save for its role as a provider of infrastructure for resource exploitation. The motivations and strategies of élites within the state, as well as the internal conflicts that inevitably have arisen – an especially frequent and telling occurrence within federal states where region-based interests are institutionalized – have been downplayed or simply ignored as not being important or relevant factors. In this way the staples approach has been prone to a certain geographic and technological determinism.

Cultural Explanations

If the staples analysis established the outlines of conventional academic opinion about the Maritimes until the 1970s, its basic line of argument was expanded upon in the writings of a new generation of scholars, such as J.M.S. Careless[10] and George Rawlyk.[11] As Michael Clow has noted, with these writers the by-now-accepted explanation for Maritime underdevelopment based on geography, technological change, and lack of resources was supplemented and reinforced by claims of a regional parochialism and conservatism that led to such deficiencies as a lack of entrepreneurship and initiative and an irrational resistance to change. 'Culture' was thus recruited in the effort to explain the historic failure of Maritime firms to diversify, invest in new technologies, or take the necessary risks in establishing or expanding manufacturing ventures. A variation on this type of explanation points to a lack of adequate entrepreneurship as a residual factor in explaining Maritime underdevelopment. Representative of this genre is the work of Roy George on manufacturing in Nova Scotia. Having found little or no real difference between the potential viability of industry in Ontario and Nova Scotia, he concludes that entrepreneurship was lacking in the Nova Scotia case as a result of 'isolation' from outside economic contacts, a statement that flies in the face of all available information on the economic history of the province.[12]

Cultural explanations for the problems of the Maritimes have also carried over into analyses of politics in the region. The standard treatment of the subject limits itself almost exclusively to an unflattering portrayal of parties and elections in the region governed in their form and content by a conservative, cynical political culture in which participation is ritualistic and patronage and corruption are rife.

The received image of politics in the Maritimes leads researchers to emphasize the distribution of attitudes towards government (which are usually portrayed as conservative and cynical), the organization and orientations of parties (which are hierarchical and pragmatic), the mobilization of partisanship (which is intense but personal rather than programmatic), and the distribution of post-electoral spoils (which, apart from the spectacle and psychic rewards of belonging to a team, is presumed to motivate the participants).[13]

In essence, politics in the Maritimes was seen to be *clientist*. This term refers to the predominant role played in political organization and processes by clientele networks, 'composed of personal networks through which individuals unequal in status, wealth, and influence exchange goods, generally material favours, for loyalty and political support ... In the parties, complex regional networks come together to form great teams of "friends" fighting for power.'[14] The stubborn remnants of this mode of analysis continue today. But where once this account of politics in the Maritimes may have been scholarly if primarily descriptive, in the current context it is ossified and increasingly irrelevant. No longer even scholarly, it has been forced into a reliance on 'occasional scandal and anecdotes' in order to paint yet again its familiar regional picture, but now on an ever-shrinking canvas.[15]

In general this cultural explanation for the backwardness and underdevelopment of the periphery complements a particular philosophy of centre-periphery relations, one that embodies to varying degrees a conception of the periphery as isolated, distant from the centre, and traditional in its perspectives. Typical of an approach to the periphery that has been characterized by Tarrow as the 'diffusion-isolation' model of centre-periphery relations, this model has deep roots in Western philosophical thought. It has attained its purest expression, however, in the work of functional sociologists such as Edward Shils. Here both class and territorial conflicts were assimilated to the zero-sum scale of adherence to a central value system. The problem for Shils's élites within this system was to diffuse their 'modern' values to society's periphery. Ruling consisted of the universalization within the boundaries of society of these central values and the rules inherent in the ordering of modern society.[16]

This model of periphery traditionalism and isolation, besides embodying, in Tarrow's words, an 'immense conservatism,' reflects the approach to the periphery of élites who seek to control, regulate, and reform it. However, vis-à-vis the élite, 'the strategy of the periphery is defensive, and it may place the mask of tradition over revolt that springs from more modern sources. And vis-à-vis the periphery, the elite must develop an ideology – like Shils' – to turn its domination into legitimized hegemony.'[17]

Elements of this 'diffusion-isolation' model of centre-periphery relations are present in macro-scale, universalizing *development theory*, a synthesis of ideas that originated in post–Second World War United States and Western Europe. The economic backwardness of the periphery was seen to be a function of its exclusion or isolation from the centre (i.e., Western industrial 'core' societies). Initially the *economic isolation* of the Third World was pointed to as the culprit. But the continuation of economic malaise despite increasing economic ties with the developed world led to analyses of the role played by the periphery's *oppressive traditional culture*. This obstacle to development could be overcome by the internal restructuring of these societies and, more generally, by an influx of developmental conditions from societies that had already completed the transition to 'modernity.' Central to this process were the international capitalist economy and the modern state, both important vehicles for the propagation of modernizing norms in traditional societies.

The Market Model

The ideas at the core of the developmental approach meshed nicely with the nostrums of mainstream neoclassical economics, and in the 1950s and 1960s Canadian economists were able to borrow from both to state with all the authority of their discipline the 'causes' of regional underdevelopment in their own 'developed' country. The general line was laid down as early as the late 1940s, when B.S. Kierstead argued the inevitability of Maritime decline within Confederation because of its location on the fringe of the tariff-protected Canadian market.[18] Other 'causes' that came to be cited in subsequent years included such factors as a dearth of entrepreneurship, a relatively poor natural-resource base, a lack of adequate infrastructure, and a small regional population. All these factors in one way or another helped to explain the economic 'retardation' of the region.[19] Remedial measures in this situation could hope to improve individual factors or facets of the regional economy to make them conform more closely to the image of economic modernity, but ultimately these were likely to be little more than palliatives designed to maintain what was essentially an uneconomic pocket of regional poverty. This form of explanation allows the analyst to continue to understand chronic regional disparities through the self-adjusting equilibrium models of the neoclassical paradigm and the ideology of the market. If it is assumed that the free play of market forces and competition leads to the most rational and efficient use of resources and the maximization of wealth-creation for a society, then significant anomalies within this scenario, such as chroni-

cally lagging regions, demand either reassessment of the model or appro-
bation of fault or failure in the operation of particular components within
the model. Above all, what is usually implied in such explanations is the
absence of the requisite entrepreneurial zeal that is a 'normal' part of the
essentially acquisitive and competitive nature of man as posited by the
utilitarian philosophy underlying neoclassical economics. If 'regional
man' fails to live up to the caricature of human motivation and action
embodied in this model, the fault is his own, or rather that of the cultural
and social milieu and influences that led to his downfall in the competitive
market-place.[20]

Causes for 'market failure' may also or alternatively be found in
'external' interference in the workings of the market, such as ill-advised
government policies.[21] Indeed, by assuming perfectly operating product
and factor markets in its models, neoclassical economics acknowledges no
valid role for politics and the state in the pattern of economic development except to provide a suitable framework for the operation of the
market (that is, conditions that encourage flexibility in prices and wages
and mobility of capital and labour). Political interference in the machinations of the market's 'invisible hand' can cause only distortions in its
beneficent effects. Thus, the historical pattern of uneven regional development is blamed on market failure brought on by circumstances and/or
the actions of policy-makers. The cure is to restore conditions in which
markets can operate more freely. Excessive unemployment is cured by
removing barriers to mobility and lowering the price of labour.[22]

This approach to regional disparities, recalling as it does the halcyon
days of free enterprise and the rule of unhindered market forces, has
struck a chord of late among modern neo-conservatives rebelling against
the expansion of state expenditures in the 1960s and 1970s, particularly
'welfare' expenditures of all sorts, whether these are directed to individuals or to lagging regions. It is indeed ironic that there should be this
reaction to state intervention in the field of regional development, considering that it was the inability of the market to solve the problem of
persistent regional disparities that precipitated this selfsame intervention.

Questioning the Market Model

Neoclassical assumptions of a self-adjusting equilibrium that operates
between the migration of labour to areas of economic growth and the
migration of capital to areas of cheap land and labour costs have been
upset in the Canadian case by the concentration of manufacturing capital

in central Canada. The 'demand pull' for labour in initial areas of high growth is supplemented by a 'migration push' that ensures the existence of a surplus urban population upon which capital may continue to draw. Meanwhile, in areas of out-migration, productive sectors of the population are lost, the tax base is eroded, and infrastructure and services deteriorate – all of which discourage capital investment. Continued out-migration, while relieving areas of high unemployment of some of that burden in the short term, is also likely to worsen the long-term economic prospects of the region. To allow such a situation to continue unabated is to incur great social and political, and ultimately economic, costs without 'curing' the original problem of regional disparities at all.

Most important, perhaps, neoclassical explanations for uneven regional development are ahistorical. They cannot conceive of the role of political decisions in shaping the pattern of development. As argued by Alexander, 'These exercises are frequently unconvincing because of their circularity: the evidence of what did happen is used in restrictive models to show that only that could happen. Little weight is allowed for the cumulative effect on a country of making the right decisions, maximizing all the opportunities, and, above all, defining economic, social and cultural goals and means independently of modal patterns emanating from metropolitan centers.'[23]

The inability of basic neoclassical models to deal with the persistence of regional disparities ultimately led to the rise of a separate school of regional science and to a diverse assortment of explanations that attribute the problems of regional development to the failure of one or more institutional factors that play some role in standard neoclassical models.[24] Within this approach the role of the state becomes that of technocratic 'fixer,' devising and implementing the right mix of policies to produce the necessary climate and conditions to entice private investment and thus begin a virtuous spiral of economic growth and diversification. In other words, a transcendent equilibrium could be achieved by state-directed adjustments in order to correct the spatial distortions generated by the operation of market forces. Thus, the notion of purposely 'stepping down' the dynamism of the core to new growth centres in peripheral regions, first elaborated upon by François Perroux and Gunnar Myrdal, led to the spread of growth-pole and growth-centre strategies as the international leitmotiv of regional planning in the 1960s and 1970s.[25]

However, like Keynes's theories on state intervention for the purpose of 'smoothing out' business cycles, regional science formulations treat 'politics' as a potential threat to the rational management of the economy. It is something to be kept at bay if state planners are to be free to discover and implement the operational measures that would ensure the rational integration of development programs and enable existing public and private agencies and actors to co-operate more effectively in the realization of desired goals. The major problem is the design and/or adaptation of government machinery for the task of supplementing what is perceived to be a generally efficient market mechanism: 'planning efforts need only be concentrated where there are breakdowns [in the market mechanism] or resolutions at less than optimum results.'[26]

Combined with a generally paternalistic view of politics in the Maritimes, this imperative of technocratic control over the planning process undoubtedly contributed to the reluctance of state élites at the centre to give up control over regional-development planning and expenditures to 'junior governments' in the regions. But even if this had not led to intergovernmental conflict over policy design and implementation (which it inevitably did), a politicization of the state planning process would have occurred in any event. This politicization occurs because state intervention in the field of regional development makes *explicit* many questions of 'control,' 'social goals,' and 'the distribution of benefits' that otherwise remain implicit – largely 'unasked' – in those other approaches that place their emphasis on aspects of the market mechanism. Who participates in the design of the plan? What are the goals and objectives of the planning process? What are the criteria to be used for the targeting of development efforts? How is a redistribution of developmental investment between richer and poorer regions to be accomplished? Thus, while some programs rather naïvely made provision for 'politics' in the form of popular participation in the plan, such participation being one means of overcoming local resistance and spreading 'modern attitudes,' this provision often backfired on regional planners by mobilizing popular resistance to planning objectives.[27] Ultimately, the application of regional science techniques to the problem of regional development in Canada, especially the 'growth centre' approach, has had rather disappointing results, and has generated serious criticism, not ·least from a number of its early advocates.[28]

Dependency: An Alternative Perspective

Alongside these theoretical developments, which as noted above have often attained concrete embodiment in diverse government policies and programs, alternative explanations of regional underdevelopment have arisen as part of a critical response to more mainstream development and modernization theories and to the implementation of policies based on their assumptions. Most important of these have been the arguments put forth by international dependency theorists, especially in Latin America. Against the dualistic conception of modern and traditional society (i.e., centre and periphery) posited by development and modernization theory, dependency theorists have argued the essential modernity of 'development' and 'underdevelopment' as two sides of the same coin, 'reciprocal conditions in a global system of capital accumulation.'[29] It is argued that a country's dependent position in an international division of labour acts as the structural source of its development or underdevelopment. Moreover, this argument has been carried farther to the contention that each country has created within itself its own underdeveloped regions. Thus the problem of regional disparities or inequalities can be explained in this approach within the context of a global system of metropolitan domination and periphery subordination that victimizes not only the so-called Third World countries, but also peripheral regions within the developed societies of the metropolitan 'core.'[30]

One expression of the dependency perspective has been studies of 'internal colonialism' as a way of understanding centre-periphery relations and regional underdevelopment within certain nation-states. By extending inwards the various propositions of theories of imperialism and/or dependency, this model describes the periphery as a 'conquered society,' condemned to an instrumental role in which economic and social development are constrained by their complementarity to that of the centre or metropolis. This situation is maintained initially by force of arms, then increasingly by political and economic coercion as well as cultural and ideological symbols and stereotypes that serve to maintain political stability and servility and to legitimate metropolitan superordination.[31]

But while theories of internal colonialism have generally tended to stress questions of *ethnicity*, *culture*, *racism*, and *nationalism* as important factors in the economic exploitation and political oppression of the periphery, within the dependency approach, first and foremost the *class* and *spatial* relationships involved in this exploitation are seen to produce dependence and underdevelopment. This pattern of relations derives from the polarization over time of the world economy such that an unbalanced division of labour, a highly skewed distribution of productive resources and income, and a territorial hierarchy of nation-states have evolved. According to this formulation, the metropolitan bourgeoisie comes to dominate socio-political forces and relations on the periphery.

As a result, the class structure of the periphery will tend to be characterized by the formation of a 'comprador' bourgeoisie or élite that mediates
the domestic operations of transnational enterprises in particular and
world capitalism in general. Because this class or élite in the dependent
society owes its privileged position to the metropolitan bourgeoisie, and
is thus beholden to it, it is seen to be incapable of acting in the true
interests of the periphery (i.e., as a 'national bourgeoisie'). Other groups
and classes on the periphery not connected to the dynamic capitalist
sector in the export enclave (the overwhelming majority of the periphery's population) tend to be either marginalized or 'superexploited.'[32]

While some formulations of dependency theory have thus posited a
direct relationship between *dependence* and *underdevelopment*, other
dependency theorists, recognizing the progressive industrialization and
rising standards of living in a select group of Third World countries, have
come to speak of a process of *dependent development* based on massive
foreign investment in manufacturing and the production of consumer
goods aimed at the periphery's growing urban middle class. Rather than
trade and unequal exchange as the dominant moment in determining the
pattern of periphery development, production for a growing domestic
market comes to characterize the 'new dependency,' a form of development based on direct foreign investment and increasing state management of the dependent economy.[33]

These shifts in the analysis of international dependency have their
counterparts in the application of this approach to peripheral regions
within the 'developed' or advanced capitalist societies. There the periphery's role as a reservoir of migratory labour is seen to be supplemented
by various forms of 'dependent' industrialization. Thus, while new industries, products, and consumer orientations may in this way be 'diffused' to
the periphery, many local businesses are destroyed in the process and
others are transformed into mere agents for big national distributors.
Profits are repatriated to the centre, and savings generated within the
region are funnelled out through a centralized banking system. And while
some new jobs are created (usually at lower wage rates than those at the
centre), many more are continually lost (through plant shut-downs,
rationalization of older industries, introduction of new technology, etc.),
while key management and decision-making positions are shifted 'up-
stream' to the metropole or are maintained within the periphery but
reserved for 'outsiders.' Moreover, the values that come to be diffused to
the periphery – part of an accompanying process of 'cultural imperialism'
– only worsen the situation for periphery residents, pressing upon them

metropolitan tastes and values that downgrade the 'indigenous' products, culture, and life-style of the periphery as inferior, while encouraging acceptance of, and aspirations to acquire, the metropolitan counterpart, even though this imitative process ensures that the periphery resident can never really 'measure up.'[34]

The dependency perspective, then, suggests a quite different role for culture in centre-periphery relations than that perceived by modernization theorists. In contrast to the modernization perception it argues that the diffusion of metropolitan culture to the periphery reinforces processes of regional underdevelopment rather than stimulating development on the periphery. And the cultural identity and autonomy of the periphery, far from being factors contributing to underdevelopment, come to be seen as essential to a process of self-reliant and self-directed development, part of the complement of resources held by the periphery that would allow the retention of a modicum of local control over values, capital, and technology.

It should be noted about this perspective, however, that barring some form of autarchy such resources would have to be employed by the periphery in such a manner so as to meet the challenge of competition within an international capitalist economy. Presumably local capital somehow would have to be husbanded and mobilized, technology controlled and adapted to local needs and circumstances, and cultural values nurtured and defended (if at the same time permitted to evolve). Politics, of course, becomes the essential medium through which these aims must be accomplished.

In the Maritimes, such alternative analyses of regional underdevelopment as those mentioned above have been spawned by the historical inquiries of regionally based academicians and researchers who have, to varying degrees, drawn upon the insights of international dependency theory and other radical critiques of capitalism. These works have refuted the 'orthodox' interpretation of a steady and natural decline of the Maritimes into economic stagnation as a result of such factors as technological change, geographic isolation, and cultural conservatism. Instead, we have been presented with a picture of a regional economy and society in a dynamic state of flux, rapidly making the transition to the new industrialism. The fact that this transition was slowed and eventually short-circuited in the 1920s, forcing many workers and other producers on the periphery to choose between emigration and a marginal, subsistence-oriented existence, was seen to be the result of a political, social, and economic framework that subordinated the regional interests of a subordinate Maritimes to the larger interest of capital accumulation at the centre.

Such revisionist scholarship on the history of the Maritimes has become solidly established and widespread among the region's 'intelligentsia' in recent years, sparking wide-ranging debates on the causes and manifestations of Maritime underdevelopment. Most of this work has to date focused on regional industrialization and deindustrialization during the half-century between 1880 and 1930, and has its origins in the seminal work of T.W. Acheson, who demonstrated that a rapid and successful industrialization had in fact occurred in the Maritimes within the framework of the tariff protection provided by the National Policy.[35] A consolidation process carried out through Montreal-based syndicates led to the 'branch-planting' of most Maritime manufacturing and was followed by the centralization of production in the post–First World War period, effectively 'deindustrializing' the region. This has suggested to many that the Maritimes, in fact, were victimized by a process of 'underdevelopment,' rather than by a lack of development. The need to explain the processes of consolidation and centralization that left the Maritimes as a marginal, underdeveloped region within Confederation, and the manner in which these processes evolved, has since become a central problem for analyses of the political economy of the region.

Acheson's original work focused on the business élite in the region, and ultimately his explanation for Maritime decline rests upon failed entrepreneurship, 'the lack of a powerful self-directed and self-confident business community.'[36] Implicit in Acheson's work, however, and more explicitly than in that of E.R. Forbes,[37] is an argument that lays the blame for the region's predicament at the door of the superior political strength exercised by central-Canadian business interests over federal policy. The resulting treatment received by the Maritimes at the hands of the federal government is perceived by these authors as a great injustice in Canadian history, one that should finally be corrected by the fulfilment of the 'promises' of Confederation by those who have inherited the benefits of the pattern of national development.

While destroying many of the myths regarding the post-Confederation history of the Maritimes, this 'fairer deal within Confederation' school, as it has been referred to elsewhere,[38] has come in for some criticism from political economists drawing upon Marxist dependency theory. Clow, for instance, has criticized the 'wishful thinking' involved in conceptualizing the role of the Maritime economic élite as a nascent 'national bourgeoisie,' a view that emerges in the work of this school. Although it may be argued that politics is an important ingredient in the explanation of the rise and fall of Maritime industry, Forbes's and Acheson's explanation does not reflect a very deep or critical penetration of the dynamics of capitalist development that provided the framework and issues of political struggle, and it contains a tendency to romanticize the process as one where 'our' (good) Maritime capitalists were beaten by 'their' (bad) ones.

Clow argues that there is no a priori reason to assume that Maritime capitalists – some of whom participated vigorously in the consolidation movement centred in Montreal that led to the initial 'branch-planting' of Maritime production – acted in some sense as a national bourgeoisie of the Maritimes. Other critics of the 'fairer deal' school, such as Gene Barrett, have argued that Acheson's work, and all other explanations that rely on *particular factors* such as entrepreneurship or individual government policies, operate within a framework based on the mistaken assumption that the institutional order was basically sound, and that regional disparities could be explained in terms of the malfunctioning of only certain parts of that order, such as the market or entrepreneurship. 'The ideological bias of these assumptions should be abundantly clear: it is outside the realm of possibility for *the structure of society* to create problems in its normal course and, even if this were possible, it is inconceivable to discuss altering that structure. The *self-balance theory* of regional disparity is rightly named: it is an equilibrium theory based on the preservation of the status quo [emphasis added].'[40]

The general approach represented by this criticism – that uneven regional development is a structural feature of capitalism – runs directly counter to those analyses found in the aforementioned 'self-balanced' category. Barrett has cited at least three variants within this critical school of thought that have been put forward as explanatory frameworks for Maritime underdevelopment: the Frankian 'development of underdevelopment' school, the 'new dependency' perspective, and the 'modes of production' approach.[41] The starting-point of all three of these approaches to uneven regional development is to point out the similarity of its occurrence in Canada to others elsewhere and to insist that an adequate understanding of it must be rooted in a solid conception of the dynamics of uneven capitalist development.

Archibald's analysis of underdevelopment in Atlantic Canada was the first systematic application of a modern theory of dependency to regional problems.[42] But his uncritical use of Andre Gunder Frank's 'development of underdevelopment' model suffers from notable explanatory weaknesses deriving from assumptions embodied in the model and from acceptance of the orthodox focus on staples and a failure to industrialize. Thus, according to Frank's theory, the periphery will experience its greatest economic development, and especially its most classically capitalist industrial development, if and when its ties to the metropolis are weakest.[43] Yet the Maritimes experienced a burst of industrialization at a time when its ties with central Canada were considerably strengthened from what they had been previously. Archibald's analysis, then, which argued the impossibility of Maritime industrialization within Confederation, was brought into question by Acheson's historical examination of the industrialization of the Maritimes.

Henry Veltmeyer's work on dependent capitalist development and underdevelopment in the Maritimes captures important aspects of the interregional relationship generated by the rise of monopoly capital at a centre.[44] For Veltmeyer, the process of concentration and centralization of capital is self-explanatory as a law of capitalist development: 'the expanded reproduction of capital at one pole (the centre) both requires and creates on the other (the periphery) conditions for a mass of "free" labour held in reserve but available for purchase ... underdevelopment in Atlantic Canada can best be understood in terms of Marx's concept of an "industrial reserve army", as a lever of capital accumulation.'[45]

Veltmeyer, in his analysis, adapts to the Maritimes Michael Mandel's (and later Samir Amin's) arguments that a labour reserve is created at the periphery for export to the centre at a lower wage in order to depress the labour market there. The argument is that this labour reserve constitutes a hidden form of surplus transfer, since the periphery has borne the costs of training and rearing this work-force. This mechanism is designed to counteract the law that shows that the rate of profit tends to fall at the centre.[46] Operating within the context of centre-periphery relations within a developed capitalist economy, Veltmeyer argues that locational attractions will be exploited during periods of recession and cheap labour siphoned away from backward areas during periods of expansion. Investments by metropolitan capital in peripheral regions have a distorting effect on the periphery's social structure since only select branches of industry are developed. In the face of this structural deficiency, labour has been kept in reserve by certain pre-capitalist relations of production that have subsidized the social-security costs of capital and sustained this reserve labour power. This distorted and truncated pattern of investment and employment explains the origin and reproduction of poverty, as well as the 'backward' class structure of the region.[47]

The third approach cited by Barrett, the 'modes of production' approach, picks up from Veltmeyer's theoretical explanation for uneven regional development and goes on to postulate and expand on the use made of pre-capitalist or 'archaic' modes of production by metropolitan capital. The leading exponents of this approach, R.J. Brym and R.J. Sacouman, have focused on the 'structural articulation of two apparent modes of production,' and the subsumption of independent commodity producers to the capitalist mode of production.[48] Their studies of this phenomenon in the Maritimes have led to the claim that the various forms and stages of such subsumption represent differing types of capitalist underdevelopment.

Critique of the Application of Dependency to the Maritimes

While these various analyses raise some important questions they are also subject to some notable theoretical and empirical weaknesses. Veltmeyer's conception of the periphery as a 'holding ground' for the 'reserve army of labour' is a rather economistic and ahistorical treatment. While the relationship of a labour reserve to capital is clear, he does not explain why it should adopt a particular spatial pattern. Certainly there are many more unemployed, in absolute terms, in the large urban centres than on the periphery. And while it is no doubt accurate to say that the Maritime provinces were unfairly burdened with the costs of rearing and training a migrant work-force for significant periods prior to the 1960s (this constituting a transfer of surplus to the centre), these costs have since been centralized through equalization and other transfer payments that now constitute approximately one-half of the budgets of provincial governments in the region.[49]

Moreover, it is far from clear that it is less onerous and/or more functional for metropolitan capital and the state to purposely maintain labour in non-capitalist modes of production on the periphery (given the resulting support expenses) than it would be simply to rely on relative impoverishment to stimulate out-migration or to revert to the straight subsidization of surplus labour through unemployment and welfare (as is the case in urban settings). This anomaly in Veltmeyer's argument points to a glaring weakness in his analysis of regional underdevelopment: the role of politics and the state and their intercession between labour and capital, centre and periphery. Veltmeyer's analysis implicitly suggests that the state plays no role other than to support the requirements of metropolitan capital through its allocations. But he nowhere discusses this; the state is left with such a role based on the theoretically imputed requirements of the process of capitalist development at the centre. Thus, Veltmeyer's analysis is lent a functionalist cast and needs to be supplanted by an empirical study of the historical role of the Canadian state in centre-periphery relations.

The real implications of dependent industrialization on the periphery are also less than clear. Is this process always a negative one? Rather than considering as self-evident the proposition that industries on the periphery always compete at a disadvantage with the centre, one should engage in analysis that is sensitive to specific factors that determine the rate of exploitation, the profitability of invested capital, and the material and non-material returns to labour: the strategic location of the industry; the demands of the market; the structure of ownership and the disposition of capital; the contribution made to physical infrastructure, material resources, and capital formation; and the skills and human resources within the local economy that are subsequently developed or suppressed.[50]

In a similar vein, Brym and Sacouman's overly formalistic 'modes of production' approach has been criticized for its assumption that the existence of primary production, which is dependent upon capital but not fully subsumed under it, is automatically part of capital's 'grand design' for underdeveloped regions. Barrett, for instance, has argued that those who utilize this approach tend to see capital as all-powerful, thus ignoring the world-wide resistance of producers in the face of monopoly capitalism.[51] While this argument may somewhat overstate the case, at least as it pertains to the position taken by Brym and Sacouman, what can be said about the 'modes of production' approach is that it doesn't appear to allow for a dynamic of class conflict that produces something new and conceivably 'better' – in the sense of 'more highly developed' – than what existed before. Thus, the clash of monopoly capital and primary producer is seen to leave only a gutted version of a previous culture and mode of existence. Class formation occurs as a *result* of capitalist underdevelopment on the periphery, a process that subverts and gnaws away at existing social and cultural resources there. What remains results only from the struggles of subordinate classes against the domination of capital.

But what about the *reciprocal impact of subordinate-class resistance* on politics, culture, and the development process? Do such struggles merely amount to a clinging to tradition in the face of threatened change, which effectively, though momentarily, 'stalemates' the development process? Are there alternative development strategies or models that can be pursued? What allies are recruited in these struggles? How are outcomes shaped or reshaped accordingly? Traits or characteristics of the periphery that Brym and Sacouman identify as indicative of capitalist underdevelopment may be, in fact, the effects of survivalist adaptations to change, a measure of periphery resistance to the penetration of capital and the diffusion of metropolitan values, or merely evidence of the slow and gradual disintegration of pre-capitalist class structures brought on by the wider social and economic processes of capitalist development.

The connections that develop between primary producers on the periphery and industrial capital may well be a case in point. Brym and Sacouman make the error of seeing primary producers only in terms of their functionality to capital and capitalism, and ascribing only negative connotations to their adaptions to the growth on the periphery of capital and capitalist social relations of production. Yet the continued salience of modes of work and life connected to part-time, seasonal, and/or semi-subsistence farming, fishing, and woodlot operations can be seen to have a rationality of their own independent of the requirements of capitalism. Besides providing a cushion against long-term unemployment, outright dispossession of the means to a livelihood, and/or the spectre of forced migration, they allow for the continuation of a particular life-style not obtainable within, or compatible with, a social and economic setting dominated by purely capitalist social relations of production. In this connection, state subsidies of various sorts can be seen to have been utilized by petty-commodity producers to buttress their marginal position.

In effect, Brym and Sacouman perceive in their surveys evidence only of *underdevelopment* occasioned either indirectly through the truncation yet maintenance of the domestic mode of production as a basis for surplus labour power, or directly through the establishment in competition with primary producers of genuinely capitalist social relations of production.[52] This finding has led others to conclude that the application of the 'modes of production' approach to the Maritimes harbours an essentially dualist conception of underdeveloped regions that is excessively concerned with the conservation of the traditional sector, or non-capitalist social relations or modes of production, without questioning whether this conservation is 'real' or, in fact, desirable. As a result, developmental tendencies and trends associated with the slow disintegration of pre-capitalist class structures brought on by wider economic and social processes of capitalist development are either ignored or misinterpreted.[53]

In his review of these debates – among what he refers to as the 'Maritime Marxists' – Clow has rightly taken issue with the economism of many of those working within a dependency framework. He admits that such economism has led to a serious lack of attention to the 'big picture' of class conflict as a social force that shapes the broad history of capitalist development in the Maritimes.[54] Clow attempts to rectify this failure to deal with politics by placing emphasis on the strategies and political agendas that are linked to the competing 'social projects' of different social classes. These projects, Clow argues, find reflection in partisan party politics and state policies. Confederation is seen to have been a political project of the Canadian bourgeoisie that set the parameters for capitalist development in the Maritimes, closing off some strategies and offering others, while putting in place the political mechanisms for the subordination of the region to the central-Canadian ruling class and its political élite.

While Clow incorporates in this formulation politics and the state in the analysis of Maritime and Canadian development, his work, like Sacouman's, still tends to convey the impression of a unilateral imposition of the mechanisms of domination, which suggests that politics – as part of the wider 'social project' of the Canadian bourgeoisie – was *necessarily* a contributing factor to Maritime underdevelopment.[55] In other words, it remains too straightforwardly reductionist in a social and political sense. What is required instead is an analysis of the capitalist state, 'which proceeds from the logic of the state itself rather than being reduced to a reflection of the needs of capital'[56] (or, with regard to Clow, the 'social projects' of capitalists).

At this point it may prove helpful to raise the prickly question of the manner in which one understands the process of *development*. The path-breaking work on the Maritimes undertaken by Acheson and Forbes, among others, and the critique that followed, invite comparisons with wider debates over the manner in which some variants of dependency theory and élite analysis attempt to explain the pattern of Canadian development. These approaches have tended to draw sharp distinctions between 'industrial' and 'financial,' as well as 'domestic' and 'foreign' capital, with the primary developmental role being allocated to the initiative and success of indigenous entrepreneurs. In the case of the Maritimes, the failure of regional capital, or its absorption by central Canada–based finance and corporate capital, is seen to be the underlying 'cause' of regional dependence and underdevelopment. Therefore, the focus shifts to indigenous entrepreneurial innovation, independence, and 'success' as the guide-posts to development and dependence.

But, as pointed out by Leo Panitch, it is hardly unusual that small industrialists cannot survive in an era of corporate capitalism.[57] In the context of a unified national market, it is not really surprising or puzzling, for instance, that the growth of centralized, monopoly capital was accomplished by the demise of a large number of smaller Maritime manufactories and the absorption of many others into consolidated Canadian corporations. Indeed, elements of Maritime capital 'rose to the top' as part of these consolidated operations, and were sometimes major movers in the process. Rather, the salient questions for understanding regional deindustrialization and underdevelopment, according to Panitch, concern the original reasons for regional disinvestment in crucial economic sectors and the subsequent failure of substantial new units of capital and production to spring up in their place. Why didn't the Maritimes continue to be a 'pole of accumulation,' a suitable site for profitable investment, during and after the transition in Canada from 'competitive' to 'monopoly' capitalism? Such questions shift the focus of analysis to the process of capital accumulation – particularly the rate and form of economic exploitation that produces capitalist profit – as the determining element in the process of development.

The foregoing can be related to a more general comment on the dependency perspective in terms of the particular understanding it imparts to the relationship between *class* and *development*. Some versions of dependency theory see the major axis of exploitation as territorial or spatial in nature, and the major villain as external, thus granting a residual or secondary status to class cleavages within the periphery community. But, just as Panitch argues that élite analysis and a Schumpeterian conception of class lead to an exaggerated emphasis and exclusive focus on distinctions within the capitalist class (and assessments of the balance of power among what are seen to be its competing segments, factions, or élites) as the key to understanding the course and pattern of development, it can be argued that a lack of attention in some formulations of dependency theory to the relationship between classes has produced a tendency to conceive of development (and underdevelopment) as the function of one class – the metropolitan bourgeoisie – that exercises complete discretion in determining the nature and pace of development that takes place, both at the centre and on the periphery. But if 'class' is understood to mean 'a contradictory social relationship between producers and nonproducers, entailing mutual dependence but also entailing mutual *power*,'[58] then the balance of power between classes is at the heart of the process of capitalist development. Thus, the analysis is redirected somewhat to the class struggles that can effectively limit the power of capital, as well as shape the policy choices of the state.[59]

Capitalist development as a process is exclusively determined neither by certain 'general laws of motion' nor by the short-term plans and ambitions of the bourgeoisie. It is an outcome of the mutual power exercised in the clash of antagonistic interests within capitalism *as mediated by politics and the state*. Outcomes are not predetermined and the process is ongoing, propelled by the emergence of new complexes of socio-political forces that arise from the process itself and become part of the subsequent reconstitution and reshaping of society and state. The role of dependent peripheries in these changes, and the nature and extent of capitalist development that occurs there, are part of this historical process.

Relations of power, then, are not a 'one-way street,' and it would be wrong to view the periphery as inert and passive, without resources or opportunity to affect or change the course of events at the centre (and, by extension, its own fate as a dependency of the centre). As previously noted, such has to often been the conclusion, or at least the implication, of various analyses of underdevelopment on the periphery, and in particular commentary on the Maritimes within Confederation. The state and capital do not plan and determine the whole of society. They adapt what exists, and what exists may be functional to the subordinate classes in their struggle for a dignified existence. The determinants of a region's role within wider national and international spatial divisions of labour cannot be limited to the requirements and strategies of capital alone. Individual capitals engaged in competitive struggle are not able simply to impose a particular pattern of spatial development upon a social formation based on their respective considered and rational assessments of optimal conditions for profitability, subsequently adjusting the latter at will to suit their needs (with abandonment of the 'space' or territory in question as the sole alternative). The ability of subaltern classes to successfully resist their increased exploitation or a radical restructuring of production relationships will also limit and shape the options open to capital in its profit strategies.

In this connection historical outcomes also depend upon the manner in which economic, social, and political struggles are resolved, if only partially and temporarily, through the mediation of the state. Thus, the spatial pattern of capital accumulation, and the spatial implications of capital's pursuit of particular profit strategies, are not determined in a historical or political vacuum. The very 'climate' and environment for profitable production in a particular region must be understood as at least partially the result of past and present state policies. Within certain political and structural constraints the periphery can utilize its political linkages to the centre to its advantage; it can seek to maximize its leverage and to take advantage of the opportunities and strategic possibilities that present themselves in particular historical conjunctures. Its ability to do so, however, is premised in large part upon the organizational and strategic capacities of political forces there.

The *organizational* capacity of peripheral social groupings facilitates political mobilization and provides the basis for sustainable political activity directed towards particular goals. Organizational capacity derives from a number of factors, such as resources, numbers, and levels of association or unionization. And the greater the unity and solidarity within a class or social grouping, the more politically advantageous, since political, economic, and social divisions may remove the basis for a united or even credible political project. The *strategic* capacities of organized social groupings refer to their analytical abilities and political skills. For instance, the formulation and presentation of demands may involve a process of 'issue expansion' whereby demands specific to a particular group or groups are redefined so as to make the issues more palatable to larger segments of the community, thus attracting the support of any potential external allies.[60] Social forces lacking the capacity to construct political alliances and to define what is at issue – and/or advance their interpretation against the alternative presented by a superior force – will either remain at the margins of political debate, without a chance of forcing their issues onto the 'formal agenda' of the state, or succumb to the alternative definitions of issues.[61]

Organizational and strategic capacities, then, are central to the ability of any subordinate grouping to define and articulate issues and attain status on the formal agenda of the state. Such capacities are also of key importance to the success of any challenge to the dominant *political discourse*,[62] which is itself an important factor in either facilitating or inhibiting the organizational capacity and political mobilization of particular classes or social groupings. With regard to centre-periphery relations, these factors – in conjunction with the broader political and economic strategies of state élites at the centre – will determine the degree to which central policies embody a measure of territorial or interregional redistribution. The question remains as to *who* on the periphery will benefit from these policies. A variety of social groupings exist there, and their interests cannot be assumed to be coterminous. If local leadership represents organized marginal social groups, a broadening of what can be referred to as the 'socially allocative range' of central policies may be permitted; alternatively, where they do not, at least effective local organization will procure a territorially more distributive effect.[63]

In this connection, Brym has argued, in his analysis of political conservatism in Atlantic Canada, that subordinate classes in the region by and large have been disorganized, lacking a sufficient level of social organization and control over material and other resources to force the party system to reflect their interests as well as those of the dominant class. Instead, the interests of the latter have been universalized through the party system as well as through other institutions. The reason for this historic discrepancy between the relative power positions of classes in the Maritimes, according to Brym, has been the underdevelopment of the Atlantic region, a process that has weakened the subordinate classes and reduced their social solidarity (and, thus, their propensity to engage in collective action). The answer to this dilemma lies in increased industrialization, which would provide the necessary support for more radical producer-based third parties to establish themselves.[64]

While Brym's analysis of the relationship between class power and social organization in Atlantic Canada is revealing and suggestive, it is misleading on at least two counts. First, it appears to assume that further industrialization would automatically result in a significant increase in working-class and producer organization, which would in turn provide the organizational base for radical politics. But this assumption poses a too-simplistic parallel between economic development and the potential for radical politics. Brodie and Jenson have argued that predictions of the 'inevitability' of class-based electoral politics in industrial societies mistakenly assume a direct relationship between economic and partisan development. A further assumption is that voters' political demands, attitudes, and behaviour automatically reflect their class position. Yet history has often defied this anticipated outcome.

Economic conditions, such as the level of industrialization, set parameters around the range of organization which is possible in any society, but they can never guarantee that particular classes will be politically active. Subordinate classes will not spontaneously recognize the political implications of their disadvantaged position in capitalist relations of production and vote according to their class position. The nurturing of this [class] awareness demands, as a prerequisite, ideological and organizational activity ... the extent to which they live politically as classes is largely the extent to which they behave as classes in elections [emphasis added].[65]

Thus, the importance of the specific historical context of a party system, 'as well as the combined impact of elections, ideologies, and political parties themselves in structuring partisan and class relations,'[66] cannot be overemphasized. In this connection, direct temporal comparisons of party politics across regions in Canada have often obscured and confused, rather than illuminated, the dynamics of each party system. In turn, such comparisons have led to vague or simplistic explanations for the perceived differences in regional party politics, explanations that refer in general terms to 'political culture' or 'levels of economic development' as the 'cause' of particular party systems.

Second, and even more important, it is a mistake to assume, as Brym did, that the historical absence of a radical third party in the Maritimes means that subordinate classes in the region have to date failed to gain any representation within the party system. It is true that subordinate classes in Nova Scotia, with some significant exceptions, have *not* been represented by their own parties, in the sense of class-based parties making a direct appeal to workers, farmers, fishermen, and other producers on the basis of their class position and class interests within a capitalist system. But this does not mean that subordinate-class interests have been bereft of representation as a result. Party and electoral competition produce certain strategies, discourses, and programs that will open or close 'space' for subordinate-class demands, both at the level of periphery politics and with regard to the voicing of regional demands at the centre. Indeed, to be electorally successful on a consistent basis, this political aggregation or incorporation of subordinate-class interests *must* occur. More pertinent questions concern the conditions under which such aggregation or incorporation takes place, the kind of political discourse utilized to do it (with what particular implications for subordinate-class interests), and the material and other concessions made to subordinate social groupings, and/or regions, as part of the process.

Examining regional development as an issue and a policy field – addressing as it does (or should) state response to the economic underdevelopment of the periphery and the regional disparities thus created – should provide a good indication of the manner in which this process has proceeded historically. As Clow rightly asserts, the 'big picture' does indeed need explanation. This book is one effort in this direction.

2 The Political Economy of Regional Decline: The Maritimes, 1867–1927

The economic structure of the Maritime provinces has been shaped by politics just as surely as it has been by geophysical characteristics. Before Confederation the region was a prosperous and strategic colony of Great Britain, sharing in the benefits of the British Empire's trade and commerce. It was peopled largely by British immigrants and United Empire Loyalists and it became a major supplier of timber and ships for Britain's expanding commercial network, giving rise to a significant indigenous group of commercial capitalists. Confederation, while not immediately changing this pattern of economic activity within the region, encouraged the reorientation of the Maritime mercantile economy away from the staples and carrying trades towards manufacturing for a protected national market. Indeed, the opportunities afforded by the prospect of industrialization within Confederation provided one of the major arguments used by its proponents within the region.[1]

In fact, the vision of the Maritimes as the workshop of a federated British North America appeared to be coming to fruition in the 1880s when the region's mercantile bourgeoisie, thwarted in their traditional pursuits by the decline in the staples trade that accompanied the onset in 1873 of a world-wide commercial depression, were left searching for other investment opportunities. The fishery at this time would not have proved to be an attractive field for investment. Trawler technology was not yet readily available,[2] and the prosecution of the fishery lay in the hands of widely scattered small producers utilizing simple, labour-intensive methods – producers who were under no pressure to give up their ownership of the means of production and offer themselves as a cheap source of labour to capital. Coal and steel production, however, was being successfully exploited on a small scale and would soon constitute a major growth industry and field for investment, but entry into this sector was difficult.[3]

In contrast to the aforementioned sectors, the production of consumer goods must have proved an attractive option. Technology was relatively mature and simple at this time, and entry costs were low. Moreover, beginning in 1879 National Policy tariffs created a protected domestic market, thus removing the considerable obstacle of low-priced competition from imports.[4] Confederation had guaranteed and then delivered a railway link to central-Canadian markets, and a favourable freight-rate structure was developed by railway management as an encouragement to local industries.[5] In this context, capitalists in the Maritimes – like their counterparts in New England[6] – shifted their accumulated capital and resources from shipbuilding and the staples trade into a program of industrialization in tariff-protected consumer-goods sectors. The effort was largely a scattered, community-based one, utilizing mature and easily available technologies and heavily reliant on the family resources and business network of the region's economic élite. But for a time it produced significant results, and in the 1880s the growth in Nova Scotia's industrial output outstripped that of both Quebec and Ontario.[7]

It was not long, however, before many of the region's infant industries found themselves hard pressed in the competitive scramble for the limited Canadian market. When faced with an economic slump in the mid-1880s, many businesses failed or were 'netted' in merger movements.[8] The response of Maritime manufacturers was to blame high freight rates for their troubles and to favour the use of railways to promote national economic integration. But lower freight rates for the Maritimes would not solve the problem of Canadian manufacturers who were made vulnerable in periods of recession by overproduction and the dumping practices of their American competitors. Instead, national firms were led towards the consolidation of Canadian production and the regulation of output as a long-term survival strategy.

One by one indigenous industrial ventures and groupings in the Maritimes were absorbed in this growing consolidation movement. By 1895, control of all the mass-consumption industries in the region had passed to outside interests, primarily Montreal-based syndicates. A second wave of consolidation in the early twentieth century extended the process to heavy industry, leaving the region's manufacturing capacity operating almost wholly on a branch-plant basis, and thus vulnerable to corporate profit strategies that would scrub or relocate what had become 'peripheral' plant capacity in the Maritimes.[9]

Dependent Development and 'Arrested Industrialization': Regional Economic Decline, 1890–1914

How did Maritime industry become peripheral to the central locus of capitalist development in Canada? Could not industry in the region have developed more specialized products and services in order to compete? If the Canadian market was limited, why were export markets not pursued? Why did the regional market itself not become a more significant one for industry, a *growth* market, and thus an attractive site for new investment and a regional base of accumulation?

One clear indicator of regional economic decline was the markedly slower growth rate of manufacturing in the Maritimes after 1890 (with the important exception of coal and steel) in comparison with the growth rates in central Canada and elsewhere. In 1880 the contribution of *manufacturing* to the Maritimes (excluding lumber and pulp and paper) was 37 per cent of total goods production as compared to 46 per cent in Canada. By 1890, a decade of industrial growth had improved the relative position of the region (in terms of gross value of manufacturing per capita), and at this time both the Maritimes and Canada ranked favourably with other developed countries in the world. But between 1890 and 1910, real manufacturing output in the Maritimes grew at only 2.3 per cent per annum compared to 4.3 per cent in Canada (and this during a period of tremendous growth in Nova Scotia's coal and steel industries).[10] The labour force in the region grew by only 0.3 per cent per annum compared with a rate five times greater in Ontario and Quebec.[11] And while the regional share of national manufacturing output in 1900 was 10 per cent, by 1920 it had declined to 7 per cent.[12]

An underlying cause for the slower growth rate of Maritime production was that, unlike Ontario's, it did not benefit from foreign investment in the manufacturing sector. More to the point, Canadian-owned industry in general was weakly represented in the then 'high tech' and high-growth sectors of chemicals, electrical goods, and products based on the application of the internal-combustion engine.[13] Instead, these industries, even at this early date, had become the leading edge of American branch-plant incursion into Canada, and in their location decisions American corporations unfailingly chose Southern Ontario as their Canadian production site.[14]

This somewhat backward structure of Canadian-owned industry in combination with a significant and growing foreign presence in the more advanced manufacturing sectors has generally been attributed to the effects of the import-substitution industrialization strategy adopted by John A. Macdonald's Conservatives after their return to power in 1878. As an economic and political strategy the 'National Policy,' as it came to be known, was highly successful. By raising tariff barriers against imports it enabled domestic industry to capture the 'home market.' The subsequent growth of industry in Canada performed the virtuous functions of helping to stem emigration to the United States (by providing jobs in manufacturing in Canada), while securing for Macdonald and his Conservatives the political support of a prospering Canadian bourgeoisie. But since priority was given to the domestic market, exports tended to be neglected or even derided. Over time the technological position of Canadian industry was accordingly weakened: freed by the National Policy of the need to compete in world markets, Canadian firms found imported second-hand technology to be a more rational and cost-effective option.

Thus, the National Policy helped breed a certain disregard for the importance of technological control at both the firm level and the national level, a lack of concern that can also be seen in the government's 'open-door' policy to direct foreign investment. Thus, American branch plants could establish themselves in the most technologically advanced sectors, a base of operations that in subsequent decades was expanded to include most of the Canadian manufacturing sector.

This pattern of industrial development was clearly detrimental to the industrial prospects of the Maritimes. By restricting the industrial horizons of manufacturing capital to the domestic market, it heightened competition for this limited market as well as conferring a distinct advantage on production sites at its centre. Moreover, because indigenous industrialization was concentrated in mature-technology sectors, with more technologically advanced sectors falling under foreign control, growth rates in succeeding decades would tend to be lower in these Canadian-owned sectors, while the option of growth through exports would be all but nullified. And finally, since foreign-owned subsidiaries located almost exclusively in Southern Ontario, manufacturing in the Maritimes remained disproportionately 'Canadian' – a fact of dubious pride since these domestically owned operations remained lodged, with the exception of the region's steel-making facilities, in relatively low-technology, low-growth areas of production.

The foregoing explains why Canada, in contrast to what G. Laxer has classified in industrial terms as other 'late follower' countries, experienced in the first decade of this century a sharp decline in its exports of end-products (or 'finished manufactured goods') as against its imports of same.[15] This *national* reversal coincided, in a developmental sense, with the stagnation of a *regional* manufacturing base in the Maritimes relative to its central-Canadian counterpart, reinforcing the impression that Canada's adoption of a course of 'dependent development' implied not only a long-term reliance on foreign capital and foreign-owned technology (with its attendant drawbacks), but immediate and direct regional costs as well.

Another factor underlying the Maritimes' relative economic decline was the slow growth of the regional market. Between 1880 and 1910 population growth was marginal as a result of the combination of low immigration and considerable emigration.[16] Moreover, urbanization in the region was not proceeding apace with that in Ontario and Quebec. Maritime society remained predominantly rural compared to central Canada's, and rural primary industries continued to employ a high proportion of the population in relatively low-income, low-productivity occupations.[17] This discrepancy in regional industrial structure at this time is attributable primarily to the Maritimes' underrepresentation in the manufacturing, trade, and financial sectors and overrepresentation (in terms of employment) in the fishery and in logging/lumbering industries. What is notable about this discrepancy is that a process of capitalist development had not yet occurred in the latter industries, which imposed structural limits on the growth of the regional market. It also made these non-capitalist sectors vulnerable to more efficient and productively organized capitalist competition originating in other regions and countries. Thus, after 1910 the Maritime lumber industry entered a long period of stagnation and decline, and while pulp-and-paper production compensated to some degree, there, too, output growth was slower than in Canada.[18]

As for the fishery, between 1884 and 1910 it was a major contributor to total output in the Maritimes; thereafter it became a major drag on output growth in the region, registering a negative growth rate of -1 per cent per annum for the 1911–39 period.[19] Because of its organization on a highly decentralized merchant/small-producer basis, productivity in the industry was kept low. Given this structure, the chief means of 'squeezing' profits out of the fishery was through cost-price differentials, ensuring a continuing interest on the part of the merchant in the payment of low fish prices to individual producers who were in competition with one another. As a result, most fishing communities tended to live a self-reliant, 'hand-to-mouth' existence, with little or no capital surplus to reinvest in the fishery. Nor was there a clear incentive on the part of the

principals involved in the fishery to engage in any sweeping reorganization of the production process. Besides restricting the richness of the
internal market by limiting the level of prosperity in rural areas, the
structure of the fishery also had negative implications for the development of those industrial and service sectors that accompany a modern
fishery, particularly shipbuilding and related marine industries.

The dynamic of the reciprocal relationship between urban and rural
areas, town and country, is a key conundrum in understanding the
process of development. Were the problems and limitations of the primary sector a factor in the failure of secondary manufacturing in the
Maritimes? Did they constitute a drag on economic growth and productivity that inhibited new investment in the region? Or was the retention of
surplus labour in these sectors (and the accompanying disincentive to
invest in labour-saving technology) a result of the insufficiently rapid
growth of Maritime towns and secondary industries, and thus the scarcity
of alternative employment opportunities for rural primary producers?

What can be said with some certainty about this 'chicken and egg'
conundrum is that a crucial *temporal* factor appears to have been operative in the process of capitalist development, and that, in the case of the
Maritimes, investment forgone in the pre–First World War period – and
thus a failure to adequately diversify and strengthen the regional economic base relative to its competitors – reduced the propensity for capital
(whether regional, Canadian, or foreign) to later engage in further
expansion and improvements to that industrial base, given the availability
of more attractive and profitable investment opportunities elsewhere.

Perhaps what is most puzzling about the historical change in the
economic prospects of the Maritimes is the apparent failure of the region
to capitalize on the obvious strengths of its nineteenth-century economy,
particularly the vitality of its shipping and shipbuilding sectors. The
Maritimes, and Nova Scotia in particular, had always been important
militarily and closely associated with the British Navy and its control of
the sea lanes between Europe and North America. The region was also
actively engaged in the carrying trade for a world-wide commercial
network. Based on these roles, shipbuilding became a major industry in
the nineteenth century. That it failed to make a successful transition from
the age of wood, wind, and sail to that of steel and steam has always been
a major part of the explanation for the region's decline.

The answer for this failure can be found in large part in the absence of
the usual customers for a modern shipbuilding and marine industry. At
the turn of the century in Canada defence-related, merchant-related, and

fishery-related vessel construction of the appropriate type was not in demand, removing any domestic base for such an industry to establish itself in the Maritimes. The role of state policies here was crucial. In most if not all of the industrializing nations at the turn of the century the state was a key customer for military hardware and technological products, thus providing a crucial stimulant to investment in industries such as shipbuilding and engineering.[20] In Canada, however, a distinct lack of concern with defence and strategic questions removed the state as a significant customer for these industries. During the First World War the federal government appeared to be on the verge of helping to insert this 'missing link' in the region's industrial structure by encouraging the addition of a ship-plate mill to the steel-making facilities in Nova Scotia, going so far as to contract advance orders. But soon after the establishment of the plate mill, in February 1920, the government, now preoccupied with other matters, cancelled its orders. The mill soon closed and was forgotten for twenty years.[21]

With regard to the role and importance of shipping in the regional economy, and thus the level of demand for both the capital and consumer goods and services associated with port development and a merchant marine, here too national policies did not bode well for regional industrial prospects. The Maritimes had expected to reap the advantages of becoming the 'winter port' for Cananda after the completion of the Intercolonial Railway (ICR). But the level of shipping activity was limited by the diversion of the trade of the Canadian interior to rival American ports. Indeed, with the acquisition of the Grand Trunk Railway (which had its terminus at Portland, Maine) in 1919, the dominion government lost any incentive it may have had for routing Canadian trade through Canadian ports. The repeated protestations and submissions to the dominion government by the Maritime ports of Halifax and Saint John to alter this situation appear to have had little effect; the routing of Canadian trade remained largely subject to 'the vagaries of a market influenced by the canvassing and promotion of railways and shipping lines.'[22] In addition, the dampening effect of the National Policy on external trade in anything other than resources – the obsession with the domestic market that this policy promoted – may also be seen as a factor in the failure of the Maritimes to continue to get significant industrial benefits from a vibrant shipping sector in the twentieth century as it had in the nineteenth century.

The fishery at the turn of the century, and for a long time thereafter, continued to be a small-boat operation reliant upon the skills of local craftsmen. The industry remained labour-intensive rather than capital-intensive and produced no demand for the larger mechanized and motorized steel-hulled vessels that would provide the kind of domestic market that would justify the large investments of capital necessary to the development of modern shipbuilding and marine industries.

Thus, what would appear to have been a 'natural' industrial sector for the region – given its strategic location, its seagoing traditions and activities, its shipbuilding history, and the presence of steel-making facilities – was largely negated in the twentieth century by the *absence* of the key customers for shipbuilding yards in other industrial or industrializing countries. These customers were: a state that had an ongoing concern with defence and strategic questions and thus an interest in an ongoing program of defence procurement; a modernizing and mechanizing fishery that grows more capital-intensive because of its utilization of larger, steel-hulled vessels and more sophisticated marine equipment; and the nation's ports and merchant marine, the development of which is the usual object of national shipping policy.

Industrial Collapse: The Early 1920s

If the Maritimes' relative position in manufacturing had been worsening since the turn of the century or earlier, the 'killing blow' for the region was the sharp national recession of the early 1920s, a recession from which the rest of Canada emerged into a new economic boom cycle but which, for the Maritimes, heralded a severe and prolonged economic crisis. In fact, this situation is not the anomaly it may seem, for the post-war crisis of Canadian manufacturing – brought on in large part by its too-rapid pre-war growth induced by the wheat boom and extensive railway construction – was in part resolved by the destruction of its Maritime segment.

The main problem faced by Canadian manufacturing in the post–First World War period was its overextension – an excess of capacity. In the frantic search for economic security in a chaotic market, Canadian capitalists scrambled to reduce costs and restrict competition. When the preferred option of a government regulatory mechanism to control destructive competition failed with the dismantling of the Board of Commerce in 1920, other strategies were pursued, including the rationalization of production, a renewed merger movement, and demands for increased tariff protection.[23] Maritime manufacturing capacity was rendered superfluous and expendable in this situation; production there could be closed down and the regional market serviced from plants located in central Canada.

The result of this process for the Maritimes was little short of disastrous. The closure or removal to central Canada of production facilities forced many workers to leave the region. The total labour force employed in manufacturing declined from 46,000 in 1919 to 27,855 in 1921. Union membership in the Maritimes was halved in the space of a few years. In 1925 the net value of manufacturing production was only 45 per cent of where it stood in 1919 and the Maritimes' share of total gross value of manufacturing had dropped sharply in the interim, from 7 per cent to a mere 4.5 per cent of national output in 1926 (a level at which it would remain for the duration of the inter-war period).[24] Steel and textiles, the most important of the region's manufactures, were particularly hard hit.[25] Net migration from the region during the decade rose to 150,000 people, or 15 per cent of the region's total population.[26]

The virtual deindustrialization of the Maritime in the 1920s ensured that the growing disparity in manufacturing capacity between regions, far from correcting itself, would become worse. Thus, while non–forest-products manufacturing comprised over two-thirds of the increase in total growth for Canada between 1911 and 1939, the size of this sector in the Maritimes (in terms of output) actually *declined* by 20 per cent. Gross value of manufacturing per capita in the region fell to 42 per cent of the Canadian figure.[27]

Nor was the primary sector in the region spared by the recession. Major internationl changes in trading arrangements, prices, products, and technology worked against regional commodity exports such as coal, fish, lumber, and agricultural products. Tariff barriers, declining prices, and product changes struck especially hard at the fishery. The revival of European competitors and the aggressive, government-subsidized pursuit of new markets by Iceland and Norway sharply constricted Canadian fish exports and helped bring about a 50 per cent drop in the price for cod between 1919 and 1921.[28] The Fordney–Micumber tariff and the cancellation of arrangements allowing Canadian fishermen to market their fish directly at American ports had a similarly harsh effect, especially on fishing communities in southwestern Nova Scotia. One result was that an exodus of vessels and fishermen to the United States took place. Others dropped out of the commercial fishery altogether and supplemented a food fishery with subsistence activities on the land. Reports of destitution became common in some areas of Nova Scotia.[29]

Both lumber and coal in the Maritimes were forced to compete with younger and more efficient rivals in the post-war era. Once the Panama canal and lower ocean freight rates had arrived, a two-hundred-year-old Maritime lumber industry was not well positioned to compete with a west-coast product culled from virgin stands of timber. Employment in Maritime lumber mills dropped from 8,000 in 1920 to 4,500 only a year later. Coal was facing growing competition from oil and hydroelectric power. Moreover, the Nova Scotia product had been displaced from the Montreal market during the war years by American coal. Tariff protection had been allowed to erode to such an extent that between 1879 and 1924 the actual level of protection for Canadian coal fell by over two-thirds. Simultaneously the iron and steel industry in the Maritimes was hurt, losing through tariff reductions on imported coal most if not all of its original locational advantages for the production of iron and steel in Canada.[30]

The economic downturn of the first half of the 1920s, then, affected virtually every sector of the Maritime economy. But it was the disastrous collapse of Maritime manufacturing that sealed the region's economic fate for decades to come. With its already developed primary sectors, the region had to rely more on expansion in the production of finished goods or export sales of services (for example, shipping) to improve its economic position.[31] Failure in both these areas crippled the basis for future economic growth and diversification and with it the potential for a significant measure of endogenous economic dynamism.

In conclusion, understanding the wherefore and why of regional economic decline and, then, deindustrialization in the 1920's has required the delineation of a number of underlying 'causes.' Some of these, the details of which are not examined within the confines of this study – such as the general economic recession and the growth of protectionism in the United States and elsewhere immediately after the First World War – are related to national and international economic conditions that provided the most immediate 'cause' for the shut-down of some Maritime industries and the loss of markets for others. But it must be remembered that these conditions exerted the particular effects and impacts on Canada and the Maritimes that they did only because of the earlier establishment of a particular national and regional economic structure. And the range of likely, indeed *possible*, responses of Canadian industry under such conditions was predetermined accordingly by structural factors that cannot be divorced from earlier political decisions taken at both the regional and national levels, decisions that greatly influenced the course of capitalist development within Canada and the Maritimes (e.g., Confederation itself and the patterns of trade and investment encouraged by the National Policy).

Besides the constraints of a particular national industrial structure induced by the policy framework set in place to encourage the growth of domestic manufacturing, other 'structural' causes for Maritime under-development had to do with certain forms of social and economic organization in the Maritime region that, in and of themselves, limited the scope of the regional market and inhibited an adequate response on the part of social classes in the Maritimes to new competitive pressures and changing market situations. Taken together, these structural factors provide a large part of the explanation for the character of Maritime industrialization and the subsequent relative economic decline of the region (which in essence began before the turn of the century).

It was this historical compendium of political decisions, economic forces, and structural constraints that 'prepared the ground' for the severe regional economic crisis of the early 1920s. These are the parameters within which more specific and immediate political factors relating to the balance of political forces (both at the centre and on the periphery) in particular historical conjunctures – for example, adjustments to the tariff and national transportation policies, a particular political response from within the region to the crisis, a delayed and muted reaction to the resulting regional protest on the part of state élites at the centre – could 'trigger' and subsequently tolerate the collapse of industry in the Maritimes without unduly disturbing either a prospering national economy in the 1920s or the stability of Canadian political institutions.

National Politics and the Decline of Regional Influence

The most immediate and readily identifiable factor that triggered the deindustrialization of the Maritimes was the destruction of the ICR as an instrument of regional development in Canada. From the beginning railway politics had been inextricably intertwined with the Confederation project. The construction of a railway link between the lower colonies and Canada was a central element of the Confederation agreement. It was, and for several decades would continue to be, one of the important compromises that stitched together governing coalitions in Canada, whether Conservative or Liberal. The commercial success of such a railway was not the prime consideration in its construction. It was a necessary expense undertaken to join and integrate British North America into a new nation-state, in the words of John A. Macdonald, 'a political consequence of a political union.'[32]

Indeed, the ICR, constructed on a rather circuitous route for strategic and political reasons, initially lost huge sums. But after the National Policy was invoked it became the key mechanism in enabling the industrialization of the Maritimes. Moreover, as its low and flexible freight-rate structure built up long-haul traffic to central and western Canada, its deficits were gradually reduced. In 1899, the year after Montreal became the official terminus of the Intercolonial, which had become the undisputed rate-maker between the Maritimes and central Canada, the railway recorded its first significant operating surplus.[33]

Government support for the 'special status' accorded to the operation of the Intercolonial began to unravel, however, soon after the Reciprocity election of 1911, when the Conservatives under Robert Borden came to power. The new prime minister, in the optimistic spirit of his age, was determined to reshape party politics and national government in Canada. 'Borden ... was rejecting the kind of politics that was marked by compromise and where decision only occurred at the lowest common denominator. Borden sought a larger vision, one which would go beyond mere consensus.'[34]

For Borden and task of government was to pursue 'an objective and definable general interest' – a 'One Canada' policy – that would burst the constraints of brokerage politics and 'depoliticize' major areas of government decision-making.[35] Finding his own caucus lacking in the necessary talent and zeal for the task at hand, the Conservative leader embarked upon the recruitment of more dynamic men from outside the traditional confines of the national party. To this end he conferred with and drew into the national party a number of 'outsiders,' whether the emissaries of the much-admired Conservative provincial government in Ontario or representatives of business interests and other newly organized citizens' groups opposing corruption, patronage, and nepotism in government and advocating in their place the merit principle and efficiency in the performance of governmental functions and activities.

Borden, then, was wedded to the new discourse of 'progressivism' with its notions of efficient, functional, business-like government. The brokering of regional interests that was the pattern of politics during the Macdonald–Laurier era was viewed as an archaic and corrupt practice, one that had to be overcome if 'the national interest' was to be defined and pursued. 'Railway politics' was a chief culprit, the epitome of old-style political corruption and back-scratching. Decisions on railway questions, thought Borden, should be made on 'business,' not political, grounds.[36] Accordingly, as part of its reform agenda the Conservative government moved to detach two key appointments to railway regulatory bodies from the vagaries of partisan politics: the chairman of the Board of Railway Commissioners and the chairman of the National Transcontinental Railway Commission.[37] By in this way distancing itself from policy-making for the railways, the government hoped to 'cleanse' the regulatory environment and leave the railway commissioners free to run the railways on business principles.

But the removal of railway operations from the constraints of traditional brokerage politics also left the new managers of Canada's railway system free to revoke the special status of a 'political' railway such as the ICR, with disastrous consequences for the Maritimes. The stage was set for this regional calamity by the growing financial crisis of Canada's overbuilt railway system. A royal commission (the Drayton-Ackworth Commission), necessitated by the near-bankrupt state of at least one major Canadian railway, recommended in April 1917 that a number of lines be nationalized and that the Intercolonial be integrated into this newly created government railway.[38]

Thus began a process that saw the ICR have its independence revoked, its management relocated, and its freight rates drastically escalated relative to general pan-Canadian increases, all in the name of 'fairness,' symmetry, and deficit-reduction. Rationalized management and freight-rate structures would eliminate inefficiency and corruption and 'equalize' the costs of transporting goods in Canada. According to E.R. Forbes, the contrast in rate-making principles between the new regulators of the railway and the 'old' Intercolonial management could not have been more striking, with the former constantly reiterating that freight rates could *not* be justified on the grounds of lessening geographical disadvantages or encouraging regional industrial development.[39] Railway policy was in this way to be purged of its 'politics,' notwithstanding the opposition and protests of Maritimers. Thus stripped in the post-war period of the essential protection of politically constructed and maintained arrangements between centre and periphery, Maritime industries would be fully exposed to the chilling blast of centralizing market forces.

Of course, in and of itself, the ideology of progressivism, and the reform of the railway regulatory bodies that, in Canada, appears to have been one its consequences, cannot alone account for the subsequent destruction of the dominion government's regionally sensitive national transportation policy. But it does help to explain the erosion of support for, and indeed the growth of hostility in Canada to, certain pre-war arrangements that served the Maritimes reasonably well. Yet to fully understand the context within which this could be allowed to happen, the impact of the war itself, as well as other salient features of the changing political landscape, must be acknowledged.

Certainly the First World War and the economic, political, and ideological changes that accompanied it represent a crucial watershed in Maritime history, dividing the relative (if limited) prosperity of the pre-war years from the post-war crash that devastated so many of the industrial towns that had grown up since the 1880s, as well as those rural communities dependent upon traditional staple industries that were suddenly faced with disappearing markets and declining commodity prices. Politically what the war did was to harden public attitudes against the old politics and especially the spectacle of political corruption and 'partyism.' The ICR was very much tainted with all of this, and little sympathy could be aroused outside the Maritimes for the defence of a discredited status quo.[40]

This shift in political discourse and values brought about by the rise of progressivism and the political effect on the public of a mismanaged war effort was part of a larger shift in the balance of political forces at the centre, which worked against the Maritimes. The region was already experiencing declining political influence at the centre as a result of its shrinking share of the Canadian population and industrial base. This decline in influence was more or less illustrated by the attempt by provincial governments in the Maritimes – at the time desperately seeking the financial means to maintain and upgrade declining educational services – to gain any ground on the question of a revision of their subsidies in lieu of the territorial expansion granted to other provinces. As it turned out, attempting to secure a quid pro quo for territorial expansion that had already taken place (the 1912 'real estate potlatch' affecting Quebec, Ontario, and Manitoba) proved an impossible task for political representatives of the region.[41] For, while Borden initially appeared receptive to the case made by the Maritimes, promising that their 'just rights' would be taken into consideration by the dominion government, the subsidies issue would never escape the 'tangle of claims and counter-claims' forwarded by the Maritime and Prairie provinces on the issue.[42]

The subsidies question highlights both the relatively weak fiscal capacity of the Maritime provinces resulting from their slower growth rates and comparatively limited resource bases and the extent to which the social and economic roles of the federal government had been limited relative to those of the provinces. Outside of tariffs, railways, and banking, the provinces had acquired substantial autonomy from federal interference or intervention. The main beneficiary of this devolution of power to the provinces was Ontario, which had pursued since the 1880s a vigorous 'Ontario first' provincialist line and repeatedly opposed any interference by Ottawa that would increase federal taxes on Ontario residents or reduce provincial powers.[43]

While provincial governments in this way gained considerable freedom to formulate policy (as well as collect revenues) in areas such as resource development and economic regulation, they were also saddled with the fiscal burdens of providing a social and economic infrastructure. Such a decentralized federalism served to entrench regional inequalities rooted in size, population, proximity to markets, and resource endowment (aided, of course, by the large swatches of dominion territory granted to all provinces but the Maritimes). It constricted the central government's capacity to limit or balance out this growing inequality (that is, if the central government was so inclined, which it does not appear to have been). In effect, as the Maritimes fell behind economically, this institutional setting effectively 'ghettoized' them within Confederation.

A more direct measure of the Maritimes' shrinking input into political decision-making at the centre, however, was the reduction in its cabinet representation experienced after the Conservative victory in 1911. Traditionally the region had been represented by three or four ministers, but in the new Borden government they had only two: Borden himself, sitting for Halifax, and J.D. Hazen, minister of marine and fisheries and member for Saint John, New Brunswick.[44] Of course, for the prime minister, the role of regional representative could not always have coexisted comfortably with his strongly held philosophical views on the proper role of politics and the state. Moreover, such onerous and comparatively petty duties could not have but receded in proportion to the attention and energies that Borden was required to give to the conduct of the war and its aftermath. Matters deteriorated even farther during the political upheaval accompanying the disintegration of Borden's unionist government after the war. For ten months in 1920, at a time when decisions were being made that had drastic consequences for the Maritimes, the region was effectively left without any cabinet representation.[45]

Perhaps the most telling indicator of declining regional influence was the failure of political representatives from the Maritimes to halt or reverse changes to the freight-rate structure. Beginning with the elimination in 1912 of the 'differential' of 12 per cent in eastbound over westbound rates between Montreal and the Maritimes – at the same time that a similar differential was being successfully defended in the United States – the pressure for increased freight rates in the East continued, spurred by demands emanating from western Canada for 'equalization of freight rates,' and from railway operators in the East trying to keep up with rising expenses and diminishing profits thanks to the inevitable costs of the duplication and overexpansion of the previous decade.[46] The Intercolonial became a favourite target of criticism during these years, repeatedly singled out by Ontario and Western MPs as 'a special project maintained at the expense of the Dominion as a whole for the exclusive benefit of the Maritime provinces.'[47]

Ultimately, regional opposition to freight-rate increases that would further erode the Maritimes' competitive position was overwhelmed by other, more 'pressing' matters: the railway crisis, the conduct of the war, and the inflation and then economic recession that set in soon afterward. In 1917 an amendment to the Government Railway Act to bring the ICR under the jurisdiction of the Railway Commission was passed in Parliament. And though this threat to the autonomy of the regional railway suddenly dissipated when, with an election imminent, the bill was permitted to lapse, the reprieve was temporary.[48] In the immediate post-war period freight rates in the Maritimes that were traditionally 20 to 50 per cent lower than similar rates in force in Ontario and Quebec were 'levelled up' by the Board of Railway Commissioners. Combined with general across-the-board increases at this time, the new policy produced a jump in Maritime rates of 140 to 216 per cent. Thus, Maritime manufacturers were faced with a growth in transportation costs relative to that of a Montreal competitor of 125 per cent in under four years, at a time when business profits were already being squeezed by a severe recession. 'Their [freight rate increases'] effect on the Maritime producer was almost as if he had been suddenly thrust a thousand miles out into the Atlantic.'[49]

Political Response to Regional Economic Crisis: The Maritime Rights Movement

Political developments in the Maritimes between the end of the war and the collapse of industry in the region bore a striking resemblance to what was happening elsewhere in Canada. Farmers and labour were engaged in the formation of their own class-based parties to challenge the discredited traditional parties. The United Farmers of New Brunswick was formed in 1918 and the United Farmers of Nova Scotia in 1920. The Maritime United Farmers Cooperative was also founded in 1920, and a farmer's journal, the *United Farmer's Guide*, was begun in the same year as an affiliate of the *Grain Grower's Guide*. Labour was also engaged in organizational and political activity. Unionization in the newer industrial communities was on the rise. The United Mine Workers in Nova Scotia (UMW District 26) reported a membership of 13,365, the largest cohesive body of organized labour in the country. Labour conventions in Nova Scotia and New Brunswick affirmed the existence of labour as a class and advocated its representation by a separate political party.[50]

When the Liberal government in Nova Scotia, in power since 1882, called a snap election in 1920 to pre-empt the organizing efforts of what had become a politically threatening farmer-labour alliance, the latter managed to poll 31 per cent of the vote and, with eleven elected MLAs, formed the official opposition in the Nova Scotia legislature. But its challenge to 'normal' two-party politics in the province proved to be short-lived. Within a few years the alliance had totally dissipated, destroyed by external ideological attacks, internal contradictions, and an economic situation that was wreaking havoc on the alliance partners and their organizations.[51] A third-party alternative in the province might have survived external ideological assault and internal schism, but not the coincidence of massively dislocating economic factors that both removed the organizational basis of the respective farmer and labour movements and undermined their nascent political discourse based on class. Above all, circumstances in the Maritimes in the early 1920s suggested a *regional* response to what was a regional economic crisis.

In fact, a regional protest movement was launched during this period under the leadership of the Nova Scotia Conservative Party in alliance with what remained of the region's business and manufacturing élite (after consolidation and closures had considerably diminished their numerical and political weight). The Maritime Rights crusade appealed to the people of the region unite behind its leadership in demanding the reinstatement of those conditions that had nurtured industrial development in the Maritimes in the first place, as well as the fulfilment of other 'promises' seen to be part of the original Confederation 'bargain.' The demands of the movement included the restoration of preferential freight rates for the region, increased subsidies to provincial governments in the region in lieu of school lands and territorial expansion, a floor on regional representation in Parliament, the greater use and development of winter port facilities in Halifax and Saint John, a protectionist national coal and steel policy, and a regionally sensitive revision of the tariff (either lower or higher depending upon the economic interest involved).[52]

The complexity of Maritime claims and their sometimes contradictory implications (as with tariff agitation) reveal the divisions of economic interest that existed within the region and the difficulty Maritimers had in pin-pointing the exact cause of the crisis. Moreover, the balance of political forces at the centre in the 1921–5 period was not conducive to a favourable reception for Maritime grievances and demands. Indeed, there was considerable hostility to the Maritime Rights movement from the representatives of other regions. Internally divided and virtually without external allies, the prospects for the successful posing of the periphery's demands were dimmed accordingly.

The agitation served as well to harden political attitudes and heighten interregional mistrust and suspicions. Antagonism within the Maritimes towards Quebec and Ontario knew few bounds during this period, as Maritimers became convinced that their economic problems were caused by the greed and callousness of their central-Canadian brethren. The actions and reactions of the latter did nothing to disarm this resentment, as politicians and the media continued to adopt 'a patronizing manner and easy expertise' towards problems in the Atlantic region, accusing Maritimers of being complainers and of laziness and lack of initiative, and resorting to other culturally based slurs.[53]

Neither were the attitudes and political positions adopted by the West advantageous for the sympathetic treatment of Maritime claims. The farmer-backed Progressives had won solid electoral support on the Prairies in the 1921 federal election, becoming the second-largest party in Parliament between 1921 and 1926, holding the balance of power as well as the attention of the minority Liberal government of Mackenzie King. The Progressives were hostile to the positions forwarded by Maritime Rights advocates on a range of issues: a return to lower freight rates for the Maritimes, an increase in subsidies to the region's three provinces, discrimination in favour of Maritime ports, and increased tariff protection for steel and coal.[54] In a head-on conflict between Maritime advocacy of these positions and the straightforward opposition of the Progressives, there was no question as to which side King and the Liberal government would favour. The cultivation of the Progressives and their enticement back into the Liberal fold was a central feature of King's strategy for short-term political survival and long-term Liberal resurgence. Given this strategy, even the appearance of concessions to Maritime demands was avoided.[55]

The irony persisted of the two regional protests against the metropolitian region dissipating their firepower against each other instead of cooperating against a common enemy. MacKenzie King's government presided over the struggle like a referee at a wrestling match, but interfering occasionally to adjust the rules in favour of the stronger contender. The contest frustrated Maritime observers, whose champions under the rules of the game appeared doomed to perpetual defeat.[56]

The Maritime Rights movement was further hampered by its own internal divisions. Maritimers had never formed a cohesive group within national parties. The issue over which they most often tended to divide was the tariff. Within King's Liberal caucus some Maritime representatives joined the 'high tariff' and others the 'low tariff' factions.

The need to mollify different factions within the Maritimes, as well as reduce the opposition of the Progressives to Maritime claims, led to a redefining and reformulating process on the part of the movement's leadership. The representation and subsidies issues, which were especially galling to representatives from the Prairies, were played down. Reference to the tariff began to disappear in the Maritime Rights movement's official propaganda. As one of the less-contentious issues, the channelling of trade through Maritime ports became more prominent in Maritime agitation.[57] In other words, in the search for external allies, or at least lessened resistance at the centre, there was a progressive moderating and watering-down of demands.

The shaping of these demands and the strategies adopted to have them placed on the state agenda owe much to the class composition of the movement and its leadership: regional businessmen and entrepreneurs, a group committed to capitalism and by and large to the National Policy. Their protest could not be expected to encompass a radical critique of the political, social, and economic status quo. Indeed, it is ironic that while the cry of 'Maritime Rights' was being raised, federal troops acting at the behest of the provincial government were being sent into industrial Cape Breton for the sixth time since 1882 to crush a labour movement struggling for recognition and the assertion of its rights, including the right to a living wage. But it is clear that at this time the rights and prerogatives of property and capital took precedence, at least in the view of the British Empire Steel and Coal Corporation (BESCO) management and provincial state élites.[58]

In contrast to the 'illegitimate' struggles of Cape Breton labour, the Maritime Rights protest was largely contained within the traditional two-party system. The movement did not require a radical political manifestation in the form of an independent protest party because its aims and leadership were not in any sense radical. When it became clear that the Liberal government would do nothing to meet the movement's demands, the Conservatives seized the opportunity to become the party of Maritime Rights. It was natural that regional business would associate itself and its objectives with a party that shared its own ideological beliefs but was in opposition to a current government that was proving intransigent. It was also understandable and predictable that the Conservative party, devastated in the region in the political aftermath of the war, would 'regionalize' itself and use the issue of Maritime rights in order to revive support for the party. A mobilization of regional sentiment *within limits* would serve the purposes of the party and its business supporters well.

Yet a moderate course in the Conservatives' prosecution of the Maritime Rights campaign was not assured, at least initially. One party faction led by F.B. McCurdy, a prominent Halifax financier and former cabinet minister who had become convinced that Canada's federal structure and the national party system prevented any fundamental redress of Maritime grievances, sought to create an all-party union within Nova Scotia that would demand fiscal independence for the province to allow it to control its own tariff. This independence was opposed by others in the party who looked to closer economic integration nationally as the solution to regional difficulties, and viewed McCurdy's scheme as a thinly disguised continuation of earlier secessionist tendencies. In the event, McCurdy and his supporters were effectively isolated, as much the result of his alienation of substantial elements within the movement on the tariff question as of fears regarding his motives and radicalism.[59]

Class Struggles outside the Regional Protest: Industrial Workers and the Fishery

BESCO and the UMW

The 'too-radical' demands and implied secessionist threat of the McCurdy faction within the Conservative party were an alternative political strategy and discourse vying for political and ideological hegemony within the Maritime Rights movement. But it wasn't the only alternative put forward in the 1920s. In the coal and steel communities of Nova Scotia a different kind of conflict, with different protagonists, dominated throughout this period.

The newly created British Empire Steel and Coal Corporation (BESCO) under president Roy Wolvin was intent upon pursuing a profit strategy that ensured a confrontation with its workers: a direct assault on production costs in the labour-intensive coal industry through wage reductions of 20 to 40 per cent and absolute refusal to recognize or countenance a steelworkers' union.[60] The end result of the classic, violent, and drawn-out confrontation between capital and labour that ensued was the bankruptcy of Canada's largest industrial conglomerate, the dissipation of its new president's dream of an international industrial empire rooted in Nova Scotia coal and steel, and the impoverishment and despair of Cape Breton miners and their communities.

Nova Scotia coal-miners formed the hard core of organized labour in the Maritimes. As a group they also exhibited considerably greater militancy than did the international organization with which they were affiliated. In the years following the end of the First World War they supported the One Big Union (OBU) movement, voted to affiliate with the Red International, and favoured the representation of labour by its own political party.[61] Their leaders were jailed for sedition and suspended by the International Union of Mine Workers.[62] Between 1922 and 1925 the miners resisted BESCO's wage cuts with lengthy strikes that saw the repeated dispatch of provincial police and federal troops into the mining areas. The resulting escalation of the conflict led to mass protests, brutal repression, rioting, bloodshed, arson, and near-starvation conditions in the mining areas.[63]

The politics surrounding the capital-labour conflict in Cape Breton in the 1920s, and the attitude of state élites to the 'industrial troubles' there, are understandable only in the context of the divisions within the labour movement following the First World War and the 'Red scare' that dictated the response of capital and the state to the challenge of organized labour and working-class militancy during this period. To the extent that the demands of workers and the actions of unions could be linked to the allegedly nefarious influence of 'Bolshevists' in their midst, repression became politically saleable and thus acceptable. Furthermore, the labour movement was weakened from within by a growing split within its ranks (between militants and moderates, left and right, International headquarters and local leadership), a split that turned the focus and energies of the labour movement inward for more than a decade, fracturing solidarity and undermining labour's presence in the political arena as a force capable of challenging the old-line parties.

BESCO's campaign to 'declaw' the industrial work-force proceeded on several fronts, but its most important weapons were its ability to blacklist agitators and its control over housing and foodstuffs, which enabled it to threaten, cajole, and punish workers.[64] The corporation was also able to count on the support of a 'company' press that launched vociferous attacks on labour militants; at the same time measures were taken to silence the *Maritime Labour Herald*, a worker's paper established in the area in 1921.[65] Support from the provincial government in the fight to 'eradicate Bolshevism' was also forthcoming through an expanded provincial police force that was deployed in the industrial area to 'pacify' the population.[66] The dominion government obliged by arguing, 'Pontious Pilate' fashion, throughout the whole episode that while they deplored the appalling conditions in Cape Breton that accompanied the protracted struggle, they could not intervene in matters that were clearly a provincial responsibility.[67]

Matters were complicated for the workers – and the split within labour reinforced – by the intervention by the American leadership of the United Mine Workers (UMW) into the local conflict on the side of those within the union opposed to radical local leaders such as J.B. MacLaughlin. UMW head John L. Lewis was determined to put an end to 'political strikes' and responded to 'acts of solidarity' on the part of UMW District 26 with the steelworkers by revoking the union's charter and placing it under trusteeship. In doing so he referred to MacLaughlin as 'an evil genius' and to the radicals' 'revolutionary masters in Moscow,' while openly co-operating with BESCO to limit the local autonomy of District 26 and force out the militants.[68]

The intervention in this instance of the international union against a militant local leadership presents a clear example of the implications for workers on the periphery of the outcome and trajectory of class struggles at the centre. The anti-leftism and economism of American trade-union leaders posed a daunting obstacle for Nova Scotia miners advocating socialism and working towards a politicized, class-concious union movement. Not only did it deprive workers engaged in localized struggles of a crucial source of support, it provided capital with an invaluable ally by undermining the class solidarity of periphery workers. The internal struggles that followed John L. Lewis's intervention would badly divide District 26 of the UMW and its membership for years, culminating in the formation in 1932 of a breakaway union in the Cape Breton coalfields.

Despite the divisions induced by this episode, the outright brutality of the BESCO management in the prosecution of its campaign against the miners and steelworkers united the work-force against the company and gave rise to a stubborn resistance in the affected Cape Breton communities. Not only did BESCO's strategy founder on the miners' staunch resistance, but it did so in so spectacular a fashion that it attracted nation-wide attention to the latter's plight and popular hostility towards the corporation. When BESCO shifted its strategy in 1925–6 to acquiring increased tariff protection for the coal and steel industries, it found few politicians and businessmen within the region who would allow them-selves to become associated with a corporation that had by then become synonomous with the external exploitation that Maritime Rights agitation had identified as culpable in the destruction of the region's economy.[69]

When BESCO went into receivership in 1927, class conflict in the coal and steel towns abated. But the events of the 1920s left behind a residue of worker discontent and cynicism and a deep-rooted distrust of all 'outside' management, which found expression in unexpectedly high levels of absenteeism and carelessness and in numerous wildcat strikes.[70] Although it was too late to save BESCO, the industrial troubles in Cape Breton did eventually contribute to action on the part of the dominion government to stabilize the Nova Scotia coal industry. Between 1928 and 1931 it enacted a series of measures aimed at supporting the production of coal and steel for the Canadian market, measures that in subsequent years would provide a significant and growing government subsidy to Nova Scotia's coal industry and its new corporate owners.[71]

The Fishery

While the Maritime Rights movement was peripheral at best to the relatively distinct class struggles associated with Nova Scotia's largest industry (coal and steel), it touched the region's fishermen and their rural communities hardly at all. The 'atomization' of inshore fishermen – their almost complete lack of organization – also meant their near-total lack of participation and influence in either the brief rise of farmer-labour politics or the Maritime Rights agitation.[72] In any event, the interests of the fishermen appeared to lie in quite opposite directions from the aforementioned movements: rather than seeking the closer embrace of the National Policy and the further integration with the national economy it implied, those engaged in the fishery had always advocated free trade and greater access to foreign markets.

This detachment of the fishery from the regional political protest movements of the 1920s, however, should not be taken as an indication of that industry's relative lack of troubles. Indeed, fishermen had suffered a drastic fall in prices and loss of markets in the post – First World War period. European and Newfoundland competition and a restrictive U.S.

tariff had resulted in a wholesale shift of some elements of the fishery to New England and a reduction in the number of active fishermen by almost one-third between 1919 and 1923. Those who remained suffered a sharp deterioration in living standards.[73]

The plight of Maritime fishermen was considered serious enough to warrant a royal commission to look into the problem. Appointed by the federal government in 1927, the MacLean Commission recommended official encouragement of co-operative organizations among the fishermen and the banning of 'unfair' competition from mechanized trawlers.[74] Unfortunately, this recommendation merely reaffirmed a superficial and totally inadequate government policy of assuaging the inshore fishermen's fear of mechanized competition without undertaking any major steps towards addressing the whole neglected question of fisheries development.

The Response to the Maritime Rights Campaign: The Duncan Commission

Mackenzie King's strategy of stonewalling Maritime demands and the Conservatives' advocacy of Maritime Rights reaped for the Liberal party bitter if predictable electoral results in the 1925 federal election. Whereas in 1921 the Liberals had taken twenty-five of thirty-one federal seats in the region, including a sweep of Nova Scotia's sixteen seats, four years later the Conservatives took twenty-three of twenty-nine seats. This reversal contributed to an overall election result that placed the Liberals in a minority situation, with fewer seats than the Conservatives. Left clinging precariously to power, King was forced into an attempt to make amends in the Maritimes. In 1926 he appointed the Royal Commission on Maritime Claims (the Duncan Commission) to investigate and make recommendations to the government. Its outcome emphasized even more the internal divisions within the Maritimes, the reduced influence of the region once its political support for the governing coalition was rendered superfluous, and the scant probability – given the dominant political discourse both at the centre and on the periphery – for state intervention of the nature and scope necessary to resuscitate and revitalize the Maritime economy.

In sum, the recommendations of the Duncan Commission addressed most of the issues highlighted by the Maritime Rights crusade, and on the whole were 'an exercise in the fine art of the possible.'[75] The tariff issue – political dynamite both nationally and regionally – was referred to the

Tariff Board for consideration. (Most of the evidence presented before the commission in the Maritimes, however, favoured closer national integration through increased tariffs as the solution to Maritime ills.) On the matter of freight rates, Duncan urged immediate action, professing belief in the wisdom and justice of using transportation policy as a tool of regional development.[76] On the subsidies issue, Duncan's recommendations were at variance with the historic *modus operandi* of Canadian federalism, and presaged a debate that would become the dominant federal-provincial issue for the Maritimes for at least the next thirty years. While avoiding direct advocacy of the principle of 'fiscal need' in federal-provincial fiscal relations, Duncan was receptive to regional arguments on this question, and urged the dominion's immediate attention to it.[77]

Duncan's report was received by the King government in a significantly altered set of political circumstances than those extant when the study was commissioned by the same government. The 1926 election results, heavily influenced by King's political exploitation of his disagreement with the governor general (Lord Byng), once again returned the Liberals to a majority position, leaving the government with greater freedom to deal with Duncan's report while at the same time defusing the agitation. The most notable opposition to the report came from the minister of finance within King's cabinet, J.A. Robb. His memorandum presenting an exaggerated estimate of the costs of implementing the report was leaked to the press and sparked a spreading campaign against implementation. Besides the finance minister, the railways were also opposed based on their concerns about the effect elsewhere of unilateral rate reductions in the Maritimes. As the debate continued, King himself began to waver in his initial support for full implementation, recalculating the number of 'political chickens' to be hatched by full implementation of the report's recommendations.[78]

Nevertheless, with expectations raised and future Liberal fortunes in the Maritimes riding on the government's handling of the report, it was clear that some compromise would have to be worked out that would satisfy Maritime Liberals and defuse the agitation. Politically it was crucial that it *appear* that the region's problems were being addressed, while in fact the fewest possible concessions were made. E.R. Forbes described the end result as follows:

They [the Liberal cabinet] ignored Duncan's suggestions on fiscal need and rigidity in transportation but conceded enough of the more prominent recommendations to permit the claim that they were implementing the Report. They granted the 20 per cent freight rate reduction but pared it down to exclude traffic on international lines or that entering through Maritime ports. They also conceded the subsidy increases ... but presented them only as temporary grants conditional upon Maritime good behaviour.[79]

Since the government program contained concessions of freight rates, port development, and subsidies – the most widely shared grievances of the Maritime Rights movement – the foundations of the agitation were undermined. But an even more important factor pointed to by Forbes in his analysis of the generally positive regional response to the government's announced program was the desire of the movement's leadership, especially the boards of trade, to attract outside investment during a period of buoyancy in the national economy.[80] Eager to erase the image of poverty and destitution that the Maritime Rights agitation had encouraged, regional businessmen and politicians were only too willing to proclaim victory and the imminence of prosperity in which all were invited to invest.[81] When, in 1928, it was realized just how limited and circumscribed the government's concessions were, there would be a belated and unsuccessful attempt by the Maritime Board of Trade's Freight Rates Commission to resurrect the regional agitation.[82]

While the King government was given greater latitude to deal with the report on Maritime claims after its 1926 election victory, this leeway was further facilitated by the demise of the 'united front' that provincial governments in the region had presented on the issue during 1925–6. This regional political unity was fractured soon after the formation of a Liberal government in Prince Edward Island, a partisan shuffle that allowed King and Robb to hive off the Island from the regional agitation. PEI was the Maritime province with the least interest or involvement in the Maritime Rights crusade. A province comprised overwhelmingly of petty-commodity producers, the Island had experienced an economic decline before the 1920s; it had been steadily losing population to the other Maritime provinces since 1881.[83] Quite simply, there was no manufacturing on the Island to suffer the collapse that afflicted industry in the neighbouring provinces.[84] As a result, the Island was only mildly infected with the spirit of anti-government protest that produced an overwhelming swing to the Conservatives in the region in the 1925 federal election. The new Island premier in 1927, A.C. Saunders, egged on by King and Robb, was quick to demonstrate a certain hostility towards, and lack of co-operation with, his Conservative counterparts in Nova Scotia and New Brunswick.

The issue that was used by King and Robb to detach PEI completely from the other provinces was that of subsidies. The Duncan Commission's award of a $125,000 lump-sum payment to PEI did not come near to meeting that province's needs. (It was almost entirely swallowed by increased highway expenditures between 1926 and 1927.) Premier Saunders was convinced by King and Robb that shunning co-operation with the other Maritime premiers in the presentation to the federal government of the province's subsidy claims would be looked upon favourably. In the end, however, it did Saunders little good; the dominion government refused to budge on a reassessment of subsidies to the Maritimes without 'a complete investigation of the various form of taxation which prevail throughout Canada.'[85]

Of course, as long as Ontario, among other provinces, remained fervently opposed throughout the 1920s and 1930s to any change in fiscal relations not based on the then-dominant legal fictions of provincial equality, autonomy, and self-reliance,[86] a resolution of the chronic fiscal crisis of the Maritime provinces was precluded – a fact of which King was well aware and generally supportive.[87] In other words, the way in which state élites at the centre dealt with the question of Maritime claims was shaped by the manner in which other political tensions and policy debates previously had been 'resolved' (in terms of the perception on the part of these same state élites that an acceptable 'equilibrium of compromise' had been attained, even if this amounted to no more than a dominion-provincial stalemate on certain matters). On the issue of intergovernmental fiscal relations, the 'margin of manoeuvre' for the periphery had all but disappeared.

Conclusion

During the heydey of the National Policy (1880–1914), a process of industrialization did, in fact, occur in the Maritimes. However, while high tariffs and 'railway politics' in this era made Maritime industrialization possible, other state policies in sectors necessary to the process of marine-related industrialization that was most suited to the Maritimes' particular resources and circumstances were either absent or inhibiting. Moreover, the class structure in key regional industries – notably the fishery and forestry – was *not* conducive to a process of capitalist development, thereby imposing structural limits on the growth of the regional market while exposing producers in these industries to the potentially debilitating competition of capitalist production elsewhere. As the process of consolidation that took place within the Canadian economy (as it did within all developing capitalist countries) reduced manufacturing production in the Maritimes to branch-plant status, and the balance of political forces at the centre became increasingly adverse for the Maritimes, the stage was set for the latter's peripheralization within the Canadian political economy.

Maritime Rights was a protest movement led by territorially bound regional capital that sought to revive the Maritimes' sagging industrial fortunes within the parameters of the National Policy. The basic objective of the movement was the re-establishment of the competitive conditions that had ben central to the original growth of industry in the region: a favourable regional transportation policy and higher national tariffs to protect the region's faltering heavy industries. The region's three provincial governments were also demanding a change in the basis for dominion-provincial fiscal relations in order to place their finances on a more stable footing. (Of course, implicit in this demand for increased subsidies was the question of the capacity of these provinces to provide a level of social and economic infrastructure and services that was comparable to that provided elsewhere in Canada – and thus the question of maintaining the competitiveness of the region in economic terms.)

The content of the Maritime Rights movement, its shortcomings in fully uniting and mobilizing the people of the region behind the regional protest, and its long-term failure to alleviate the damage done to the regional economy and reverse the deindustrialization of the region (and thus its relative underdevelopment) cannot reasonably be attributed to any sort of cultural conservatism that inhibited the 'entrepreneurial spirit' or somehow enjoined regional élites to capitulate to centralizing forces instead of negotiating or 'holding out' for a better deal for the region within Confederation. Nor was the region's fate merely the inevitable outcome of its geographical location, or the limitations of its resource base.

In order to truly understand the predicament of the Maritimes in the first quarter of this century, attention must be paid to the concatenation and reciprocity of separate developments rooted in a regional class structure and industrial configuration shaped by the pre-Confederation history of the Maritimes and the response of regional capital to the National Policy. The adverse effect of these factors on the competitiveness of the regional economy laid the basis for the subsequent course of development in the region, and in particular the economic crisis of the 1920s. The failure of Maritime Rights to redirect state policy at this point

is indicative of the constraints that were placed on the regional mobilization of political resistance to underdevelopment associated with the
internal political, social, and economic divisions produced by the region's
complex economic and industrial structure, as well as the adverse balance
of political forces at the national level.

The underdevelopment of the Maritimes, then, had diverse roots: the
effects on the regional economy of a structural change from competitive
to monopoly capitalism within the confines of a national economic
strategy that ultimately favoured central Canada over the peripheries; the
absence or weakness of state planning and participation in those sectors
crucial to the region's transition to an industrialized maritime economy;
the impact of capitalist competition on non-capitalist modes of production in the region; poor management of the region's huge steel-and-coal
conglomerate; and the declining ability of the region's political envoys to
defend the interests they claimed to represent and to significantly alter
the course of state policy at the centre.

These diverse roots were demonstrated in the political response to the
onset of the crisis. The Maritime Rights movement was only superficially
a unified regional response to the crisis; its main themes and demands
emerged only after competing development strategies and discourses –
such as McCurdy's radical, bi-partisan, sovereignty-association position
and the revolutionary socialist alternative advocated by the more militant
leaders of the organized industrial working class – were side-tracked,
suppressed, or co-opted. Yet even the Maritime Rights movement's
minimalist campaign proved impossible to sustain politically, *given the
extent of internal divisions and conflicting interests within the region and
the unfavourable balance of political forces at the centre.* By the end of the
1920s local business élites, industrial workers, and fishermen can be said
to have won Pyrrhic victories of sorts: concessions – in the form of the two
Duncan commissions and the MacLean Commission – that brought
limited gains within an overall context of political and economic defeat.
In the end, the deindustrialization of the Maritimes proved problematic
neither for the stability of Canadian political institutions nor for the pace
of national economic recovery in the 1920s. The region, in both a political
and economic sense, had been relegated to the status of periphery.

3 After the Fall: Economy, Politics, and Centre-Periphery Relations, 1925–39

The Regional Economy, 1926–39

The Maritime economy did not stagnate completely after the cycle of disinvestment in the early 1920s had hobbled the region's industrial base. However, neither was there any compelling reason for manufacturing capital to reinvest in the region, with the notable exception of the expanding pulp-and-paper industry. In the production of consumer goods, small units of regional capital faced the barrier of large, consolidated firms content to control the limited national market from their central-Canadian base of operations. This situation was further solidified by the onset of the Depression, which acted as a severe inhibitor to the establishment of any new units of productive capital, let alone in relatively disadvantaged regions such as the Maritimes.

The Depression also had the effect of slowing the erosion of rural class structures in the Maritimes, even reversing this process to some extent by reimposing a reliance on a form of semi-subsistence rural economy based on farming, fishing, and woodlots. At the same time, during these years large capitalist firms – pulp-and-paper mills and fish-processing plants – used small, independent producers as a source of cheap supply, purchasing commodities embodying cheap labour rather than labour power itself. Indeed, the availability of such supplies of raw material at very low prices was an important factor in maintaining the profitability and production levels of these firms during the Depression, but the burden had to be borne by the small producer and the community.[1] One result of this increasingly prevalent interconnection in the Maritimes between capitalist enterprise and independent commodity producers would be the growth of producer co-operatives as a means of establishing some countervailing power in the primary producer's relationship to capital.[2]

Agriculture

The farmers' protest in the Maritimes immediately after the First World War had been brief and rather meek when compared to its Western or even its Ontario counterpart. Part of the reason for the short duration of agrarian protest in the region (or at least the brevity of its overtly political manifestation) was the strategy adopted by newly formed farmers' parties, especially in Nova Scotia, to join forces with labour, a marriage of convenience that was rife with contradiction and ideological division. The farmers' movement was also undercut by the economic crisis of the early 1920s. Agricultural co-operatives went out of business. Urban markets for farm produce were constricted. Emigration from rural areas, one of the chief concerns motivating the farmers' movement during the period, accelerated.

In the 1930s, this outflow from rural areas in the Maritimes was reversed, but only because of the general economic situation and the lack of employment opportunities elsewhere. Thus, farm income dropped sharply between 1927 and 1932, while subsistence farming became more prevalent. In Nova Scotia this return to marginal farm operations as a shelter from the Depression was encouraged by a provincial-government policy of farm resettlement that saw unemployed miners and others on the dole given abandoned farms to work.[3] While co-operative marketing became widespread during this period, it was hampered by small commercial output. The relative inefficiency of most Depression-era farming operations is further revealed by the fact that between 1928 and 1935, at the very time when there were increased numbers in the region either choosing or being forced to remain on the farm, meat imports into the Maritimes quadrupled.[4]

Of the three Maritime provinces, Nova Scotia made the worst showing in terms of the efficiency and productivity of its agricultural sector. It ranked far behind New Brunswick and PEI, and even farther behind Quebec and Ontario, in important farm indices such as the average acreage in improved land and field crops, or expenditure per farm on fertilizers. Moreover, whereas in the Maritimes at this time 23.6 per cent of farm operators considered their principal occupation as something other than farming, this figure rose to 31 per cent for Nova Scotia.[5]

Of course, this non-commercial, small-holder structure had its benefits for the rural population during the Depression. By permitting the dovetailing of agriculture with fishing, lumbering, and other economic activities, it tended to provide a cushion for employment where there would otherwise be only very meagre welfare relief.[6] Of course, it simultaneously placed real constraints on the indigenous market for the development of agriculture. As a result, this same economic structure in rural areas that would prove an invaluable cushion for Maritimers in the Depression years would later come to be labelled as a liability to the region, and the principal reason (according to some analysts) for continued interregional disparities in per capita incomes.

Forestry

In the 1930s the trend towards an increasing duality in the forest sector in the Maritimes was reinforced, with lumbering and sawmills giving way to the production of pulp and paper as the most important wood-using industry. This transition was aided by the American tariff of 1930, which placed new obstacles in the way of Maritime forest products other than pulp and paper. But the trend was also the result of the loss of traditional lumber markets on the eastern seaboard to Pacific-coast producers and the decline of Maritime competitiveness in the U.K. market relative to northern-European rivals.

Employment in the industry was shaped by the shifting pattern of forest utilization, the ownership structure of forest lands, and the interconnections between large pulp-and-paper mills and small producers. A large percentage of the forested land in the region was privately owned. In Nova Scotia in the 1930s such land amounted to 87 per cent of the total, of which half was in small holdings that included the most-accessible stands for exploitation. Thus, the woodlot became a major feature of both agriculture and forestry in the Maritimes.[7] Operations were generally confined to the winter months, making possible the employment of off-season labour from other sectors, especially agriculture and fishing. S.A. Saunders estimates that in the early 1930s there were 10,000 part-time woods workers in Nova Scotia, and even more in New Brunswick, engaged in production either as wage-earners or as independent producers.[8] This work-force was largely unorganized and incapable of bringing about improvements in either remuneration or conditions of work.[9]

As well, a great deal of manufacturing employment in Nova Scotia and especially New Brunswick was linked to wood-using groups. (Once again, Saunders estimates that one-third of all manufacturing employment in New Brunswick fell into this category in the 1930s and about one-fifth in Nova Scotia.)[10] The increasing importance of this sector during this period is shown by the fact that it was the only branch of manufacturing in the region to substantially increase its output between 1929 and 1939.[11]

Mining

Despite the bankruptcy of BESCO and the declining fortunes of Nova Scotia's heavy industry in general, one-sixth to one-fifth of the population of that province (depending upon the estimates used) continued to be directly dependent on the steel and coal industries and their subsidiaries.[12] Saunders estimated that there were 16,000 men engaged in the mining and handling of coal in the province in the mid-1930s, and that coal made up from 80 to 90 per cent of the total value of minerals produced in the province.[13] Yet coal production had reached its peak in 1913. Continued high levels of employment in the industry were maintained because of the coal companies' strategy of 'spreading the work around.' While this served the salutary purpose of retaining an abundant reserve labour force for the mine operators, it also meant that relatively high hourly wage rates were not reflected in weekly, monthly, and especially, yearly pay packets, which on average tended to be very low.[14]

The production of coal dropped off from seven million to four million tons between 1927 and 1932, but a gradual recovery took place such that, by 1937, the production levels of the late 1920s were actually exceeded. This increase in production was primarily the result of the recovery of the iron and steel industry from its low point in 1932, and of increased penetration of central Canadian markets for bituminous coal by Dominion Steel and Coal Corporation (DOSCO). In 1935–6 DOSCO had approximately 70 per cent of the Quebec market (as compared to 61 per cent in 1928) and 11 per cent of the Ontario market (up from 0.6 per cent in 1928).[15]

This increased market for Nova Scotia coal – and the recovery of production and employment levels through the 1930s that it engendered – hinged on the coal-and-steel policy of the dominion government, which provided bonuses for Canadian coal used in gas and coking plants (1927); subventions for transportation of Nova Scotia coal to central-Canadian points (1928); bonuses for Canadian coal used in the production of coke for the manufacture of iron and steel (1930); and increased tariffs on imported coal (1931). This increasing level of government support for the Nova Scotia coal industry was reflected in the growth of disbursements from the dominion treasury to fund the various measures cited above: from $65,809 in 1928 to $1,480,795 in 1933, to $2,307,671 in 1937.[16] The result was that by the later 1930s a fairly high and stable level of employment in Nova Scotia's heavy industry had been achieved.

The Fishery

The fishing industry in the Maritimes had always been dominated by a large number of small individual producers, and to a great extent this continued to be the case in the inter-war period. Saunders described the fishery for the 1937 Royal Commission on Dominion-Provincial Relations (Rowell-Sirois Commission):

The fishing industry of the Maritime Provinces is not, as, for example, in British Columbia, a highly centralized industry. Operators are to be found in practically all the many bays and harbours along the extensive coast line of the three provinces, and the individual fisherman is still, in many branches of the industry, working on his own account and is largely responsible for the methods employed in catching, and very often in processing, the fish ... fish canning and curing establishments are organized in small individual units ... The export trades are concentrated in the hands of comparatively large firms, but many of these firms are merely dealers in fish, having practically nothing to do with processing. In all branches of the industry, therefore, with only a few exceptions, it is very difficult to obtain uniformity in the finished product and to introduce new methods and processes.[17]

This industry structure made the fishery a labour-intensive sector, but it also produced, in the person of the inshore fisherman and in the hundreds of fishing communities in the region, the lowest-income group in the Maritime provinces, the poorest educational facilities, and the least adequate medical and social services.[18] Developments in the 1930s both supported the continuation of this kind of fishery and undermined the long-run viability of the industry.

A number of factors can be cited that exerted pressures on the traditional fishery is the inter-war period. Drastic declines in the price of fish, major inroads into traditional Maritime and Newfoundland salt-fish markets by more efficient northern European competitors, and the imposition of American tariffs combined to constrict markets and slash the real incomes of Maritime fishermen. While in the period immediately after the First World War the response on the part of a number of fishermen and fishing operations to such external pressures was to relocate to the United States, there was no comparable reduction in the number of Maritime fishermen occasioned by the Depression. Instead, between 1928 and 1935 there was an increase in the numbers engaged in the fishery, despite a drop in prices of between 30 and 45 per cent over the same period.[19] In other words, the fishery, like Maritime agriculture, had become a haven of sorts during a period of crisis and contraction in the capitalist economy.

At the same time it appears that certain adjustments were taking place within the fishery in reaction to the obstacles it faced. Since the problems were most severe for the trade in salt cod, there was an expansion of trade in fresh and frozen fish during this period and a shift to species other than cod. Coterminous with and related to these developments was a consolidation process within the industry that saw the rise of several major catching and processing firms and the greater concentration of fishing effort and processing operations in a few large ports.[20] In many ways the decline of the salt-fish trade, which in its organization, techniques, and technology was a form of petty-commodity production 'par excellence,' sounded the death-knell for the 'independent commodity producer–fish merchant' relationship that had always been the fundamental social and economic basis of the Atlantic fishery. Given the existing structure of the industry, the demands of the fresh- and frozen-fish trade (cold storage and packing facilities, filleting and quick-freezing technology, fast transportation services, a large dependable supply of fish) were leading inexorably towards greater control of fishing and processing operations by large, vertically integrated firms employing large vessels that fished year round and delivered their fish to central processing facilities.

Movement in this direction, however, encountered stiff resistance in the inter-war period, particularly with regard to certain aspects of modernization such as the adoption of trawler technology. Opposition to such technology came from an impressive political coalition of inshore fishermen, large-schooner owners, and fish merchants, all of whom saw the introduction of this 'industrial' technology as contrary to their interests. This coalition had been successful in forcing the government as early as 1908 to pass restrictive legislation on the use of trawlers, and it reached the peak of its influence in 1929 with state actions inspired by the recommendation of the Royal Commission on Fisheries (the Maclean Commission) to severely restrict trawler competition. The resulting government legislation – a program of restrictive licensing with a tax on trawler-caught fish – reversed the trend towards the increasing use of this technology in Nova Scotia, effectively reducing the number of trawlers in use from ten in 1927 to three in 1939.[21]

The ability of this political coalition in the region to 'fend off' the threat of capitalist competition employing new technology is further evidenced by the failed attempt in the late 1920s by American capital – utilizing

American-owned quick-freeze technology, cheap second-hand English steam trawlers, and purchased Nova Scotia fish-processing facilities – to follow through with a plan to turn Nova Scotia into the 'Fish Pier of America.'[22] With the help of the government-imposed trawler restrictions, and collusion among Nova Scotia fish buyers and schooner captains, the American firms in question were forced either to withdraw or to sell their operations.[23]

With direct capitalist competition safely shackled, the way was clear in the 1930s for a consolidation process to proceed within the Nova Scotia industry. Out of this process of the bigger swallowing the smaller, less-efficient firms emerged two large corporations: Atlantic Coast Fisheries and the W.C. Smith–Lunenburg Sea Products consortium. This consolidation and vertical integration, while yielding significant profits for the corporate owners, continued to rely on mercantile techniques, a cheap and abundant labour supply, and very low wages.[24] The net effect was to saddle the Nova Scotia industry with antiquated and inefficient technologies and forms of organization. Fish catching, holding, and processing remained heavily labour-intensive. Capital in the industry, when faced in the 1930s with the strategic alternatives of either further technological and organizational transformation to enter the U.S. market on a competitive basis, or cutting prices to achieve the same ends, by and large chose the latter route. In this situation fishermen and plant workers were forced to bear the brunt of the losses, with drastic effect on the relative position of fishermen's and fish handlers' incomes.[25]

The Co-operative Movement

The lot of the inshore fisherman and the general economic and social conditions that prevailed in the region in the depths of the Depression called out for some form of redress, a movement of social protest and reform, and the formulation of alternative development models to the one that had seemingly gone so wrong. If there was an emergent alternative that expressed the interests and aspirations of rural primary producers in the Maritimes at this time, it was to be found in the region's several co-operative movements. And the most notable of these was the Antigonish movement, whose Catholic founders put forth a forceful and far-reaching critique of Maritime society and Canadian capitalism. In its stead they articulated a democratic-socialist vision of society that the movement's leading figure and spokesman, Mgr M.M. Coady, claimed would return the necessary control to producers to make them 'masters of their own destiny.'[26]

The difficulties of uniting individuals within this class of rural primary producers behind some sort of common social and political project aimed at changing the status quo were considerable. In the fishing industry the progress of co-operation was that it was forced to overcome a traditionally competitive and individualistic ideology, as well as a great diversity of methods and techniques. In the agricultural sector the non-commercial nature of much of the farming taking place during the Depression also reduced the incentive to engage in co-operation, since the latter was usually undertaken for the purpose of marketing the agricultural products of the more prosperous farming locales.[27] In contrast, subsistence or semi-subsistence farming tended to 'atomize' the farmer socially.

In the case of the Antigonish movement these obstacles to collective social action were overcome by the religious/ethnic/cultural homogeneity of the small fishing and farming communities of eastern Nova Scotia, and by the articulation of a binding ideology – presented almost as a form of religious expression – by the sole viable source of leadership and 'intelligentsia' available to this community that might conceivably be disposed to formulate and support a challenge to the dominant social and economic order in a time of crisis: the Catholic church and its affiliates.[28]

Unlike that of other co-operative movements in the region, the Antigonish movement's leadership was not content simply to confine itself to setting up producer co-operatives for the purpose of improving the economic lot of their 'constituents.' Instead, they seized the opportunity to play a larger social role through the establishment of 'people's schools,' study clubs, credit unions, and co-operative housing projects. According to Coady, the movement was at once an educator, a fulcrum of power that would allow the common people to squeeze their fair share out of the economy, and 'a way to the good and abundant life.' It was, for him, the expression of Christianity in the economic sphere, 'an answer to the "isms"' that would remove the necessity of revolution by abolishing the proletariat and 'making owners again of all.'[29]

While it can be said, then, that the overall aim of the Antigonish movement was the construction of a radical and far-reaching alternative to the status quo, it must also be admitted that the movement had certain characteristics that limited its potential for attaining this goal on its own. One of its most serious deficiencies was that it could not or would not seek to provide the organizational base for a protest party that could challenge the old-line parties for political power (as did, for example, the co-operative movement in Saskatchewan) with a view to implementing over time the broad program of social and economic reforms required to realize the movement's co-operative vision of society. At root this 'deficiency' in ability to bring about the long-term social and economic changes thought necessary to the realization of the movement's democratic vision lay both in its specific ideological underpinnings (as well as in the nature of that vision itself) and in the limitations placed on co-operation among subordinate-class groupings in the Maritimes by the division of class interest occasioned by the region's fragmented and unevenly developed economic structure.

The Antigonish movement, then, while it can be said to have been radical in its advocacy of sweeping changes to be brought about through 'people power,' was also a conservative force in politics. Papal social encyclicals provided the inspiration for the movement, and this source also tempered its radical character, especially in light of the Catholic church's outspoken opposition to socialism in the 1930s, and led the movement to avail itself of conservative sources of funding (e.g., the Catholic Scottish Society and the Carnegie Foundation). In the opinion of the noted Catholic theologian Gregory Baum, the Antigonish movement consciously sought to dissociate itself from 'socialism' – or for that matter any radical political alternative – and to emphasize instead its religious identification. It sought such identification both because it bestowed a legitimacy with a deeply religious people the movement could not otherwise have achieved and because it afforded the movement resources – of the church, St Francis Xavier University, the Carnegie Foundation – that would not otherwise have been forthcoming.[30]

The movement was also more 'romantic' than 'realistic' in the vision it sought to realize. In a very real sense, it sought to keep people 'down on the farm.' Its objective was to revive a society of prosperous, 'God-fearing' independent commodity producers making an honest living from the resources at hand.[31] Based as it was on a rural ideal that had long since been made obsolete by processes of industrialization, urbanization, and the development of the productive forces within Canada and other capitalist societies, the development model upon which the vision rested and the strategy of societal renewal it proposed could have been conceivable as a viable option only within the context of the Depression. In fact, it was not sustainable once an end had come to the particular circumstances and conditions in the region associated with the Depression and the process of capital accumulation – with the inevitable further urbanization and expansion of capitalist social relations of production this occasioned – had resumed.

Neither was the Antigonish movement particularly successful in bridging the gap between its social base in the rural villages and the industrial working class, for largely the same reason. In this sense, C.B. MacPherson's comments on the inherent limitations of the co-operative vision of Henry Wise Wood that motivated the United Farmers of Alberta are also salient when applied to the Antigonish movement. 'The cooperative order which was to be the essence of democracy was envisaged as a harmony of producers, of groups of citizens in their capacity as producers. To expect such harmony, it must be assumed that the sole or main conflict of interest in competitive society is that between producers ... The assumption was invalid, for it left out of account the conflict of interests between employed labour and capital.'[32]

Like the ideas of Wood, the philosophy of the Antigonish movement was rooted in 'the world view of small-holding independent commodity producers,' one that 'ignored the entirely different social relations that linked and divided labour and capital.'[33] This world-view was exemplified not only by the relatively minor attention given to the problems of the industrial working class by the movement, not to mention Coady's own discomfort with the complaints and concerns of urban workers, but also in the strained relations between the Antigonish movement and the co-operative and labour organizations of industrial Cape Breton. These organizations evolved under completely different circumstances, adopted different forms, and were estranged from the Antigonish movement by ideological and practical differences, in addition to 'hidden but felt religious tensions.'[34] It might also be presumed that the relative material prosperity of mining from the mid-1930s on moderated the appeal of the Antigonish movement and presented something of a barrier to the emergence of any 'common front' of industrial workers and rural producers under the umbrella of a common leadership and philosophy.

The relationship of the co-operative movement to the worker in the coal and steel communities of Nova Scotia, where capitalist social relations of production actually existed, was very different from the link that was forged between the primary producer and the Antigonish movement. The working class was in no position to gain greater control over the production and marketing of the fruits of their labour or their conditions of work through the co-operative movement. As distributors of consumer goods, co-operatives helped to relieve some of the burden imposed on the worker by the 'pluck me' company stores, and by so doing the British Canadian Cooperative Society in Cape Breton became for a time the largest consumer co-operative society in North America.[35] But co-operative organization could not otherwise contribute to any real improvement in the workingman's lot. Indeed, during periods of heightened industrial conflict and worker militancy they ultimately proved to be a conservative force rather than an instrument of struggle for the workers. The main vehicle of class struggle remained the union; co-operatives confined their operations to those of a business enterprise and organizer of occasional community events.[36] This suggests that the co-operative movement differed dramatically in its meaning and role, depending upon the social and material base of the movement in question.

The Antigonish movement was the logical organizational form for the expression of the class power of independent commodity producers within a crisis-ridden capitalist economy. It sought to stabilize and reconstitute a traumatized and disintegrating community and a threatened way of life. As such the movement represented the classic populist response of the rural *petite-bourgeoisie* (and their representatives) to the pressures exerted upon them by changes in the capitalist economy – pressures that tended to undermine their position as producers within that economy. While it is difficult to assess whether the co-operative movement in the Maritimes actually *diverted* attention from 'politics' as a means of bringing about widespread and far-reaching social reform, it is clear that it was either incapable of or averse to the prospect of transforming itself into a political movement by providing the organizational and ideological basis for a new political party. Such an orientation nullified to a great extent any political challenge it may have represented to the dominant social and political order.

Nova Scotia Politics, 1925–33

At the provincial level, the chief political consequence of the economic troubles and industrial strife in Nova Scotia during the 1920–5 period was the crushing defeat of the Liberal party at the polls after forty-three years of uninterrupted power. The Maritime Rights movement, initiated by the Nova Scotia Conservative Party in 1922 and endorsed by the Maritime Board of Trade in September 1923, provided the Conservatives with the vehicle to reverse the disastrous electoral losses they had incurred at the beginning of the decade, so that in 1925 it was the turn of the Nova Scotia Liberal Party to be reduced to a shadow of its former self.[37] And while the challenge facing the provincial Conservatives after 1925 was the not-inconsiderable one of consolidating their new-found voter support, the Liberal party faced what might have been presumed to be the more daunting task of making itself over and presenting a more palatable image to a provincial electorate that seemingly had been utterly alienated by the previous Liberal regime.

Provincial party politics in Nova Scotia during this period can be understood only within the context of the regional economic crisis and the coincident bitter struggle between capital and labour in the province's steel and coal towns. The events of the 1920s and the shift in the balance of political forces that accompanied them brought about a significant change in the strategies and discourse utilized by the old-line political parties in the province. In particular, the re-emergence of genuine party competition after an extended period of one-party dominance served to revalue the support of labour within the province, and altered the terms upon which that support was to be garnered. At the same time, the accumulated weight of past partisan contests and the continuing needs and demands of party organization did not simply evaporate with the onset of the crisis and the defeat of the Liberal political establishment. Indeed, such imperatives would reassert themselves with a vengeance in the aftermath of the Tory victory in 1925, much to the chagrin of the new provincial government and the delight of a dethroned and repentant Liberal party.

The initial rebirth of the Conservative party in 1922 was largely the result of the efforts and resources of a few prominent individuals: notably W.H. Dennis, who placed his two Halifax newspapers 'unreservedly at the disposal of the party' after the débâcle of the early 1920s; and two other individuals – national party leader, the Hon. A. Meighen, and Nova Scotia textile manufacturer Frank Stanfield – who apparently footed virtually the entire cost of party reorganization and the provincial leader's expenses.[38] While at first glance the support for the provincial party at this time was dismal (the Conservatives had finished third in the 1920 election with only three seats and 26.6 per cent of the vote), political prospects were brightened by the apparent inability of provincial Liberals to entice their federal counterparts to take some action to limit the severity of the regional depression[39] and by the virtual dissolution of the official opposition in the Nova Scotia legislature (the Farmer-Labour coalition).[40]

In addition, the declining popularity after 1922 of the radical variety of political representation provided by the leadership of the Independent Labour Party (which had ties with the communist Workers Party of

Canada) put the support of the industrial work-force in the province 'up for grabs.' Beginning in 1923 the Conservatives took advantage of this, attacking BESCO and the labour policies of the Liberal government, and portraying that government as the puppet of big business in the province. So flagrant (and unexpected) was the courting of the workingman by the Conservatives that frustrated Liberals took to hurling charges of 'Bolshevik' and 'Communist' at their opponents for their all-too-ready sympathy with the cause of Nova Scotia miners.[41]

The Conservative party, however, was careful not to allow its political manoeuvring to alienate key business supporters. When the party's provincial leader in 1923, H.W. Corning, put forward a resolution in the provincial legislature on secession and the establishment of Nova Scotia as an independent dominion, the response of the party executive was to immediately convene a meeting; there it was decided to quietly drop secession as an option and instead concentrate on the matters of 'Maritime rights in trade and commerce' and the issue of the Intercolonial Railway.[42] Later, more elaborate interventions on the part of the provincial executive would be required to derail the radical McCurdy faction in order to ensure that the provincial Conservative party remained a 'safe' alternative – in the eyes of business and the national party – to the Liberals.[43]

In the 1925 provincial election the Conservative party was able to capitalize on the obvious failures of the provincial government in either stemming the deindustrialization of the province or halting the fierce industrial conflict then raging in Cape Breton. The Conservative leader, E.N. Rhodes, promised that his first act if elected premier would be to intervene personally in the latter confrontation and bring an end to the prolonged strike. On 25 June the Liberals were swept from office, with the formerly invincible 'government party' winning only three seats in the entire province. In industrial Cape Breton the Liberal vote completely collapsed in the rush to the Conservatives, swamping the four sitting Independent Labour candidates in the process.[44]

On assuming office Rhodes immediately implemented a series of measures aimed at resolving the BESCO crisis and solidifying his political support among the miners. Col. G.S. Harrington, a Sydney lawyer who had identified himself with labour and defended the radical union leader J.B. MacLaughlin against sedition charges, was given the mines portfolio. The hated provincial police force was hastily decommissioned. The new premier immediately began a week-long series of meetings with BESCO and UMW officers aimed at securing a negotiated end to the stand-off. His recommendations, which included the appointment of a provincial royal commission under Sir Andrew Rae Duncan (who would later be called upon by Mackenzie King to head the federal Royal Commission on Maritime Claims) to fully investigate all aspects of the Nova Scotia coal industry, were accepted by both parties, bringing to an end the most bitter strike in the history of the province.[45]

The sympathetic overtures to labour on the part of the Rhodes government did not stop here. Throughout 1926 the government continued to vigorously criticize BESCO and to make known their hostility to the corporation's management. Moreover, after the corporation had failed and its constituent parts had been rearranged into the Dominion Steel and Coal Corporation (DOSCO), the government expressly forbade the new management from engaging in retail merchandising, effectively putting an end to the hated company stores.[46] Such concessions to labour paid handsome returns in the 1928 provincial election when the Tories gained solid majorities in the chief mining areas of the province (comprising ten seats in all), a block of support that provided the government with the margin of victory in a close contest.[47]

While the 1928 provincial election confirmed the Conservatives' upset in 1925, more striking was the phoenix-like recovery of the Liberals, who came within three seats of winning the election. The core of this Liberal resilience was in rural Nova Scotia where the party's support was rooted historically in being on the 'right side' of the great Confederation and tariff questions. And since the distribution of seats heavily favoured the rural areas of the province, an immediate advantage was conferred upon the Liberal party. The latter also benefited from the practical advantages of having been the sole dispenser of government patronage for more than four decades before 1925. Political allegiances and debts built up over this time could not be wiped out as suddenly or as completely as the Liberal majority in the House of Assembly. And in its rebuilding efforts the party could tap the resentment of numerous individuals in all parts of the province who had been the beneficiaries of Liberal largesse in years past but suddenly found themselves 'out in the cold' with a provincial Conservative government.[48]

The Conservative government, however, found that sudden control over the mechanisms of patronage afforded by the formal assumption of government power in the province was at best a dubious advantage. In the aftermath of their first electoral victory in more than forty years the Conservatives were riven by internal strife. The expectations of their supporters after so many years in the political wilderness could not begin to be satisfied, while the removal of the Liberal appointees of generations past provided the opposition with a highly motivated cadre eager for the revival and return to power of *their* party.

Matters were made worse for Rhodes and his colleagues, however, by the manner in which the party élite had manipulated internal party affairs prior to the 1925 election. McCurdy's faction within the party had been isolated, and the provincial party leader – W.L. Hall – had been cut out of the leadership in order to make way for the more attractive Rhodes, an Ontario businessman who had not resided in the province for more than a decade. While this series of moves created some resentment among Tories, Hall's subsequent treatment at the hands of the new premier – specifically Rhodes's failure to keep his promise of a cabinet post for the former leader – further antagonized Hall's supporters within the party and led to the retreat from active party affairs of a number of prominent Conservatives (including Frank Stanfield).[49]

Nevertheless, the Conservative government did survive the 1928 election, and with a general economic upturn in the province between 1927 and 1929,[50] the prospect that they would henceforth command sufficient support to ensure the genuine alternation of political élites in Nova Scotia was perhaps better than average. These positive signs for the provincial Conservatives in the late 1920s were quickly erased, however, when the weight of the Depression laid low the provincial economy. While the widespread unemployment and human suffering generated during this period were certainly sufficient to deliver a crushing blow to the electoral prospects of whatever government happened to be in power, the provincial government in Nova Scotia added to the certainty of its demise through its response to the exigencies and constraints of the situation.

First, Premier Rhodes abandoned his provincial colleagues in 1930 to accept R.B. Bennett's offer of a cabinet post in his newly elected federal government. Then the remainder of the provincial cabinet (now under the leadership of Col. Harrington) chose to postpone, cancel, or cut back popular programs in order to weather the Depression within the stringent guide-lines of fiscal orthodoxy.[51] In addition, the solid labour support that the Conservatives had cultivated since the early 1920s was eroded by the sharply rising unemployment figures and by the internal fracturing of the miners' union.[52] The government's fate was sealed when an ill-advised, last-ditch attempt to salvage their electoral prospects by rigging the compilation of the voter's list became an election issue. The resulting scandal turned an impending electoral defeat into a political rout.[53]

The provincial Liberal party, which stood to gain from the Conservatives' trials and tribulations, had itself gone through a period of self-criticism and stock-taking after the 1925 election, so that it was able to present a very different face to voters when the provincial election was finally called in 1933. Two years earlier it had held its first-ever party convention to choose a new leader and formulate a platform. At the convention speaker after speaker rose to repudiate the policies of the post-war Liberal governments of Murray and Armstrong. Time and again the assertion was made that the Liberal downfall in 1925 was a result of the party's entanglement with corporate interests to such an extent that the people could no longer support it. The clear message was that the party had to change both its image and its policies. It did both. It switched its appeal to emphasizing the need for new social legislation: aid to hospitals, an eight-hour workday, the fulfilment of an earlier Tory promise of a department of labour, free school books, and a general declaration that a Liberal government would put the interests of the people before those of private corporations and monopolies.[54] The party also chose a new leader for itself, one that suited the shift in policy and reinforced the impression of a reformed party. Angus L. Macdonald, a handsome and eloquent war veteran, was an unexpected late entry into the leadership race who had not previously been a prominent figure in provincial politics. Indeed, as an academic, he had the distinct aura of an 'outsider.' In the context of the Liberals' search for a new image and direction, a new leader untainted by any association with big business was perceived as a distinct asset to the party. Macdonald swept the convention on the first ballot.[55]

To affirm their new direction the Liberals immediately began a populist campaign that slammed the activities of big business in the province and sought to portray the Rhodes-Harrington government as a mere puppet of the big interests. Accordingly, the government was pilloried for allowing what was in fact the reincarnation of BESCO (but this time under a new name) and for their links with the Mersey Paper Company, which was condemned in Liberal propaganda as the source of the problems of Nova Scotia woodlot owners.[56]

The party's 1933 election platform emphasized social reformism and government activism. It promised an independent inquiry into 'the conditions which cripple the economic life of Nova Scotia,' and the presentation of its findings to the dominion government with the province's full support for the implementation of its recommendations. It also promised Nova Scotians that a Liberal government would push hard for a range of social-welfare measures: an expanded public-works program, direct relief of the unemployed through an unemployment scheme, the payment of old-age pensions to Nova Scotians, and improvements to the provincial education system. The provincial bureaucracy would be improved through the addition of a department of labour and a tourist bureau, along with the reorganization of the Department of Agriculture. Coal-and-steel operations within the province would be investigated and 'placed on a sound foundation,' a major program of highway paving would be undertaken, and unspecified actions would be taken to ensure the development and greater prosperity of the forestry and fishing industries.[57]

In the aftermath of a disastrous regional depression and bitter class struggles in the province's coal towns, the provincial Conservative party in Nova Scotia had opportunistically cast itself as the defender of the regional interest and a friend to labour. The political success of this strategy shifted the ground for political competition in the province. It forced reforms within the Liberal party and altered the political discourse and electoral platforms of both parties in order to avoid association with the discredited discourse and policies of the 1920–5 Liberal government. At the same time, the parties exercised their overweaning influence over the parameters of the political debate to exclude radical options from active consideration as serious alternatives to the political status quo. Secessionist and socialist tendencies were, for the most part, excluded or pushed to the margins of political debate, to be replaced with moderate programs of reform and a more 'balanced' approach to conflicts between capital and labour in the province.

However, such discursive and programmatic changes did not herald the demise of more traditional bases of political support and competition in the province. Indeed, a continued basis for parochial patronage politics was buttressed by the deindustrialization of the 1920s and the enforced economic and social regression of the Depression years. And here the 'dead hand of party organization' exercised a strong influence over the course of party politics, preoccupying party leaders and organizers with questions of patronage and in the process re-creating the basis for a politics based on the 'Ins' and 'Outs.' Thus, no 'new politics' associated with the rise of class-based or protest parties advocating radical reforms emerged during this period in Nova Scotia, or the other Maritime provinces as it did in western Canada. Instead, a superficially remade and relatively progressive-sounding Liberal party prepared itself for a return to power in the midst of the Depression.

The Jones Commission

Within a year of its landslide election in 1933 the new Liberal government in Nova Scotia launched its investigation into the province's economic situation: the Royal Commission of Provincial Economic Inquiry (the Jones Commission). The Liberal government's instructions to the commission left little doubt as to where they believed the onus for Nova Scotia's economic difficulties lay. The commissioners – J.H. Jones (chairman), A.S. Johnston, and H.A. Innis – were asked to investigate and consider the effect of the dominion's fiscal and trade policies on Nova Scotia and the adequacy of the financial arrangements between the dominion and Nova Scotia in light of the powers, responsibilities, and obligations of each under the federal constitution, and further, to make recommendations based on their findings that would contribute to the removal of any economic, financial, or other disability that was preventing the economic advancement of Nova Scotia.[58]

The provincial government itself drove its point home in a brief submitted to the commission on its behalf by Norman MacLeod Rogers (shortly thereafter to become the federal minister of labour). He argued before the commissioners that national tariff and transportation policies had led to the closing down and consolidation of Nova Scotia's manufacturing capacity and raised the production costs of the province's export industries. In effect, the tariff had acted as a tax on Nova Scotia and a subsidy to central Canada. It did not represent a fair compromise among conflicting provincial interests within the dominion.[59] On the matter of subsidies, Rogers advocated dropping the per capita subsidy formula, which ignored the reality that the revenue capacity of a province had more to do with its economic development than its population, and replacing it with a subsidy based on the principle of *fiscal need*.[60]

In their report the commissioners agreed with the substance of the provincial brief. The tariff had indeed brought about a diversion of industry and trade that benefited central Canada at the expense of Nova Scotia. (That this was a perception held not just by the provincial government seems clear from the numerous individual and group submissions before the commission calling for secession or some sort of Nova Scotia free-trade zone.)[61] But at the same time, in the industrialized eastern portion of Nova Scotia, coal and steel production was highly dependent upon a protected domestic market and increasingly as well, with regard to coal, on federal transportation subventions. The commissioners responded by advocating even greater transport subventions and a purchasing policy on the part of the railways for both coal and rolling stock during periods of recession.[62]

On the subject of freight rates, the commissioners were highly critical of the manner in which the Maritime Freight Rates Act (MFRA) of 1927 had been applied by the railways. The intention of the act clearly had been to restore the pre-war relationship between rates from the Maritimes and those of other Canadian regions (in line with the Duncan Commission's recommendations). Yet, in practice, rates were so reduced in central Canada after 1927 as to again destroy the relationship supposedly re-established by the MFRA, a development that the federal regulatory authority (the Board of Railway Commissioners) did nothing to halt because of their acceptance of the railways' pleas that they were required to grant special rates in central Canada in order to counter water and road competition there. Jones and his fellow commissioners became convinced that what was needed was a better mechanism to oversee the MFRA to ensure that the spirit of the legislation remained intact in its implementation.[63]

With regard to financial arrangements between the dominion and the province, the commissioners advocated one of two courses to solve the problem of equity: the dominion could seek to establish equity on its own by taking over from the province certain services that fell within the latter's jurisdiction or by establishing a fund for allocation among the different provinces in accordance with their fiscal needs.[64] The commissioners on their part advocated the transference of certain services to the dominion: old-age pensions, unemployment insurance, technical education, and public health, with the rationale for this transfer being the development of such services to a common standard across Canada.[65]

Finally, in response to the many complaints before the commission about unfair trade practices, regional dumping, and unjustifiable price spreads, the commissioners recommended that the dominion consider instituting a federal trade commission along the lines of that established in the United States.[66]

While the brunt of the Jones Commission recommendations were thus aimed at dominion-designed and administered national policies, and were dependent for their implementation upon the agreement and will to act of the dominion government (and in some cases the agreement of other provinces), the commissioners did suggest some things that the province itself could do to improve its situation. Most important, they argued the need for a permanent civil service in Nova Scotia, to enable consistency and continuity of administration, a greater degree of control over the exploitation of natural resources, and the collection and collation of data to guide provincial policies.[67] It was also thought that a provincial economic council should be established as an advisory body on matters relating to trade and industry. Other measures, such as a program of road-building and rural electrification, could directly meet employment needs while upgrading the province's economic and tourist infrastructure.[68] Finally, it was the commissioners' opinion that the appalling conditions of the fishery at this time provided just cause for the removal of control over the fisheries to the province, with sufficient allocations from the dominion for its administration. Improving fisheries infrastructure, banning steam trawlers, and invoking legislation encouraging the development of co-operative enterprise in the province were advocated as complementary measures to this jurisdictional change.[69]

In his complementary report, University of Toronto political economist H.A. Innis offered his own insightful analysis of Nova Scotia's disabilities within Confederation. As might be expected from a scholar who had become widely recognized for his ground-breaking studies on the historic relationship between centre and periphery in the process of economic development, Innis's argument demonstrated an acute awareness of the factors impinging upon the balance of power in this relationship, and furthermore the importance of such power relations to the process of development. Stripped bare, Innis's argument made three essential points: that a clear divergence of interest within the province of Nova Scotia (between an export-oriented, commodity-producing western region and a domestic market-oriented, industrialized eastern region) had weakened it politically in its dealings with the centre; that low productivity, low standards of living, and poor working conditions in the fishery and in forestry were largely the result of the methods of production and poorly organized work-forces that characterized these sectors; and most important, with regard to state policies, that the Ottawa civil service had failed to avoid piecemeal solutions and contradictory policies in its dealings with the periphery, resulting in a failure to address fundamental problems and the growth of bitterness on the part of certain groups against Confederation. Thus, if the province was to overcome the obstacle of the Ottawa civil service, it must build one of its own 'in order that the evils of existing central control may be checked.'[70]

It should be noted that in the 1930s Nova Scotia had no counter to the dominion bureaucracy, no 'state capacity' to take charge of its own development policy. Under depression conditions, argued Innis, there was a real danger of further centralized control, which demanded the extension and improvement of regional governmental machinery.[71] In considering future trends and provincial strategy, Innis emphasized the evident importance to the province of a development policy carried out in co-operation with the dominion government. For the good of the province, the trend had to be towards 'a marked expansion of provincial control and a narrowing of central control except insofar as it can coordinate and assist provincial and regional development.'[72]

[This] implies the cornerstone of a provincial civil service. Unified provincial direction is fundamental ... [A new] National Policy must be intensive and regional in character and must depend on a strong provincial civil service ... We [the commissioners] are convinced that the trend toward centralization in banking, railways, finance, and industry tends to become less efficient in relation to the outlying areas and must be offset by a definite reversal in terms of developmental policy. Increasing centralization must be offset by increasing devolution if the more distant regions are to guard more effectively their interests.[73]

The analysis offered by Innis and the other commissioners in 1934 suggests that Nova Scotia's disabilities were in large part a function of political and bureaucratic decision-making at the centre. But it was also apparent to them that there were other factors that were limiting or debilitating in nature: the internal divisions that politically weakened the periphery, an underdeveloped state structure that sharply circumscribed the ability of the province to exert any control over its own economic development, and the presence of internal obstacles to the development of major resource industries such as the fishery and forestry as a result of the continued utilization of archaic methods of production and the lack of organization among workers, which left them weak and divided and, therefore, unable to force improvements in their wages or working conditions.

The provincial government, for its part, acted on a number of the commission's recommendations, while ignoring others. A Nova Scotia economic council was established on the recommendation of the Jones Commission to advise the government on matters of economic development. Legislation was brought in to aid the establishment of co-operatives. The government also sponsored the Civil Service Act of 1935 in line with the recommendation of the Jones Commission that the province needed an effective permanent bureaucracy. But there were so many exceptions, omissions, and loopholes in the act that the standard mode of operation was left virtually intact.[74]

In addition, there were a number of state actions to counter the debilitating effects of the Depression. The province used deficit financing and dominion grants to embark upon a large-scale program of highway construction.[75] Increased tariffs and subventions led to a recovery in the key coal and steel industries, and the resource sector began to show some growth.[76] Combined with an increase in public works and the widespread return to rural, semi-subsistence activities, the improved economic situation removed tens of thousands from the welfare rolls. As early as 1935 provincial-government officials could boast of a reduction in the numbers on relief of more than two-thirds.[77]

By the mid-1930s the crisis conditions in Nova Scotia wrought by the Depression had eased and a measure of economic stability had been restored. The populist streak exhibited by the Macdonald Liberals in the early years of the decade did not extend very far on fiscal and economic matters, and government under Angus L. Macdonald proved quite compatible with the continued operations of big business in the province. When Macdonald next went to the polls in 1937, there were no major issues in the campaign, nor were there further promises of sweeping reform, and the government was easily re-elected on a 'stand-pat' platform.[78]

The one significant ripple of political discontent in 1937 was the apparent resurgence of support in industrial Cape Breton for a radical third-party option. In 1937 this took the form of the Cape Breton Labour Party (CBLP), which arose from nowhere and almost stole a seat from the Liberals. Two years later, after the CBLP had been reconstituted as the CCF (NS), it did win a seat in the provincial legislature, the first CCF victory east of Ontario. This success was repeated in the 1940 federal election when CCF candidate Clarie Gillis was elected as the member for Cape Breton South.[79]

This renewed support in industrial Cape Breton for a radical socialist alternative in the arena of party and electoral politics signalled the end of a long period of internal conflict that had divided the labour movement ideologically and organizationally. When finally the rift was narrowed in 1936 with a general return to the UMW, former leaders of both leftist and rightist factions within the labour movement joined together in their endorsement of a new party – initially the CBLP and then the CCF.[80] With an army of volunteers at its disposal in the mining commmunities, the party became an instant force. But in future decades it would fail to grow beyond its origins as an 'enclave' party, defined, shaped, and staffed by its miner and steelworker constituency in industrial Cape Breton, drawing local political strength from this close affiliation while at the same time restricted to its narrow confines.

Centre-Periphery Relations in the 1930s

Throughout the 1920s Canada's Liberal prime minister W.L. Mackenzie King had balked at extending the role of the dominion government in the economy or embarking upon any redistribution of the powers and responsibilities of governments in Canada. Moreover, the issue of increased subsidies was allowed to remain deadlocked with the Prairie and Maritime provinces putting forward mutually incompatible claims and Ontario stubbornly resisting both as an unjust 'leeching' of Ontario taxpayers in order to subsidize the residents of the poorer provinces. The prosperity of the 1920s for most of Canada other than the Maritimes merely affirmed the stance of the more well-off provinces in their resistance to those proposed changes to dominion-provincial financial arrangements, or to the Constitution, that threatened to reduce their autonomy.[81]

Indeed, far from heeding the increasingly insistent distress calls coming from the Maritimes as the decade wore on for some kind of rebalancing of fiscal relations in order to rescue foundering provincial governments in the region, provinces such as Ontario and Quebec were content to demand in successive dominion-provincial conferences that the dominion government turn over to them the field of income tax,[82] This measure would have sharply increased already large and growing disparities between provinces by undercutting any actual or potential role for the central government in the geographic redistribution of wealth in Canada. Indeed, the dominion government's response to demands was to use its role in regional redistribution to justify its rejection of central-Canadian demands for it to vacate the field of income tax in favour of the provinces. [83]

In fact, the actual extent to which the dominion government used its taxing power to play an equilibrating role was extremely limited. As already noted, subsidies to the provinces were maintained at their low per-capita level, totally divorced from the actual capacities of provinces to raise the necessary revenues to provide a comparable level of infrastructure and services to their residents. Moreover, the further involvement of the dominion government in the provision of social welfare was forestalled by the reaction of King and his cabinet to the decision rendered by the Judicial Committee of the Privy Council in case of *Toronto Electric Commissioners* vs *Snider* (1925). This ruling, which prevented the central government from using its general grant of power to legislate in the area of industrial disputes, not only made it incumbent on the provincial governments to manage industrial relations, it also provided the premise for King to argue that the dominion had no constitutional authority to provide unemployment relief.[84] And while political exigencies forced a reluctant dominion government into the design and implementation of an old-age pension scheme, beginning in 1928, the Maritimes – the provinces most in need because of their relatively older populations, lower incomes, and employment crises – were prevented from taking advantage of the program because of the relatively high cost of accepting the dominion's conditions for entry (i.e., that the provinces were expected to pick up one-half of the costs of the program).[85]

Taken together, the practical political balance within the Canadian federation, the sanctioned legality of a judicially interpreted constitutional division of powers and responsibilities, and the ideological predilections of the dominion government (and especially the ever-cautious and calculating King) worked against any amelioration of the Maritimes' predicament. A raised level of subsidies was blocked by the dominion government's parsimony and its ability to exploit sharp provincial disagreements on the issue in order to resist any further outlays; any serious discussion of a reallocation of government responsibilities in light of new realities was thwarted by the opposition of the larger, well-off provinces who effectively stood in the way of constitutional change; and the possibility of an enlarged scope for direct federal intervention in the field of regional economic development, or in the provision of social welfare, was dampened both by court decisions unfavourable to the prospect and, perhaps more important in the final analysis, by a genuine ideological aversion on the part of state élites at the centre to embark on such a change of course.

In effect, the Maritime provinces were 'ghettoized' within Confederation in the 1920s, thus allowing the other governments of Canada to get on with the accumulation function in a boom period of economic growth and prosperity. Moreover, as long as economic depression and fiscal crisis remained a 'localized' problem, and barring some major shift in the balance of political forces at the centre or a sharp political seizure such as Maritime secession, this state of affairs could have been expected to continue indefinitely.

The great stock-market crash of 1929 and the Depression years that followed changed the calculus of the situation, though not immediately. Initially the conditions fostered by the Depression made little impact on the willingness of state élites at the centre, or those running the larger provinces, to engage in any wholesale re-evaluation of the federal system in Canada. Instead, there was wrangling over the immediate exigencies of the economic crisis, especially the costs of unemployment relief. The Bennett government in Ottawa, which had inherited the crisis upon its assumption of office in 1930, asserted that the prime responsibility for the provision of welfare fell on the individual, the municipality, and the province, in that order. And since the provinces were not ready to hand over jurisdiction on the matter of relief to the central government, there was little that Ottawa could do. As a result, 'little was achieved at a 1933 Dominion-Provincial conference besides the endorsation of existing methods of funding relief to the unemployed.'[86]

It was only in the second half of the decade that a significant shift began to take place in the balance of political forces within Confederation, one based on new calls from various quarters for more concerted action on the part of the central government. Opinion within the dominion government itself moved away from stubborn adherence to fiscal orthodoxy and 'limited government' towards the greater application of the fiscal power of the central government as a corrective to defective market forces. As well, the whole question of dominion-provincial relations in Canada was handed over to a royal commission in 1937 for the most extensive study of the Canadian political economy undertaken up to that time.

However, the return of Mackenzie King and the Liberal party nationally in 1935 did not immediately herald a change in political discourse. King himself remained orthodox on both fiscal and constitutional matters. He continued to believe that governments should balance revenues and expenditures and that each level of government should be responsible for its own policies and programs and for collecting the money to implement them.[87] His choice of finance minister confirmed this conservative approach. Charles Dunning was chosen by King because he represented fiscal conservatism. Dunning opposed any 'orgy of expensive social reform without regard to how it is to be paid for.' As minister of finance he would 'stand for stability, non-interference with legitimate business, sanctity of governmental contracts, and prevention of provincial raids upon the Federal Treasury.'[88] Such views, while undoubtedly reassuring to Canadian capitalists, did not bode well for the unemployed or the financially strapped poorer provinces.

Given the conservatism of King and his finance lieutenant, and the continued intransigence of the wealthier provinces on the matter of a rearrangement of federal powers and responsibilities, the prospects for making progress on resolving the long-standing issues of Confederation at the 1935 dominion-provincial conference were dim. On the agenda were the amendment of the BNA Act, financial relations between the dominion and provincial governments, unemployment relief, and social services. However, any resolution of the first two of these items was deferred by the first ministers, with discussion of the subject of amending the BNA Act commended to its own conference at an unspecified later date and the question of social legislation set aside pending the outcome of the dominion government's reference of Bennett's 'New Deal' legislation to the Supreme Court.[89]

Given this determination to defer or shelve these central issues, Nova Scotia's appeal at the conference for a change in financial arrangements and the division of responsibilities went nowhere. Nevertheless, Premier Angus L. Macdonald made the province's case, citing as evidence a provincial deficit accumulating every year since 1923 despite a very frugal administration. The fundamental problem, it was argued, was a restriction in the available sources of revenue, and the only clear solution was the assumption by the dominion government of the full costs of certain social services borne by the province.[90]

Little headway, then, was made on the questions of constitutional reform or social legislation, but the King government did assent to bearing the full cost of relief for individuals classified as permanently unemployable, while also offering immediate and substantial increases in federal grants to the provinces for relief. This weakening of the dominion government's resolve to protect its financial position proved quite temporary, however, and it was soon stiffened by a rising federal deficit that was sufficient incentive to snap the federal purse shut again and provoke an across-the-board cut-back in grants to the provinces.[91]

Nor did Nova Scotia succeed in altering the position of the dominion government on the subsidies issue. While there was no formal response to the Jones Commission on the part of the dominion government, King did appoint yet another royal commission, this time one on the financial arrangements between the dominion and the Maritime provinces (the White Commission). The report that followed resoundingly closed the Duncan Commission's tentative opening to the idea of a continuing federal commitment to deal with regional disparities through some form of annual subsidy readjusted on the basis of fiscal need. The White Commission attempted to put this idea to rest. It clung to the ideal of provinces as self-sustaining entities and attempted to resurrect the 'solution' of a 'once-and-for-all' settlement of claims.[92]

Other initiatives taken by King upon his return to power were the appointment of a national employment commission to study the unemployment problem (though this was undertaken mainly with the hope that it would dramatically reduce relief costs by eliminating various abuses of federal funds),[93] and the proposal of reforms to dominion-provincial financial relations designed to reduce the amount of dominion aid to the provinces. Perusing the actions of the prime minister between 1935 and 1937, historian H.B. Neatby was led to conclude that 'King did not yet see that the fundamental problem was the financing of all government activities in Canada and that the financial problems of the federal government could not be resolved separately.'[94]

It was not until the late 1930s that the dominion government moved away from the old orthodoxies (both fiscal and constitutional), and then only because of the impetus of an impending political crisis within the government if it did not do so. The change of approach was brought about by the urgings of senior bureaucrats who were becoming convinced of the need for the central government to adopt a larger social and economic role and the growth of a similar political sentiment within the cabinet. That action by senior bureaucrats led directly to a conversion plan to aid the near-bankrupt Prairie provinces and to the launching of a grand inquest into dominion-provincial relations – the Royal Commission on Dominion-Provincial Relations (the Rowell-Sirois Commission).[95]

The most concrete manifestation of a change of direction, however, came in 1938 when the minister of labour, Norman MacLeod Rogers, came before cabinet with a program of public works totalling more than $75 million. Although King had appointed the cabinet committee headed by Rogers to devise a program of public works, he was stunned at the size of recommended expenditures, as was Dunning, his finance minister. But like many of Ottawa's senior bureaucrats, Rogers, who had always favoured a major social role for the central government, had been converted to the economic doctrines of John Maynard Keynes. He stood firm on the cabinet committee's proposed public-works program and threatened resignation. Many in the cabinet supported his position. There were also bureaucratic supporters for a change of direction, prompting King in January 1938 to refer pejoratively to senior civil servants such as Skelton, Clark, Mackintosh, and others as 'these men ... who have been working jointly to seek to bring about a change in constitutional relations which will lead to a centralization of powers and away from the present order of things.'[96] In a bid to head off a political crisis within his government, King encouraged a mediated solution to the sharp conflict within his cabinet. The result was a recovery program in 1938 that marked a significant extension of federal economic intervention.[97]

The Rowell-Sirois Commission was appointed in 1937 with the idea that a constitutional conference would be called to discuss its recommendations. The division between rich and poor provinces in Canada once again became clear in provincial submissions made to the commission. Nova Scotia argued for a redistribution of national wealth to compensate disadvantaged regions of the country to be accomplished by establishing dominion-provincial financial relations on the basis of fiscal need. The province also advocated the consolidation of welfare – mothers' allowances, old-age pensions, unemployment insurance – under federal jurisdiction in return for the exclusive right to levy succession duties and income tax.[98] Ontario's premier Mitchell Hepburn, however, felt that his province had already been asked to give too much to the federal government to pass on to the poorer provinces. He rejected any notion of national minimum standards, arguing instead that every region should fix and finance its own level of social services. In a biting tone, Hepburn concluded that Canadian unity would be achieved only 'when Ontario is no longer the milch cow of the rest of the country.'[99]

When the commissioners finally submitted their report to the dominion government in 1940 they had totally rejected the position of the Ontario government and embraced that of the Nova Scotia government. Developments since 1867 and the economic collapse after 1930 had destroyed any 'logical relationship ... between the local income of any province and the constitutional powers and responsibilities of that province.' Moreover, federal grants-in-aid were a 'thoroughly unsuitable' means of financing programs. The commissioners suggested instead that the federal government take responsibility for the employable unemployed. 'The provinces would withdraw from the field of income tax, corporation taxes, and succession duties, and all existing subsidies would cease. In return federal authorities would assume the entire burden of provincial debt and pay over to the provinces *National Adjustment Grants*. These would permit the provinces to provide services equal to the Canadian average without imposing above average taxes.'[100]

The Rowell-Sirois Commission, then, accepted fiscal need as the governing principle in dominion-provincial financial relations, and its recommendations were aimed at relieving the excessive burden shouldered by the poorer provinces in the provision of social services and the uneven quantity and quality of such services that resulted. But while the commission's recommendations would ensure the financial security of the smaller provinces and establish minimum national standards in the provision of social services, these were primarily compensatory measures that attempted to deal with the effects of uneven regional development. The sources of this pattern of economic development would remain if not addressed by other state initiatives in various policy fields.

In the dominion-provincial conference called in 1940 to deal with the Rowell-Sirois report, Ontario, Quebec, British Columbia, and Alberta opposed the implementation of its recommendations. But the country had been plunged into another war in Europe, and King had already received a confidential memo from the governor of the Bank of Canada urging immediate action on the commission's recommendations to avert chaos in provincial finances, ruinous competition for tax room, and the enormous social problems that would be associated with post-war unemployment.[101] Thus, while agreement on the recommendations of the Rowell-Sirois Commission was not achieved at the conference, there was sufficient consensus to allow for an amendment to the constitution giving the dominion government jurisdiction over unemployment insurance, and a temporary way was found to centralize and expand fiscal power (via tax-rental agreements between Ottawa and the provinces) as a necessary measure to finance and conduct the war. For the duration of that war, however, questions of constitutional reform, the appropriate division of revenues and responsibilities between governments, and the role of state policy in precipitating and perpetuating regional economic imbalances in Canada would be placed in abeyance.

Conclusion

The economy of the Maritimes, devastated by a severe regional depression in the early 1920s, demonstrated a brief spurt of recovery between 1927 and 1929 before being plunged back into deep recession in 1930. The general nature of that recession encouraged a return to subsistence and semi-subsistence production in the Maritimes (where such an option was still a possibility for many), and a rise in the numbers of those engaged in farming, forestry, and fishing. State policies that encouraged the resettlement of abandoned farms, and all-but-banned the use of relatively capital-intensive trawler technology in the fishery, facilitated this process. The predominance of small-holding and independent commodity production, however, did not bode well for the competitiveness of the region's farm, wood, and fish products as more efficient and productively organized operations elsewhere made inroads into traditional regional markets, both locally and abroad. Capital in the Maritimes – whether 'industrial' as in pulp-and-paper production or 'merchant' as in the fishery – maintained the profitability of its operations in this period by lowering the cost of the supply of raw material through exploitative pricing arrangements with individual primary producers. As noted by Nova Scotia's Jones Commission, the economic and organizational weakness of primary producers inhibited development within certain sectors of the Nova Scotia economy. It also provided the material basis for clientist politics in the region and gave impetus to the co-operative movement. That movement, which tended to be either narrow and limited in its economic goals or conservative and romantic in its political and social outlook, could not by itself offer a credible and durable alternative to the capitalist system it sought to replace (or at least moderate). In the Maritimes there was no conflating of the aims and discourse of the co-operative movement with the political and social goals of the organized working class; no radical political alternative to the status quo with both urban and rural roots (a 'Red-Green' alliance along the lines of the defunct Nova Scotia Farmer-Labour Party) could re-emerge in the inter-war period.

This state of affairs left the two old-line parties without serious challenge in the electoral arena. But it did not preclude changes in the strategies, discourses, and policies of the Liberals and Conservatives as they manoeuvred for electoral support and sought to stabilize the situation in the context of an extended economic crisis in the province. This manoeuvring involved processes internal to the parties themselves as well as a certain dynamic of issue construction and redefinition spurred by the sudden renewal of more genuine two-party competition in the province. Thus, a political struggle within the provincial Conservative party over contending strategies and discourses determined the political form that the regional protest would adopt: a more radical non-partisan, quasi-secessionist tendency was isolated, while the support of industrial workers was courted. The latter took place in the context of an extended period of extremely bitter industrial conflict in the province that appears to have been the occasion for something of a shift in the balance of power between capital and labour in the province. The ability of the miners to confront and at length overturn a brutal profit strategy pursued by BESCO management in the 1920s also contributed to the demise of a Liberal provincial government that had been pursuing a policy of straightforward support for capital in the dispute. The Conservative successor to the 1920–5 Liberal government consciously pursued a more even-handed approach and even demonstrated a measure of hostility towards the 'absentee' management of the huge coal-and-steel conglomerate. For its part, the dominion government, after adhering to a self-serving 'hands-off' policy throughout the conflict (which did not prevent the repeated dispatch of the military into the area), finally bowed to pressures to support the region's coal and steel industries and enacted a series of measures to this effect between 1928 and 1931.

While the Conservative party in Nova Scotia was in this way able to win over the province's industrial workers, the rural political base of its Liberal rival survived the unprecedented defeat of 1925 relatively intact, and provided the means for a political resurrection of sorts three years later. But the experience of the last Liberal government and the resultant political successes of the Conservatives did have a salutary affect upon the Liberal party, which publicly repudiated its earlier policies, especially its complicity with big business in the province, adopting instead a more populist discourse, a 'clean,' 'independent' leader, and a reformist policy platform. This reformation left the Liberals well-positioned to take advantage of the crumbling of political support for the Conservatives in the early 1930s, and to a degree pre-empted the possible rise of a more radical alternative to the political status quo in the province. The emergence of such an alternative was made unlikely in any event not least by the organizational and ideological rifts that divided the largest body of organized workers in the province – the miners – from the early 1920s until 1936. It was not until 1936 that a significant measure of organizational unity and political solidarity and activism was recaptured, although on a more limited scale and a narrower geographic and social base than had been the case immediately after the First World War.

In 1934 the new Liberal government in Nova Scotia gave a royal commission the task of divining the causes of Nova Scotia's economic disabilities within Confederation. The commission report noted the divisions within the province on such matters as the tariff question (and the political implications of such divisions). It also argued that though important regional measures had ostensibly been won (e.g., the MFRA), these had been subsequently undermined by the railways and the actions of federal bureaucratic agencies. H.A. Innis's adjunct report took the argument farther by stating that the federal civil service had failed to address coherently the fundamental development problem of the region, instead contributing to its lack of resolution through its own piecemeal solutions and contradictory policies. Any further centralization brought on by the Depression, therefore, would be anathema to the design and pursuit of an effective development policy for Nova Scotia. The neglect of the fisheries, its starving of both a coherent development policy and resources, was singled out as a particularly glaring example of the 'dead hand' of centralist administration that justified the 'repatriation' of this sector to the province.

Of all the recommendations made by the Jones Commission aimed at removing Nova Scotia's disabilities, those most salient to dominion-provincial relations in the 1930s (and for some time thereafter) dealt with the need for changes in the Constitution and intergovernmental financial arrangements in order to relieve the poorer provinces of the excessive burden of welfare and social-service costs. Even though the Maritime provinces were forced to settle for a lower level of such services in comparison with the wealthier provinces, they nevertheless remained hamstrung in fiscal terms. In effect, the situation of the Maritimes in the inter-war period was taking on the characteristics of a regional 'ghetto,' whereby relatively impoverished areas have their disadvantages reinforced and accentuated by a system that makes no provisions for any redistribution of wealth between richer and poorer regions, but instead sanctions the ever-increasing growth of interregional disparities through a constitutional compartmentalization of revenues and responsibilities into federal and provincial containers.

Centre-periphery relations at this time were governed by the narrow provincialism of the larger provinces within Confederation and the fiscal conservatism of the King government in Ottawa. The former rejected any revision of powers and responsibilities that would reduce their autonomy while the dominion government clung to fiscal orthodoxy and a 'hands-off' watertight-compartment view of jurisdictions. Such a view precluded any major intervention or revision of financial arrangements to address the mounting fiscal crisis in a number of the poorer provinces. Only in the late 1930s did the balance of political forces supporting the status quo begin to shift at the centre as an increasing number of senior bureaucrats and cabinet ministers accepted the economic theories of Keynes and the need for a Canadian 'New Deal' that would permit expanded use of the federal spending power and greater centralized management of the economy. Of course, the adoption of such policies would also entail a stronger central government and an end to the highly decentralized federalism of the inter-war period.

In the end, the question of whether a compartmentalized 'ghetto federalism' could have continued unscathed by the crisis of the Canadian peripheries, or would be reformed by converts to Keynesianism, was rendered moot by the exigencies of the country's participation in the global conflagration of 1939–45.

4   The Decade Following the War: The Post-war Regional Economy and Political Impediments to State Intervention

The Maritime Economy

In 1944, Nova Scotia's Royal Commission on Provincial Development and Rehabilitation (the Dawson Commission) made clear the impact of the war on the regional economy and the development problems facing the province as the conflict drew to an end. R. MacGregor Dawson pointed out in his report that of $714 million in government investment in expanded industrial capacity to 1 January 1944 the Maritimes had received a meagre 2.46 per cent, most of which went towards the construction of temporary facilities.[1] Thus, while central Canada provided with greatly enlarged industrial facilities as a result of the war, the contracts awarded to Nova Scotia served only to create serious problems of labour adjustment arising from the attraction to wartime jobs of farm and fishery labour.[2] It was estimated that the war brought a 75 per cent increase in employment in the Maritimes, three-quarters to four-fifths of which was thought to have come from people not previously employed (industrial unemployed, women, young persons), the balance from farms and fishing villages. There was a reduction of 40 per cent in those engaged in fishing and 25 to 30 per cent of those engaged in farming.[3] In effect, the war 'drained off' surplus labour in the rural areas and eroded the self-reliant, subsistence-oriented rural economy prevalent throughout much of the region in the 1930s. But if this newly mobilized labour force was to remain 'absorbed' into the wage sector after the war – and a process of 'labour dumping' back into rural primary industries (and significant out-migration) avoided – a continued high level of economic activity and industrial expansion within the region would be required.

In fact, over the period from 1940 to 1958, the three Maritime provinces – Nova Scotia, New Brunswick, and Prince Edward Island – would experience an advance in gross provincial product (GPP) of 76 per cent, 75 per cent, and 65 per cent, respectively. But Canada as a whole would see a 119 per cent rise in gross national product (GNP). In other words, aggregate growth in Canada was 1.5 to 1.8 times that of the three Maritime provinces for this period.[4] Thus, while there was growth in the Maritimes, it lagged behind the nation as a whole.[5] This disparity is further reinforced by comparing the average 2.4 per cent annual growth in GPP for Nova Scotia over the decade from 1950 to 1960 with the 5 per cent average annual growth in GNP over this same period.[6] A sector-by-sector analysis, however, is more revealing of the dynamics of change within what appears to be in aggregate terms a slow-growth regional economy. It shows that in general the primary sector – agriculture, forestry, the fishery, and mining – was experiencing a process of expansion and/or rationalization over the 1940–60 period.

Agriculture

Agriculture was the 'hardest hit' in terms of a decline in employment and the number of operating units. While this decline in the number of farms and farmers had been going on since 1911, it picked up pace considerably during the war and in the post-war years.[7] In 1941 agricultural labour made up 26 per cent of the labour force in the Maritimes; by 1961 it was down to 5.1 per cent in Nova Scotia, 7 per cent in New Brunswick, and 26 per cent in Prince Edward Island.[8] While participation in farming was clearly declining, the small average size of farms, the small percentage of commercial farms to total farms (only 38 per cent in Nova Scotia in 1956), and very low capital investment continued to be identified as problems in post-war Maritime agriculture.[9] Production levels between 1945 and 1962 barely increased, while during the same period Ontario and Quebec experienced a 20 per cent rise in real net value of production and Canada as a whole, a 95 per cent increase.[10] Studies of Maritime agriculture in the mid-1950s showed a startling regional deficit in a wide range of food items.[11]

Yet within this overall picture of relative stagnation in production, there were signs of movement and change. The region experienced a massive 39 per cent reduction in farm acreage between 1941 and 1961 (as compared to 6 per cent for Canada),[12] with a corresponding increase in the average size of Maritime farms. Thus, if non-census farms are excluded from the 1961 census, the average size of farms in the Maritimes grew at a rate almost double that of central Canada for the 1941–61 period. Of course, the fact that the reverse is true when *non-census farms* are included in the calculations indicates the relatively large number of small, semi-subsistence operations that were still in existence at this time.[13]

The more one 'fleshes out' the profile of the agricultural sector, the more the contradictions within Maritime agriculture continue. While the Maritimes in 1961 had a larger ratio of *small* farms to total farms than did central Canada, and the smallest ratio of *commercial* farms to total farms,[14] over the 1941–61 period the increase in the capital/output ratio and capital/labour ratio in Maritime agriculture was greater than for central Canada, leading to larger overall productivity gains for this period.[15] Since this increased capital intensity and productivity were accompanied by the decline of small subsistence farms, the suggestion is that some (perhaps much) of this statistical increase in productivity can be attributed to the stepped-up abandonment of marginal and subsistence farms. In addition, a progressive concentration of farming in the more highly productive locales was occurring, as well as a shift away from cereals and livestock (disadvantaged by competition from producers elsewhere) to dairy and poultry production and export crops such as potatoes.[16] Finally, by the latter part of the 1950s the construction of food-processing plants within the region (for meats, potatoes, and frozen fruits and vegetables) was under way.[17]

With regard to the Nova Scotia government's position on 'what to do about agriculture,' submissions to both the Royal Commission on Canada's Economic Prospects (the Gordon Commission) in 1956 and the Special Senate Committee on Land Use in Canada in 1957, as well as the recommendations of its own Royal Commission on Rural Credit (1957), are clear: greater availability of long-term credit for farmers was crucial to a continued process of farm consolidation and expansion. The conservative loan practices of the Canadian Farm Loan Board in particular were singled out for criticism, with the solution seen to be greater federal-provincial co-operation to assure liberalization of the process of extending credit for farm improvement and expansion.[18] In its own recommendations the Gordon Commission urged a government program to finance the consolidation of farm holdings where possible and the re-allocation of marginal farmlands in the region for forestry purposes.[19] Soon after these reports, the federal government, through the Farm Credit Corporation, and the provincial government, through the Farm Loan Settlement Board, substantially increased the size of loans available to farmers.[20]

Forestry

Forestry, which included the pulp-and-paper, logging, lumber, and wood-using industries, was by 1961 the region's most important export sector, with pulp and paper alone accounting for 40 per cent of all exports in value (fish and fish products were a distant second, at 19 per cent).[21] Production gains in pulp and paper between 1940 and 1958 were significant: a 100 per cent increase in real terms in *gross value* and *employment* in New Brunswick, and increases of 65 per cent and 37 per cent, respectively, in Nova Scotia.[22]

In contrast to this expansion of the pulp-and-paper industry, and the change in forest utilization it wrought (for instance, pulpwood production in New Brunswick increased tenfold between 1919 and 1958), lumber and sawmilling production was halved between 1919 and 1958. Admittedly, there was some modest growth in this industry in the post-war period, but employment was stagnant, and both government and private-sector studies warned that without substantial improvements the small average size, low efficiency, and lack of product differentiation that characterized lumber operations in the region did not bode well for the industry's future.[23]

With regard to logging, R.D. Howland's study for the Gordon Commission pointed to its *seasonal amplitude* and the high proportion of the cut carried out by *small operators* as the main factors explaining the low net value per worker. The latter was related by Howland to the *pattern of land ownership* in the Maritimes, which, as a region, had a much higher percentage of its forest land privately owned than did the rest of Canada, and much of this in small parcels, often with absentee landowners.[24] Howland considered this to be an obstacle to efficient, large-scale development for forestry purposes achievable through the application of greater amounts of capital, as well as sound management and conservation practices.

As for the seasonality of logging in the Maritimes in the 1950s, this was specifically addressed in a joint study prepared by the federal and Nova Scotia departments of labour. According to this study, one of the contributing factors to increasingly high levels of seasonal unemployment in the region was the disruption of traditional work patterns in which logging was a fall and winter activity for rural persons. Post-war developments in both logging and fishing – occasioned principally by the demands of pulp-and-paper mills and larger fishing vessels – had altered and lengthened work seasons, making it increasingly difficult for individuals to combine logging in winter with small-scale farming or small-boat fishing in the summer.[25] Moreover, the same complaints made by Innis and the Jones Commission in 1934 – very low prices and wages for both woodlot owners and loggers, poor working conditions, and a badly organized labour force – continued to characterize the logging industry in the Maritimes as late as 1961, constituting at that time, according to one federal study, a major source of poverty in a number of the region's rural counties.[26] Nova Scotia woodsmen earned slightly better than one-third the average wage of BC loggers in the early 1960s, and the educational level of the former was the lowest of all major census groups.[27]

Howland's study for the Gordon Commission also suggested that the industry's low wage structure actually discouraged seasonal participation since it was difficult for the workers to earn very much more by working in the winter than could be collected in unemployment insurance and social-welfare benefits.[28] Indeed, the availability of such 'external' benefits – a new development in the Maritime economy – could not but alter both the future basis for successful accumulation within the region and the strategic calculations of subordinate groups and individuals. In other words, national politics and policies in this instance contributed to a de facto shift in the balance of power between classes in the region that demanded a new response on the part of capital, and ultimately a reorganization of the affected industries.

In effect, the extension of state benefits to workers in low-wage, low-productivity industries would gradually make it incumbent upon capital to alter its methods, organization, and profit strategies. Moreover, the industrial adjustment thus encouraged would be facilitated and 'directed' by making available government-aid packages to the affected corporations. Thus, just as the government response to problems in Maritime agriculture was to advocate and implement policies aimed at furthering the consolidation of holdings and the greater application of capital, so in forestry the major thrust seems to have been, at least in the case of Nova Scotia, the acquisition of increased acreage to bring Crown holdings to a bigger percentage of the total forest.[29] The forest could then be made available for efficient exploitation on a profitable basis. The Gordon Commission itself, based on its analysis of Maritime problems as rooted in the disproportionate number of people engaged in marginal activities (including part-time or seasonal logging), similarly advocated the consolidation of holdings as well as assistance in the relocation of rural-dwellers and the better use of 'underutilized lands' (and here the commissioners deferred to the then recently established Special Senate Committee on Land Use).[30]

The Fishery

For centuries, a widespread, seminal economic and social activity in the Atlantic region, the fishery perhaps best illustrates the perceived development problems and conundrums of the rural-based primary sector at this time. A gravitation of labour from rural to urban areas, from fish plants to higher-paying industrial jobs, which began to occur as the Depression lifted, picked up pace with the onset of the war. By 1942 there was an unprecedented labour shortage in the fishery, a development that focused attention on the deficiencies of an industry that had up until that point depended upon an abundance of cheap labour.[31] Concerned about stagnating production, the federal government offered subsidies and depreciation allowances for the construction of draggers and trawlers and in 1944 provided grants for long-liners and other craft over fifty-five feet in length.[32] The large companies were the first to exploit these new programs, and the result was extended mechanization of the fishery. At the same time, the continued need for labour in the processing plants led to the increased employment of women and the importation of labour from Newfoundland.

After the war, government-imposed restrictions on trawlers were gradually lifted and federal-government subsidies extended for the further construction (and under certain conditions the importation) of new trawlers, draggers, and long-liners.[33] Beginning in 1943 the provincial government extended large capital contributions for freezing plants and financial assistance for port facilities (the latter leading directly to the construction by two large processing companies of major plants in Louisbourg and Petit-de-Grat in 1950 and 1953, respectively). The enactment by Ottawa of the Fisheries Improvement Loan Act in 1955 added to state assistance for the purchase and/or overhaul of vessels and equipment. One of the main beneficiaries of this change in state policy was the giant National Sea Products (NatSea), chartered in 1945 as an amalgamation of eighteen companies and their subsidiaries. By 1953 the new company had phased out its archaic schooner operations to be replaced by seven mechanized trawlers.[34] By the end of the decade over one hundred long-liners would also be built with government subsidies, and the number of Canadian trawlers in the Atlantic fishery would rise to thirty-seven,[35] while investment in small boats would decline to a fraction of its 1935 level.[36] In addition, capital expansion in numerous areas of the region to build fish-processing, packaging, and cold-storage plants was under way. To circumvent American duties on processed fish NatSea also expanded its U.S.-based fish-processing operations.[37] The cumulative effect of these changes was that while employment in the fishery remained relatively constant, output was quadrupled.[38]

Nevertheless, the fishery continued to be dominated, in terms of numbers if not volume of catch, by *inshore fishermen*. The low productivity and incomes of the latter, in the opinion of the Gordon Commission, dragged down average industry results, leading to the suggestion that further centralization and capitalization were needed.[39] It was anticipated by the commission that the trend to more sophisticated means of production, larger and more mechanized plants, and increased productivity would continue, accompanied by declining opposition within the region to these developments. The most advisable course for government under such circumstances was to extend further assistance for the necessary capital expenditures to modernize the industry – an inflow of capital which had to be matched by a parallel outflow of labour if higher incomes and earnings were to be generated. It was not in the industry's interest to resist this trend![40]

One significant reason for the continued low incomes of Nova Scotia fishermen and fish-plant workers in the post-war years ignored by the Gordon Commission was the history of labour relations in the industry. Declining real incomes and wage cuts in 1938–9 had led to a surge of organizing among fishermen. Four simultaneous strikes by fishermen and plant workers in Halifax, Lunenburg, and Lockeport in 1939 met with little success. Only the plant workers were successful in getting the provincial government to recognize their status as a legitimate union (and only after they had returned to work).[41] It wasn't until 1943, however, that plant workers broke away from the Canadian Fishermen's Union (CFU) to create the Canadian Fish Handler's Union.

The problem of recognition for the fishermen remained throughout the war years because of the Nova Scotia government's position that the share system made deep-sea fishermen 'co-adventurers' with processors and vessel-owners, and therefore ineligible to form or join a union. After the National War Labour Relations Board denied certification to the CFU in 1946, the two unions reunited to form the Canadian Fishermen and Fish Handlers' Union (CFFU). After a bitter and prolonged strike by the CFFU in 1947, the Nova Scotia Supreme Court ruled, in the *Zwicker* decision, that the granting of union status to fishermen was invalid on the basis of their status as co-adventurers rather than employees.[42] Continued attempts by the CFFU to force a change in its legal status through various actions were finally ended by the onset of Cold War hysteria and the successful campaign by companies and government to discredit the union leadership as 'communist' for its unholy association with the communist-led Canadian Seaman's Union (CSU). The CFFU found few allies in this ideological struggle. Both the union movement and the CCF had conducted and would continue to conduct their own anti-communist campaigns. In the atmosphere of the Cold War they scrambled to dissociate themselves from the taint of communism and thus shelter themselves from the political fall-out of anti-communist hysteria.[43] Ironically, the failure of the unionization drive within the fishery in the immediate post-war period not only deprived workers in that industry of an organizational base to defend and promote their interests, it also undoubtedly hurt the long-term prospects of the CCF in the region, since the spread of unionization among workers in the fishery harboured at least the potential for increased political support in rural areas for a radical alternative in the realm of party politics.

In the event, the demise of the CFFU was followed by amendments to the Nova Scotia Trade Union Act in 1947, which, 'restricted collective organization among fishermen to one organization, the Fishermen's Federation of Nova Scotia, and excluded all groups in the industry, except the offshore fishermen, from membership. The act further limited organization by county, frustrating either industry-wide, or even company-wide bargaining ... the Act restricted bargaining to only two items: the terms or conditions of sharing, and work conditions.'[44]

This amendment effectively ended the drive for an industrial-type union of all fishermen.[45] By in this way legally preventing the effective organization of workers in the fishery, the government was party to maintaining conditions of underdevelopment within the industry. By ensuring that the balance of power would remain heavily weighted towards the companies, the latter could continue to pursue profit strategies based on cheap wages, outmoded and inefficient technology, and poor working conditions without fear of worker militancy or the compulsion to seek to maintain productivity and profit levels through other means. Indeed, the inability of Nova Scotia fish companies immediately after the war to increase production when the opportunity presented itself is indicated by the complaints of a shocked Nova Scotia minister of industry that Nova Scotia companies were refusing the new business that his efforts had generated! Thus, the minister was led to urge the premier to overrule the historic opposition of Nova Scotia companies and recognize the need for *new capital* in the industry. (It appears that the minister had an able and willing American firm in mind!)[46]

Mining

Mining is the last of the primary-sector industries to be considered. As late as 1958 it was estimated by the Atlantic Provinces Economic Council (APEC) that 25 per cent of the Nova Scotia economy was in some way based on coal.[47] At the end of the Second World War there were more than 13,000 coal miners in Nova Scotia mines, and if the industry had a troubled past, its future was even more clouded. In 1946 the Royal Commission on Coal (the Carroll Commission) reported its findings. It recommended that the federal government continue to assist Nova Scotia coal production, but in the form of transportation subventions rather than the wartime policy of production subsidies.[48] Also based on the Carroll Commission's recommendations was a campaign of modernization and mechanization that received a federal contribution of $7.5 million in loans under the Maritime Coal Production Assistance Act (MCPAA) of 1949 and a DOSCO investment of $5 million.[49]

As for the miners, throughout the war and again at its end they called for public ownership of the mines. When the 1947 contract negotiations stalled, union leaders bit the bullet and launched the first general strike by District 26 of the UMW since the great 'Standing the Gaff' strike of 1925. Poorly planned and executed, with little in the way of support from International headquarters or other unions in Canada, the strike was a dismal failure. After three months the miners were forced to return to work with little to show for the effort. The 1947 strike 'certainly shattered whatever belief had ever existed that the union could beat DOSCO in a strike confrontation.' To make matters worse, the debts incurred from the ill-fated strike led to the loss of the *Glace Bay Gazette*, the only worker-owned daily newspaper in Canada (and the only Canadian daily to support the CCF).[50]

The years following the 1947 strike would witness internal bickering, anti-communist and anti-leftist campaigns by an increasingly conservative union leadership, and the signing of 'sweetheart' contracts (including a three-year wage freeze in the mid-1950s) – all this against the backdrop of an increasingly uncompetitive industry with shrinking markets. Indeed, the bleakness of the profit picture for DOSCO's mining operations in the

1950s was apparently sufficient to convince union leaders to shift their attention from the company to the government, perceiving that further government assistance to DOSCO was the only alternative to major wage concessions on their part.[51]

The coal industry in the 1950s clearly represents a case of industrial decline sliding towards a crisis. In 1946 the two largest consumers of Nova Scotia coal were the national railways, yet by 1960 not one locomotive was using coal.[52] The problem of dieselization of the railways was exacerbated by competition from alternative fuels and hydroelectricity, which was rapidly shrinking traditional thermal-generation markets in Atlantic Canada, Quebec, and eastern Ontario.[53] To keep Nova Scotia coal competitive, federal-government subsidies were increasing: from 1945 to 1959 total subventions amounted to $74 million on 26.5 million tons of coal. This spending rose sharply in 1959, reaching $15 million on 3 million tons of coal. And while there were productivity gains in the mines in the post-war period (between 1945 and 1955, productivity was raised by 47 per cent, while there was a corresponding drop in employment from 13,200 in 1946 to 11,300 in 1955, to 10,200 in 1958),[54] even greater productivity gains were being made in American mines as a result of mechanization and massive labour reductions, continuously undercutting the relative competitiveness of Nova Scotia coal in remaining Canadian markets.[55]

The government response to the problems of the coal industry in the 1950s was twofold: continued subsidies and subventions to try to maintain the competitiveness of Nova Scotia coal in its traditional markets, and assistance with capital funds for the mechanization of mining operations. Representative of this policy was the Liberal government's 1949 legislation; the Diefenbaker government's Atlantic Provinces Power Development Act (APPDA) in 1958, which forwarded financial assistance to encourage the use of coal for the production of thermal power in the Atlantic provinces; and a revised Maritime Coal Production Assistance Act (MCPPA) in 1959, which provided further government loans for the mechanization of DOSCO's mining operations.[56]

By 1960, another royal commission on coal (the Rand Commission) was forced to come to grips with what seemed by then to be the inevitable decline of coal mining in Nova Scotia. Its basic recommendations were aimed at government-aided adjustment. Subsidies were to be aimed at maintaining at least skeletal operations and conserving mining investment values. If social disruption in mining communities was unavoidable, the process should be graduated. Production should be cut back to the most economical mines and the drive to mechanization continued. Government acquisition of the mines was not seen as a solution; nor would it improve matters, from Rand's perspective. In effect, the coal industry as it existed was being given the 'kiss of death,' with few concrete suggestions for alternative economic activities to replace it (tourism, vocational training, animal husbandry, and 'new industry' were mentioned).[57]

Manufacturing and the Public Sector

Manufacturing in the Maritimes has traditionally been closely related to the resource industries already discussed, as well as the manufacture of those products that have had a natural advantage in the local market (for instance, various perishable goods). But in the wake of the National Policy and its creation of a tariff-protected national market for secondary manufactures, a number of significant manufacturing concerns were also established, producing a wide variety of durable and non-durable consumer and producer goods. This manufacturing sector underwent a process of consolidation and centralization in the 1890–1920 period, with disastrous results for Maritime manufactories and the employment base they provided for many Maritime communities.

In Nova Scotia, some gains were made during the war years, only to be lost in the period immediately after the war.[58] The situation was worst in industrial Cape Breton. In contrast to central Canada, there was little in the way of new productive capacity added to the industrial base present in the Sydney basin before the war. The only new development was the rehabilitation of the steel-plate mill for ship construction that had been abandoned in 1920. Yet, just as a federal-government decision caused the shut-down of the plate mill after the First World War, so it did after the Second World War. As the war was winding down, the federal government offered DOSCO a financial incentive to cease producing ship's plate. DOSCO obliged, and the mill's assets were sold. At the same time, the size of the plant's work-force was slashed. By May 1947, fully one-half of Nova Scotia's 20,000 unemployed were in Cape Breton. A year later, industrial Cape Breton (along with Pictou County, Nova Scotia) was termed the worst spot in Canada's employment picture by the federal department of labour.[59] The employment situation eased, however, with the coming of the Korean War. Indeed, in 1952 employment at the Sydney steel works could reach a post-war high of 5,200.[60]

In contrast to the outcome of the 1947 miners' strike, Nova Scotia steelworkers were able to secure gains as the result of their participation in a national steelworkers' strike in 1946. They benefited from strong *national* bargaining by the United Steelworkers of America and from strong, almost universal, local support. Even so, DOSCO management, claiming inability to pay, held out after Canada's other steel companies had accepted the terms of a national agreement. DOSCO settled with its work-force only after face-to-face negotiations with reconstruction minister C.D. Howe had netted the company a federal subsidy to cover the cost of the increased wages the settlement would entail.[61]

In terms of the overall performance of the manufacturing sector in the post-war period, a comparison of the percentage contributions of important economic sectors to GPP and GNP for 1951 demonstrates the lagging contribution of manufacturing to the Nova Scotia economy as compared to Canada as a whole, while that of service industries and government was much higher than the Canadian average.[62] Between 1948 and 1955, real gross value in secondary manufacturing in the province (other than resource-related manufacturing) rose by less than 20 per cent, a pattern similarly exhibited in New Brunswick.[63] By 1958, there were almost ten thousand fewer employees in secondary manufacturing in the province than there had been in 1943–4.[64]

It is apparent that this crucial sector was not performing the same role of creating new employment opportunities in the post-war period in the Atlantic region that it was elsewhere in Canada, as evidenced by a regional comparison of employment increases in the sector for the 1949–57 period: central Canada, +18 per cent; Prairie provinces, +17 per cent; British Columbia, +27 per cent; Atlantic provinces, +1 per cent. In New Brunswick and Nova Scotia manufacturing employment actually *declined* by 3.8 per cent during this period, with major job losses experienced in the textiles and knitted-goods industry, with the latter's share of manufacturing employment in the region dropping from 7.2 per cent in 1949 to 2.9 per cent in 1958.[65] (At the same time gross value of production was cut in half, ruling out the possibility of job loss due to the introduction of labour-saving technology.)[66] As would be expected, the region's share of salaries and wages in manufacturing also declined during this period, from 4.6 per cent of the Canadian total to 3.7 per cent.[67]

The respective contributions of the *public* and *private* sectors to economic growth in the Maritimes are also revealing. These figures indicate that it is primarily retarded private-sector investment that explains the relatively poor performance of the region in the late 1940s and the 1950s. In the area of construction, for instance, government accounted for one-half of the expenditure on durable physical assets in PEI, and around

40 per cent in New Brunswick and Nova Scotia, as compared with only 25 per cent in central Canada and between 23 and 33 per cent in the West. Yet the regional values for total construction differed little on a per-capita basis, suggesting a comparatively larger role for the state in the Atlantic region in building and maintaining physical infrastructure during this period.[68]

If the rate of *new capital investment* over the period 1950–60 is measured as a percentage of gross product, it is again apparent that a considerably smaller portion of this investment went into the private sector in Nova Scotia (68 per cent) than in Canada as a whole (81 per cent).[69] Total capital expenditures per capita in Nova Scotia were also much lower than for Canada (58.8 per cent of the Canadian average over the 1949–56 period), though capital investment by the public sector alone approached the Canadian average.[70] This suggests the relatively dismal performance of private capital in Nova Scotia at this time, as well as the failure of the state to make up the difference through sharply increased public-sector investment (i.e., per-capita public-sector investment would have had to have been appreciably higher than the national average to compensate for the private-sector deficiency).

Summary and Assessments of the Regional Problem

What was the impact of these various changes on the overall structure of the regional economy, and Nova Scotia's economy in particular? While Nova Scotia experienced an 8 per cent rise in employment between 1950 and 1960, the primary sector – agriculture, fishery, forestry, mining – experienced employment reductions as small-scale production by small units became increasingly uncompetitive and uneconomical, and consolidation into larger, more mechanized production units with a smaller overall work-force and higher output per worker proceeded apace. This decline of employment in primary industries, however, was not offset by significant increases in construction and manufacturing employment: these remained static as a source of employment in the 1950s. Also, what expansion did take place within manufacturing – mainly food and beverages – resulted in the displacement of male by female workers. This displacement was also a feature of the increase in service-sector employment in Nova Scotia, which rose from 104,000 in 1950 to 134,000 in 1960. (One-third of this increase was the result of an expansion of defence services,[71] the rest attributable to a general increase in the 'white collar' clerical, sales, teaching, health, and other service occupations, jobs generally unavailable to those male manual workers experiencing redundancy in the goods-producing industries.)[72]

Though in general the regional economy was experiencing growth in output and productivity, modest increases in overall levels of employment, and increased personal incomes (real income per capita in the Maritimes increased by 94 per cent between 1926 and 1955, as compared with an 80 per cent increase for the rest of Canada), the Maritimes were clearly lagging behind the performance of the rest of Canadian economy in the 1950s. Employment and investment in key sectors stagnated, preventing movement of the labour force from the labour-shedding primary sectors to labour-absorptive secondary-manufacturing and construction sectors, while growth in the service/public sector drew disproportionately upon female and more highly educated workers. In this milieu the out-migration of young males from the region was significant and inevitable, while a 'surplus' rural, non-farm population increased in size. Thus, although farm population in the three Maritime provinces declined by 26 per cent between 1951 and 1961, urban population remained constant as a percentage of the regional population at 55–56 per cent. Meanwhile rural, non-farm population rose to 35 per cent of the regional populace. In 1961, fully one-third of the total population of Nova Scotia fell into this latter category.[73]

This rural non-farm population created by the changing production methods associated with the effects of capitalist development in the primary sector constituted a relatively impoverished group, even by Maritime standards. Their situation was thought to be central to the 'regional problem' as defined by the Gordon Commission.[74] Maritime poverty was seen by the Commission as primarily a problem of *rural poverty* associated with the relatively large number of non-commercial or subsistence-oriented farmers–fishermen–loggers in the region. The solution put forward was to quicken the pace of development in the resource industries through an infusion of public capital for basic facilities and for private capital to raise productivity and further reduce the primary-sector work-force. The out-migration of the inevitable surplus population would have to be facilitated through the state provision of financial assistance.[75] (Of course, as has been shown, this solution ignored entirely other problems associated with the decline of heavy industry, the stagnation of manufacturing, and the heavy reliance on public-sector spending and employment that were also characteristic of the regional economy.)

So while the rationalization and mechanization of primary industries in the Maritimes gradually proceeded in the post-war period with state assistance and encouragement – a process characterized by the expansion of both foreign and domestic capital in these sectors, the continuing erosion of rural class structures, and the decline of petty-commodity and semi-subsistence or household modes of production – there were no state policies to ensure the parallel expansion of investment in regional manufacturing industries. And while some of the labour being released from the primary sector was absorbed through the growth of the public and service sectors, this absorption was not sufficient to produce levels of economic growth comparable to the rest of the country. Such an economic structure generally restricted the scope and diversity of employment opportunities such that a process of out-migration from the region quickly resumed after the war, accompanied by the enforced marginality of an increasing number of those who remained behind in the region, rural-dwellers in particular.

By the early 1960s what appears to have been a substantial measure of agreement emerged among economists on the region's development problems. Although exhibiting some small differences in specifics, major studies by A.C. Parks, A.K. Cairncross, and J.F. Graham pointed to the same obstacles inhibiting economic development in the region, and offered similar conclusions as to the proper 'development path' that public policies should encourage.[76] The solution to low incomes in the rural areas was a continuation of the trend towards rationalization and mechanization of the primary sector, which would lead to increased productivity and higher incomes in resource industries. But this pattern of growth was also part of the problem since the expansion of capital in resource industries and not in other manufacturing with greater labour-absorptive capacity prevented the movement of the labour force from labour-surplus sectors to the extent that this shift had occurred in other parts of the country.[77] The result of this process was a large and persistent surplus of labour that had only two avenues of release: even larger migration movements out of the region or considerable expansion of secondary manufacturing.

The probability of a labour surplus even after allowing for these avenues created a strong argument for federal subsidies to encourage the further expansion of secondary-manufacturing industries in the region.[78] And state assistance for this purpose could be justified on grounds of efficiency: it would reduce the loss of manpower, production, and revenues that results from local underemployment. Migration alone would not address this problem, for 'there were limits to the scale on which labour transfers are possible without inflicting lasting damage on the economic and social life of both types of area [centre and periphery].'[79] Moreover, there were also other kinds of limits on the scale of 'labour transfers' or interregional migration. Impoverishment, age, sentimental attachments to family and community, and skill levels might all impinge upon such migration, and state policies aimed at overcoming these impediments to out-migration could prove to be politically very unpopular.[80]

If the relative decline of the Maritimes in the post-war period was not clear to all concerned before the report of the Royal Commission on Canada's Economic Prospects (1957), it certainly was thereafter. Even so, the analysis and recommendations of the commission, which followed from the various submissions and studies with which it was presented, represented but a point of crystallization for what was becoming an improved 'climate' for aid to the region and a wider movement advocating government policies and programs to specifically address development problems in the Maritimes. In his study for the Gordon Commission, *Some Regional Aspects of Canada's Economic Development*, R.D. Howland noted the change in the tone of the then recent discussions on the Atlantic region, from the highly legalistic anti-productive squabbles of the 1920s and 1930s, to a focusing of attention on the design of possible policies and programs to produce improvements in the regional economy 'at reasonable cost'; in other words, the debate was not so much a matter of *if* federal aid for economic development purposes was justified, but of *what kind* of special program of assistance to the region should be forthcoming. The trend at that time, as Howland noted, seemed to be to supplement fiscal aid with economic assistance primarily in the field of resource development.[81] In fact, these observations on what Howland referred to as 'an improved political climate' for assistance to the Atlantic region for economic-development purposes were soon to be verified by just such an increased state presence, at both the federal and provincial levels, in the field of regional development.

Where did government transfer payments for welfare purposes fit into this pattern of development? What was the role and impact of unemployment insurance, family allowances, social assistance, and pensions? While *earned income* per capita (excluding transfer payments) in the Maritimes fell from 75 per cent of the Canadian average in 1945 to 66 per cent in 1958, the inclusion of *government transfer payments* sustained per capita incomes in the region at 70 per cent of the national average, suggesting the important role the state was beginning to play at this time in maintaining the level of personal incomes in 'lagging regions.'[82] This state role of compensating for a delinquent private sector was also apparent in a relatively high level of defence spending and in the construction of physical infrastructure, where a level of public-sector activity approximating the national average compared favourably with a dismal private-sector performance.

Government transfers of various types undoubtedly slowed out-migration from rural areas by providing a supplementary source of income that allowed rural dwellers in particular to knit together a sustaining income and facilitated the formation and/or continuation of modes of existence that in and of themselves had come to be associated with the problem of rural poverty and underdevelopment as diagnosed by economic analysts. This seeming contradiction in state policies remained and remains unresolved. For, while the promotion of growth and efficiency in the economy may demand one set of policies, the need to win and retain political support often results in other policies that interfere with an efficient process of economic transformation. But in buttressing the position of the subordinate classes by giving them access to non-market sources of income, state policies have discouraged some modes of accumulation in favour of others. Certainly accumulation based upon abundant supplies of cheap labour has become less viable. Instead, modernization and the substitution of capital for labour increasingly has become a necessity for competitive survival; in effect, the state has become the handmaiden of modernization. And especially in regions and industries where accumulation based upon extensive exploitation has been the rule, the state, in a haphazard way, has been drawn into the planning and subsidization of the modernization process.

Centre-Periphery Relations and Post-war Reconstruction Proposals, 1945–6

Wartime Politics

In the space of a few short years, the war had exercised a strong influence on the direction and content of Canadian politics. By 1943–4, the Co-operative Commonwealth Federation (CCF) – with a string of by-election victories, official-opposition status in Ontario, and election in Saskatchewan as the first socialist government in North America – had become a serious electoral threat to the Liberal party. The prime minister, Mackenzie King, was deeply disturbed by the socialists' rising strength and felt that it had to be countered by an increased emphasis on the post-war policy of his government.[83] As a result, Leonard Marsh, a prominent member of the League of Social Reconstruction and the CCF, and one of the authors of *Social Planning for Canada* (1935) and *Democracy Needs Socialism* (1938), was commissioned by the Cabinet Committee on Reconstruction to produce a report on social security that would parallel the Beveridge Report in Britain. Furthermore, in response to the rise of CCF fortunes, the Liberal caucus and National Liberal Federation were called together for a series of meetings, consultations, and planning sessions.[84]

The main strategic response on the part of the Liberal government to emerge from all this frantic activity was an electoral campaign aimed directly at those Canadians leaning towards the socialist alternative as represented by the CCF. With the slogan 'For a New Social Order' the Liberals offered voters a welfare program in 1945 that 'stole just enough of the Socialists' thunder to make it a credible reform platform, but was eminently practical and within the capacity of the government to implement without seriously disturbing the balance of power between government and business.'[85]

The proposed post-war program also fit in well with the changing ideological complexion of state élites at the centre who had by the mid-1940s shed the fiscal conservatism and economic orthodoxy of an earlier period; in its stead they had adopted a centralist Keynesian perspective on the proper post-war role for the federal government, with, as it turned out, certain important and uniquely Canadian caveats and adaptations.[86] Indeed, while the political exigencies of the 1943–5 period, and especially the electoral threat posed by the CCF, may have been the key factor in nudging the federal cabinet and Liberal party down the road of social reforms, such a policy course already had considerable support and sympathy within the upper ranks of the federal bureaucracy. And by 1945 this group – a powerful clique of senior civil servants – was wielding unprecedented influence over government policy-making.[87]

But co-optation of personnel and policy was not the only response to the socialist electoral threat. There was also a surge of vitriolic propaganda aimed at the CCF and its program, warning of the party's diabolical intent and the dire consequences should it succeed in its goals.[88] In 1945 the new party was successful in resisting this onslaught only in those few areas where it had acquired strong organizational support. Saskatchewan, where the CCF had formed the government in 1944, is the best example. The party also did well in parts of British Columbia where organized labour was well established and highly politicized. It could boast only 'pockets' of support elsewhere, including industrial Cape Breton where an impressive degree of local organizational support existed for the party.[89]

But further union-party links of this type, which the national leadership of the CCF wholly expected to become commonplace, proved elusive. The leadership of the Trades and Labor Congress (TLC) preferred to work with the Liberal government of Mackenzie King rather than to throw its support behind the socialist alternative.[90] And only a year after the CCF had been endorsed by the CCL leadership as the political arm of labour in 1943, the CCL Congress repudiated its stance and, like the TLC, turned its efforts to lobbying the federal government.[91] By 1945, the party by and large had been left to its own devices by the union movement to face the old-line parties and a hostile press, and it did not fare well. In 1945 the Liberal party won election victories both at the federal level and in Nova Scotia. This victory ensured that post-war reconstruction would take place under the party that had been in power in Ottawa since 1935, and in Nova Scotia since 1933.

Preparing Nova Scotia's Position

At the end of the Second World War many Nova Scotians were of the opinion that the dominion government would not allow the Maritimes to return to a condition of economic stagnation, and that a program of public investment aimed at full employment would be undertaken. This was certainly the opinion expressed by R. MacGregor Dawson in his 1944 report to the Nova Scotia government on post-war rehabilitation. Dawson argued that any benefits from the dominion's full-employment policies for the post-war years would accrue primarily to central Canada. The political, economic, and financial centralization required to carry out Keynesian programs, and the concern those programs manifest for the grand total of the national income, did not bode well for such provinces as Nova Scotia. Dawson feared that, on the one hand, this increased centralization would lead to a demotion of the provincial government, while, on the other, 'there was likely to be a distinct lack of concern over the sources and the distribution of the sources of [national] income.'[92]

To counter this eventuality, Dawson drew on the moral, political, and economic reasoning of the Jones Commission to make a case for dominion assistance in regional development. A federation's primary purpose, argued Dawson, was to shape its policies such that they would promote the welfare of all its component parts. Nova Scotia's capacities had to be developed to the utmost, and this could only be done, given the circumstances in 1944, through *direct government expenditures on plant expansion in the region*, at least restoring the relative position of Maritime industry in pre-war terms, along with special efforts to further the progressive development of industries in the region through such initiatives as a comprehensive development plan for the fisheries.[93] Other studies concurred with this analysis. A continued role for the national government in carrying out sound employment and investment schemes after the war was mandatory. The profitable production of resources and manufactured goods in the Maritimes in the post-war period, at decent wages, was likely, 'only if a full employment programme of public investment [was] carried out with full fiscal authority.'[94]

Organizations such as the Cape Breton Citizens' Committee for Full Employment, the United Mine Workers, and the Nova Scotia Federation of Labour fully endorsed Dawson's report regarding the requirements for the development of new industries in Nova Scotia, and were especially adamant in their insistence that 'lack of capital' was not an acceptable excuse for the failure to establish such new industries. Though they recognized that C.D. Howe's Department of Reconstruction was committed to private enterprise to maintain full employment, they laboured under no such delusions when it came to their region. Government would have to fill the breach created by the preference of private capital to invest elsewhere: 'if private capital will not provide the machines of production then public capital must.'[95]

But the political influence of organized labour in Nova Scotia was not great. Its real political power did not extend beyond the confines of industrial Cape Breton where labour support had given the CCF its only seat in the whole of Canada east of Ontario. In other areas of the province, organizational support for a radical political alternative was almost completely lacking. The political pressure on the government to act on these demands was, therefore, less than compelling. And the level of acceptance or enthusiasm for a major, direct post-war role for the state in regional economic development was by no means great among key government decision-makers. When this situation became clear to Dawson, he expressed shock and dismay in a letter to the Nova Scotia premier that only the labour unions and the CCF seemed to be taking his report seriously. Instead, the Nova Scotia government was using the royal commission primarily as a means of strengthening its hand at the dominion-provincial conference. Indeed, it appears to have established the royal commission for this express purpose.[96]

Certainly Premier Macdonald, who many times demonstrated his adherence to economic orthodoxy and fiscal conservatism during his long tenure in office, was much more concerned with the dangers posed to provincial autonomy by the trend to centralization and bureaucratization than with obtaining or undertaking a major program of public investment in the provincial economy. The latter issue remained largely unaddressed while Macdonald pursued another crusade in the post-war years: the struggle for continued provincial autonomy and integrity in the face of a massive centralization of fiscal and bureaucratic power in Canada at the end of the Second World War. This political discourse would govern Nova Scotia's response to federal reconstruction proposals, rather than concerns about industrial development or planning for full employment in the post-war era. While the CCF and labour unions strained to place the full-employment efforts highest on the political agenda and make that issue the central one in the province's post-war provincial elections, it was the federalist discourse of Macdonald's Liberalism that would dominate and shape the role of the provincial government in the reconstruction era.

That Macdonald was deeply concerned about centralizing tendencies in Canadian federalism, there can be no doubt. His liberalism and provincialism, and his experience in Ottawa, contributed to this wariness of centralism and bureaucracy. Moreover, the Jones Commission in 1934 had warned against the nefarious effects on provincial economic development should control over this area be further centralized. Macdonald's correspondence in the post-war period is filled with familiar refrains voicing such concerns. He felt sure that the continued encroachment of the dominion government on direct-taxation fields occupied by the provinces would demote the provinces to

nothing more than the recipient of grants from the Dominion government with all their own taxing powers gone ... Raising the ante [on the part of the Dominion as enticement to the provinces to relinquish the right to tax] might be alright for the moment but the fundamental question is just how far the Dominion will go in its invasion of the direct taxation field. If it goes to the limit the Provinces will of course have nothing left to tax and they will be mere agents distributing funds allotted to them by the Dominion. The result would be that nobody would bother with provincial politics, and a few controllers or directors appointed from Ottawa would be running the nine provinces of Canada.[97]

Macdonald received support for this perspective from various quarters. He exchanged letters with noted political scientist J.A. Corry and economist H.A. Innis, soliciting advice on the appropriate response to the dominion proposals. Macdonald's admission that he was compelled to seek such advice outside of his own provincial bureaucracy because of the lack of knowledgeable expertise available to him there[98] provided substance for Corry's warnings that *the real threat to provincial autonomy came from the gross imbalance in dominion and provincial civil services in terms of competence, expertise, experience, and resources.* The narrowing of the provincial fiscal base posed further dangers for provincial autonomy and made more likely the prospect that the provinces would become mere agents for the central government. Corry linked this issue with that of equalization: if some sort of equalization payments based on fiscal need were not forthcoming, the central government would be provided with strong grounds for taking over yet more government functions. The province had to look to a strengthened civil service and the desire of local people to 'run their own show'; this alliance would prove formidable in resisting further centralization.[99]

Innis's advice to Macdonald was that the dominion did not require the exclusive right to the three tax fields in question in order to stimulate and stabilize employment. Indeed, he argued that the dominion was far too optimistic that centralization of taxation would produce the results claimed. Rather, bureaucrats in Ottawa had been carried away by their enthusiasm for Keynes, the Bank of Canada, and by bureaucratic and wartime interests and necessities. By relying only on centralized fiscal and monetary policy to produce high and stable levels of employment, they were courting disaster. Moreover, the Maritimes would suffer a further drain of industry, population, and revenues to central Canada under this scheme. As a result, he counselled against handing over major revenues to the dominion until there was much more evidence that the latter would 'work through the complications of specific problems of a regional character,' and recognize the need for special measures to overcome the handicaps of the tariff and other national policies.[100] Indeed, on further reflection, Innis expressed the opinion that *under no terms must the province's taxing power be alienated, since it remained the most important means of assuring continued governmental sensitivity and responsiveness to the electorate.* And he, too, like Corry and Dawson, emphasized the importance of the principle of fiscal need as the basis for dominion-provincial financial arrangements; this principle had to be kept in the forefront of provincial demands.[101]

The Dominion Offer

In his budget speech of 6 August 1945, J.L. Ilsley, the dominion minister of finance, made a number of proposals regarding post-war dominion-provincial relations and social security. These included the withdrawal of the provinces from three fields of taxation – corporate, personal, and succession duties – in return for a grant from the dominion of $15 per capita, to increase as population and national income increased. In addition the provinces were asked to give up their constitutional right to collect personal income tax and the right to subsidies received from the dominion, as well as the collection of corporate taxes and succession duties. The dominion government also advanced proposals for a program of health insurance, extended old-age pensions, assistance for the development of natural resources, and dominion participation in public-investment programs carried out at a time designated by the dominion.[102]

These proposals were considered at the meeting of the Co-ordinating Committee of the Dominion-Provincial Conference. Health insurance was soon separated from the other financial proposals of the dominion, and a continuing economic committee was struck to negotiate the content of the dominion proposals and the positions of the respective provincial governments towards them.[103] It was during these meetings of senior officials from both levels of government that the intentions of the dominion government with regard to economic assistance for lagging regions became clear. It was first pointed out that while public investment was part of the whole dominion reconstruction plan, it was not necessarily a *major* part. It was also made clear that there would be *no grants to private companies* under the dominion scheme, *no grants to public utilities* where there was direct competition with the private sector,[104] and *no direct budgetary aid to the provinces*; rather dominion assistance would be in the form of a 50 per cent contribution to planning costs and a 20 per cent share of total costs in provincial projects meeting the stipulations laid down by the dominion.[105] Moreover, it was revealed by the dominion government that the thrust of its public-investment program was primarily to be directed towards expediting the exploration and development of new resource wealth; designed, in other words, to assist in the opening of resource hinterlands or frontier sections of Canada.[106]

Such a program was, of course, of little use to Nova Scotia, or to the Maritimes in general. It was also indicated by senior dominion officials that dominion assistance for public investment was primarily intended as a countermeasure to the onset of Depression conditions – the more prolonged and severe the depression, the larger the percentage of the cost of public-investment projects the dominion would agree to assume.[107] In this context, officials warned provincial representatives that local or even province-wide unemployment conditions 'would not necessarily receive dominion assistance if the rest of the country was enjoying a more or less high level of employment.'[108]

Macdonald's Response

Both the Nova Scotia government's written submission to the 1946 Dominion-Provincial Reconstruction Conference and Macdonald's part in plenary and committee discussions followed closely along the lines determined by his own predilections, fears, and concerns as confirmed by his exchange of views with Corry, Innis, and others. That is, there was a strong expression of concern over the prospect of perpetual loss of provincial autonomy and total dependence on grants from the dominion, and an equally strong assertion of the importance of making fiscal need the operative principle in dominion-provincial financial arrangements by taking into account the relative wealth and taxable capacity of each province when determining the size of dominion grants to the provinces (rather than population alone, or population and GNP growth together). Reference was also made (yet again) to the injurious effects of national policies – tariffs and transportation in particular – upon the province, and the need for more than budgetary subsidies from one government to another if the material and economic level of the people of the province was to be noticeably raised. (These remarks, it should be noted, were fully endorsed and reiterated by New Brunswick and Prince Edward Island.)[109]

Macdonald's dissatisfaction with the dominion 'offer' as a result of the Dominion-Provincial Conference of 1945–6, and the federal government's determination to proceed with bilateral agreements with provincial governments after a general agreement failed to materialize, led him to seek a provincial political alliance to hold out for another conference and/or changes in the dominion offer to the provinces. In this quest he allied himself with Ontario's premier George Drew. Macdonald's Maritime counterparts in New Brunswick and PEI, however, quickly agreed to the dominion offer along with several other provinces. Drew urged Macdonald to 'stand firm,' as this would demonstrate that opposition to federal encroachment was not limited to the wealthier provinces alone, but rooted in principle.[110]

Apart from such odd bedfellows as George Drew, Macdonald found few allies for his 'principled' opposition to the dominion offer. His own bureaucrats were not unfavourably disposed towards it, guaranteeing, as it did, more favourable financial returns for the province.[111] The other Maritime premiers, John McNair (NB) and J. Walter Jones (PEI), had already acquiesced to the temptation of increased federal payments; and in Jones's case 'acquiescence' was accompanied by the gleeful proclamation to Island MLAs and constituents alike that this was the best agreement that PEI had reached since Confederation.[112] Prime Minister King, on his part, was promising a return to the conference table to discuss 'mutually satisfactory arrangements relating to public investment and social welfare ... once satisfactory financial arrangements [between dominion and provinces] have been agreed upon.'[113] Yet Macdonald continued to balk at giving up legislative control and taxing power in areas of provincial jurisdiction. 'From a purely financial viewpoint we [Nova Scotia] would be better off if we accepted the budget offer ... On the other hand, I think that the provinces, if they are to continue as provinces, must now take a stand against what I fear is a determined effort to centralize more power at Ottawa. If the provinces do not take that stand now when they are being asked to give up the greatest fields of taxation available to governments in this country, I do not think that they can ever hope to take it successfully again.'[114]

Macdonald's continued intransigence on this matter eventually gave occasion to intervention by the Nova Scotia caucus of the federal Liberal party – not on the side of Macdonald, but in an effort to persuade him to relent. Both Gordon Isnor and Robert Winters, the latter soon to be 'political minister' for Nova Scotia, informed Macdonald of the Nova Scotia caucus's support for the dominion proposals and urged him to enter the proposed agreement as soon as possible.[115] It appears that it was, in fact, party pressure that eventually brought Macdonald to heel. In a response to Drew, who had written him in May 1947 to again encourage him to 'stand firm,' Macdonald admitted to his belated accession to the dominion proposals, citing the attitude of the party as the key factor. Macdonald's participation in an upcoming federal by-election in Halifax may also have been salient; he could not refuse such a role, he argued, because of the perception of party workers that he was 'letting the side down.'[116]

Shaping the Political Discourse in the Post-war Period

The thrust of the federal government's reconstruction plan was a return to reliance upon private investment to power the economy and the export of Canadian natural resources as the engine of growth. Under the auspices of reconstruction minister C.D. Howe, the close wartime integration of Canadian and U.S. production, as represented by the Materials Co-ordinating Committee and the Joint War Production Committee, was de facto extended into the reconstruction era as American corporations took advantage of the federal government's bargain-basement divestiture of Crown corporations at war's end to increase their branch-plant capacity in Canada, or to invest heavily in Canadian resources.[117] This sell-off policy reinforced a pattern of development – staple exports and import-substitution industrialization – that had already shown itself to be detrimental to the development prospects of the Maritimes. The region did not fit comfortably into the role of staples hinterland for American investment, as did the northern parts of central Canada and the West. Nor were the Maritimes in line for any significant expansion of manufacturing and industrial output on the basis of the peacetime reconversion of industrial plant built up through extensive capital investments made for the prosecution of the war, as was central Canada's 'golden triangle.' And increased levels of American ownership would only worsen the regional maldistribution of manufacturing industries in Canada.[118]

The growth-oriented, continentalist, business-minded Liberal government in Ottawa at the end of the war, then, proved averse to implementing the type of program that the royal commission in Nova Scotia, the CCF, the unions, and other private-sector analysts were calling for as a necessary part of any reconstruction package for the Maritimes. It also appears that there was a particular aversion in Ottawa, especially on the part of C.D. Howe, to the 'public-works shelf' – that back-up government plan for massive public investment that was never put into effect. Howe believed such a plan to be superfluous since there was no immediate economic crisis. Instead, with a perceived labour shortage in the post-war years (unemployment bottomed out in 1951 at 2.9 per cent) and aggregate national figures on production that told Howe that the economy was in good shape, there was a conscious and conspicuous de-emphasis on government planning.[119]

The disappearance of the Department of Reconstruction within a few short years of its establishment signalled the official termination of plans for state intervention in the economy to counter a prophesied economic downturn in the immediate post-war years. Healthy national economic growth also meant continued respect and support for Howe and his policies as reconstruction minister and later as minister of trade and commerce. And the effects engendered by the surge of defence spending and private investment associated with the Korean War (1949–53) – presumably a 'legitimate' form of government spending on goods, services, and personnel that also happened to produce some benefits for the Maritimes (especially Nova Scotia) – only reinforced his stature within cabinet, and that of the Liberal government within the country. 'The relative prosperity of the economy made Howe's political position inside the Cabinet and as a public figure virtually unassailable.'[120]

The reconstruction program of the dominion government was blatantly neglectful – and as the proceedings of the Reconstruction Conference's Continuing Economic Committee reveal, intentionally so – of the uneven regional incidence of its policies. There would be no special consideration or measures for the Maritimes, regardless of the demonstrable facts of its necessity and the groundswell of regional expectations and opinion at the end of the war favouring major state initiatives in this area. Moreover, it appears that this federal position went largely uncontested by the Nova Scotia government, and by Maritime representatives in general. There was no strong submission from the latter quarters advocating a major public-investment program at the end of the war along lines recommended by the Dawson report and demanded by community organizations and labour unions in Nova Scotia, as well as the CCF. Behind this stance may be discerned an ideological acceptance on the part of Maritime governments of the dominion government's commitment to private enterprise, deference to superior dominion economic and technical expertise, and evidence of the political atmosphere of the post-war period.

The balance of power extant in the post-war years at once stymied an alternative political discourse that questioned the return of control over the economy at war's end to private capital without safeguards or provisions that would ensure a more equitable regional distribution of economic growth and capital investment, and at the same time narrowed the margin of manoeuvre for political forces on the periphery in their dealings with state élites at the centre. Indeed the alternative political discourse, though in many respects echoed in the findings of Nova Scotia's Royal Commission on Postwar Rehabilitation, was largely ignored by the government of Nova Scotia in its negotiations with the dominion government. Moreover, the political and ideological conditions that might have made the dominion government more receptive to such an approach – with or without the support of the relevant provincial governments – were absent in 1945, as they were for some time thereafter.

Instead, the three Maritime governments concentrated on intergovernmental financial arrangements, and especially the establishment of the principle of fiscal need as the basis for these arrangements, as their primary objective in intergovernmental bargaining. The ability to inflate provincial budgets without incurring major deficits must have seemed a much more immediate, likely, and compelling proposition for these fiscally conservative governments with their narrow tax bases than a 'radical' and unprecedented program of direct dominion expenditures in the realm of regional economic development. And Macdonald's lonely crusade for the protection of provincial autonomy and democratic decentralization, while recognizing the very real dangers to provinces on the periphery of the trend to centralization, proved to be a largely futile exercise given the balance of power within the federation at the end of the war.

But what would Macdonald's stand have accomplished in any case? Wittingly or not, it did serve the partisan ideological purpose of defining the issues at stake for Nova Scotia in post-war reconstruction as ones of federal control versus provincial autonomy, rather than the economic and class issues associated with the question of government responsibility for the rehabilitation of the Nova Scotia economy or comparative strategies for maintaining full employment in the post-war period. These were not issues that Macdonald's Liberal government chose to dwell upon; while they *were* the issues of the socialist CCF and the labour unions, those groups continued to remain outside the charmed circle of power at both the federal and provincial levels. In the event, Macdonald's principled protest on the matter of Nova Scotia's autonomy in the post-war era was doomed by the province's fiscal and political weakness, with the final indignity being his own accession to the exigencies of party politics and internal party discipline.

Centre-Periphery Relations: The 'Government Party' and the Cold War

The Government Party

The centralism of Canadian federalism in the post-war years and the domination of the Liberal Party of Canada by its parliamentary caucus – and more particularly by key political ministers within the caucus – finds further illustration in the preparation, proceedings, and outcome of the 1948 National Convention of the Liberal party. While at first the prospect of King's retirement and a national convention raised the hopes of those who felt the need for renewal and innovation in both policy and leadership, these hopes soon dissipated as King continually hedged on a retirement announcement while behind-the-scenes machinations prepared the way for King's chosen successor, St Laurent, with the minimum of opposition or the untidiness and embarrassment of a serious questioning of Liberal policies. Chubby Power's penned comments to A.L. Macdonald concerning the preparations, machinations, and 'atmosphere' in Ottawa leading up to the 1948 convention register the frustration felt by a number of senior Liberals at the time.

'[A] hasty bitch begets whelps' ... This is doubtless what will happen in connection with the convention. The blind whelps will go to the convention eager only to accept whatever is handed down to them from on high. I see little hope for reform and for formulation of Liberal policies ... As to Leadership, present indications are that St Laurent would win on the first ballot ... So that, with leadership out of the way and policy neglected, I fear that the much prayed for convention, instead of marking the beginning of a Liberal resurgence, will be the last nail in the coffin of both traditional Liberalism and new liberalism ... At any rate, there is not a glimmer of hope here in Ottawa.[121]

Other Liberal insiders expressed similar, if less colourfully stated views to Macdonald as he engaged in almost daily correspondence with key Liberal contacts in Ottawa and the West between February and April 1948, in order to glean rumours regarding likely entrants into the leadership race and their level of support, 'testing the waters' regarding his own chances.

To say the least, these intraparty power relations and arrangements presented considerable difficulties for those Maritime Liberals who wished to place regional concerns and demands on the agenda of the national party, as two incidents clearly reveal. Dalton Camp, in his recollections of the 1948 convention, relates the strategy of the New Brunswick delegation to articulate and register on the convention agenda the policy recommendations of the Maritime delegates. This would be accomplished through the candidacy of the Nova Scotia premier (who would, upon completion of this role, withdraw from the race). But the whole scheme was quashed after the new political minister for Nova Scotia, Robert Winters, got wind of it. The unity of the Maritime delegation fizzled as various members refused to take part in the strategy and Macdonald himself was persuaded not to enter the race at all. As noted by Camp, the Maritime resolutions were appended to the general policy statement, 'accepted with perfunctory dispatch and as quickly forgotten.'[122]

To add insult to injury, Maritime versions of draft resolutions were watered down by the convention, bled of their region-specific and policy-specific content. One example is the Nova Scotia draft resolution on transportation. At the time of the convention, sharp horizontal increases in freight rates had just received approval, provoking a gathering storm of protest in the Maritimes as provincial governments and the Maritime Board of Trade marshalled their resources and arguments for a reversal of the decision.[123] The attempt by the Nova Scotia delegation to link the Liberal party's resolution on transportation to the railway act, freight-rates policy, and the stimulation of economic and industrial growth in all parts of Canada did not see the light of day; instead a resolution quite different in its policy implications, omitting any reference to those specific characteristics and aspects of transportation policy referred to by the Nova Scotia draft, was given the official recommendation of the Resolutions Committee.[124]

Within a year of the Liberal convention the Royal Commission on Transportation (the Turgeon Commission) was appointed to look into recently imposed rate increases that were producing an uproar in the Maritimes. In order to ensure the most effective and unified of regional responses, Macdonald and the other Maritime premiers joined forces with the Maritime Board of Trade Transportation Commission (MBTTC: a permanent standing committee and research agency on transportation matters affecting the Maritimes).[125] The outcome of the Maritime appeal before the commission says much about the narrow 'space' available for regional development in the political and ideological atmosphere of the post-war period, when special regional concerns in such matters as national transportation policy were not accorded a great deal of legitimacy. The commissioners rejected the Maritime appeal with the riposte that the Maritime Freight Rates Act of 1927 was a 'once and for all' measure that had 'performed all the functions for which it was designed.' The region was once again left exposed to the play of 'market forces,' and the introduction of 'competitive rates' in central Canada was allowed to progressively undercut the relative position of Maritime shippers in the 1950s.[126]

The Korean War and Defence Spending

In the 1950 Federal-Provincial Conference, intergovernmental financial arrangements and social security were again on the agenda, this time against the backdrop of the Korean War. The federal government was devoting $1 billion, or 30 per cent of its budget, to defence, a fivefold increase in expenditures over 1947. According to the federal minister of finance, under these conditions, and in light of a major federal proposal in the field of old-age security, tax-rental renewals with the provinces could not mean major new expenditures. Indeed, since the federal government was following a policy of balancing the budget, it would be forced to cut back on non-defence expenditures, especially construction and other capital expenditures. In St Laurent's words: 'Until there is convincing evidence of an end to the menace of communist aggression, a large and growing share of the manpower and resources of our country will have to be devoted to defence purposes.'[127]

This policy left less for other purposes, especially considering the need for the federal government to avoid contributing to a new round of inflation. Thus, both the Cold War and orthodox economic concerns threw cold water on any Maritime arguments for increased federal expenditures in the region for economic-development purposes. In this context Macdonald's repetition of earlier arguments that increased federal subsidies, while needed, were not the solution to either the problem of fiscal relations, or the attainment of a state of greater economic prosperity and happiness in the Maritimes, made little headway.

The Nova Scotia premier, like his provincial colleagues, did not quibble with the federal government's characterization of the external demands placed on the country by the international situation in 1950 (ergo, the priority of a defence build-up). In such a political and ideological milieu the federal government easily obtained the compliance of nine provinces (Quebec alone abstaining) to an extension of tax-rental agreements for the 1952–7 period (with a raise in the guaranteed minimum return to the provinces) and provincial agreement on a constitutional amendment to give the federal government jurisdiction to establish a contributory system of old-age security. No equalization scheme or regional-development program was adopted, or even mooted in anything more than brief, vague terms.

In any event, in light of the benefits accruing to Nova Scotia as a result of the high level of defence spending at this time (temporary though such benefits might be), arguments stating the need for further development assistance to the region were likely to be somewhat deflated. Between 1951 and 1961, defence employment in the Atlantic provinces grew by over 100 per cent. And two-thirds of all defence employment in the region was in Nova Scotia, where salaries and wages from this sector accounted for 10.2 per cent of personal income (as against only 2.6 per cent for Canada). Halifax, in particular, remained heavily dependent upon defence expenditures. In 1961, fully 25 per cent of that city's labour force was directly engaged in defence services. But the *type* of defence expenditures made in the region is also revealing. Ontario and Quebec together received over 90 per cent of the value of defence contracts for equipment purchases in 1960–1 (compared to 4.9 per cent for the Atlantic provinces, and this largely related to shipbuilding and repair).[128] In other words, while *defence spending* was important to personal incomes and employment in the region (primarily to Nova Scotia), *the federal government's purchasing power was not used to provide any significant boost to the region's industrial base.*

None the less, the high level of defence spending in the 1950s did provide significant material benefits to parts of the Atlantic region. Larger defence budgets in this way gave material substance to political strategies and discourses that made use of Cold War rhetoric, particularly the need for military preparedness in the face of the 'Soviet Threat,' to garner public support for a particular political party or government. In effect, it became part of 'the material base for compromise' in the Maritimes: the tangible benefits thus provided to an underdeveloped region needful of the resources presumably helped to legitimate a political regime that might otherwise have been seen as sorely neglectful of that region's welfare.

The Canadian Merchant Marine

The ideological milieu created by the Cold War was also a factor in removing the deep-sea merchant marine as an element in the economy of the Maritimes. The merchant fleet and its Canadian seamen were largely a product of the Second World War. At the end of hostilities the federal government, which initially claimed the government-owned fleet to be important to national security and external trade, sold off the ships to Canadian operators with the provision that they would continue under Canadian registry and employ Canadian seamen. Soon after the transfer, however, shipowners began 'reflagging' ships and hiring foreign crews. By 1948–9 this phenomenon of sell-off and replacement crews amounted to a 'steady haemorrhage' of the Canadian merchant marine.[129]

The main obstacle to the speedy progress of this process of eliminating the Canadian deep-sea fleet was the communist-led union representing the Canadian crewmen, the Canadian Seamen's Union (CSU). After the war, the union campaigned to no avail to have 50 per cent of Canadian exports carried in Canadian bottoms (a policy adopted by the United States to cover shipments under the Marshall Plan).[130] In 1948–9 contract negotiations they faced shipowners determined to gain concessions including wage cuts and elimination of the hiring hall, and unwilling to give any assurances that the fleet would not be sold off or reflagged, or that its Canadian crews would be replaced by foreign crews.[131] When the union resisted by going on strike, strike-breakers from the American Seaman's International Union (SIU) were imported with the compliance of the Canadian government to displace the CSU on Canadian ships. The CSU's communist ties were a ready justification for such actions. By portraying CSU resistance to what was happening in Canadian shipping as a communist plot, potential opposition to the policy of importing SIU thugs to break the strike and ultimately the CSU was neutralized; indeed the trade-union movement became a willing accomplice in the act when the CSU was expelled from the Trades and Labor Congress (TLC).[132]

By 1952, seventy-four Canadian deep-sea vessels had been sold off to foreign buyers, with only two replacement vessels built with the proceeds of the sales. It appears that the rest of the money from the sell-off of the deep-sea fleet went towards the construction of modern lake boats to ply Canada's inland sea, the Great Lakes.[133] In effect, over a period of several years an ocean-going fleet with obvious linkages to marine-related industries and services in the Maritime provinces was traded in for a Great Lakes fleet constructed and based in central Canada! Thus, the low priority the government in Ottawa had always placed on ocean shipping, shipbuilding, and port development, in spite of Canada's position as a major trading nation, continued unabated into the post-war period.

Nova Scotia Government and Politics, 1945–54

If it can be said that the federal government was resistant to dabbling in regional development at the end of the war, it is also the case that there were no notable provincial initiatives at that time. Constricted finances were no doubt a major factor, but so was Macdonald's economic orthodoxy, which, while a fairly constant feature of his premiership, seems to have grown into a deepening social and economic conservatism in his later years.[134] A budget surplus became the overriding objective and proudest accomplishment of his regime, even if this meant considering the abolition of the provincial fisheries department in order to cut provincial government expenditures![135] Moreover, neither Macdonald nor his minister of industry, Harold Connolly, betrays in his correspondence a burning interest in the problems of Nova Scotia industrial development. Industrial loans were extended only very tentatively and sometimes bedrudgingly, and often as not to applicants who were not 'industrial' at all, such as hotels and other tourist-related activities.[136] According to E.A. Manson, the Conservative minister of industry who took over the portfolio in 1956, 'there were just two fellows in the department. No one was travelling. They were just sending out a circular letter. The first thing I did was to cancel the bloody thing.' Neither did the Nova Scotia government have any expertise on the steel industry available to it, despite the fact that this industry represented 17 per cent of the manufacturing capacity of Nova Scotia at the time.[137] Macdonald's fiscal conservatism and his anti-bureaucratic and anti-planning philosophy impeded any move to build up a provincial bureaucracy that could oversee a more effective, substantive, and systematic development role on the part of the provincial state, despite recommendations to this effect from two provincial royal commissions. In expressing his government's opposition to the Dawson Commission's recommendations regarding a rationalized, strengthened provincial bureaucracy,[138] while at the same time voicing deep concern and fear over the implications of the encroachment of federal bureaucrats, Macdonald revealed a certain ideological consistency, but also the dilemma faced by liberals of his ilk in the post-war period. The positive state had been gradually imposing itself upon all jurisdictions since at least the First World War, as regulations, supervision, and administration of economic activity and social relations became ever more requisite and expansive. Within the Canadian federal system, not all of this increased state role could or would be assumed by the central government. And as we have seen with regard to negotiation over federal-provincial fiscal relations, even if the severe constriction of provincial resources inhibited provincial initiatives in various fields, the constitutional division of powers and responsibilities forced constant accommodations between governments over the design, funding, and delivery of diverse government policies and programs 'sponsored' by state élites at the centre.

Thus, between 1900 and 1956, the annual revenues of the province of Nova Scotia grew from less than $1 million to $60 million; the provincial bureaucracy from fewer than 300 government employees to more than 4,000 and from 3 government departments to 14. Macdonald himself oversaw a good deal of this growth, including the creation of the Departments of Municipal Affairs (1935), Mines (1939), Trade and Industry (1939), and Public Welfare (1944), and the provincial treasurer (1947).

Successive provincial governments also engaged in considerable 'farming-out' of regulatory, quasi-judicial and advisory functions to various boards and commissions, such as the Board of Public Utilities, the Nova Scotia Power Commission, the Nova Scotia Liquor Commission, the Workmen's Compensation Board, the Labour Relations Board, the Nova Scotia Economic Council, the Nova Scotia Research Foundation, and the Industrial Loan Board, to name some of the major agencies that came into existence between 1914 and 1946.[139]

Yet Macdonald's attitude towards the Dawson Commission's recommendations on the provincial civil service attests to the remnants of a stubborn political resistance to the abdication of still more power and discretion to the bureaucracy for the ostensible purpose of making the latter a more efficient administrative apparatus. The passing of the Civil Service Act in 1935 (on the recommendation of the Jones Commission) had failed to stem charges of political interference, manipulation, and patronage; the many exceptions and omissions in the employees covered by the act and the continuing lack of an adequate system of gradation and classification were among the loopholes in the strict mandatory provisions of the act.[140]

Nevertheless, there was discernible progress towards the practices that had been advocated by the Jones and Dawson commissions, and it is perhaps noteworthy that the advent of the new Conservative administration under Stanfield in 1956 was the first in which there was no outburst of dismissals as the result of a change of government.[141] The information-gathering and analytical capacities of the provincial bureaucracy remained strictly limited, however, as demonstrated by the Nova Scotia submission to the Gordon Commission wherein the largely descriptive submission of the provincial government, which lacked any concerted analysis of the problem areas of the province's economy or possible solutions to its woes, itself condemned the lack of information and statistics on the regional economy.[142]

As will become apparent, many of these perceived bureaucratic weaknesses and inadequacies would gradually be rectified as the apparatuses of the provincial state became more involved with, and essential to, continuing economic development, and attuned to that overriding objective. One of the developments that advanced this process was provincial-government access to greater fiscal reserves as the result of the inauguration of equalization payments in 1957 and the extension of the equalization formula thereafter. Equalization helped to loosen the financial restrictions that can be seen to have inhibited earlier provincial expenditures on economic development. Similarly, increased federal involvement in the field of regional development had as its corollary a sharp increase in provincial state expenditures for this purpose and major changes in the provincial bureaucracy's capacities and complexity.

This suggests that the central government's former intransigence on the inclusion of an equalization component in intergovernmental financial arrangements, and its extreme reluctance to consider programs and policies that would specifically address the chronic economic problems of the Maritimes, were major inhibitors of the growth and modernization of the provincial state. The persistence of small, unprofessional, and ineffective states in the Maritimes, not to mention the region's petty patronage politics, can be at least partially understood as a consequence of the repeated failures on the part of the region's political representatives both to secure the reform of intergovernmental fiscal relations in order to place them on a more rational and regionally equitable basis, and to extract from the federal government a substantive political commitment to regional development. The implication here is not that such a commitment necessarily would have ensured the resumption of a process of private investment in industry in the region; rather it implies that provincial states and political processes in the region would have been substantially altered as bureaucratic organizations, resources, and processes were expanded and 'modernized' within the context of capitalist state functions – i.e., progressively disciplined to the requirements of the province's role in some larger state strategy aimed at the state-assisted expansion of private-capital accumulation in the region.

Fiscal Arrangements: Equalization

A first step in the direction of more regionally equitable intergovernmental fiscal relations was the adoption of an equalization-payments scheme at the 1955 Federal-Provincial Conference. The main item on the agenda of this conference was the renegotiation of federal-provincial financial arrangements. As might be expected, the Maritime premiers were arguing for the principle of fiscal need as the basis for tax-rental agreements, to be achieved through an equalization formula or National Adjustment Grant, which would take into account the tax-raising ability of each province.[143] Premier Henry D. Hicks of Nova Scotia (Macdonald died in 1954) went so far as to explicitly link Nova Scotia's participation in any shared-cost scheme for health and welfare programs to some form of equalization payment, arguing that, for all intents and purposes, the two were inseparable.[144] Unlike the situation at past conferences, however, it seemed that this time the federal government had come around to viewing the prospect of some form of equalization with greater equanimity. Indeed, the claim was made that the aim of previous tax agreements had in fact been 'to make it financially possible for all provinces, whatever their tax base, to perform their constitutional functions themselves and to provide a reasonable Canadian level of provincial services without an abnormal burden of taxation ... This is the principle of paying an element of fiscal need subsidies to provinces with lesser tax potential than others.'[145]

The federal government then announced that it was prepared to extend this fiscal-need subsidy in a new set of tax agreements. In effect, the wheels were set in motion for negotiation over the formula for the routinized disbursement of equalization payments, as an integral part of federal-provincial finances.

On the issue of federal assistance for economic-development purposes, the Maritime premiers were less successful. During the meetings of the Preparatory Committee for the 1955 conference, federal officials made known to provincial representatives their negative view of federal involvement in 'the provincial field of development.'[146] During the conference itself, St Laurent continued to stonewall on the matter of federal contributions for development projects, arguing that federal intervention in this field could only be undertaken in exceptional circumstances and justified on national grounds. The 'normal' costs of growth that accrued to provinces and municipalities could not be construed as requiring federal intervention.[147] This was a direct rebuff to Premier Hugh J. Flemming of New Brunswick, who in both the preliminary and main meetings had made strong statements calling for a comprehensive system of federal assistance for development purposes that would take into consideration the differing needs and financial capabilities of provinces.[148]

As demonstrated by the submissions of provincial Liberal governments from the Maritimes at successive federal-provincial conferences in the post-war period, strongly voiced demands for a redress of Maritime grievances and special consideration on the part of the federal government of the region's 'unique problems' were a persistent feature of post-war federal-provincial relations. But little was gained in the way of either acknowledgment or action during the long period of Liberal dominance between 1935 and 1957. This tough federal against a more interventionist role for itself in regional development is indicative of the conservatism of the post-war Liberal governments on matters requiring an innovative role for the state, and Ottawa's belief that basically all was well with the Canadian economy. Instead the main concerns continued to be fiscal relations between governments and the slow extension of income and social-security programs. And there is some evidence to suggest that the former was primarily a concern not because of the repeated harping of Maritime provincial governments, but because of the 'dangerous isolation' of Quebec, which had refused to extend its tax-rental agreement with the federal government. Both Maurice Lamontange, St Laurent's adviser on federal-provincial relations, and J.J. Deutsch, in the Department of Finance, worked to come up with a plan that would require no agreements to be signed and no tax fields to be rented to the federal government, yet would guarantee a fairly large element of subsidy to poorer provinces. Equalization payments were the answer since Quebec could continue to impose its own taxes and still be eligible for the equalization grant. Discrimination against Quebeckers would be ended. St Laurent was strongly in favour of the plan for this reason and because it would leave the federal government free to determine the size of the payments without negotiation.[149] In finance minister Walter Harris's presentation of the plan to Parliament, he explicitly cited the Quebec situation as the reason for the design of the plan. It would be 'a substitute for a system which was not acceptable to the government of a province containing almost one third of our people, and which had won only the reluctant acquiescence of the governments of two other provinces containing more than one-half the rest of the people of Canada.'[150]

It would appear that while the influence of unallied Maritime interests at the centre remained something less than politically determinant in the motivations of Ottawa's policy-makers and in the design of national programs, a shared interest with Quebec at this point in the comprehensive reform of intergovernmental financial arrangements was sufficient to 'move' state élites at the centre.

Even so, the equalization formula settled on by the St Laurent government – a formula that 'equalized' only three tax sources (corporate, income, and succession taxes) – was strictly limited. As such, it created a real problem for the Atlantic provinces because of the low yield of tax sources other than personal, corporate, or succession taxes. In the case of Nova Scotia, for example, subsidies and equalization together would cover only 30 per cent of the provincial budget in 1957. This led the Atlantic premiers to argue that what was done for three tax fields needed to be extended to the whole range of provincial revenue sources if there was to be equalization in fact as well as name.[151] In the assessment of Hugh J. Flemming, the New Brunswick premier, the formula arrived at by the

federal government in 1955 'does nothing to improve our relative financial position as compared to other provinces ... The promotion of economic development must of necessity involve provincial governments in
greatly increased expenditures. We must have more flexibility in our
budgets if we are going to undertake those things which are essential for
economic growth.'[152]

The federal government had symbolically nodded in the direction of
regional equality in the public sector. It would be more than a decade,
however, before something close to full equalization would be realized.
Achieving an approximate result in the private sector would prove a
much more daunting task.

Conclusion

The Second World War exercised a profound effect on the Canadian
political economy. In the Maritimes, however, only a tiny fraction of the
Canadian state's wartime investment went towards increased productive
capacity. This level of investment ensured that the end of hostilities
would be accompanied by a severe downturn in the regional economy.
Moreover, in important sectors – for example, the fishery and mining –
workers' struggles at the end of the war to unionize or to improve wages
and benefits were defeated. In the long term this merely permitted capital
in these industries to delay making necessary adjustments in production
processes and productivity levels that eventually would have to be made
in any case if competition were to be met and worker demands accommodated.

The role of the state policies in post-war class struggles and development tendencies was contradictory. The provincial government supported capital in the fishery in its anti-unionism. The federal government
gradually extended social-welfare benefits that in some sectors made the
continuation of archaic methods of production based on cheap, abundant
labour more difficult, while buttressing such production in other sectors.
The state also extended subsidies to the declining coal industry in Nova
Scotia, while spurning more comprehensive intervention aimed at restructuring or even replacing the industry. But such apparent contradictions were inevitable given the separate root causes of their design and
implementation and the lack of any co-ordinated regional industrial
policy in the post-war era.

The failure of state policy-makers to address coherently the economic
problems of the periphery in the post-war period once again can be

related to the balance of socio-political forces at the centre and on the periphery. With massive central-state intervention during the Second World War and the embrace of a limited Keynesianism in the post-war reconstruction period, inaction – allowing market forces to hold sway and adjust the factors of production – was gradually supplemented with the distribution of welfare as the state response to regional disparities. The federal government was reluctant, however, to go beyond a minimal social-welfare program or to adopt a national policy of interprovincial fiscal equalization. There was even less inclination in the decade following the war to design regional-development policies that would involve the state directly in restructuring the economy of the periphery.

Neither the centralist and private enterprise bias of the dominion government nor the anti-statist liberalism of the Nova Scotia premier produced a political discourse that was open to direct state intervention in the regional economy as part of state planning for post-war reconstruction. Moreover, the Cold War rhetoric and resurgence of defence expenditures that characterized the late 1940s and early 1950s supported continued political and economic centralism and relative political quiescence on the periphery. It also provided a hostile environment for left-wing parties and unions in Canada, who also happened to be the main advocates at the end of the war of a program of public-sector investment for the Maritimes. In at least two instances unions that were actively defending and promoting the interests of groups of workers in the Maritimes – the CFFU and the CSU – were attacked for their communist links and effectively destroyed through the use of propaganda, court actions, legislation, and strike-breakers. The outcome in the case of the CFFU ensured that fishermen would remain relatively powerless in their relations with fish processors and vessel owners; the destruction of the CSU removed the last remaining obstacle to the scrapping of the Canadian merchant marine, with obvious and immediate implications for marine-related industry and services in the Maritimes, and the future potential for same.

Granted, the post-war years did witness unparalleled national economic growth and prosperity and the political hegemony of successive Liberal governments rested easily on this surge of economic expansion. National economic prosperity helped to breed a distinct complacency on the part of the federal government to the growing concern of various groups in the Maritimes that their region was being left behind. With the end of the Korean War, however, the relative stagnation of the Maritimes could no longer be obscured by high levels of defence spending in the region. Emergent within the Maritimes in the 1950s were new political coalitions and governmental initiatives that pointed the way to a larger state role in regional economic development. Within a few years the narrow 'space' for regional-development concerns in the political and ideological atmosphere of the post-war period would give way to a new balance of political forces, a new political discourse both at the centre and on the periphery, and a new state agenda.

5 Entry into the Field of Regional Development: Constructing the Issues and Attaining the Agenda, 1955–62

There were aspects of politics in 1950s Nova Scotia that suggest that significant changes had taken place in the province since the inter-war period – changes with economic, social, and cultural implications. Whereas petty-commodity producers and regional resource capital dependent upon the export of primary products, on the one hand, and import-substituting manufacturing and industrial capital and their workforces, on the other, were the main protagonists engaged in a free trade–protectionist debate between the 1880s and the 1920s, by the 1950s changes were evident in this economic and class structure, and in the 'politics of development' that accompanied it. In the 1920s the Maritime Rights movement had been primarily concerned with the rehabilitation of a regional bourgeoisie within the framework of the National Policy (to be achieved through freight-rate reductions, tariff adjustments, subsidies, etc.). By the 1950s the notion of development as internally spawned and generated (if perpetuated by favourable national policies) was giving way to a concept of development as something that 'comes from away,' a condition of modernity acquired by the region via the importation of industries.

Given this change from an endogenous conception of development to what may be labelled a 'dependent' one, the main thrust of state intervention was to design and implement policies that would attract capital into the region (whether foreign or Canadian, resource-based or manufacturing-based). Transplanted industries became the perceived catalyst of economic growth and diversification, thus increasing the scope and range of opportunities for both regional capital and the regional workforce. The implication of this analysis, of course, was an admission that the regional economy no longer harboured any internal dynamism. By the 1950s, regional political and economic élites appear to have accommodated themselves to the fact that *dependent development* had become the only available framework within which development in the Maritimes could proceed, and from the beginning an attitude of dependence was pervasive in the new politics of regional development.

If development had to be artificially 'imported' or 'transplanted,' then there would have to be a concerted campaign to attract private capital into the region, and there would have to be direct state involvement in this campaign. Towards this end, a coalition of social and political forces in the Maritimes engaged themselves in the articulation and promotion of a political project: to obtain state assistance for regional development, initially through greater direct involvement on the part of provincial governments, but more importantly through the promotion of a regional campaign to define federal assistance for regional development as a charter right of the poorer provinces. In part, the first of these goals could be accomplished through the election of more activist, business-oriented provincial governments with which regional business élites could co-operate in the design and implementation of provincial programs of promotion and assistance. But the financing of such programs, if tied to the state of provincial finances, was problematic: 'freeing up' discretionary spending for economic development within relatively small and constricted provincial budgets would be largely dependent upon federal-provincial financial arrangements.

The second objective – involving the federal government in regional development – was therefore crucial; achieving this meant assembling the elements for a much more forceful, unified, and informed regional lobby than had existed theretofore, one that could effectively place the issue on the federal agenda, and keep it there. Past experience left no illusions about the necessity of a sustained campaign that did not end with the first sign of concessions. Ongoing pressure and continuous monitoring of federal commitments was required. Regional capitalists – through a closer liaison with political parties and provincial governments, through the stepped-up activities of their existing trade association, and through the creation of new, special-purpose organizations – would have to vigorously pursue government financial assistance for the 'modernization' of the regional economy and the expansion of private-capital accumulation in the region.

Regional Disquiet and Electoral Upsets

The centralism and élite dominance that came to characterize the national Liberal party during its long tenure as the dominant party in the

Canadian political system made it extremely difficult for Maritime representatives to divert the focus of the party leadership from national policies that did not benefit their region. For Maritime Liberals, adherence to party discipline in the post-war period meant acceptance of the fact that there would be no special consideration for their region, despite its singular economic difficulties.

While there was not an open revolt in response to this persistent lack of regional sensitivity, there were doubtless some 'defections to the enemy' within the Liberal camp, and in the post-war period a gradual erosion of Liberal political support within the region is discernible. This erosion manifested itself first at the provincial level, where Progressive Conservative governments were elected in New Brunswick (1952) and Nova Scotia (1956), and finally bore fruit at the federal level in 1957, when a significant shift of voter support in the Maritimes to the Diefenbaker-led Conservatives increased the latter's seat total from five to nineteen of twenty-six. In Nova Scotia their total jumped from one to ten of twelve seats. This proved to be a key regional component in the national swing of seats that resulted in a minority Progressive Conservative government in 1957.

The electoral success of the Conservative party in the Maritimes after two decades of defeat can be understood as a 'boiling-over' of accumulated frustrations with the intransigent centralism and élitism of the post-war Liberal regime, a state of affairs that had repeatedly blocked attempts to secure greater federal attention to regional grievances and problems. Yet it was also made possible by the transformation of the Progressive Conservative party into a vehicle that was both sympathetic and progressive in its orientation towards the periphery, and therefore open to the use of the federal government as a means of redressing regional disparities. Clearly, this had not always been the case. During the twenty years of Liberal dominance from the mid-1930s to the mid-1950s, the Conservatives did not offer an attractive alternative to Maritimers. Indeed, if anything, the party tended to be more conservative, market-oriented, centralist, and élitist than its Liberal counterpart.

That Maritime representatives within the Conservative party prior to Diefenbaker's ascendance to the leadership were just as much captive to a generally unsympathetic national party establishment as were Maritime Liberals is evidenced by the early experience of George Nowlan, MP for the Nova Scotia riding of Digby-Annapolis-Kings from 1948 to 1965, and minister in the Diefenbaker cabinets of 1957–63. Nowlan had gained for himself something of a reputation as a 'Red Tory' during the war years for his advocacy of government control over medical services, changes to dominion-provincial financial arrangements, and more regional input into the determination of national policies.[1] He thought the federal government should intervene to offset the operation of market forces that handicapped the Maritimes, and he envisaged programs that would bring about a decentralization of industry in Canada: federal aid to help Maritime industry modernize, a regional purchasing policy, incentives to private industry to locate in depressed regions, and even separate regional fiscal policies.[2]

Most of Nowlan's blueprint for regional development reflected the arguments and accepted wisdom of business and producer groups within the region who in the post-war period were clamouring for the state-supported creation of a modern industrial economy there; Nowlan himself was advised by prominent Conservative businessmen and professionals who continued to perceive the federal government as both the *cause* of and the *resolution* to the region's problems.[3] But just like his Liberal counterparts, the Conservative member for Digby-Annapolis-Kings encountered stiff resistance within his own party, and his aspirations for a concerted regional-development policy found little sympathy within the national party establishment or resonance in Conservative election platforms between 1945 and 1955.[4]

The Conservative parliamentary caucus during these years was a right-leaning group emphasizing 'fiscal responsibility.' Dominated by Ontario representation, it exhibited a growing uneasiness about welfare measures of all kinds as the Liberal government's limited Keynesian program was put in place in the post-war years. By emphasizing reduced expenditures and taxation in a period of economic expansion the party precluded regionally specific concessions and repeatedly courted electoral disaster on Canada's eastern and western peripheries; Nowlan was only one of two Conservatives returned from Nova Scotia in 1949, and the only one elected in 1953.[5]

The fortunes of the provincial Conservative parties in the Maritimes were similarly bleak until the 1950s. Then, in 1952, H.J. Flemming's Conservatives unexpectedly defeated the McNair Liberals in New Brunswick. The next year, the Nova Scotia Conservatives under Robert Stanfield's leadership continued to whittle away Macdonald's majority, gaining five additional seats in the legislature (for a total of thirteen) and rising to 42 per cent of the popular vote (up 10 per cent over 1945). The thrust of Stanfield's campaign in 1953 concerned his critique of the incumbent government's economic-development efforts, particularly the chronic failure to attract new industry to Nova Scotia. The Nova Scotia

Department of Trade and Industry was portrayed as lethargic, unimaginative, and ineffective. Stanfield proposed that if elected he himself would take over the industry department and give it some direction. He would assume direct responsibility for industrial development.[6]

Despite the slippage in Liberal support in Nova Scotia, the provincial party under Macdonald remained securely in power. In particular, its hold over the Catholic voters of Halifax and Cape Breton seemed unshakeable. This sectarian aspect of Nova Scotia politics could 'cut both ways,' however, as shown by developments within the party after Macdonald's death in 1954. The subsequent Liberal leadership convention was marred by religious controversy as Henry Hicks took the Protestant vote to come from behind and defeat the favoured Harold Connolly, who was supported by Catholic delegates.[7] Later that year in the Halifax South by-election to fill Macdonald's seat, the Irish Catholic vote split between Liberal and Conservative candidates as it had never done before, and in an upset Halifax South returned the Progressive Conservative candidate.[8]

In the 1956 provincial election campaign, Stanfield once again attempted to make Nova Scotia's lagging economic development the issue and proposed a 'Nova Scotia Industrial Development Organization' as a means of stimulating industrial growth.[9] This time, in the estimation of Dalton Camp, a key Conservative 'insider' and orgnizer of the Stanfield campaign, Cape Breton Catholics proved to be the margin of victory for Stanfield. The Tories took away five of the ten Liberal seats on the Island, winning twenty-three seats overall to the Liberal's nineteen and the CCF's one. As in the 1920s, it was the province's enclave of industrial workers that deserted the Liberals for a more promising alternative in the form of a revived Conservative party. As noted by Camp: 'In the end, the margin of victory came from embattled coal miners, the steel men, and the hard-pressed merchants in the urban areas [of Cape Breton], all of whom for years had given their sentimental support to Angus L. They had no such feelings for Hicks. Instead, they turned to Stanfield, who looked to them like a man who might do something.'[10]

What of the CCF, the party of Cape Breton's miners and steelworkers? It was suffering a fate similar to that of the national and Ontario parties. In the 1953 provincial election the Nova Scotia CCF managed to put up only sixteen candidates, down from twenty-one four years earlier. It managed to re-elect two MLAs with increased majorities, but its overall vote was down. In the run-up to the 1956 election, there was very little activity on the part of the party. After a strenuous effort, only eleven candidates were nominated, and many of these were token. When the results were in, only one of the sitting MLAs had survived, and the party had captured a paltry 3 per cent of the vote. Provincial-party membership quickly dropped to fewer than two hundred, and party organization was in tatters. An executive council meeting in early 1957 expressed the fear that the end of the movement in Nova Scotia was in sight.[11]

Nova Scotia politics in 1956 was a straight contest between the long-dominant Liberals and a surging Conservative party. Nevertheless, it is easy to exaggerate the swing of voter support away from the government party. The Tories just barely surpassed the Liberals in popular vote – 48.6 per cent to 48.2 per cent – and if the Liberals had polled just 598 votes more in nine key ridings, they would have won a landslide with twenty-seven seats.[12] Moreover, the substantive differences between the major parties on issues and approach cannot be said to have been dramatic nor had they ever been. As Beck points out in his history of Nova Scotia politics and government, the provincial-party system has historically been characterized by the notable absence of clear-cut party philosophies. Both major parties have tended to be pragmatic and 'generally supportive of business' (or at the very least non-threatening to its interests). This historical reality, Beck argues, has tended to accentuate the role of political leadership and party organization in Nova Scotia politics, commodities over which provincial Liberals appear to have had a distinct advantage from the 1880s to the 1950s.[13] Dalton Camp offered the same assessment with regard to the 1956 election: the distinction between one party and another came down to differences in political leadership, 'the quality of the chieftain.'[14] According to Camp, Stanfield possessed the necessary qualities for this role: an 'anti-politician' with a rather patrician demeanour and a strong sense of 'noblesse oblige,' he exuded honesty, sincerity, and integrity.[15]

Stanfield's selection, then, while representing a decisive break in the Liberal dominance of Nova Scotia politics, may also be seen as reaffirmation of the historically important position of political leadership and party organization in a system of party competition largely devoid of meaningful philosophical or ideological differences; in other words, a confirmation of the dominance of traditional, small 'c' conservative-party politics.

But the ideological homogeneity of Nova Scotia politics can also be interpreted as evidence of the historic hegemony of the dominant class in the province, aided and abetted by the lack of organization on the part of the subordinate classes, particularly the province's rural primary producers.[16] And those instances of radicalism in Nova Scotia party politics that have occurred (the separatist movement of the Confedera-

tion period and the 1880s, the Farmer-Labour movement of the post
–First World War period, the working-class politics of industrial Cape
Breton) have introduced a variability that has exercised important effects
– in specific historical conjunctures – on party strategy, on political
discourse, and on electoral outcomes.

Looking Outward and Looking Inward: APEC, IEL, and VEPB as Vehicles of Business-Government Collaboration

APEC

The freight-rate increases of 1948–9 that had so upset Maritime manufacturers and politicians, and led to their co-operation in an unsuccessful
attempt to have the spirit of the Maritime Freight Rates Act take
precedence, brought home the need for an *ongoing* research and promotion agency in the region that could monitor the effects on the regional
economy of national policies. The Maritime Board of Trade began to
promote the idea of an economic council. After enlisting the co-operation
of the four Atlantic premiers in the project, politicians and businessmen
met in conference in September 1954.[17] A decision was taken to set up
the Atlantic Provinces Economic Council (APEC), a non-governmental
agency with the following tasks: a / to undertake a survey of the factors
affecting economic development in the region; b / to develop united
action on matters of common concern; c / to co-ordinate the efforts of all
those interested in the economic welfare of the Atlantic provinces,
including other specialized agencies such as the MBTTC.[18] APEC was also
given a committee structure (on agriculture, trade and industry, tourism,
and power) charged with the task of carrying on research in particular
areas and advancing concrete proposals. An overview of committee
composition reveals the extent to which APEC at this juncture represented
the Maritime business élite.[19]

One of APEC's first major efforts was its submission to the Royal
Commission on Canada's Economic Prospects (the Gordon Commission). It was proudly cited by APEC's executive manager, O. Nelson
Mann, as 'a complete statistical review and forecast of potential prospects
and possibilities of the region,' in a form and manner never before
attempted by the Maritime provinces. The main message APEC sought to
convey to the Gordon Commission was the dire need for new methods,
new capital, and greater productivity, and that labour being displaced
through the modernization of the resource sector needed to be provided

with employment through the growth of the manufacturing sector.[20]

Within a few short years of APEC's founding, an annual Atlantic premiers conference was established (later to become the Maritime Premiers Conference with the withdrawal of Newfoundland), and the government-funded Atlantic Provinces Research Board (APRB) was initiated to co-ordinate an extensive program of economic research. Moreover, a direct channel of communication was established between APEC and the federal government. In addition trade shows, economic conferences, promotions, fact-finding studies, market surveys, and regional economic analyses were being carried out.

The founding of APEC, then, filled a large gap in the organizational and strategic capacities of both regional-capital and provincial governments in the region at this time. The agency provided an ongoing ability to gather, analyse, and diffuse information relating to the regional economy. It served in promotional and co-ordinative capacities, maintaining at least a superficial overall unity in the campaign for regional development. APEC also provided a direct service to those elements of regional capital planning business expansion and investment through its publication of 'quarterly reports' on economic conditions in the region and through specific market-research studies undertaken for private firms.[21] But most of all it was a regional agency that could monitor government actions in the regional-development field and lobby government decision-makers on pertinent policies and issues. Such a capacity at the regional level was clearly needed to counter bureaucratic agencies and advisers at the centre.

With regard to Maritime provincial governments, unity in their representations to the federal government on the issue of regional development was in no way assured, but it improved markedly over what it had been in the inter-war period and in the first decade after the war. Before Stanfield's election in 1956, New Brunswick's Conservative premier, H.J. Flemming, who had been aggressively 'taking the point' in representations to Liberal Ottawa, was having difficulty in gaining the co-operation and support of his Liberal counterparts in the other Maritime provinces.[22] One result of this was that midway through Stanfield's 1956 election campaign there was an unexpected donation of 'tangible assistance' from Flemming's New Brunswick finance chairman, in addition to a substantial injection of aid from Progressive Conservative national headquarters, 'for the first time in a long time.'[23]

It would appear, then, that Stanfield's 1956 campaign was the most soundly supported Conservative campaign in the province for some time, and that this was partly the result of the New Brunswick premier's wish to reduce the partisan obstacles to a united Maritime front. The extent of active business support for the Stanfield campaign remains something of an open question, though there can be little doubt that Stanfield (whose family remains a notable member of Nova Scotia's business élite) immediately developed a close working association with the province's business élite after his ascension to the premiership, whether they were Conservative or Liberal in their politics. In a series of secret meetings after his election, Stanfield invited a group of 'business luminaries' – including known Liberals as well as Tories – to offer advice on the options for promoting industrial development. He was convinced by them to make the proposed Industrial Development Corporation a completely publicly funded agency, which led to the creation of Industrial Estates Limited (IEL), a provincial Crown corporation totally financed by the provincial government.[24]

IEL

The birth of IEL in 1957 may have heralded a new era in the provincial state's development role, but its inspiration, composition, and *modus operandi* suggests that the state in this instance was little more than the agency's sponsor and banker. The real significance of the Crown corporation was that it provided a focus and venue for Nova Scotia capital to utilize and expand its business network to 'sell' the province to other venture capitalists. As such IEL represented another variant of the emergent business-government collaboration aimed at the promotion of regional development.

Stanfield's secret meetings with Nova Scotia businessmen determined not just the corporate form IEL would adopt, but the ground rules of its operation as well. In effect, the agency was handed over to Nova Scotia's business élite, while Stanfield accepted the 'political headaches.' 'Government would provide the money ($23 million to start) but it would keep its nose out of IEL. Businessmen would run the agency, and they'd do it as unpaid volunteers ... Manson was the sole Cabinet minister on the IEL board ... Not government but IEL would announce its agreements with industry clients, and only after they'd been signed and sealed.'[25]

The rationale for a business-staffed and -run agency was a straightforward recognition of business practices: 'money talks to money.' There was also a clear division of labour demarcated between IEL's development role and that of the provincial government. IEL's purpose was 'to encourage the promotion, expansion, diversification, and development of industrial activity in Nova Scotia,' but with regard to light or secondary industry. The provincial government would devote itself to the problems of resource development and heavy industry.[26] It was also stipulated that IEL-induced industries could not be competitive with any similar industry existing or operating in Nova Scotia.[27]

The services and incentives which the agency had available to offer potential investors were multiple. 'Industrialists! Have Industrial Estates Ltd. finance and build your plant in Nova Scotia! The company will develop the site of your choice, finance and build your plant, lease it to you at low rental and, if and when you wish, sell it to you at book cost.'[28]

The inspiration for this type of Crown agency came from the British experience with industrial estates in northeastern England. The key link here was Major-General Kenelm Appleyard, an acquaintance of the Nova Scotia industrialist R.A. Jodrey and agriculture minister E.D. Haliburton. As chairman of Northeastern Trading Estates – a state-funded, business-run, British Crown corporation with a regional-development mandate – Appleyard was recruited by the Stanfield government to advise them on the establishment of a similar agency in Nova Scotia.[29]

If the model for IEL was British in origin, the motivations of the agency's business directorship were deeply rooted in their own concern over Nova Scotia's growing economic crisis. The chief business figure in IEL over the first decade of its existence was its president, Frank Sobey, whose ownership of the largest chain of supermarkets in the Maritimes had provided the basis for diversification into investment funds, real estate development, and directorships on approximately twenty corporations.[30] In 1957, the economic prospects of Sobey's Pictou County home base were anything but bright. Once an important mining district, coal production had been dropping steadily through the 1950s when a January 1957 fire in the last operating mine destroyed an industry upon which 2,700 people were 'wholly dependent.' Sobey's immediate response was to see Stanfield with suggestions for a government-aid package for the area.[31] While Sobey undoubtedly felt the urgent need to do something for his home town, 'what was good for Pictou County, as a rule, was good for Frank [Sobey].'[32] On such matters personal and community interests coincided, as was the case with other IEL directors who either had some interest in IEL clients or a clear financial stake in a revived Nova Scotia economy.[33]

The gradual collapse of Nova Scotia's coal industry and the economy of the towns dependent upon it not only supplied the urgency that led to Sobey's direct involvement in IEL, it was the reason for the establishment of the agency's first subsidiary company – the Springhill Development Corporation. Formed after two major mining disasters in 1957–8 brought an end to coal mining in the town of Springhill, the subsidiary company was given authority to offer special incentives over and above the usual IEL fare to attract industry to the town.[34] The extreme urgency of the Springhill situation was an exception to IEL's usual mode of operation, which consisted of an extended period of 'contacts' and meetings with potential investors, many of which were organized through the corporate connections of IEL directors or advisory-board members. It was through such business 'net working' that doors were opened and 'deals' arranged. To facilitate this process, IEL named a new advisory board in 1961 to tap a Nova Scotia 'old boy' network of Canadian and American corporate 'heavyweights.'[35]

IEL's pitch to foreign firms, particularly labour-intensive manufacturing industries in the United States, was that Nova Scotia had a readily available, stable, cheap labour force.[36] According to IEL's management, the preferred corporate profile was 'a company which, for reasons of its youth, aggressiveness and growth, had a shortage of working capital and therefore needs our plan of financing.' It was also preferable if the company was 'nobody's subsidiary,' as time and again big companies had begun their cost-cutting in recessionary times by closing a branch operation in the Maritimes.[37]

As a state-funded vehicle for deal-making within the extended business network of Nova Scotia's corporate élite, IEL scored a number of successes in terms of the adoption of Nova Scotia locales for plants or factories.[38] But the Nova Scotia agency also had its downside in terms of financial fiascos,[39] industrial conflict,[40] excessive concessions to corporate friends,[41] unreasonable secrecy,[42] and simple overconfidence and/or incompetence.[43] By the early 1970s, it was operating with a much lower profile (if with a larger staff), its role increasingly made redundant by the activities of the federal Department of Regional Economic Expansion (1969) and the provincial Department of Development (1970).

Voluntary Planning

While IEL may be seen as one means by which the corporate interconnections of Nova Scotia–based capital could be exploited to encourage external investment (Canadian or foreign) in the province, the Nova

Scotia government went on to sponsor a further innovation aimed at improving the internal lines of information and communication between business and government: the Voluntary Economic Planning Board (VEPB). In 1962 APEC president W.Y. Smith extolled the virtues of improved business-government communication and of state planning in the regional-development effort.[44] O.N. Mann, executive vice-president of APEC, would later reiterate the potential benefits that would flow to regional capital as the result of state intervention of this sort. A regional plan elaborated at the federal level in co-operation with the Atlantic provinces 'would be of considerable help to the private entrepreneur in reducing the area of uncertainty within which he must always operate. As a result he would become more willing to take the kind of risks traditionally expected of him.'[45] But he also chided business to make itself aware, and to take advantage of the state efforts made on its behalf.

'The businessman must keep informed of changes in development policy and programming as they occur. He must be prepared to cooperate in such efforts and above all be alert to *the profit possibilities which the overall development effort is intended to point out and make available*' (emphasis added).[46]

The VEPB was inaugurated in 1962 by the Stanfield government after a fact-finding mission to Britain and France had convinced the provincial minister and deputy minister of finance that economic planning on a provincial level was both possible and desirable. Business participation in the various sector committees was initially enthusiastic, and there were ambitious projections of the benefits that would flow from the exercise. Overall planning, pronounced the government-appointed secretary of the VEPB, would be seminal in achieving the primary objective: 'maximum economic growth with profits.'[47]

Industry representatives, however, while ostensibly given a major role in formulating the provincial plan, would not be obliged to incur any commitment to assist in carrying it out. It was to be economic planning completely free of regimentation or compulsion.[48] In effect, this careful demarcation of the planning exercise such that it in no way trod on either the absolute prerogative of capital to plan its own activities and investments or government's freedom to accept, reject, or modify the final product made VEPB mainly an exercise in communications and information exchange between the provincial state and virtually every sector of the economy.[49] At the very least, the program would serve as a medium for providing reliable information to both government and industry. It would also be a medium within which industry could attempt to solve its own problems and have *direct access to government for whatever assistance may be appropriate and within its power.*[50] In Stanfield's words, the VEPB would afford 'not only a thorough opportunity for government understanding of the business point of view, but will also enable the various business sectors to make representations to government on a continuing basis.'[51]

Both IEL and VEPB, then, were provincial innovations borrowed from abroad that were meant to provide Nova Scotia capital with vehicles for influencing the rate and nature of corporate investment in the province as well as those aspects of the provincial government's policy, planning, and legal framework that could encourage and/or restrict sectoral developments. The prime motivation for such innovations, and the sense of urgent necessity that brought both government and business to actively participate in their establishment, was the crumbling of Nova Scotia's traditional industrial base in coal and steel, and the need, as a result, to quickly fill the yawning gaps that were beginning to open in the provincial economy.

Industrial Relations and the JLMSC

Organized labour in Canada had made substantial gains during the war in terms of membership, living standards, and favourable legislation. But with the retreat of the Canadian state from the economy in the post-war years (in terms of both ownership and regulation), unions were called upon to consolidate and extend these wartime gains. Thus, in 1946 alone, more than 4.5 million person-days were lost through strikes in Canada. One major victory for labour was the outcome of the United Autoworkers strike when Justice Ivan C. Rand gained a settlement of the strike under which payment of union dues was to be mandatory while union membership was to be voluntary. The 'Rand formula,' which in effect conceded the union shop (i.e., union security), established a firm precedent for the organizing struggles of other workers throughout the country. The outcomes of labour–management clashes in Nova Scotia in the post-war years were less heartening for the labour movement. In both mining and the fishery industrial unionism encountered defeats or setbacks that left workers in a weakened bargaining position vis-à-vis capital. What was for the most part a quiet provincial labour scene in the 1950s, however, was shattered by the 1957–8 Nova Scotia Gypsum strike.

The Gypsum Strike and the McKinnon Report

The Gypsum strike was a thirteen-month-long struggle for union security by four hundred members of the Nova Scotia Quarry Workers Union (QWU) in Windsor, Nova Scotia. The employer in this case was the Canadian Gypsum Company, a wholly owned subsidiary of United States Gypsum. The bitter strike was marked by demonstrations, arrests, and industrial sabotage. It sharply divided the community and ultimately brought a threat from the Nova Scotia Federation of Labour (NSFL) of a general strike if the provincial government did not intervene to force a compromise solution. The Stanfield government did appoint an industrial inquiry commission, but it did not make its findings binding. When the commission's recommendation that the principle of the 'closed shop' be accepted was rejected by the company, the basis for a settlement disintegrated. In the end, with strike support dwindling and gypsum again being shipped, the union was forced to give up its key demand and negotiate a return to work.

The Gypsum strike is notable here not for its length and its bitterness, but for its implications for organized labour in Nova Scotia, and for the pattern of industrial relations in the province more generally. During the strike both sides made repeated appeals and demands to the provincial government to involve itself in resolving the strike in favour of the party in question. For labour, the strike outcome discredited industrial action as a means of obtaining basic protections for trade-union principles. Instead, meetings between strike leaders and politicians in 1957–8 laid the basis for an alternative avenue of acquiring such protection: provincial legislation. At its 1959 and 1960 conventions, the NSFL put forward unanimous resolutions supporting provincial legislation to guarantee union security. In a brief to the provincial cabinet, the federation argued that such legislation would greatly reduce the kind of industrial strife in Nova Scotia that was characterized by the Gypsum strike. Not content, however, to limit its appeal to formal resolutions and recommendations, the NSFL for the first time directly suggested and supported the changes it desired in the form of Bill 116, put forward in the Legislature in March 1960, by CCF leader Michael McDonald. The Stanfield government's response was to establish a 'Fact-Finding Body on Labour Legislation' headed by Judge A.H. McKinnon in order to assess the extent to which such legislation elsewhere contributed to industrial peace. In his report McKinnon shunned more restrictive legislation as a solution to industrial conflict, instead drawing on the Swedish model of voluntary co-operation and internal regulation as the way to industrial peace.

One is forced to the conclusion that restrictive legislation has driven an ever-deepening wedge between management and labour and has made much more difficult the voluntary cooperation which is vital to the welfare of industry and its employees. A continuation of this trend could very well mean an ever widening rift between the parties and a not remote possibility of a renewal of a class struggle which besmirched the record of the last century ... representatives of labour and management in Nova Scotia [should] undertake an exhaustive ... examination and study of the Swedish plan, with a view to adopting those features which may be suitable to conditions in this province.[52]

The Joint Labour-Management Study Committee

Concurrent with McKinnon's investigation into labour legislation, representatives of management and labour, facilitated by the activities of the Dalhousie Institute of Public Affairs, were making tentative moves towards acceptance of more co-operative labour-management relations in Nova Scotia.[53] With the release of the McKinnon Report in March 1962, these efforts were increased, culminating in the creation of a Joint Labour-Management Study Committee (JLMSC) under the auspices of the Institute of Public Affairs and the chairmanship of its director, Guy Henson. The JLMSC brought together labour representatives from top leadership positions in provincial labour councils, the NSFL, the UMW, and the CLC with individual owner-managers representing a regional and sectoral cross-section of Nova Scotia companies.[54]

The initial role envisaged for the JLMSC by its founding members was essentially that of a highly informal discussion group that would study a limited range of problems associated with the collective-bargaining process in the private sector with a view to improving what all agreed was a soured atmosphere for industrial relations in the province by gaining a measure of consensus on certain problems facing both management and labour. However, both the scope of the JLMSC's concerns and its mode of operation would change as it became more established. Both internal and external pressures demanded that the committee either disband or evolve beyond its modest beginnings to assume a more active and responsible role on the province's industrial-relations scene.

The provincial government was quick to give its approval and support to the new body, which it viewed as a promising means to reduce the level of industrial conflict; for its part, the government pledged not to initiate any changes to the Trade Union Act without first consulting the JLMSC. In fact, for a number of years running, the government passed into law only changes to the act that had been recommended to it by the committee.[55] Within a short time after the inception of the JLMSC, three-way communication between business, labour, and government had become the norm and the deputy minister of labour had become a sitting member of the committee. The relationship was further solidified when the JLMSC agreed to become Labour-Management Advisory Council to the VEPB, and to prepare reports or reviews to be incorporated into the provincial planning process.[56]

The labour members of the JLMSC were not universally supported in their decision to co-operate with management in removing obstacles to smoother industrial relations. However, continuing support and legitimacy was derived from the fact that the NSFL appointed its members to the JLMSC as a federation committee that would report each year to the annual convention. In contrast, employer members of the committee were not directly responsible to an organization that could give their actions and agreements wider import and legitimacy. Their only mandate to negotiate for employers derived from a yearly JLMSC conference attended by key representatives from both sides (for example, the Nova Scotia branch of the Canadian Manufacturers Association, municipal and regional boards of trade, industry organizations).[57]

In the mid-1960s, the JLMSC encountered its first crises: provincial government decisions to enact minimum-wage legislation and extend the provisions of the Vacation Pay Act. In both cases not only were business and labour members of the committee divided over the legislation, but each group came in for criticism from their respective constituencies for co-operating with the government in the introduction of the legislation. Business representatives on the committee felt most threatened by the course of events because of their weak mandate to negotiate for employers and the lack of a body to which they could refer for guidance. With growing pressure on them to work out common positions on issues, management members began exploring the question of an employers' association from which they could draw direction and legitimacy. However, divisions remained as to the advisability and necessity for such an organization in Nova Scotia, and nothing concrete emerged from discussions on the question.[58] It appears that there was not sufficient compulsion or self-interest at this time (nor would there be in subsequent years) to force employers in the province to give up to a small group of representatives engaged in centralized negotiations with labour leaders a significant measure of their traditional independence and freedom of action in dealing with their work-forces.

The answer to these crises was found in the committee's decision to proclaim its non-involvement and non-position with regard to the controversial legislation. Forced to define its relationship to broader questions of labour standards and social legislation, the Fifth Labour-Management Study Conference, in November 1966, produced an agreement that recognized the government's right to 'take action, on its own initiative, to set minimum standards as to wages, working conditions, and fringe benefits for the purpose of fixing levels of certain workers. Although labour and management should consult as much as possible and seek joint action on all matters of common interest, the moratorium with respect to separate approaches to Government [on the part of labour and management] should apply only to the Nova Scotia Trade Union Act.'[59]

The agreement confirmed the committee's narrow focus on industrial relations while not completely ruling out more wide-ranging discussions on social issues. This did not end discussion of the most desirable labour-management-government relationship. The growth of industrial conflict in the province in the late 1960s, and attendant government concerns over the damage done to the provincial economy and its 'industrial image' by the rise in work stoppages, produced a number of government overtures for closer, more formal tripartite arrangements.[60] But while the JLMSC would continue to contribute to the achievement of agreements in specific sectors, a larger role for it would not come to pass. Instead, new circumstances and new governments would conspire to dramatically alter the province's industrial-relations climate and bring an end to the JLMSC and its pursuit of a Swedish-style 'basic agreement' between labour and management in Nova Scotia that would provide the framework for internal self-regulation and industrial peace.

The Diefenbaker Revolution and a 'Positive' Role for the Federal Government

The election of Progressive Conservative governments in New Brunswick and Nova Scotia was undoubtedly an important factor in the major Conservative gains in the region in the federal election of 1957. The national party had been stalled for a number of elections at 30 per cent of the popular vote and fifty seats, most of them in Ontario. But there were sweeping changes occurring within the party which, in the opinion of

John Meisel, were born from concern over the party's survival and growing dissatisfaction with its policy orientation. Internal critics, however, were not part of the party 'establishment,' and their views were usually defeated when and if they were given a hearing (recall Nowlan's frustrated attempts to advance 'Red Tory' views within the party).[61] By the mid-1950s, an incipient rebellion against this ruling élite was given its opportunity: the resignation of the post-war party leader, George Drew. The leadership and policy convention that followed would not only dramatically alter the image and policy orientation of the party, but harbour long-range consequences for the social and geographic composition of Conservative voter support.

From the beginning, John Diefenbaker was the favourite to win the 1956 leadership campaign. 'He had been a leading figure within the party since 1940, was recognized as one of its most able parliamentarians, and had acquired a national reputation for his advocacy of civil rights and progressive social legislation.'[62]

Attempts on the part of the party establishment – representatives of wealthy party supporters from Toronto and English-speaking Montreal[63] – to find a candidate of national stature and appeal from outside the caucus to oppose Diefenbaker's leadership bid (his third) had failed, leading to reluctant establishment support for Donald Fleming.[64] However, the general feeling among the party élite appears to have been that on this occasion Diefenbaker could not be stopped; to that eventuality those opposed to Diefenbaker's candidacy appear to have been reconciled. 'Though he would be difficult, if not impossible, as a leader, and a failure, after one election he would retire and the party could then find a younger, abler man. Diefenbaker had been around a long time, so let him have it. The Grits would win the next election anyway.'[65]

But Diefenbaker's landslide leadership win at the 1956 convention was far more portentous. It occasioned a significant shift of power within the party away from the traditional Conservative hierarchy and away from traditional conservatism. Diefenbaker had a Canada-wide reputation as a liberal, a champion of the 'little man' against the big interests and of the poorer provinces against the wealthier ones. This view of him no doubt explains why he was distrusted in Toronto and Montreal financial circles. But he was also opposed in his third leadership bid by almost the whole of the Conservative front bench, the former and acting party leaders, and the party president. His election was also accompanied by a progressive moderation of official Conservative policies by convention delegates, with labour and natural-resource development given greater pride of place, unqualified support pledged for the Canadian Wheat Board, and the removal from official policy of some earlier 'ultra-Conservative' resolutions.[66]

It was in the 1957 election campaign, however, that the real nature of the change in the Progressive Conservative party became evident. Diefenbaker's hinterland, populist outlook was reflected in the party's campaign organization, issue selection, and policy orientation. He chose as a close adviser and speech-writer Dr Merrill Menzies, who urged the party to abandon its traditional distrust of positive government action and advocated a new national policy based on the national energy grid, a comprehensive policy on natural–resource development, and the establishment of various incentives for development.[67] *One of the major thrusts of the campaign became an appeal to those left out of the prosperity.* In the Maritimes the Tories were successful in exploiting a growing discontent and sense of grievance. Under Diefenbaker, 'the party of the big interests' would be transformed in the eyes of many voters into a populist party of the hinterland and the underdog.

The transformation of the Progressive Conservative party under Diefenbaker gave greater credibility to the electoral strategy and platform of Atlantic-region Conservative candidates. At the centre of this regional platform was the 'Atlantic Manifesto,' a series of resolutions (largely devised by George Nowlan and Dalton Camp) that included financial aid for New Brunswick's Beechwood Power Project, subsidies for coal-fired thermal-power generation in the region, defence production contracts, a capital projects commission (modelled on the Gordon Commission's recommendations), a Canadian coast guard, and special Atlantic adjustment grants.[68]

The 'Atlantic Manifesto,' a regional platform devised by regional representatives, was a break with past Conservative practice. Such supplemental activity by a regional grouping of MPs and candidates in conjunction with Tory provincial governments (Stanfield and Flemming) represented a considerable decentralization in platform construction, issue-making, and policy-making within the party.[69] In response the Liberals scrambled to make some last-minute or interim concessions to the Maritimes on power development and freight rates.[70] Moreover, the Liberal budget did include a small increase in some transfer payments to individuals. But the latter measures were too little, too late, and were merely ridiculed by Diefenbaker for their 'niggling smallness.'[71]

Following Diefenbaker's narrow victory in the election, the Maritime premiers were not long in pressing their claims on the new federal government, which responded by quickly delivering on several of its promises to the region. In his opening address to the 1957 Federal-Provincial Conference, Diefenbaker signalled a newly sympathetic federal stance on the Maritimes' grievances and demands. The intention of the government actively to promote the development of all of Canada's regions was emphasized. To accomplish that, 'positive government' was considered necessary at both the national and the provincial levels. In line with this approach, assurances were given with regard to a range of federal commitments: assistance for power development in the Maritimes, further subventions to coal producers in Nova Scotia, the extension of seasonal unemployment-insurance benefits, and more money for Canada Mortgage and Housing Corporations's low-cost housing program. On the topic of fiscal relations, the pressing need for some form of special assistance to the Atlantic provinces as a result of their relatively lower taxable capacities was cited.[72]

The foremost concerns of the Nova Scotia government were made evident in Robert Stanfield's address to the conference. He took immediate aim at his primary concern: the equalization formula devised to determine payments for the 1957–62 period. Stanfield argued that the formula, which included only three tax fields (corporate, income, and succession duties), was totally inadequate and that it was imperative that the formula be extended to cover all relevant tax fields.[73] He also urged that the 'special assistance' for the Atlantic provinces alluded to by Diefenbaker be in the form of an adjustment grant (as promised in the 'Atlantic Manifesto'). Such assistance was the minimum required if the provinces in question were to be able to meet rising educational costs, increased demands from municipalities, and the financial commitments arising out of the new Hospital Insurance Plan.[74]

As if in justification for these claims on the federal treasury, Stanfield made explicit reference to developments within the Atlantic region that indicated a new era of 'self-help' in finding ways and means whereby the region could share in the nation's industrial growth: the Conference of Atlantic Premiers was pointed to as a positive step towards regional co-operation and solidarity; IEL signalled an innovative departure in the campaign to attract industry to the province; APEC was proving to be an invaluable research and advisory agency for regional governments.[75]

In 1957–8 the federal government enacted a number of measures to aid the Atlantic provinces. There would be special adjustment grants for a four-year period (Nova Scotia's share of which amounted to $7.5 million annually). There was also special financial assistance for power development in the Maritimes and increased freight and coal subventions.[76] In 1959, the Maritime Marshlands Rehabilitation Act (MMRA) was updated and extended, and the Farm Credit Corporation established. Royal commissions on Transportation (the MacPherson Commission) and Coal (the Rand Commission) were appointed; the former would attempt to deal yet again with a problem area of special significance to all three Maritime provinces, while the latter was of great significance to Nova Scotia's major industry. Such concessions to the Maritimes, while gratefully accepted, were not in any way considered a sufficient federal commitment to reducing regional disparities and promoting regional development. The goal of *a greater federal role in all aspects of regional development* continued to be pursued by the four Atlantic premiers, the regional business association, and associated development agencies.

To this end the Atlantic premiers had begun in 1956 to meet in regular (semi-annual or annual) conferences towards the adoption of common positions on federal policies affecting regional development. In the May 1957 meeting a continuing committee was struck to ensure continuity. Observers praised the institutionalization of the conference and its objective of regional unity as the main hope in the struggle to achieve 'better terms within Confederation.'[77] In 1958 agreement was reached on a broad, idealistic program to ignore all provincial boundaries in the region with regard to regional development proposals. A committee was appointed to recommend ways and means by which research into the general problems of regional development could be brought about. At the same time APEC, at the request of the Maritime Board of Trade, resolved on the project of an overall survey of the region's industrial and economic potential. The conference also received the report of its Capital Projects Committee, set up as the result of an earlier meeting of Atlantic premiers to examine the implications of the Gordon Commission's recommendations to the federal government.[78]

By 1959, the discrepancy between the expectations and objectives of the region's political actors and the actual 'goods' delivered by Ottawa was beginning to take its toll on the initial enthusiasm and goodwill extended to the Diefenbaker government. It was becoming apparent that the 'Atlantic Manifesto' was to be more or less the full extent of the federal response to regional grievances, and political pressure began to mount on the government to produce a coherent plan of action for the Atlantic provinces. As early as 1957, New Brunswick premier H.J. Flemming (later a federal cabinet minister under Diefenbaker) was warning that what was really needed was a committee of senior officials

within the federal government to study the regional problem and determine what combination of measures would be necessary to influence
industrial location so as to achieve more balanced regional economic
growth.[79]

Private-sector agencies and advisory bodies, and the regional press,
also began stressing the need for a more wide-ranging and substantive
measure of federal aid and movement towards co-ordinated state planning. The usually staid *Halifax Chronicle-Herald* officially ended the
'honeymoon' with the government with a series of editorials assailing the
federal government's ad hoc approach to the problem of Atlantic development. 'The present federal administration ... have approached the task
of repairing the weakened structures of the outlaying parts of the nation
with bits and pieces, and the result has been, to date, a patchwork effort
with no appearance of sound permanency.'[80]

Whereas the Gordon Commission had earlier been condemned by the
Chronicle-Herald for daring to suggest that the federal government give
assistance to the people waiting to leave the Atlantic region (which
conjured up visions of a modern-day Highland Clearances), the Gordon
Report was now approvingly cited for its rejection of piecemeal solutions
to the region's economic problems and its advocacy of 'a bold, comprehensive and coordinated approach to the underlying problem of the
region.' Subsequent editorials went on to elaborate a 'Blueprint for
Atlantic Advance': special taxation concessions to industries willing to
operate in the region (similar to those operative in the U.S. possession of
Puerto Rico, the happy results of which were approvingly noted); a major
revision of the national freight-rate structure; special low-rate capital
loans for industries willing to locate in the region (similar to those offered
by the British government in its own regional-development program, and
to proposed U.S. legislation); special consideration for new highways,
water transportation, and electric power generation; a greater regional
allocation of defence contracts and other public works; and increased
sensitivity to regional needs in tariff negotiations. This major program of
state intervention, however, would have but one aim according to the
paper's editorial staff: 'the restoration of a climate in which private
enterprise can operate successfully.[81] Furthermore: '*The creation of conditions which will attract private capital*' – that is the key to the whole
question of what is holding back the progress of this part of the Canadian
nation and of how to go about bringing it into step with the rest of the
country ... We must have more of that good old-fashioned private
enterprise.'[82]

At the 1960 Federal-Provincial Conference, the Maritime premiers continued aggressively to pursue by-now familiar regional themes: equalization, social programs, incentives to industry, and capital expenditures in the region. All were cited as areas in which greater federal contributions were necessary and fully justified on the basis of national concerns and obligations. Stanfield focused on social programs and equalization. Subsidies and grants from the federal government for education, social welfare, and public health services had to be continued for as long as the need existed. The regional concentration of income and wealth in Canada imposed limitations on the ability of the Atlantic provinces to raise revenues for educational and social services, yet through providing a protected domestic market for Canadian manufacturers and educating large numbers of Maritimers who migrated to other parts of Canada, the region was contributing to national welfare and prosperity. Despite the fact that education was a provincial responsibility Nova Scotians had a *right* by virtue of citizenship to the best educational facilities that *Canada* (as opposed to its constituent parts) could afford to offer; education was a matter of *national* concern.

The same spill-over effects and social-entitlement rights were operative in the fields of public health and welfare; a level of federal involvement was required sufficient to provide a reasonable standard of essential services to all Canadians.[83] A continuation of the pattern of growth of federal payments to the provinces – both equalization payments and those for use in social programs – was thus defined as a *right of citizenship* and a *national obligation*.[84] The tax-sharing plan and Atlantic adjustment grants would have to be supplemented by increased revenues if Nova Scotia was to maintain national standards in education, health, and welfare. Full recognition on the part of the federal government of the principle of fiscal need was required.[85]

New Brunswick's premier Louis J. Robichaud, while supportive and reiterative of Stanfield's position on federal-provincial fiscal arrangements, directed more of his comments to the need for special federal incentives for manufacturing in the region. The Gordon Commission's findings and recommendations were cited as useful, particularly the idea of a capital projects development fund that would allow for federal contributions towards capital projects in the region. But further tax concessions and grants for manufacturers were needed if work was to be brought to the worker, thus taking advantage of the economic and social infrastructure already in place.[86]

The federal government, however, gave no indication of major new initiatives of the sort demanded by the Maritime premiers at the 1960 Federal-Provincial Conference. All Diefenbaker had to announce was a winter-works program to ease seasonal unemployment and a raising of the federal share of the cost of training unemployed workers from 50 per cent to 75 per cent.[87] In addition, a fourth provincial revenue source – natural-resource revenues – was to be included in the formula for calculating equalization payments. Such concessions, however, constituted a great deal less than what the Maritime premiers were requesting. Stanfield was to later argue that this formula was totally inadequate for the maintenance of the national standards in education, social welfare, and public health in his province.[88] Either the federal government's commitment to the concept of equalization was a narrow and limited one, premised merely on the utility of the mechanism of an equalization formula for standardizing and universalizing federal-provincial fiscal relations in the face of growing provincial disenchantment with tax-rental agreements (and Quebec's non-participation), or the full incorporation of the principle into intergovernmental financial arrangements had stalled in the face of a slow-down in national economic growth.

It had become clear by 1960, then, that the response of the Diefenbaker government to chronic regional disparities was strictly limited and ad hoc, both in the way the problem was conceived and in the resources allotted to solving it. Populist rhetoric and initial concessions to the Atlantic region were never followed up with a more co-ordinated, long-term policy to reduce regional disparities and promote regional development. The creation of a new department for this purpose, or the appointment of a responsible minister, was apparently not even contemplated. Instead, the Liberal 'ministerialist system' was renewed, and designated regional representatives in cabinet were given wide latitude in handling questions pertaining to their province; 'regional concerns never became regional policy.'[89] A more sympathetic hearing for Maritime problems was the chief advantage gained with the new Progressive Conservative government over the former Liberal administration.

That the Diefenbaker Conservatives were, in fact, more attentive to the Maritimes than the previous Liberal government had been seems clear. There was action on the 'Atlantic Manifesto,' the 1957 election platform of Conservative candidates in the region. And the manifesto itself seems to have embodied much of the 'conventional wisdom' of the time about the development problems of the region and what government could do about it. Moreover, the source of much of the 'blueprint for action' came from within the region: from provincial governments, associated agencies such as the Atlantic Premiers Conference, and advisory bodies such as APEC. Provincial initiatives *were* given paramountcy.

In 1961, the calls for a change in federal-government approach to the regional problem were joined by the Special Senate Committee on Manpower and Employment, which came out strongly in favour of a 'co-ordinated program' of economic development for the Atlantic provinces, including capital 'on attractive terms' to build new productive facilities. The Senate Committee warned that 'sporadic incursions into this problem and random flourishes are not going to bring results.' They further rejected massive migration of the population as 'neither socially nor economically advisable.'[90] The findings and recommendations of the Senate Committee on Land Use, as well as the 'Resources for Tomorrow' Conference (1961), confirmed and reinforced this call for a greater federal effort.[91]

It was at this point that the Diefenbaker government's first major initiative in the field of regional development was launched: the Agricultural Rehabilitation and Development Act, later renamed the Agricultural and Rural Development Act (ARDA). The ARDA legislation was put together and enacted under the aegis and 'protection' of the influential minister of agriculture, Alvin Hamilton, who took on the new agency as a 'pet project.' Not surprisingly, the early part of ARDA's life-cycle reflected the concerns of the grass-roots Prairie politician, operating very much in the 1930s tradition of farm resuscitation and local projects. As such, ARDA was essentially a populist response to the economic problems of the poorer farmers who had struggled under the former Liberal government's 'business approach' to agriculture. Only later, after the return of the Liberals to power, did ARDA move towards state-sponsored programs of 'social adjustment' in rural areas as the key to reducing poverty in the Atlantic region.[92]

The creation of ARDA was followed in 1962 by the inauguration of the Atlantic Development Board (ADB). This agency was to act in an advisory capacity and its primary task would be the preparation of a development plan for the Atlantic region. But it came near the end of the Conservative government's life, and with the defeat of the Conservatives early in 1963 the admittedly sketchy outline of the ADB's planning role was supplanted by the incoming Liberal government with agency responsibility for the disbursement of a $100-million development fund (raised to $150 million in 1966).[93]

That the ADB was initiated primarily in response to mounting political pressure from the Atlantic region for a more coherent and comprehensive regional-development policy, rather than an internally generated policy measure, is suggested by its terms of reference. Five full years into the Diefenbaker government's mandate, the board was directed to *initiate* an assessment of the regional problem and then recommend appropriate remedial policy measures. Evidently no such assessment had been undertaken within the bureaucracy during the life of the Conservative government.[94]

The mandate given the ADB is revealing. Part of the reason for the shortcomings of the federal government's regional-development role in the Diefenbaker years was a simple lack of knowledge about regional-development problems, especially how regional development as a process fit into national economic growth, and how a federal role in regional economic development fit with its more customary task of national economic management. This lacuna within the federal bureaucracy could only be rectified by means of some form of *political sponsorship* for the introduction of new expertise and structures that would strengthen the capacity to research and analyse the regional problem as a basis for policy development in a new field of state intervention. In lieu of such federal expertise, it was to be expected that initiatives and actions with regard to regional development would be predominantly provincial in origin, with the federal contribution largely limited to that of 'banker.' The Conservative government was just beginning to move beyond this limited role when it was defeated. The Diefenbaker years were an important transition period, however, one in which regional political forces were given an opening at the federal level that led to a higher profile for regional development as an issue of national concern and an appropriate area for federal intervention.

The Liberal Party: Renewal, Adaptation, and a Revamped Policy Agenda

While the Diefenbaker government's commitment to reducing regional disparities may have been poorly conceived, and as a field of policy development less than compelling in terms of actual policies and programs, the elevation of regional development to the state agenda at the national level did have a discernible effect on the sensitivity of the Liberal party to the issue. This change can be attributed in large part to the dynamic interplay of strategies, discourses, and policy platforms that is a potential consequence of the electoral competition between political parties. In order to effectively 'compete' in the political arena, parties may be forced to respond to the discursive and programmatic elements embodied in a successful or *potentially* successful opposition party's strategies and tactics.

Such was most assuredly the case with the Liberal party after its overwhelming defeat in the elections of 1957 and 1958. The trauma of losing control over state power was made all the more complete by the significant reduction of the party's political support base and the ranks of its elected members. The Liberals clearly had been outflanked by the Diefenbaker Conservatives, 'beached' in terms of their strategic positioning and policy orientation by a shift in both the discourse and actual policy outlook of late-1950s Progressive Conservatism, and the public's perception of that party and its leader.

Where formally the Conservative Party had stood for balanced budgets and restricted economic intervention by government, it now, under the leadership of Diefenbaker, appeared to be favouring a welfare-statism that places it to the left of the Liberals on a left-right continuum. Its six-year period of rule featured such items as increased old age pensions, extended and enlarged unemployment insurance benefits, and heavy financial assistance to the provinces – most notably the Prairies and the Maritimes.[95]

The completeness of the defeat in 1958 did have one beneficial effect for the Liberals. It 'purged' the party, not only in the sense of removing the overweaning influence that extended years in power had granted to the aging, élitist, small 'c' conservative party establishment, but in actual physical terms as well. Between 1958 and 1962, a generational change of personnel occurred, opening up both ideological and physical space within the party. The result was greatly increased influence for the younger, more progressive, left-of-centre elements of the party: those more strongly Keynesian and welfarist in policy orientation, more favourably disposed towards state intervention in the economy and technocratic planning, and in strategic terms, covetous of the electoral support of the growing urban middle class.

In fact, there had been rumblings of discontent within Liberal-party ranks for a decade previous to the 1958 cataclysm over the centrism, élitism, and conservatism of the party leadership. The 1948 leadership convention had provided a focus for this dissatisfaction, though the latter was masterfully suffocated by party élites.[96] The appointment of the Royal Commission on Canada's Economic Prospects (the Gordon Commission) in 1955 provided further evidence of both the expression and subsequent stultification of those forces within the party advocating a change of direction. Impetus for the commission came from an article sent to the deputy minister of finance by Walter Gordon, who hoped to deflect the government from some of C.D. Howe's policies. Seized upon by the finance minister and his department, the decision to appoint a royal commission was taken in Howe's absence in order to avoid his opposition to what inevitably would amount to a questioning of his policies. In the event, the government set aside the recommendations embodied in the commission's preliminary report as cabinet closed ranks behind Howe in the face of opposition criticism.[97] After 1958, however, the way was clear for Liberals of Gordon's ilk to exercise a much more profound influence on party policy and organization.

The 1958 national Liberal convention, which elected L.B. Pearson as leader, produced a spate of resolutions on the Atlantic provinces. Most of these were disconnected concessions to various disparate interests, apparently designed to woo this or that particular constituency, adopted at the urging of one or another Liberal power-broker within the region.[98] There were among these, perhaps, a couple of substantial policy offerings, most notably the adoption of the Gordon Commission's recommendations for an Atlantic provinces capital assistance fund for the purpose of financing large projects essential to the development of primary industries and electric-power facilities in the provinces. However, the resolutions taken as a whole reveal a clear lack of recognition of the need for a comprehensive regional development policy for the Atlantic provinces. Nor did the resolutions represent a departure from the traditional forms of intervention undertaken by the Canadian state, as offers of assistance were limited to furthering the development of resource industries in the region. Such assistance would require no major policy or program innovation on the part of the federal government; it did not offer any conception of a *qualitatively different role for the state in managing or regulating the regional distribution of industrial activity in Canada.* Furthermore, it suggested nothing that might be construed as state interference with the prerogatives of capital and as such remained non-threatening to a Canadian capitalist class accustomed to the sympathetic treatment and non-interventionism of past Liberal governments.

The need for a major overhaul and reconstruction of the Liberal party after the 1958 election had both an ideological and, therefore, policy dimension and an organizational dimension. The revamping and redirection of Liberal party ideology and policy began with the Study Conference on National Problems, better known as the Kingston Thinkers Conference, in 1960. Papers were presented by emergent figures within the party such as Maurice Lamontagne and Tom Kent. Their progressive, left-leaning policy prescriptions (somewhat at odds with past Liberal practice) incited charges by prominent business elements within the party that they were embracing socialism.[99] In fact, what Lamontagne and Kent were advocating was something more closely approximating a comprehensive welfare state – 'the completion and refinement of the postwar edifice of social security' – including medical insurance, a prices review board, a council of economic advisers, tax incentives and public investment for depressed areas, retraining for the unemployed, and a massive state investment in education.[100]

Lamontagne's paper at the Kingston Conference, entitled 'Growth, Price Stability and the Problem of Unemployment,' argued that the Keynesian revolution had to be transcended. 'We must develop selective policies and we must try to give a regional and industrial formulation to our national policies.' According to Lamontagne, one of the policy implications of coming to grips with the end of the post-war period in Canada was a special program for the Atlantic provinces that included cheaper power, better transportation, a special lending policy, an industrial development fund, and special tax incentives. He also called for federal co-ordination of this comprehensive regional-development policy with the four provinces concerned and with APEC.[101] Kent's paper addressed the problem of relocating capital. In his view manpower training was not enough; government was responsible for bringing work to the workers, rather than vice versa. A regional program of public investment would provide the necessary inducement to private capital to relocate to depressed regions.[102]

The 1961 National Liberal Rally provided the first opportunity following the Kingston Conference for an official review of party policy, and a subcommittee on the Atlantic provinces duly confirmed and/or incorporated policy prescriptions generated by the Gordon Commission and the Kingston Conference. Most significant was the recognition that a slow-growth Atlantic economy represented a productivity drag on the national economy, and far from conflicting with the maximization of national economic growth, the reduction of regional disparities was deemed essential to this goal and to the future economic well-being of the country as a whole. This analysis, in turn, provided the philosophical basis for a series of proposed measures aimed at encouraging industrial expansion and job-creation in the Atlantic region: a capital assistance fund administered by a special federal agency, a broad scheme of regional tax incentives to private capital, promotion of the vigorous use of the Industrial

Development Bank in the region, a program of assistance for highway construction within the context of a regional transportation policy, and a coal policy with special treatment for the chronic unemployment in coal-mining areas.[103]

The transformation of the Liberal party after 1958 wrought by the ascent to a position of influence of progressive, 'social democratic' Liberals can be overstated. David Smith, in his excellent study *The Regional Decline of a National Party: Liberals on the Prairies,* makes the point that under Pearson there was, in fact, a marriage of 'old guard' and 'new guard' Liberals.[104] This alliance took on the concrete expression of right-left factional splits within Liberal cabinets. The organizational and electoral strategy of courting the urban middle class and the 'calculated flirtation' with the New Democratic Party after the minority election victories of 1963 and 1965 – while helping to give impetus and substance to Walter Gordon's vision of a moderately leftish, moderately nationalist Liberal government – produced a backlash against what were seen to be 'socialistic' policies among representatives of business within Cabinet and the more right-wing, small 'c' conservative Liberals of western Canada.[105] In addition, the Liberal minority governments of 1963–8 were under mounting pressure from the provinces, particularly Quebec, which was in the throes of its 'Quiet Revolution.' It is within this political context that the Liberal response to the regional-development issue, and more generally the treatment accorded to the interests of the poorer Atlantic provinces, must be situated.

Conclusion

In the inter-war period political forces in the Maritimes engaged in a futile campaign to have national policies redesigned or overturned and the system of fiscal relations between the federal and provincial governments fundamentally overhauled. When at the end of the Second World War a much more centralist political system rejected any special role for itself in those regions (primarily the Maritimes) that were lagging economically in preference for a more conventional Keynesian role for itself in aggregate economic management, provincial governments in the region appear to have reconciled themselves to a subordinate, peripheral status within Confederation.

Regional complacency in the post-war period, abetted by the continued political hegemony of entrenched Liberal regimes and the renewed defence spending in the region occasioned by the Korean War, was finally shaken by the relative economic stagnation of the 1950s. Regional development once again became an issue around which political forces on the periphery began to mobilize. However, in the interim the issue had been substantively redefined; development was now seen to be dependent upon the attractiveness of the region as a site for non-indigenous investment. Viewed thusly, the strategy pursued was one of promoting the region and enticing investment. Both the provincial and federal governments would have to be active sponsors and participants in carrying out this strategy, underwriting the search for potential investors and funnelling state resources into the region as either contributions to expansion and modernization of the infrastructure there or as direct subsidies to capital.

The more direct involvement of the state, however, awaited political changes at both the regional and the national levels. The monopsonistic structure of Liberal-party dominance in the post-war period stultified new initiatives in the field of regional development, while alternative political vehicles were in some way incapacitated for the role of promoting and carrying out the task. The upshot was that regional development was by and large kept off the political agenda during this period.

With the defeat of the Liberals in both Nova Scotia and Ottawa in 1956–7, a greater 'space' was created for the elaboration of the theme of regional development and the construction of new policies and programs to address the problem. The Stanfield Conservatives in Nova Scotia co-operated closely with the province's business élite and with the other governments in the Atlantic region in organizing a regional-development campaign. This move on the part of the provincial government towards a more activist role, including more innovative mechanisms for promoting private investment in Nova Scotia, was given urgency by the growing crisis in the coal industry, a sector upon which a sizeable proportion of the population – and thus business activity in the province – continued to depend.

At the national level the unexpected election of the Diefenbaker Conservatives in 1957 – an electoral upset in which the Maritimes played a major part – brought a significant change of attitude at the federal level towards regional demands and grievances. Diefenbaker's ascent to the leadership of the Progressive Conservative party the previous year had dramatically altered the party's embrace of economic conservatism and its image as the party of Big Business and Ontario, with the consequence of greatly expanding the party's appeal on Canada's eastern and western peripheries. In fact, the new leader's sympathy with the grievances of both the Maritimes and the West did lead to a number of specific concessions and innovations in policy terms. But the overall policy record of the Diefenbaker government also suggests the lack of substance or depth in the prime minister's populist discourse. In terms of an economic or social analysis that would provide the ideological and intellectual underpinnings for a regional-development policy, no coherent program of measures followed logically from the government's expressions of sympathy for the plight of the periphery, other than various ad hoc concessions. This poverty of strategy and policy development at the political level was not likely to be compensated for at the bureaucratic level. As will be indicated in chapter 6, Ottawa's senior bureaucrats, openly hostile to the concept of a regional-development policy, formed an entrenched opposition that constituted a major obstacle to the formulation and implementation of new structures, policies, and programs in this uncultivated field. Given this bureaucratic resistance and the lack of firm political commitment of sponsorship for something more than sporadic incursions into the realm of regional development, the federal government as a whole remained aloof from the problem, with little expertise, analysis, or bureaucratic capacity developed such that the government might undertake a more general and co-ordinated intervention in this area.

Diefenbaker's political success and his championing of the hinterland regions did have an impact on the Liberal party, however, ensuring that the problem of regional development would be given greater attention in the course of the party's renewal and transformation. Many of the programs rejected by past Liberal governments were now openly embraced. Regional development was, as a result, firmly ensconced on the political agenda, becoming an essential component of the platforms of political parties intent upon competing for the support of voters in Atlantic Canada.

6 Restructuring the State 1963–8: Obstacles to the Ascendance of a Regional-Development Technocracy

The preceding discussion raises a number of theoretical questions regarding the historic relationship between party and policy at the national level in Canada and, further in this connection, the salience of bureaucratic structures in determining the nature and extent of state intervention to address the economic problems of the periphery. This chapter will indicate how the issue of regional development was differentially incorporated into party platforms and government policy agendas at the federal and provincial levels, depending upon the composition of the governing coalition, its base of support, and its electoral strategy. An assessment of the nature of the constraints placed upon regional development as a policy field will also be undertaken in light of the tendencies and functions of existing bureaucratic structures at the national level. Finally, the role of local political forces will be assessed – the nature and extent of their influence over the course of events on the periphery and their impact on the role assumed by the state.

These theoretical questions will be probed through an examination of intergovernmental and interagency controversies swirling around the federal government's regional-development policies and programs, and the response of governments to the crisis of heavy industry in Nova Scotia. Together these elements go some way towards explaining why, the federal government should on the one hand, adopt a wide range of welfare measures to more or less complete the edifice of the welfare state in Canada, while, on the other, taking a very limited, tentative, and haphazard approach to more basic problems of economic structure on the periphery, with its attendant symptoms of higher-than-national rates of poverty, unemployment, and underemployment.

Throughout most of the 1960s the main thrust of federal intervention in the regional-development field was in the direction of rural development, following from the analysis of the Gordon Commission that the disparities between the Atlantic region and the rest of the country were primarily attributable to the problem of rural poverty. This analysis ignored the question of the region's lack of economic diversification, particularly its weak and narrow manufacturing base, and the looming crisis in coal and steel, a central pillar of Nova Scotia's economy since the turn of the century. When state élites were finally forced to consider these problems, the nature and limits of the federal commitment to regional development, as gauged by its willingness to involve itself directly in the rehabilitation of regional industry, would become clearer.

Regional Economic Performance in the 1960s

For most of the 1960s Canada rode the crest of an economic boom. Unemployment rates dropped substantially from the highs experienced during the 1957–61 recession remained relatively low (between 3.6 and 4.8 per cent) from 1964 to the end of the decade.[1] Rates in the Atlantic region followed the downward trend. Although slow to emerge from the recession that began in 1957, all four Atlantic provinces made substantial gains in the mid-to-late 1960s in economic growth, capital investment, and employment creation. Between 1961 and 1968 gross regional product rose by 85 per cent (Nova Scotia's by 76 per cent), income by 112 per cent, and investment by 140 per cent.[2] With $9.5 billion in new capital investment in the region between 1961 and 1969, there was a sharp rise in construction employment (up 54 per cent in 1966 over 1961 levels). Housing, institutional services, and government accounted for the largest share of this both nationally (40 per cent) and regionally (44 per cent),[3] while in Newfoundland and New Brunswick utilities proved to be a particularly large contributor to the growth of capital investment.[4] And while the economic boom pulled people from the region at an unprecedented rate in the 1961–6 period, the outflow was stemmed in the second half of the decade. By the early 1970s, Nova Scotia was actually experiencing net in-migration.[5]

Despite these encouraging signs of increased growth and prosperity in the 1960s, serious problems with the regional economy remained. The absolute improvement in economic conditions in the Atlantic region during this period did not substantially reduce the relative disparities separating it from the rest of Canada. Even with the steady decline in unemployment figures (the regional unemployment rate dropped from

11.2 per cent in 1961 to 6.4 per cent by mid-decade), unemployment in the Atlantic provinces remained high compared with rates in the rest of Canada at this time.[6] And the problem of seasonality of employment in the Atlantic region remained, actually worsening in amplitude over the course of the period from 1956 to 1969.[7] Labour participation rates for every one of the Atlantic provinces continued to remain well below the national level, even when the employment gap narrowed briefly in the early 1970s. Finally, the most obvious measure of relative prosperity – per capita incomes in the Atlantic region as compared to those in the rest of Canada – showed some improvement between 1961 and 1971, but the gap remained large and the rate of its closure agonizingly slow.[8]

The Primary Sector

The primary sector in the Atlantic region was a site of significant new investment in the 1960s, producing large increases in output and productivity while reducing the employed work-force. This sector's share of regional employment dropped accordingly from 24.2 per cent in 1961 to 15.2 per cent in 1969. The numbers of those engaged in *agriculture* in the Maritimes dropped precipitously: while there was a considerable decline of 19 per cent in agricultural employment in Nova Scotia between 1961 and 1966,[9] the rate of employment reduction more than doubled to 40 per cent in the latter half of the decade. (There were declines of 50 and 33 per cent in New Brunswick and Prince Edward Island, respectively.) By 1971 just 4 per cent of the labour force in Atlantic Canada was engaged in agriculture, only 3.3 per cent in Nova Scotia. Average farm size continued to grow, increasing 80 per cent between 1951 and 1971.[10]

To some extent these figures obscure the persistence of subsistence agricultural activities in the rural areas, at least up to the mid-1960s. As recently as 1965, 33 per cent of all Maritime farms were not statistically recognized as farms because of their small size and non-commercial nature. These 'non-farms' help explain the large rural 'non-farm' population recorded for the region in the mid-1960s: approximately 33 per cent of the population of the three Maritime provinces as against 17.3 per cent for the rest of Canada.[11] It seems a higher proportion of Maritimers remained on the land while not engaging in commercial farming, instead acquiring sufficient income to subsist through other means. It was this relatively impoverished rural population that the federal government sought to affect with the rural adjustment programs designed by ARDA.

Forestry also experienced decreases in the overall size of its work-force, as well as a continued shift to pulpwood production in line with increased pulp-and-paper output. In Nova Scotia, pulpwood production quadrupled between 1960 and 1976, while employment in this particular subsector increased by 25 per cent.[12] In a province where a large proportion of the forested land remained under the control of private landowners with less than 1,000 acres, the expansion of pulp-and-paper production also connoted expanded commercial relations between woodlot owners and industrial capital in the form of the pulp-and-paper companies. With the growth of such linkages, the pattern of landownership in the province began to present obstacles to the efficient exploitation and management of the forest resource. After 1967, the harvest from small ownerships would decline in proportion to the increase in output from large ownerships and Crown lands. By the mid-1970s, it had become apparent to state managers that small ownerships were producing 'a fraction of the yield of the forest products that they could produce.'[13] This would lead to the growth of state assistance for management programs and for the formation and operation of woodlot owners' cooperatives.

In the *fishery*, employment actually increased by 11 per cent over the first half of the 1960s, once again demonstrating the distinctiveness of this sector from other primary industries. Independent inshore fishermen continued to dominate the industry in terms of numbers, but increasingly they dealt with large-scale processors who were expanding their year-round mechanized trawling operations. The growing competition among processors even began to transform the United Maritime Fishermen (UMF), the co-op federation started by M.M. Coady and the Antigonish Movement in the 1930s. In the 1960s, the UMF moved to amalgamate and centralize co-op management, and to purchase two large offshore vessels to obtain a secure supply of fish. Although at odds with its original philosophy of small, independent producers who would democratically control locally-owned and managed co-ops, UMF management justified the restructuring in financial, managerial, and market terms. In attempting to compete with private capital, the co-op was being forced to remake itself so as to resemble other corporations in the fishery.[14]

The fishery was changing in other ways, too, that suggested its ongoing transformation into a more thoroughly industrial and capitalist enterprise. Throughout the Atlantic region in the 1960s unions were still restricted to representing shore workers. But pressure was building on fish companies and the state to extend 'normal' collective-bargaining rights to fishermen, which culminated in the long and bitter Canso strike in 1970–1. During the course of this strike there were court injunctions, jail sentences, walk-outs by unions elsewhere in the province in support of the fishermen, a special industrial inquiry commission, and even the veiled threat of a general strike. In the end, both the companies and the government accepted and facilitated the unionization of Nova Scotia's offshore fleet.[15]

But while the strike against two foreign-owned processors by fishermen in three eastern Nova Scotia communities led to a change in government legislation that legitimized the right of fishermen working on large, mechanized trawlers to be represented by a union of their choice, it did not do the same for inshore fishermen (one of the original demands of the strikers). Moreover, though fishing companies throughout the Atlantic region began granting voluntary recognition to CLC-affiliated unions to represent the fishermen on offshore vessels, the West Coast union that organized the Canso strike (the militant United Fishermen and Allied Workers Union – UFAWU) was shut out by the companies, with the co-operation of the Canadian Labour Congress.[16]

Within a few years of the Canso strike, however, preoccupation with unionization struggles within the fishery would give way momentarily to a growing general concern with a severe decline in fish stocks that was sharply curtailing catches in the ground and pelagic fisheries. By the mid-1970s the stage was set for federal-government intervention to limit foreign fishing and exert control over the management of stocks. This was accomplished by vastly increasing the size of the territorial waters over which Canada claimed sovereignty, and by initiating state-determined quotas on all catches within these waters.[17] Suddenly the rules of the game were dramatically changed, in the process entwining the state much more directly with a diverse assortment of class and group struggles within the industry.

Manufacturing and Services

In the 1960s manufacturing in the Maritimes reversed the decline it had experienced in the 1950s, registering a significant increase in employment levels.[18] In Nova Scotia, manufacturing's share of new capital investment exceeded the national share between 1964 and 1968.[19] But, even so, manufacturing remained a much lower net contributor to total net value in Atlantic Canada than in Canada as a whole (36.9 per cent versus 54.7 per cent in 1967).[20] Part of the reason for this trend was the manufacturing sector's continued heavy reliance on primary-sector activities. This aspect of regional manufacturing remained virtually unchanged. Thus, in 1973 Nova Scotia, which had the most diversified of the provincial economies in the Atlantic region, employed 25 per cent of its manufacturing labour force in fish-processing and forestry, approximately the same as in 1961. This industrial structure not only inhibited the overall growth of manufacturing in terms of employment and the contribution of this sector to total net value (and thus the growth of incomes and profits), but also perpetuated the problem of seasonality of employment. (Fish-processing, in particular, continued throughout this period to be characterized by seasonality and relatively low wages.)[21]

The greatest gains in employment and growth terms in the 1960s occurred in the public and service sectors: health, education, government, and trade and services. Federal transfers to the provinces for education, health, and social services increased dramatically; by 1971 60 per cent of all provincial expenditures were in these three areas. In the process, the public sector became a major source of expanding employment opportunities and the most important provider of income in the region.[22] This factor must be considered as having key importance in raising personal income per capita in Nova Scotia from 72 per cent of the national average in 1956 to 78 per cent in 1971.[23]

In sum, then, the 1960s were years of general economic expansion. During the latter half of the decade the Canadian economy operated at something close to capacity. Private investment in the economy of the Atlantic region showed a dramatic improvement over that of the 1950s, not only in the resource industries, but also in the manufacturing sector. Overall growth rates were high, unemployment was low, incomes were rising, and inflation was not yet a serious problem. It was within this context that the federal government fully embraced the welfare state, a development that benefited the Atlantic periphery more than any other region. Capital spending and employment growth in the public sector provided most of the fuel for an expanding Atlantic economy during these years.

Far from attenuating the demands of Atlantic Canada for a greater national commitment to reducing regional disparities in the country, the general prosperity of the 1960s made the idea of regional development seem a more attainable goal, if only the Canadian state would commit itself to the task. Besides, there was ample evidence of continuing, even worsening poverty and economic stagnation in the midst of plenty. Modernization in the primary sector was drastically reducing the demand for labour even as it raised output and productivity. And the problems of

Nova Scotia's heavy industry threatened to undermine the economy of the whole of eastern Nova Scotia. Indeed, it would be the unfolding coal-and-steel crisis that would finally direct the attention of state élites to the fundamental problem of regional industrial structure, a problem that refused to dissipate of its own accord, regardless of the level of prosperity of the national economy.

Bureaucracy, Cabinet, and Policy Formation

The chief difficulty encountered by those attempting to alter state structures and policy-making processes to deal with a 'new' problem such as regional development – that is, a problem which draws the attention of the state because of the success (for reasons explored herein) of a new constellation of social and economic forces in pressuring for a change – is the fact of *existing* state structures and policy-making processes that have shown themselves to be in some way inadequate or unsuitable for the task.

A large part of the reason for the shortcomings of the federal government's regional-development effort in the Diefenbaker years was the resistance of the department of finance and its minister to any proposals for an ambitious program to reduce regional disparities or to extend equalization. The 'narrow attitudes' exhibited by the department and its cabinet representative evidently proved to be a never-ending source of frustration for regional-development advocates and allied 'progressive elements' within cabinet.[24]

For some, opposition to new expenditures from the 'guardians of the federal treasury' during a period of economic recession – the first major recession since the Depression years – can hardly be considered as surprising. Unfavourable economic conditions for virtually the whole of the period the Conservatives were in office meant that a raft of economic management problems could be pointed to by the finance department as taking precedence over any *new* government intervention in the economy. That a concerted campaign to reduce regional disparities faded from view as an important item on the government's agenda as its troubles mounted and the national economy continued to sputter is evidenced by the austerity program announced by the prime minister only six days after the 1962 election. The program included temporary surcharges on about half the country's imports, substantial cuts in government expenditures, and the imposition of a tight-money policy.[25] When the national economy was labouring under a recessionary yoke, 'regional development' inevitably took a back seat to state measures aimed at restoring national economic growth, a lesson to be driven home again in the later 1970s and early 1980s. In any event, as pointed out at the time by at least one regional-development analyst, 'no regional development policy will have any lasting effect on higher standards of living unless you are sharing in a national economy which has a rapid rate of growth.'[26] (It might have been added that no such policy was even likely to be contemplated unless such conditions existed.)

But the Diefenbaker period was also the height of the era of Keynesian economic management, when increased government spending might have been expected as an anticyclical device. And here the limits of the federal bureaucracy's commitment to Keynesianism is apparent, as is the crudeness or perhaps irrelevance of that approach to economic management – at least in the form in which it was employed by Canada's department of finance – for the purposes of regional development policy. Throughout the 1960s there evidently was little or no sentiment within the ranks of the senior civil service in favour of the concept of regional development. Indeed, quite the opposite appears to have been the general rule. Most senior civil servants were in agreement with C.D. Howe on this matter: GNP was the important indicator; people seeking employment should move to areas of high growth. State intervention to stem migration from a depressed region by attempting to stimulate economic activity there was an ill-advised, counterproductive course of action.

This attitude on the part of federal bureaucrats towards any increased federal role in the field of regional economic development – which, by and large, was a constant throughout the 1950s and 1960s – meant that any major new policy thrust in this area had to be initiated and shepherded by the government of the day. This was one instance in which any 'policy vacuum' at the highest levels was unlikely to be filled by senior bureaucrats.[27]

But the Diefenbaker Conservatives arrived in power with a poorly thought-out strategy on regional development, and the new government was ill-equipped to deal with the magnitude of the problem or with the manipulation and/or redesign of a state apparatus with which they were unfamiliar. To make matters worse, relations between the Conservative government and an Ottawa bureaucracy that had worked 'hand-in-glove' with the Liberals for two decades were less than easy.[28] Mutual distrust and a natural self-serving resistance on the part of senior bureaucrats to the emergence of some new centre of bureaucratic power (i.e., a potential source of alternative advice and policy development, as well as a 'pole of attraction' for scarce resources) combined to inhibit the possibility of any new departure on the part of the government to establish innovative bureaucratic structures to oversee regional development.

This situation might have been expected to change with the return to power of the Liberals in 1963, especially given that individuals who had shown themselves to be favourably disposed towards a more comprehensive and coherent regional-development policy had now assumed senior positions within the new government: Walter Gordon became minister of finance, Tom Kent became program co-ordinator in the PMO, and Maurice Lamontagne was made president of the Privy Council (a position that allowed him to deal with what he and Pearson both saw as the new Liberal government's most urgent problem – English-French relations).[29]

Almost from the moment Gordon assumed his cabinet post, however, he faced the resolute opposition of his own senior bureaucrats, as well as that of the Canadian business élite and its allies within the cabinet (particularly Sharp and Drury) for his nationalist, interventionist agenda. Forced to retreat on his first budget, Gordon became the subject of numerous criticisms, conveyed to Pearson by 'old guard' Liberals, former bureaucratic colleagues, and the Liberal party's corporate supporters, leading Pearson himself to vacillate in his support for Gordon and his ideas.[30] By 1965 Pearson appears to have been alternately intimating to corporate and bureaucratic friends that after the next election the finance department would be headed by 'old guard' corporate executive Robert Winters or former senior bureaucrat Mitchell Sharp. Gordon's own role in persuading Pearson to call the 1965 election sealed his fate when the outcome yielded only two additional seats for the Liberal government instead of the anticipated majority. Gordon's resignation from cabinet was accepted by Pearson, and his cabinet post was filled by Sharp. Winters was given the ministry of trade and commerce.[31]

If the challenge to continental corporate capitalism represented by Gordon's nationalism was too much for 'old guard' Liberals and big business, there was room for some compromise, within the context of an expanding Canadian economy, on programs that addressed the problem of regional disparities. Indeed, the first and most prominent item on the agenda of the Federal-Provincial Conference of 1965 was regional development. Pearson opened the conference with a statement recognizing the inadequacy of general fiscal and monetary policies for this purpose and acknowledging the need for 'special policies' to encourage the full development of all parts of Canada. Noting that special incentives for investment in depressed areas were 'an important ingredient in the economic policies of the most industrially advanced countries,' Pearson proceeded to elaborate upon his own government's approach, and in so doing clearly signalled its welfarist, full-employment thrust. In effect, with the conservative tenor of federal economic policies firmly established in the wake of Gordon's demise, regional development was brought onto the state agenda through the 'back door' as part of the government's package of social-welfare reforms.

Thus, the object of industrial incentives was *not* to further advance well-established areas with good growth rates, but to bring jobs where they were most needed. Special assistance to industry was to focus on areas suffering chronic, long-standing conditions of unemployment and underemployment. This particular interpretation and understanding of the problem and the policies it called forth, while perhaps easily incorporated into the political discourse and policy debates of the Liberal government under Pearson, was destined to generate a significant measure of confusion and controversy within the affected provinces and the relevant development agencies, as well as within the federal bureaucracy itself. The nature and course of these disagreements will be explored below.

ADB and ADA

The problems associated with introducing and financing new state agencies concerned with the economic development of poorer regions, yet not under the immediate sway of finance department officials, are central to understanding the design and the fate of federal regional-development agencies in the pre-DREE era. The Diefenbaker government produced two such agencies as a response to political pressure on the government to produce a co-ordinated plan of action for the Atlantic provinces. ARDA's inauguration in 1961 was followed, in 1962, by the establishment of the Atlantic Development Board (ADB). Just as ARDA was shaped, nurtured, and protected by the Conservative minister of agriculture Alvin Hamilton, the ADB became the special concern of J.W. Pickersgill, a senior minister in Pearson's cabinet. According to Anthony Careless, 'The ADB was ... Pickersgill and "Pickersgillian". It was moved from its arms length quest for broadly appropriate government policy and placed squarely inside the government under Pickersgill as secretary of state, and with a $100 million budget to spend. So personal was the ADB to Pickersgill that he took it with him to the Department of Transport when he became its Minister.'[32]

Pickersgill was evidently aware that 'the independence of departments each with their own priorities' would spell disaster for the ADB if the board attempted a 'difficult and vague role of coordination,' or if it was dependent in any way on other departments to take up its recommendations. 'Having its own fund, the board could engage in projects without being at the mercy of other departments; and being a board with a "gapfiller" role there would be a minimum of political conflict with existing or proposed federal policy among departments ... Its spending function also made it political, for it provided its own visible indication of its choices and activities.'[33]

This analysis of the ADB gives full recognition to Pickersgill's commitment to a particular kind of ADB and his willingness to defend the board and its expenditures before cabinet. He did so with a fair degree of success. In the 1965–9 period the board spent $135 million, more than the total of the other three major regional development agencies (ARDA, ADA, and FRED) combined.[34] According to Careless, the adoption of the ADB by a powerful and very political minister willing to reshape its role and purpose within the federal government salvaged the board from what would inevitably have been an irrelevant existence on the margins of the Ottawa bureaucracy. The key to its salvation was to remove it as a threat to the priorities of other federal departments and give it an independent existence by simply tacking it onto the existing bureaucratic and policy-making structures. Without in any way changing the policies or procedures of the federal bureaucracy, the board was allowed to become the titular administrator of a fund similar to the Atlantic Provinces Capital Assistance Fund advocated by the Gordon Commission and endorsed by the 1961 National Liberal Rally. Since the monies disbursed from this fund produced a significant number of high-profile, temporary jobs, they naturally were used for political advantage and reward. Such financial outlays could be profitably labelled as Liberal-party expenditures, 'with obvious implications for the voter at election time.'[35]

The ADB was needful of powerful political protection and representation precisely because the board was alien and potentially threatening to federal bureaucratic structures and policy-making processes. But even the performance of a gap-filler role that minimized conflict with other federal departments did not leave the ADB free from central control over its spending. The board was allowed little autonomy within the confines of the 'Ottawa system.' It had no authority to make expenditures without the prior approval of the cabinet and Treasury Board. This dependence proved to be both a constant source of frustration for board members and a regulator of the pattern of board expenditures. (Thus, the fact that the Treasury Board favoured infrastructure expenditures strengthened the tendency for the board to submit infrastructure projects for the Treasury Board's approval.)[36]

If the mechanisms of central control limiting the autonomy of the ADB can be said to have constituted a serious defect in agency design from the regional point of view, making the board less representative of the region and more subordinate to policy-makers at the centre, the social and political composition of the board also gives cause for criticism that to the degree the board *did* represent the regional interest, it did so only in a very narrow sense. Of the twenty-six persons appointed to the board over six years, all were wealthy businessmen and/or lawyers with partisan connections to the government in power, with the exception of one token representative of labour, appointed to the board in 1968.[37]

ADB expenditures were heavily weighted towards infrastructure provision and resource development and only marginally concerned with assistance to secondary industry.[38] A great deal of this spending went towards large power-development projects. The development rationale for this type of expenditure reflected an emphasis on resource industries that was consistent with the role of hinterland regions in the Canadian economy.

It is generally agreed that the availability of adequate amounts of reasonably priced power is an important factor in the development of industry, particularly of power-intensive industries such as pulp and paper, mining and mineral processing. Hence, from its inception, the Board was interested in solving the problem of providing sufficient quantities of low cost power as quickly as possible ... Major industrial expansion is either going forward or planned in New Brunswick and Newfoundland as a result of these power projects.[39]

Nova Scotia, bereft of major opportunities for conventional hydroelectric-power development, had to settle for a large amount of ADB expenditure on the building and rehabilitation of trunk highways and general-purpose buildings, as well as site preparation and provision of fresh-water supply to fish plants and the like.[40]

Judging from this spending pattern, it is clear that the ADB was not concerned with the need for *structural change* in the regional economy and an increase in the size and number of labour-intensive industries, particularly secondary-manufacturing and service industries. The latter, of course, was exactly the thrust of the Stanfield government's development strategy pursued through such agencies as IEL and VEPB. There-fore, it should not be surprising that the ADB came in for criticism from the Nova Scotia government and regional-development agencies such as APEC. In its 1967 *First Annual Review*, APEC questioned the broad development strategy of the ADB. It was thought that a 'conceptual inconsistency' existed between the ADB approach to regional develop-ment, on the one hand, and the general APEC-VEPB-IEL approach, on the other. This difference of approach had first to be resolved before federal and provincial agencies could 'work in concert in the general interest.'[41]

In his study of Canadian federalism and regional economic develop-ment, Anthony Careless asserted that friction between Nova Scotia's VEPB and the ADB was rooted in the exclusion of the VEPB from consulta-tions and negotiations between the ADB and provincial departments, and that this annoyance (on the part of the VEPB) 'was converted into a protest against the ADB that became the official Nova Scotian line.'[42] Such an explanation overlooks the predictable resentment felt by regional actors and agencies towards the control exercised over ADB expenditures by policy-makers at the centre. It also ignores the fact that the differing approaches of the federal body and the regional groupings were, in fact, rooted in divergent ideological, social, and political interests that pro-vided the respective bases for the institutional design, purpose, and operation of the ADB as opposed to those of APEC, IEL, and VEPB. As a result, conflict and bitterness, as well as mutual incomprehension and criticism, were destined to figure prominently in federal-provincial and interagency relations.

From the beginning the Nova Scotia government had argued that the ADB's infrastructure expenditures needed a complementary program of federal incentives to secondary industry, similar to the sort used in northern England, to bolster Nova Scotia's efforts in this area.[43] But no sooner had the new Liberal regime in Ottawa inaugurated the designated-areas program – to be administered by the Area Development Agency (ADA) within the Department of Industry – than it came under attack from development agencies and provincial governments in the Maritimes, and in particular from APEC and the Nova Scotia government. From the standpoint of the latter, the problem with the new federal agency, and with Liberal regional-development policies in general, was that they were motivated, designed in accordance with, and indeed were 'part and parcel' of the national Liberal party's advocacy of a number of changes and extensions in the field of social-welfare policy, the expansion of which was central to the public philosophy and electoral strategy of an important segment of the Liberal party as it was constituted under Pearson. Thus, the ADA and its policy instruments – tax incentives and grants – were directed to slow-growth, high-unemployment areas. In effect, 'regional development,' as one of the components of the Liberals' reform package in the area of social policy, became a concept associated with the need to reduce regionally concentrated pockets of poverty and inequality.[44]

One result of Ottawa's manner of targeting incentives was the exclusion of the relatively prosperous Halifax–Dartmouth region in Nova Scotia as an area eligible for assistance. Even after the ADA program was revised in 1965 (as a result of pressure from the region) to extend grant limits and the tax holiday proffered to new manufacturers and processors, and to extend coverage to 'almost all the Atlantic provinces,'[45] the government of Nova Scotia continued to express reservations about the federal program. 'We feel Ottawa's conception is still faulty. If an area like Halifax–Dartmouth is excluded, for example, it would be a limitation to any serious effort to get the Nova Scotia economy moving rapidly ahead. It would be inconsistent with economic thinking and the present thinking in the old country (the U.K.) where they have come around to the view that if a region needs help you should support and accelerate growth of the part of the region that already is going ahead.'[46]

Stanfield's endorsation here of the 'growth centre' concept was also reflected in the analysis of APEC, whose preferred development scenario became the growth-centre strategy. The path being followed by the federal development agencies in the mid-1960s – the ADB and ADA in particular – was not congruent with APEC's stance, leading APEC to suggest to the ADB that it re-examine its policies for economic development. More specifically, APEC advocated a concentration of development spending on eight intense-growth centres in the Atlantic region, areas 'ready' for concentrated industrial development. Attempting to spread industrialization too thinly throughout the region was counterproductive. Much of the assistance then being granted under the ADA could well have been going to areas of little growth potential, resulting in no great stimulus to the economy as a whole. This was criticised by APEC as a form of *welfare assistance*, rather than the most beneficial form of *economic stimulus*. 'Areas for assistance should not be chosen on the basis of surplus labour without regard to the potential of such areas for viable economic development; rather, we suggest the Atlantic region be designated as an area for assistance and a number of centres within the region be designated as growth centres.'[47]

This division of opinion over the proper role and approach of federal agencies such as the ADA and ADB is revealing of more deep-seated federal-provincial differences regarding 'regional development.' The Nova Scotia government and regional capital, along with their associated development agencies, on the one hand, and the Liberal federal government – political élites, bureaucratic advisers, and regional-development agencies – on the other, had adopted approaches rooted in fundamentally different conceptions of 'regional development' as a consequence of the manner in which such development was co-opted, as an *issue* and a *policy field*, into particular political strategies, discourses, patterns of compromise over state policies, and structures of representation.

The provincial government, APEC, and the other development agencies were acting primarily as the representatives and purveyors of the interests of regional business. While this occasionally manifested itself in a crude instrumentalist sense, more often it can be understood as the logical consequence of their conception of what was necessitated if the process of capitalist development in the region was to go forward. The strategy was clear (what Claus Offe and Volker Ronge have called 'administrative recommodification'): federal and provincial governments would together 'jump-start' the process of capital accumulation in the region through the design and implementation of policies and programs aimed at supporting the expansion of private capital in primary and secondary manufacturing, modernizing and diversifying the economic base, and accelerating job creation in the process. Such state assistance should not attempt to arbitrarily redistribute growth and investment within the provincial/regional unit, or in any way further distort, hinder, or impinge upon the prerogative of capital to decide on the location of its investment, since such actions could undermine the larger project of 'economic resuscitation.'

By the mid-1960s, APEC, strongly influenced by the technocratic reformist impulse underpinned by new regional science techniques (and the growth-pole concept in particular), came to advocate active discrimination in the pattern of state assistance in favour of those locales that had already demonstrated some attraction for capital and were already the most urbanized, 'modern,' and 'developed' parts of the region. (Though the political perils of openly advocating government favouritism for some within the region – with the logical corollary of discrimination against others – appears to have led at a later point to some softening of this position on the part of the agency.)[48] Thus, both APEC and the Nova Scotia government were opposed to the targeting of development assistance *within provinces* on the basis of such criteria as income and unemployment figures. In contrast, Ottawa approached regional development as a variation on the national theme; regional-development policies and programs would be a variation on the national policies being pursued by the Liberal government, which emphasized the extension of social welfare and the amelioration of economic inequalities. Programs such as the ADA tax incentives and grants could be sold within cabinet and the federal bureaucracy if placed within this social-welfare context. Substantially, 'regional development' meant nothing more than raising income levels in the Atlantic region or alleviating pockets of chronic high unemployment. Demands from within the region to extend aid coverage to include Halifax and more prosperous locales generally met strong resistance at the federal level.[49] Such expenditures were not easily justified: they did not fit comfortably into the welfarist notions of redistribution or relief from distress conditions, nor had the technocratic reformist impulse associated with the nascent regional-development technocracy at the federal level sufficiently established and justified itself, its ideology, and its programs within an otherwise hostile federal bureaucracy.

If anything, the Liberal government formed after the 1965 election was likely to confirm this line of reasoning within the federal government, as ministers more representative of the views of big business and/or senior bureaucrats were handed the important economic portfolios. With Gordon's 'leftish nationalism' expunged (or at least diluted), presumably to be replaced with a more conservative, orthodox economic orientation, it could also be expected that 'regional development' would not be well received within the broad confines of federal economic and industrial policy.

It can hardly be considered surprising, then, that the ADA program of industrial incentives remained a relatively insignificant expenditure item until 1967–8, and was always to remain narrow and limited in its conception and role under the aegis of the Department of Industry. That department, which had a well-defined and vocal central-Canadian constituency already in place, was disinclined to engage in regional industrial development or restructuring.[50] Instead, the administrators of the ADA opted for the narrower goal of addressing the problem of chronic and severe unemployment in specific locales. This is clearly evident in the 1965 report of the Department of Industry: 'The Area Development project, as operated by the Department of Industry, is essentially *an extension of the national full employment policy of the federal government. In this context, the elements of regionalism in the area development program are incidental to the main purpose*'[51] (emphasis added).

While the Department of Industry's use of the ADA incentive package suggests the basic welfare orientation of the program (which may also help explain the low levels of expenditure), it may also be understood as a particular usage of industrial incentives more appropriate to the needs of central Canada. In relation to those needs the ADA incentives could serve as a means of relieving pockets of relatively high unemployment and retarded growth in an otherwise buoyant economy. Conversely, such incentives were quite inappropriate in a province such as Nova Scotia where the general characteristic was one of high unemployment and retarded growth while buoyancy was confined to specific pockets.

In addition, the newly created Department of Industry (1963) was an unlikely promoter and 'guardian angel' for programs embodying new and somewhat alien objectives. J.E. Hodgetts's comments on the creation of the new department are instructive: 'It is clear from the debate that arose in connection with the creation of this department that the government expected it to remain a very modest size, concentrating on co-ordinating, informational, and possibly inspirational functions with respect not only to its clients but also to the resource-oriented departments and other departments that might have certain peripheral concern for secondary industry.'[52]

Rianne Mahon has interpreted Hodgetts's description as indicative of the subordinate status of the new department. Its weakness was ensured by the decision to recruit staff for the new department from the private sector, resulting in a staff complement that was narrow in its perspective and out-of-step with 'the general ideology which prevailed throughout the civil service.' During the Department of Industry's short existence such anomalies 'inhibited the establishment of a good working relationship with the other departments' and likely contributed to the foreshortening of the department's independent existence.[53] It is also likely that Industry's reintegration with Trade and Commerce muted the former's protectionist bias and brought it more closely and surely under the purview and control of those senior officials in departments concerned with economic policy who claimed 'that expansion in export markets [was] the most effective way of increasing the productivity of Canadian industry: this emphasis on exports is consistent with the philosophy that the limited size of the domestic market constitutes the chief obstacle to the development of efficient manufacturing industries in Canada.'[54]

When adjustment assistance aimed at the 'rationalization of Canadian industry and gaining access to foreign markets' is the predominant concern of federal industrial policy, how can the latter also reflect the goal of interregional redistribution of industry in Canada? How could it be expected to design and implement policies to foster the development of secondary industry in underdeveloped, peripheral regions of the country? The simple answer is that it *could not* and *would not* do both, and most probably it wasn't expected to do so.

The designation of Bud Drury as minister of industry and Simon Reisman as his deputy minister would seem to confirm this. For while the creation of the new department was largely the work of left-of-centre Liberals such as Gordon, Lamontagne, and Kent who envisaged a more active government role in ensuring the health of Canadian industry,[55] those in whose care the new department was placed were distinctly averse to government intervention in the economy, and were certainly not sympathetic towards special measures and incentives to address regional disparities.[56] However, such a situation is illustrative of the awkward, often contradictory results of the compromises necessitated by the Liberal government's ideological composition, and the need to reassure and placate business and their representatives within cabinet if ostensibly 'nationalist' or 'interventionist' objectives were in some fashion to be pursued.

ARDA and FRED

Unlike the ADA, which developed a centrally designed and administered program of industrial incentives, the ARDA evidently developed a close working relationship with the provincial governments as a matter of policy. This policy led to claims by at least one of its officials that 'the whole ARDA program developed in a manner which [was] more sensitive to individual regional needs than most national programs,' and by 1964 a planning process for rural-development projects had been worked out jointly between ARDA officials and the provinces.[57] But like those of the ADA, ARDA's program expenditures did not match early ambitions for the agency. By 1966 only $62 million had been committed by the federal government and only half of that sum had been spent. (Only Quebec and Saskatchewan used their total allotment.) It seems that only token efforts were being made in many provinces.[58] Also apparent with ARDA's early programming, as with that of the ADA, was the reluctance of the federal government to undertake what one senior ARDA official differentiated as *development* programs, as opposed to an *adjustment-oriented* approach confined to areas of severe rural poverty.[59] In addition the 'designated area' concept central to ARDA's rural-development planning quickly came in for criticism from agencies within the Atlantic region. APEC expressed concern that there would be a large expenditure of federal funds on rural areas with little development potential, and that ARDA's restricted planning and programming focus would create disincentives to mobility *within provincial boundaries*. At the very least, APEC argued, ARDA's designated areas should ensure the inclusion of at least one significant growth centre.[60]

The half-measures and limited financial and program commitment that characterized the federal approach to the regional-development problem were finally superseded in June 1966 with the establishment of a $300 million Fund for Rural Economic Development (FRED). The fund was one of a number of measures undertaken in 1965–6 'to get the government moving again' and to 'consolidate a new policy thrust.' A strengthening of ARDA and ADA was part of this push, as were new manpower training and mobility measures, and the introduction of need-related programs such as the Guaranteed Income Supplement (GIS).[61] It was intended that progress in the bureaucratic implementation of this range of measures, styled as the Canadian 'War on Poverty,' would be reported directly to the prime minister through the Special Planning Secretariat (SPS), a newly created central agency headed by Tom Kent. With bureaucratic anomie and resistance coming to be perceived by Kent and others as a major obstacle to 'moving ahead,' the SPS had the ostensible purpose of giving greater 'weight' within the bureaucracy to the policy thrust represented by the 'War on Poverty' package of reforms.[62]

FRED would prove to be the single major federal-provincial exercise in devising and implementing comprehensive rural-development plans. With its inauguration, technocratic imperatives in the conduct of regional policy began to assert themselves in earnest, with important and wide-ranging effects for the content and conduct of regional-development policy. Not least among these effects was the growth of state machinery at both the federal and provincial levels concerned with the physical, spatial, and social components of the process of 'development.' That the new federal initiative would require a parallel expansion of provincial bureaucratic capacity was clearly spelled out in a description of FRED by L.E. Poetschke, at the time of writing a senior regional-development technocrat in the Ottawa bureaucracy.

While the many programs (associated with a FRED plan) are actually undertaken by government departments and agencies at the national or provincial level, our experience indicates that responsibility for management of the plan as a whole must be with a competent body working within the region. For this reason we insist that the province establish an effective program development and management group before entering the second phase of the planning process and we carry a large part of the cost.[63]

It was expected that these provincial groups, by gaining experience through the implementation of FRED plans, would 'undoubtedly provide the core of the much stronger overall provincial government administration required to play a role in real development activity.'[64] Indeed, beginning with FRED, strengthening and transforming the capacities of weak provincial bureaucracies was to become a necessary and essential part of federal-provincial development agreements. Quite simply, the enhancement of a provincial state's 'in-house' capabilities was part of the process of providing such provinces with the resources that would enable them to do the kinds of things that were done in other provinces where the provincial state was better able to do so.[65]

However, the federal 'management group' – the regional-development technocracy that had begun to emerge within the Ottawa bureaucracy – also needed to strengthen *itself* and secure its own place and function within a sometimes hostile, and an almost always unyielding and ill-adapted bureaucratic environment. As L.E. Poetschke noted in 1968: 'The present (bureaucratic) machinery was created in an era when the government role was largely *administrative* and hardly, if at all, *developmental*. Up to the present time Canadian governments have been trying to adapt and use this machinery to carry out these new functions and in a socio-economic–political environment which is vastly different than in the past' (emphasis added).[66]

The problem, then, was to adapt and create new governmental structures in order that government might perform the new 'developmental' function. And because of the demands and exigencies of federalism, these new structures would have to exist at the provincial as well as the federal level. This general requirement for *more or less coterminous growth of both the federal and provincial developmental technocracy* led to further technocratic imperatives related to planning, communication, and co-ordination. 'Jurisdictional rigidities' became a major problem, and intergovernmental committees and bodies of various sorts arose as a response. FRED was ostensibly to provide a framework within which such problems could be worked out.[67]

The structure and *modus operandi* of FRED is revealing of the changing perceptions, emphases, and analyses of regional development within the state that accompanied the growth and specialization of the developmental technocracy. FRED's work would be carried out by provincial program-development and management groups in conjunction with federal ARDA staff. Its proposals would be reviewed and filtered by an advisory board made up of deputy ministers and assistant deputy ministers from ten federal departments and agencies. This board would 'provide a forum for review, comment, and amendment to the proposals in light of broader federal government policy considerations,' prior to submission of the plan to cabinet.[68]

The comprehensive planning and co-ordinated approach that FRED was intended to promote, and provide the state machinery for, was seen by the technocrats themselves as a logical and progressive step. Then, as now, *the plan* and *planning*[69] was the 'raison d'être' of the developmental technocrat and the key to his role as 'social engineer.' Through the plan the technocrat could gain control over the process of change. But any attempt to gain control over change by transforming policy-making into a rational intellectual process, the goals of which were 'given,' was doomed to failure. To begin with, as noted by Tom Kent (the first deputy minister for Regional Economic Expansion), regional-development agencies 'cannot be expected to plan good regional development strategies unless there is a national industrial strategy of which regional programs are part and with which they can be coordinated. We do not have such a strategy.'[70]

This basic 'inadequacy' from a planning point of view merely exacerbated the tendency in a capitalist economy for control to be usurped by 'market forces.' In effect, attempting to exert control in this environment merely means that the technocrat becomes an agent who aids and abets the logic inherent in capitalism by 'rationalizing' or 'modernizing' society's structure of relations, a process by which a more appropriate environment for the operation of market forces is nurtured. 'Success' in this endeavour, of course, remains dependent upon private economic power, and the question of 'whose utility function is to prevail'[71] is more or less a foregone conclusion.

In the event, the primary goal of the emergent developmental technocracy turned out to be the relatively modest one of 'adjustment.' Nevertheless, in the eyes of the technocrat this compared favourably with previous state intervention in the field of regional disparities, considered rather disparagingly as 'subsidy' or 'compensation'. 'The tendency has been to modify the effects of decline either through subsidization which has had the effect of slowing down the adjustments in industries such as coal, shipbuilding, fishing, dairy, etc., or by augmenting welfare and neutral transfer payments to compensation for changes. In large measure these are policies of reaction to change and reflect the difficulties of organizing for a more positive response to gain control of this environment of change.'[72]

It was inevitable that the distinction drawn here between equalization and social welfare, on the one hand, and the proper role of regional development policies, programs, and expenditures, on the other, would be maintained within the lexicon of the developmental technocracy. The principles embodied in the former – universalizing and equalizing basic services and infrastructure without regionally discriminatory levels of taxation – were *not* synonymous with the transformation of an underdeveloped regional economy exhibiting lower levels of productivity, employment, and per-capita income. For the latter to be rectified, a structural transformation and process of modernization had to be encouraged.[73]

Even earlier ARDA policies came in for criticism for what was seen as an excessive concern with 'conservation' rather than 'adjustment.' For example, ARDA's alternative land-use programs allowed underemployed labour to remain on marginal and submarginal lands and prolonged myths surrounding the potential benefits of resource development. In this context, the inauguration of FRED was seen as a positive step forward by regional-development technocrats. Moving as it did towards comprehensive development programs that included educational and labour training, growth centres and relocation schemes, social capital expenditures and economic infrastructure assistance, FRED was seen to emphasize *socio-economic adjustment* rather than *rural conservation*.[74] It represented a full-blown state strategy of 'administrative recommodification': ceasing to rely upon subsidized protection for those unable to maintain themselves as market commodities, but instead using various means to recommodify those values, to change them or give them attributes that would once again make them marketable.

Besides the ARDA and FRED, the newly created Department of Manpower and Immigration (1966) under Jean Marchand as minister and Tom Kent as deputy minister became an important instigator of new programs aimed at facilitating 'adjustment' in peripheral regions. Manpower training and mobility became a priority concern for the federal government. During the Diefenbaker years the federal government had become more directly involved with manpower training through the Technical and Vocational Training Assistance Act (TVTA, 1960). This act enabled agreements to be signed with each province that provided large federal cash contributions for the rapid expansion of provincial capacity for technical and vocational training as designed by each province. But TVTA actually ended by discriminating against the poorer provinces since funds were distributed on the basis of the province's ability to match the federal allotment.[75] This fact, and the lack of federal control over TVTA expenditures, led to its demise under Marchand and Kent. If the federal government was to gain control in this area, then TVTA had to be ended.

At the 1966 Federal-Provincial Conference on Financing Higher Education, Marchand informed the provinces that Ottawa was getting out of contributions to the funding of provincial secondary-school systems (through TVTA) to play a larger role in adult occupational training and retraining for 'productive employment.' Manpower training had become directly and increasingly related to full employment and improved productivity, and was therefore of 'current, vital, direct concern' to the federal government. Accordingly, the government had decided to pay 100 per cent of the cost of occupational training for adults, but only for training in occupations that the federal government judged to be in current and future demand. The new federal program – the Occupational Training Act (OTA) – when combined with manpower-mobility measures, would better enable the federal government to achieve its objective of 'facilitating an efficient adjustment between the demand for and the supply of labour on a Canada-wide basis.'[76] Only the federal government could assess whether the provision of training on a Canada-wide basis made sense.

This position naturally raised some objections and concern among regional-development agencies such as APEC and provincial governments in poorer regions. Because the OTA's training and mobility measures would not be *regional* in design or scope but *national*, a potential conflict existed with the objectives of regional-development agencies such as the ADB and ADA, which, it was assumed, were there to encourage a faster rate of growth of job opportunities *within* the region, rather than to facilitate further mobility out of the region.[77] As a concession to these fears, the mobility measures did not become an operational part of manpower policy, though the national labour market remained the basis for manpower-training programs.[78]

All these new policies were formulated on the premise that not only should federal interventions into the field of regional development avoid interfering with spatial reorganization on the periphery, they should augment 'an efficient path of transformation.'[79] Regional planning (or manpower planning) could reduce the social and economic costs to society by removing obstacles to change and making a positive contribution to the transformation process. The expectation was that ultimately the periphery would come to exhibit those conditions and possess those characteristics of a 'modern' economy that would meet the perceived needs of capital and the process of capital accumulation, thus enticing the previously scarce private-sector investment needed to ensure a continuous, self-sustaining process of growth and structural change (i.e., 'development').

The new discourse of technocratic reformism and the anticipated policy-program matrix that was to take shape around the planning process faced an 'insidious' threat, however, from the pragmatism and political opportunism of political élites and the seemingly pervasive influence of local politics. For some technocrats, this challenge to the integrity of the plan was best dealt with by 'insulating' regional-development agencies such as the ARDA from political pressures. If planners were not in this way freed from political fetters, situations would inevitably arise in which economic principles would have to be compromised and projects accepted regardless of their economic merits.[80] Others addressed that threat as primarily a communications problem to be resolved through a continuous dialogue between 'planner' and 'planee' before, during, and after the construction of the plan.[81] Indeed, such consultation and local involvement was seen as crucial to successful planning, harbouring as it did an important element of 'exhortation' of local populaces. Planning could serve as a vehicle to get people to 'change their traditional attitudes' and 'catch up with the modern world.'[82]

More fundamental and telling, however, than popular 'resistance' or 'interference' at the local level, or politically motivated interventions at the élite level, was the struggle for *legitimacy* and *resources* within the bureaucracy itself. The elaboration of regional-development policies with accompanying programs and expenditures was encountering stiff resistance and even hostility within the senior bureaucracy, especially from Department of Finance officials who continued to be primarily interested in macro-economic policy of a Keynesian sort.[83] Moreover, these same officials were accustomed to exercising a wide-ranging control over the formulation of economic priorities and the management of expenditures, a function that had always been exercised within the context of policies for *national* growth under the direction of *federal* departments.

Regional economic policies implemented, administered, and at least partially designed by provincial bureaucrats constituted a sharp break with this tradition of centralization and national focus and were perceived (quite accurately, it might be said) as a threat to Finance's control over the federal government's economic policies. There was thus a great reluctance within Finance to see the disposal of federal funds (and in some cases decision-making power as well) concentrated at a regional level, as regional development agencies were wont to do.

Apparently, Finance officials also rejected economic arguments for 'abandoning a policy of identical, unified, or equivalent policies throughout the nation based on formulae and simple criteria in favour of deliberate discrimination and differentiation in favour of those regions which are most disadvantaged.'[84]

Reducing gaps between rich and poor regions in this way, so ran arguments for the latter, had become necessary for the acceleration of growth and productivity of the national economy as a whole. The redistribution involved, then, would be a *relative* one, not an *absolute* one. But to the dismay of regional-development technocrats and their supporters, Finance officials continued to see regional development as a 'welfare' program. In response to proposals for new programs and greatly increased expenditures in this field, they adopted a new role for themselves, 'as defenders of a balance between economic proposals for maximizing "welfare" (regional aid) and those for "efficiency" (national productivity). To this end they challenged the artificial, disproportionate division of funds under ARDA, ADA, and later DREE to underpin regions of lower productivity and slow growth and strove to achieve a balance between these and other federal policies for fast-growing regions in which Canada's prosperity was generated.'[85]

As asserted by Tom Kent, Anthony Careless, and others, in the 1960s finance department officials and the finance minister became the chief bureaucratic opponents of the developmental technocracy's proposals for increased regional-planning activities and regional-development expenditures on the part of the federal government.

The experience of federal development agencies such as the ADB, ADA, ARDA, and FRED is instructive of the political, ideological, and organizational forces that shaped this initial state foray into the relatively unknown field of regional development. It suggests that the obstacles in the Canadian context to establishing a powerful and relatively autonomous state agency or agencies that could undertake the design, coordination, and implementation of a coherent set of development policies for the Atlantic region (or provinces within that region) were perhaps insurmountable. The most promising candidate for such a role in the pre-DREE era – the proposed ADB-ECC planning body – proved to be a non-starter in the primary task envisaged for it at the ADB's creation (and subsequently incorporated into the latter's terms of reference as stipulated in the July 1963 amended legislation): 'to prepare in consultation with the Economic Council of Canada an overall coordinated plan for the promotion of economic growth in the [Atlantic] region.'[86] But a distinct ADB planning division charged with the task of undertaking various sectoral studies and integrating them into a comprehensive regional plan was not even formed until 1965, and never did submit or complete a regional plan, despite the best intentions of its chairman[87] and executive director. The latter, Dr E.P. Weeks, recognized the ongoing 'complications' faced by the agency in carrying out its appointed task: 'One is almost bound to be torn between the view of planners, who wish to withhold action until projects can be carried out in the context of a total plan, and the impatience of those who are confronted with what appears to them to be a pressing, immediate issue on which action should not, under any circumstances, be delayed.'[88]

Ultimately, the hopes held by the ADB's directorate for its planning function proved to be unfounded. Instead the ADB's legacy (it was folded into DREE in 1969) would be various cabinet-approved expenditures on basic infrastructure projects, much to the chagrin of advocates of the regional-plan idea and those agencies that placed a greater emphasis on development of the labour-absorptive manufacturing and service sectors.[89]

Yet the board's fate could have been worse. The impossibility of its proposed planning function would have rendered it completely redundant had a more 'practical' and political role for the board not been prescribed and implemented by the Liberal cabinet.[90] This was so because of the structural obstacles presented by the fundamental organization of, and the prevailing discourse within, the state apparatus. This shaped, limited, and in some cases obstructed the role of the state in regional development. Given the political context of the early 1960s, ministerial intervention was successful in carving out a niche within the state apparatus for regional-development agencies. But it did not, indeed *could not*, supersede the organizational and political obstacles to the establishment of regional development as a functional priority of the Canadian state.

On the Periphery: The DOSCO Crisis

The DOSCO crisis is revealing of the character of the federal government's commitment to regional development in the mid-1960s, and by extension the nature of the compromise among state élites at the centre that underlay state intervention in this field. In December 1966, the federal government decided to place DOSCO's Cape Breton collieries under public ownership after the British-owned corporation had announced its decision to cease coal-mining operations in Nova Scotia; within a year the federal government had decided *not* to take over the same corporation's closely related steel operations when their imminent closure was announced. Why?

From the turn of the century the coal and steel industries in Nova Scotia formed the heart of that province's industrial base. As late as 1960, one-fifth of the provincial labour force continued to be dependent upon what was by then a declining industrial base. In particular, the Nova Scotia coal industry – bedevilled by the spread of new fuels and technologies, and undercut by American coal producers who were sharply raising output and productivity through a process of modernization and rationalization that brutally cut the labour force by tens of thousands in the span of a few years – was threatened with impending crisis. The Dominion Coal Company, a branch of DOSCO, although in receipt of subsidies, subventions, and modernization grants from the federal government to help make its product saleable on the Canadian market, was not keeping apace with developments elsewhere, and was becoming less and less viable as a profit-making operation.

The second Maritime Coal Production Assistance Act (1959), which increased the level of government assistance to DOSCO, did not prevent the closure of a major pit in Cape Breton the following year, and the political alarm bells were immediately set ringing. The government response was the Royal Commission on Coal (the Rand Commission). It decreed that the decline of coal-mining in Nova Scotia was inevitable, and that measures should be taken to salvage through modernization and mechanization only the most profitable operations, the bulk of coal operations to cease with, of course, massive reductions in the work-force.

The postwar combination of dwindling markets and rapidly escalating operating costs created a major dilemma for industrial Cape Breton. Survival of the coal industry required rehabilitation of the collieries but even massive rehabilitation would not guarantee job security for the miners. Modernization would increase productivity and reduce the labour force required unless markets could be found for much higher tonnages of coal. The rapidly declining demand made that unlikely. Mechanization of the mines and a decision to reduce output provided an even less attractive option, given its drastic impact on Cape Breton employment.[91]

The steel industry, its history interwoven with that of Cape Breton coal, was not much better off. As part of DOSCO's operations it too had stagnated since the war years. It failed to experience the growth that characterized the Ontario steel industry during this period, and by the 1960s it was a relatively small operation by Canadian standards, and in addition one badly in need of modernization.[92] DOSCO had been the subject of a successful take-over bid in 1957–8 by the British multinational Hawker-Siddeley, through its Canadian subsidiary, A.V. Roe Canada, Ltd. The theme of DOSCO's new management quickly became 'retrenchment in coal; re-orientation in steel.' In an appearance before the Rand Commission, the company's new president, A.L. Fairley, Jr, stated that the corporation had no choice but to close down three collieries employing 2,614 workers. He also asserted that failure to place the whole industry on a more sound basis would result in bankruptcy, with 9,000 men thrown out of work instead of 2,000.[93] The corporation's strategy was twofold: to cut back on its coal operations and mining labour force and to grab a larger share of the growing central Canadian steel market. In its wage negotiations with the union, a substantial wage differential between Sydney and Hamilton was demanded as the price of continued operations; from the federal government, DOSCO management called for increased freight assistance; from the City of Sydney, it demanded a large reduction in municipal taxes.[94]

All of these 'prerequisites' demanded as the price for keeping steel-making alive in Nova Scotia did not, however, guarantee the plant a secure future. Shortly after Hawker-Siddeley's take-over of DOSCO in the late 1950s the decision had been taken to build a whole new steel complex at Contrecoeur, Quebec, to which Sydney, supposedly, would supply basic steel. By the mid-1960s, however, it was becoming apparent that even this restricted role for the Sydney plant had no place in Hawker-Siddeley's long-term plans.[95] The Sydney plant continued to be run down and stripped of its more profitable operations over the objections of the union, the local community, and the Nova Scotia government.[96] Indeed, the latter made several attempts to deter DOSCO from its course of action without success. Principally, and rather pathetically, it tried to induce DOSCO to establish its new rolling mills at Sydney rather than Contrecoeur.

This was the problem that we as a Government were working on, in an atmosphere of private enterprise. to try and induce a company doing business in this province to expand. Even if we would supply all the money at our cost, and looked after all the transportation, they weren't interested! ... We begged these people to take money from us – on our hands and knees – to get an investment on their part, to get something on that liability sheet that they – Hawker Siddley or DOSCO – would have to meet, with regards to the Sydney steel plant, and that they could not walk away from it [sic]. They would not do it.[97]

The coming crisis for coal and steel in Nova Scotia, then, must have been quite apparent to state élites. Yet neither the federal nor the provincial government made any move to derail the coming crisis, or developed any policy to deal with a shutdown of DOSCO operations. Instead, the governments in question responded only in the midst of the crisis itself, and then in a less-than-satisfactory manner from the point of view of restoring heavy industry in Nova Scotia to a more secure footing.

There was little in the way of organized political resistance or credible alternatives to the course taken by the Stanfield government. The provincial election of 1963 had removed the sole surviving CCF/NDP member from the Nova Scotia legislature and left only four Liberals to form the opposition. Both opposition parties were in a state of disarray. The NDP, which polled only 4.3 per cent of the vote in 1963, remained without an official leader until the party president accepted the post in 1966. With the succession of the CCF by the NDP in 1962, control over the party shifted to a small Halifax-based group of academics and professionals. This gave the party a more middle-class orientation at a time when 70 per cent of the party's vote came from the working-class area of industrial Cape Breton.[98] On the question of DOSCO's Sydney steel operations, the new party leadership abandoned the CCF's long-standing policy of straight public ownership, instead opting for the milder radicalism of a government purchase of DOSCO shares sufficient to 'obtain a seat on the Board of Directors.'[99] By the mid-1960s the party had virtually disappeared from the provincial scene. The Liberals, having lost three successive elections by increasingly wide margins, were in the throes of a leadership change-over and a rebuilding effort.

The crisis at DOSCO finally came, in double-barrelled fashion, in 1966–7. In 1965, DOSCO had brought in British experts to size up mining operations and make recommendations. The resulting demand for $25 million in government aid to rehabilitate existing collieries and open a new one at Lingan elicited a positive response from a federal government then engaged in an election campaign, but the aid was tied to yet another royal commission on the Nova Scotia coal industry, this one headed by

J.R. Donald. Donald's report, *The Cape Breton Coal Problem*, was submitted to the federal government shortly after DOSCO announced, in April 1966, its intention to close the mines. A tense nine months followed before the federal government acted, announcing the creation of a Crown corporation – the Cape Breton Development Corporation (DEVCO) – to phase out Cape Breton's collieries, while establishing new industries on the Island to take the place of coal-mining.

This form of state intervention conformed in most respects to Donald's recommendations. He had suggested that the coal industry be phased out over a fifteen-year period and that a federal Crown corporation be established to strengthen the area's economy through the promotion of new industry. In Donald's opinion, no constructive solution to unemployment and the social needs of Cape Breton could be based on coal-mining. To prevent excessive privation for displaced miners, Donald suggested a generous preretirement pension financed by funds that otherwise would have been expended on further subventions on rail shipments of coal (some $22 million in the 1960–5 period).[100] The federal government chose not to stick with Donald's rigid timetable, however, nor did it see fit to advance as generous a preretirement pension as Donald had recommended.[101]

The decision to nationalize DOSCO's coal operations and create Crown corporation charged with securing the diversification of the Cape Breton economy was not taken without internal division over the matter. As was often the case with Cabinet squabbles during Pearson's tenure as prime minister, this internal division took the form of a Left-Right split over the wisdom and necessity of government intervention in the economy. A strong presentation of the case for nationalization by MacEachen and others was not insignificant in the outcome.[102] But in explaining and justifying the outcome the government was careful to isolate the Cape Breton situation from government policy in general; to emphasize the uniqueness of its circumstances; and to confirm its status as a 'special case.' Those state élites who supported direct state intervention appear to have seen the alternative to nationalization as the collapse of a major portion of the Nova Scotia economy and an unprecedented social and economic crisis in that part of the country into which the government would inevitably be drawn in any case. In any event, the attendant social disruption was something that 'no modern government could permit to happen.' Instead, the federal government would simply have to alter its form of subsidy to the regional economy.[103]

NDP and Conservative opposition members in Ottawa reacted to the

Liberal government's creation of DEVCO by joining with the unions involved in demanding the simultaneous nationalization of DOSCO's steel-making facilities at Sydney. It was argued that leaving steel unattended was ignoring half the problem, making another employment crisis imminent. But, on this occasion, federal-government spokesmen on the matter replied that acquisition of DOSCO's steel mill, as well as its coal-mines, would be an excessive burden on the new Crown corporation. Besides, the situation in the steel industry was not critical enough to warrant such drastic action. In any case, the government's ideological distaste for further public-sector involvement in Cape Breton was made obvious in response to NDP arguments that DEVCO be permitted not only to dole out money to the private sector but to initiate public enterprises as well. The Liberal government countered with professions of belief in private enterprise as the best vehicle for diversifying Cape Breton's economy. MacEachen quipped that the government had no intention of turning Cape Breton into 'a socialist island.'[104]

The point here, one ably made by Alan Tupper in his study of DEVCO's creation, is that the state's intervention was premised on *welfare* rather than *development*. It was the social and political costs of not acting that provided the rationale for state intervention. In any event, the creation of DEVCO simply represented an extension of the subsidies that the federal government had already been providing, a varying degrees, for a number of decades. DEVCO was a concession won within the parameters of a discourse that viewed the role and purpose of such subsidies in welfarist terms. These subsidies were not extended in the context of any development plan or strategy.

While the federal decision on Cape Breton coal was being taken, DOSCO management began a series of drastic cut-backs in the steel-plant work-force. Between September and December 1966, more than seven hundred men were laid off. A few months later, however, Premier Stanfield, on the eve of a provincial election, calmed fears about the steel industry with assurances that DOSCO president C.H. Drury (brother to the federal minister of industry, C.M. Drury) had intimated to him that there was no danger of further lay-offs at the plant. Just a few months after this, on 13 October 1967 – henceforth known in Cape Breton as 'Black Friday' – DOSCO announced that the Sydney Steel plant would cease operations by 30 April 1968. Technological obsolescence and geographical location were given as reasons for the closure.[105]

Now only a year after DOSCO's first announcement, the second shoe had been dropped. The federal government condemned the move, but gave no hint of federal intervention in the matter, citing the need to await the province's decision on its actions. The province emphasized that the crisis was a national concern, and that DEVCO should be brought into operation at the earliest possible moment. However, in an emergency session of the House of Commons on 16 October the government stated its unwillingness to consider nationalization and that the federal government would not take the lead in solving the crisis, instead leaving the initiative to the province. Within the government those opposed to further nationalization argued that Ottawa had already made a large commitment; that steel, unlike coal, was *not* a declining industry needful of state support; and that, in any case, there was no future for steel in Cape Breton. To those who may have advocated further nationalization in order to incorporate the steel industry into DEVCO's development mandate (and here it might be granted to MacEachen that he so argued in the cabinet's deliberations, though there is some question as to the vigour with which he pursued the inclusion of steel under federal ownership), it evidently became clear fairly early on in discussions that nationalizing Sydney steel 'just wouldn't go.'[106]

Political tactics dictated, of course, that appropriate means of justification be brought forward for the decision *not* to intervene and here the jurisdictional question was dredged up as a fall-back position for the government. MacEachen's speech to the House of Commons on 16 October 1967 laid down the government's defence of its actions (or more appropriately in this case its non-action).

Bearing in mind that the Sydney steel plant is one part of a growing and competitive industry in Canada, it would present difficulties if a national government selected a single plant to be operated and supported with public funds in competition with other plants involved in the same industry in other parts of Canada ... I do believe that apart from the question of finances the constitutional or jurisdictional case is stronger for a provincial authority to undertake this job than for a federal authority.[107]

The federal position having been made clear, the provincial government, working very closely with the steelworkers' union, began a hasty consideration of its options. Nova Scotia's minister of trade and industry was dispatched on a frantic search to find a private-sector buyer. Canadian and Japanese steel interests were approached, and DOSCO itself was requested to run the plant for a further four months, with all operating deficits to be paid by the province.[108] When all potential private investors had rebuffed the province's overtures, Smith's primary concern became negotiations with the federal government over the size of its contribution to any provincial take-over of the steel plant.

The popular response in Cape Breton to 'Black Friday' and the events that followed was first shock and disbelief, then outrage. Mass public meetings were held to damn DOSCO and demand government action. The general feeling was that an absentee management with no commitment to the people of Sydney or to steel-making in Nova Scotia had undermined the plant. DOSCO was charged with running the Sydney operation from the beginning with the purpose of skimming off profits and eventually selling the plant's various operations to others. Tax concessions and the acceptance of lower wages than elsewhere were all for nought.[109] The growing protest in Cape Breton culminated in a mass march through the streets of Sydney on 19 November 1967. Organized by the Sydney City Council Steel Committee and the Steelworkers' Union (with the co-operation of numerous other groups), the 'Parade of Concern' saw some 25,000 people, including representatives of the government and all the political parties, engage in a non-partisan demonstration of support for some concrete action on the steel crisis. Both provincial and federal politicians pledged that governments would not stand idly by and watch the plant close.[110]

While the political impact of this display of community solidarity was evidently less than decisive in the deliberations of federal decision-makers, the same cannot be said with regard to the provincial government. On 20 November 1967, the day following the 'Parade of Concern,' the province announced that it would purchase the plant from DOSCO and create the Sydney Steel Corporation (SYSCO). The federal government continued to balk, however, at committing itself to any aid to SYSCO beyond 30 April 1968. In the end, the federal government agreed to contribute a financial-aid package to the new provincial Crown corporation, including a $2 million grant to the province and the purchase by DEVCO of the steel plant's coke ovens for $4 million. In a final exchange of letters on the matter in March 1968, Pearson made clear to the Nova Scotia premier that the federal-aid package was final and that thenceforth the problem lay with the province.[111]

Demands for further federal intervention occasioned by the announced closure of the Sydney steel plant that had followed so quickly upon the heels of DEVCO's creation ran up against those political limits that governed the Canadian state's welfare role. In the federal government's response to the second stage of the DOSCO crisis, its main concern was to limit the scope of its involvement in the regional problem, not to seek development solutions to that problem. The jurisdictional issue and even the 'competitive industry' argument were convenient if flimsy justification for shifting the problem onto the narrow shoulders of the province. Acquiescence to the state's intervention in regional economic problems on the part of those state élites opposed to such intervention was tied to the government's social-welfare role and agenda. The idea of state-planned, state-initiated, and state-run industrial development on the periphery was outside the boundaries of political bargaining and ideological acceptability. It was simply not 'part of the bargain.'

Conclusion

In the 1960s the Atlantic periphery was the beneficiary of a spate of new personal and intergovernmental transfer payments associated with the belated completion of Canada's welfare-state edifice. The subsidization of workers on the periphery supported by an ideology that emphasized the distribution of welfare to compensate for the shortcomings of the market had finally become the predominant response of state élites at the centre to regional disparities, one made viable and attractive by a period of unprecedented economic expansion. Thus, as accumulation and development at the centre leaped ahead, the economy of the periphery was buoyed up by rapid public-sector expansion and a broadened range of income supports for its residents. But while this strategy was successful in shoring up the economic base of the Atlantic periphery at a time when its traditional industrial base was undergoing potentially devastating changes (with rationalization and mechanization in the primary sector and a precipitous decline in heavy industry), it did not directly address the need for the structural transformation of the periphery's economy if further deterioration of its relative position within Canada was to be forestalled.

The reason for this one-track policy in the 1960s is clear. The Liberal party's embrace of a reformist social-welfare agenda was tempered on its return to power by the existence of ideological divisions within the cabinet and staunch resistance on the part of senior bureaucrats to any qualitative change in economic and industrial policy-making or to any significant federal intervention in the field of regional development. This ideological split lent a conservative tenor to federal economic policies and prevented the incorporation of regional development into any overall economic and industrial strategy at the federal level. Instead, regional policies were smuggled in through the 'back door' as part of the government's 'War on Poverty' social-welfare package.

The character and scope of state intervention in the regional field, and the balance of forces that determined such a role for the state, were discernible in the origins, strategies, and spending patterns of federal regional agencies. In contrast to the Stanfield government and development agencies representative of business interests on the periphery (all of which, to varying degrees, favoured co-ordinated regional planning, a growth-centre approach, and a major program of industrial incentives), federal policies and programs towards the periphery were shaped and limited by Liberal political strategy and by political and bureaucratic opposition at the national level to federal economic interventionism. Indeed, even as regional planners in the ARDA and FRED were using federal resources to expand the planning and administrative capacities of provincial bureaucracies in the Atlantic region, they remained peripheral within the Ottawa bureaucracy. And the ADB was specifically designed *not* to interfere with 'business as usual' within the federal government and federal bureaucracy and it remained subordinate to priority-ordering mechanisms at the centre. The class and partisan composition of the board further ensured that its activities and expenditures would remain non-threatening and non-offensive to state élites at the centre.

The fact of the matter is, development agencies and planners at both the regional and national levels did not like the social-welfare orientation of the federal government's regional policy. In general they argued that 'social adjustment,' intraregional migration, urban infrastructure, up-grading of labour skills, and assistance to capital, all in the context of co-ordinated state planning, were the only logical way to proceed with the modernization and 'reindustrialization' of Atlantic Canada's economy. Subsidizing older, declining industries and marginal economic activities in rural areas, or directing funds to short-term job creation in areas of high unemployment, was misguided and detrimental to development objectives. However, their more technocratic approach to the problem of regional development failed to find much resonance within the federal cabinet and bureaucracy before 1968. This failure can be attributed to the fact that such a strategy, if seriously adopted and fully implemented, had far-reaching implications for a number of federal departments and for the co-ordination of sectoral programs and federal-provincial efforts. At the very least it would require more direct and extensive government intervention in the regional economy. Given the traditional role and focus of federal economic policy, the new discourse germinating within the 'developmental technocracy' met considerable resistance and hostility from state élites at the centre and made little real headway as a result.

Occurring, as it did, at the height of a period of unparalleled national economic expansion, the DOSCO crisis represented something of an acid test for the federal government's regional policy. The escalating crisis of the coal-and-steel industry in Nova Scotia, despite a high level of ongoing state subsidy for the private corporation involved, considerably raised the potential costs (both economic and political) of maintaining a purely welfarist response to the problem of regional development. Thus, the need to move away from this strategy towards a more direct role for the state in restructuring and modernizing the periphery's economy was made abundantly clear, and in the context of national economic prosperity, politically necessary. But the DOSCO crisis also made clear certain inherent limits to federal-state intervention imposed by the welfare basis of the government's regional policies and the nature of the compromise between ideological factions within the Liberal cabinet. And while community outrage and solidarity in the face of DOSCO's announced shutdown of its steel-making facilities may have forced the provincial government to intervene when the federal government would not, the province's purely reactive and defensive response to the 'second stage' of the DOSCO crisis was determined by its past failures to persuade DOSCO's foreign owners to modernize their Nova Scotia operations, by the government's ideological aversion to state ownership and management of productive facilities, and, following from it, their lack of preparation or strategy when the task was thrust upon them.

No doubt the DOSCO episode also contributed to the rise in salience of the regional-development issue and the further sensitization of the political élite in Canada to the nature and scope of the problem. Certainly the political importance granted to regional development by this élite – and the resources subsequently placed at the disposal of the developmental technocrats – would change significantly with the 1968 election of Pierre Elliott Trudeau as Liberal leader and prime minister of Canada. The next chapter will deal with this change and the failure of state élites (both at the centre and on the periphery) to restructure state apparatuses, procedures, and policies so as to better promote economic development on the periphery.

7 Window of Opportunity? The Politics of Regional Development, 1968-75

The legacy of the manner in which the DOSCO crisis was resolved in the 1966-8 period did not bode well for the rehabilitation of Nova Scotia's industrial base. It further fragmented the responsibility and decision-making necessary to cope with the crisis and map out a viable development strategy. By limiting the federal commitment it greatly handicapped the future for steel-making in the province. However, the whole episode did heighten the salience of the issue of regional development at the centre by highlighting the crisis conditions that existed in some parts of the Atlantic region at a time when economic growth and prosperity had attained unprecedented levels throughout most of the country. More-over, it reinforced criticism regarding the ad hoc manner in which, for the most part, the regional problem had been handled by the federal government and it forced state élites to consider more seriously their role in the regional-development field. This strengthened the hand of those both within and outside the state who were advocates of a more techno-cratic, planned approach to regional development, one that would pro-mote and support a managed adjustment process on the periphery free from the type of wrenching crisis and potential social disruption asso-ciated with DOSCO's announced intention to shut down Nova Scotia's coal and steel industries.

Within this context the arrival of new governing coalitions on both the federal and provincial stages at the end of the 1960s would provide the occasion for a shift in state policies. In Ottawa regional development would be incorporated into Trudeau's 'national unity/just society' dis-course and given institutional legitimacy through a new government department charged with responsibility for regional development. Making operational the new department's ambitious mandate would prove another matter entirely. In Nova Scotia a faltering provincial-de-velopment strategy would create the political conditions for a change of government in 1970. But the promised improvements of a new Liberal administration in the co-ordination of provincial economic development would not materialize, despite a shift towards more direct bureaucratic involvement in the province's development policies and programs. Instead, there would be a period of policy drift at the provincial level and a de facto closer linking of provincial programs and expenditures to federal initiatives.

While the technical problems of policy co-ordination and the intracta-bility of the problem itself to amelioration through state intervention no doubt presented considerable obstacles to successfully altering the pat-tern of economic and industrial development on the periphery, more fundamental to the inadequacies of state structures and policies in this area was a particular balance of class and political forces at the centre and on the periphery. This balance provided a state agenda and policy orientation (or lack thereof) that shaped the timing, mode, and scope of state intervention in the regional-development field. The 1968–75 period marked the height of the state's commitment to doing something about uneven regional development in Canada. The discussion that follows will argue that this 'window of opportunity' for the Atlantic periphery was more apparent than real.

DREE

The Trudeau Agenda

The election of Pierre Elliott Trudeau as leader of the Liberal party and then prime minister in 1968 would also bring a change in the importance accorded to regional development by the federal government, both as a political issue and as a policy field. But even prior to Trudeau's ascen-dance there had been signs of a shift in the government's perceptions of regional development and its new exalted status on the formal agenda of the state. The federal government was determined to bring a halt to the decentralization of power to the provinces that had been occurring during the 1960s. Regional development – calling as it did for a strong central government capable of intervening to redress regional economic dispari-ties – rose in federal priorities. Accordingly, at the 1968 Constitutional Conference the federal government for the first time framed a policy commitment to the attainment of regional equality of opportunity. This policy was linked to the preservation of national unity and the attainment of a morally just society.[1]

The pleas and warnings of provincial premiers from the Atlantic region on this occasion regarding the need for a comprehensive federal attack on regional disparities proved to be nicely in tune with federal strategy on other matters. The Atlantic premiers, who, like federal political leaders, were wary of the trend to decentralization, made declarations of support for the maintenance of a strong central government in Canada, 'with sufficient power and resources to address itself to the regional needs of the nation.' Premier Robichaud of New Brunswick noted that if economic equity for the poorer provinces was ever to be attained, then continuing 'strength at the centre' had to be ensured.[2]

Trudeau's personal mission in coming to Ottawa in 1965 was to prevent what he saw as the gradual separation of Quebec from Canada. The growing Quebec–Ottawa split was reaching crisis proportions by the mid-1960s, and the trajectory of Quebec nationalism seemed clearly headed towards the break-up of Confederation. In the early 1960s the response of the federal government by and large had been to accede to Quebec's demands. But Trudeau and other francophone federalists in Ottawa did not believe that the answer to the growing crisis was to give the government of Quebec everything it demanded. Nor would mere symbolic concessions such as bilingual federal cheques or a distinctive new 'non-British' flag make the problem go away. What really caused concern for Trudeau and his cohorts from Quebec was the lack of an overall federal strategy for dealing with Quebec nationalism and the French-English question in general.

In the 1968 federal election that resulted in a renewed Liberal mandate, the first election in a decade to confer a majority on the governing party, 'the campaign revolved around Trudeau, with few issues besides his leadership and his ability to defend federalism in the face of growing demands for greater autonomy in Quebec capturing the electorate's attention.'[3]

With Trudeau ensconced as party leader and prime minister the federal government's focus on national unity increased, and government priorities shifted accordingly. The language issue, not surprisingly, took precedence. The official Languages Act was passed with the avowed objective of creating a bilingual federal bureaucracy that would act as an alternative pole of attraction to Quebec City for Quebec's francophone middle class. At the same time the status of 'regional disparities' as an issue was raised by Trudeau and related to the ethno-linguistic question. Both were seen as threats to national unity. 'If the underdevelopment of the Atlantic Provinces is not corrected – not by charity or subsidies but by helping them become areas of economic growth – then the unity of the country is almost as surely destroyed as it would be by the French-English confrontation.'[4]

The regional problem, however, was seen to be much broader, to extend beyond the Atlantic region. The Atlantic Development Board (ADB) or some such special agency for that region alone would not be sufficient.

That is why we are establishing a department with nation-wide responsibilities, and not, as has sometimes been suggested, a special agency for the development of the Atlantic region ... The problem is not confined to the Atlantic region. It is much the same over large parts of eastern Quebec. And it exists for smaller numbers of people in other areas of Canada. If we see regional development as we should as a nation is concerned, some of the necessary programs must operate on a nation-wide basis, in all of the areas where opportunities are lagging, and economic growth can be speeded up ... *We will not make the unity and identity of Canada secure unless we can remove large disparities between the conditions of life in the regions of our country.*[5]

In conjunction with this emphasis on national unity, Trudeau was also determined to implement a major program of *administrative reform*. Of course, bilingualization of the federal civil service was one aspect of this reform that was motivated primarily by the national-unity question. But the project went well beyond this issue and related to a much broader objective: 'the introduction of greater rationality and planning into the whole federal decision-making process.'[6] The decision-making reforms introduced during Trudeau's first government were motivated by an insistence upon order and rationality in politics in reaction to the perceived disorder and disarray of the Pearson years.[7] Under Pearson, cabinet decisions had been mainly a function of crisis management, with no real possibility of long-term planning, or even medium-term planning, and limited opportunity or possibility for co-ordination of the government's actions and activities.[8] As Trudeau noted in 1969, 'We're setting up machinery which will permit us to deal with the important and not only with the urgent ... We must avoid becoming Coney Island cowboys, just shooting at targets as they appear and doing a little bit here and a little bit there to solve the problems as they arise.'[9]

Innovations were made to overhaul and strengthen the cabinet-committee system and to redefine and expand the role of the central agencies. This change would allow cabinet 'a framework that would permit detailed and rational discussion amongst ministers; to develop mechanisms for long-range planning, coordination, and priority-setting; and in keeping with his [Trudeau's] view of bureaucratic power as essentially undemocratic, to wrest more of the real decision-making function away from top officials and back to the elected officials.'[10]

Ministers would be given and would make political choices, and they would be involved in the actual shaping of policies outside their own departments; theoretically the exercise of power would shift from individual ministerial fiefdoms to a collectivity.[11]

Regional development – as an issue, as a policy field, and as a new function of government – was also to be articulated with this discourse of 'administrative reform' that was to generate so much internal activity within the federal government over the next number of years. Calls for greater co-ordination of federal measures in the field of regional development had become commonplace by the late 1960s, providing both the necessary political demand and a source of external support for a major change in federal policy in this field. In 1966, the Economic Council of Canada (ECC) had advocated the development of a deliberate and consistent focus on the regional problem within the federal bureaucracy, stressing the need for greater efficiency of administration and co-ordination of policies and programs. In the opinion of the ECC what was required was an overarching co-ordinative mechanism within the central machinery of government 'to appraise the overall regional impact of all federal operations.'[12] It was suggested that this new capacity might best be located in the Treasury Board.[13]

From the point of view of at least some state élites, the alleviation of regional disparities would be a proving-ground of sorts for new techniques of state intervention and for new bureaucratic structures for planning and co-ordinating government policy. Henceforth there would be a greater receptivity at the highest levels for the technocratic reformist views emanating from development agencies within and without the federal government, views that emphasized the need for comprehensive or overarching regional planning and the co-ordination of government policies for regional development.

In sum, demands for a rational, co-ordinated, comprehensive federal approach to the regional problem nicely meshed with the strategies and discourses of the new government: an expanded regional role would facilitate greater federal political visibility in regional economies, thus helping to stem the decentralizing tide that was carrying Quebec out of Confederation. It also supported the thrust towards administrative reform that was a second and related priority of the new Trudeau government in Ottawa.

Bureaucratic Machinery and Development Strategy

After the Liberal election victory in 1968, work began on laying the foundation for the new governmental machinery that would be required for an enhanced federal role in regional development. Jean Marchand, who had been named minister of forestry and rural development, was given the task of overseeing the project. On his recommendation, Tom Kent was appointed by Trudeau as deputy minister designate. A number of options were considered for the new bureaucratic structure. Evidently Trudeau and Marchand both saw merit in the position of the Economic Council of Canada and were also deeply impressed with the success of the French DATAR (Délégation à l'Aménagement du Territoire et à l'Action Régionale), which had been established in 1963. The essential characteristic here was a substantial co-ordination ability and influence over line departments.[14] But such a 'super department' in Canada – essentially a new central agency with a program-delivery function – aroused the opposition of the Ottawa bureaucracy, which saw the proposed department as too powerful. It also suffered the disapproval of Trudeau's political advisers, who feared that the locating of so much power and prestige with a single cabinet minister would divide the cabinet and place the prime minister in a difficult position.[15]

In the end, it was decided that the new regional-development role would be carried out by a typical line department that would encourage other federal departments to contribute to the regional-development effort. Evidently it was thought that Marchand's easy access to Trudeau and the priority accorded to regional development by the government would be sufficient to ensure co-ordination. Originally tagged as the Department of Regional Development, it finally materialized, with the Government Organization Act of March 1969, as the Department of Regional Economic Expansion (DREE).[16]

In announcing the new department Trudeau stressed the importance of planning and co-ordination to its success. Moreover, senior DREE officials were apparently of the opinion that the elevation of planning from the provincial to the regional level was one of the principal motivations behind the establishment of the new department.[17] But if such was the case, allocating responsibility for regional development to a line department exclusively was a less-than-efficacious means of achieving the desired objective, regardless of who headed the new department. Perhaps the decision to rely on DREE and its cabinet representative reflected an overly optimistic faith that the administrative reforms then being instituted would fundamentally change cabinet decision-making processes such that policy co-ordination and long-term planning would be possible. In any case, from the very beginning there were sceptics regarding the ability of the new governmental machinery to do the job. Robert Stanfield, leader of the opposition in Parliament in 1969, articulated the general concern that DREE would be left alone to carry the entire load of promoting regional development, while other federal departments would simply go on with their own sectoral responsibilities.[18] Speaking for the NDP, Ed Broadbent characterized DREE as an inadequate response to the regional-development problem and representative of the government's lack of commitment to planning.

What is needed is the establishment of a national plan which sets down national objectives and priorities. The governments has not established such objectives into which regional growth and development programs can be fitted ... The result of this will be the continuation of programs frequently with conflicting goals arrived at by a number of competing agencies. There will be little or no indication of how the system is supposed to work, how one region is related to another in the national context or what should be the timing of specific steps. The only difference from the past will be that this will now go on within one department instead of many.[19]

Such criticisms at the time of creation of the new agency would prove prescient indeed. In succeeding years DREE would fail utterly to develop a comprehensive regional-development strategy and to involve the resource of other federal departments in a sustained and co-ordinated attack on regional disparities.

While the federal government's new state managers had compromised on a line department, rather than a central agency, for regional development, they did not abandon the notion of an approach to the problems of the periphery that would provide the necessary impetus and wherewithal for economic 'adjustment' in the lagging regions rather than simple subsidy or welfare. To this end DREE adopted the fostering of industrial 'growth centres' in the disadvantaged regions as its development strategy.[20] For years regional development agencies such as APEC and Nova Scotia's

Voluntary Planning Board had advocated the concentration of industry in a select number of areas or 'growth centres' within the Atlantic region. Moreover, the second set of ARDA agreements (1965–70) had already gone some way towards incorporating such a notion into its planning and program framework.[21] Now DREE sought to implement the approach through the use of two program instruments: the designation of *special areas* to which infrastructure support and expenditures would be funnelled; and the Regional Development Incentives Act (RDIA), which would provide industrial assistance in the form of grants to firms deciding to locate in *designated regions*. The two programs were intended to be complementary, with their combined benefits encouraging the expansion of private-sector investment in locales favoured by DREE.[22]

That the new federal department had wholly embraced the growth-pole concept was made clear by Trudeau and Marchand. In announcing DREE Trudeau noted that earlier ARDA and FRED programs had excluded the relatively prosperous urban areas in the Maritimes – Halifax, Saint John, Fredericton – and that this had to be changed. 'It is no use thinking that we can get new industries to locate in all the most remote areas ... If industrial development is possible, most of it will have to be in some of the cities and larger towns.'[23] Marchand went further in explaining the basis for the federal government's faith in the growth-centre concept. In a speech in Newfoundland, in September 1969, he refuted economic-development models based on the notion of a more efficient and comprehensive exploitation of resources. Instead, the new agents of economic development were to be found in cities.[24] Indeed, 'the region' itself would come to be more and more focused on its urban centres. That would be where employment growth would take place. Slow-growth regions were, in effect, regions that lacked vigorously growing urban centres. 'Our regional development programs must reinforce the strongest points, the "poles de croissance" ... we must build into their urban centres a new range of attractions that will permit them to negate the disadvantages that have accumulated during previous decades of relative stagnation ... the growth of the urban community is the key to the progress of the people of the region.'[25]

So it was that the vehicle for, and the shape of, systematic federal intervention on the periphery to address the problem of regional disparities were revealed soon after Trudeau and his new governing coalition assumed power. Yet this design would not, indeed could not, remain inviolate given the nature of the governing coalition and the demands and exigencies of managing a capitalist economy. The sorting out of priorities under stress would bend some policies and priorities to the needs of others, and it would soon become apparent that the federal government's new regional-development agency could expect most often to be on the receiving end of this process.

Other Priorities: The Economy, Quebec, Social Policy

The role of politics and the state in regional development cannot be understood simply in terms of those limited state actions in that discrete policy field carved out by state élites that is generally referred to as 'regional development policies.' Broader state strategies and discourses set the parameters within which the problem of 'regional development' would be considered. Understood properly, the 'terms of the compromise,' as it were, that underlay the attainment of the state agenda and subsequent rise in the priority status accorded to regional development were not likely to support, or even to suggest the necessity of a long-term, comprehensive approach to enhancing the industrial-development prospects of the periphery. That this was so became clear even during the heady days of Trudeau's first mandate, a period that in retrospect marked the high point of the federal government's commitment to regional development as a priority item on the state agenda and as a field for concerted state action. It should not be surprising, therefore, that shifting economic and political conditions at the centre would transform and further restrict an already limited federal commitment to reducing regional economic disparities. Not only would this lead to a downgrading of the problem as a priority item on the formal agenda of the state, but over time the nature and scope of the problem itself would be redefined, as would the prescription for state intervention best suited to addressing it.

In the mid-1960s national economic policy was favourable from the perspective of regional development. Federal budgets during these years were expansionary, aimed at the achievement of sustained economic growth and a high level of employment. Large annual increases in GNP and low rates of unemployment seemed to justify the general thrust of federal economic management. But changes in the material base for state policy-making were under way, resulting in the rise of new concerns in the formulation of national economic policy that would impact sharply upon the field of regional development.

David Wolfe has argued that the sharp rise in trade-union membership in Canada in the mid-1960s, under conditions of relative full employment, underlay a trend to increased labour militancy and significant wage gains for workers in the second half of the decade. Wolfe documents the increasing concern of state élites charged with the economic-management function as inflation edged upwards, despite the government's application of 'the brakes' through the adoption of relatively restrictive monetary and fiscal policies in 1966 and 1967. This led these same élites to the conclusion that Canada was experiencing a new type of 'cost push' inflation that undermined the effectiveness of fiscal and monetary policy in checking wage and price increases.[26] More drastic measures would be required to control inflation.

In 1969 the government embarked upon a two-pronged strategy to control inflation. Voluntary controls on prices and incomes were attempted through the formation of the Prices and Incomes Commission (PIC). In addition, finance minister J. Edgar Benson, emphasizing the 'fight against inflation,' introduced a succession of highly restrictive budgets in 1968, 1969, and 1970. Finally, throughout most of this period monetary policy was tied fairly closely to the goals of federal fiscal policy and the PIC. By early 1970, the economic slow-down produced by these policies had become quite marked, and unemployment had risen significantly, virtually doubling between December 1968 and February 1971.[27]

When the finance minister warned glumly in June 1969 that, 'We really mean business in the fight against inflation,' he did so with full confidence in Trudeau's support for 'tough measures.' The prime minister ignored warnings from the Economic Council of Canada at the end of 1969 about the damage being done to the economy and strongly endorsed the 'get tough' philosophy that had its origins in the finance department and the Bank of Canada. According to Marc Lalonde, throughout the whole crusade against inflation, Trudeau was reacting to advice from the latter agencies, whose arguments he accepted virtually without qualification.[28]

It is difficult not to conclude that the position adopted by the federal government during this period was in fact undermining its effort in the field of regional development. Although DREE's budget was increased during this period despite an announced freeze on federal spending and major job cuts in the public service, the overall effect of federal economic policy was to take away with one hand what it was giving with the other. DREE officials, led by Kent, argued strenuously against this policy, citing the damage to their efforts to ameliorate regional disparities.[29] But despite protestations that a buoyant economy was essential to the success of these efforts, the government continued to put the squeeze on the economy, clamping it down 'by increasingly painful turns of the screw.'[30] The regional effect was similar to the national: at the height of regional-development spending, unemployment in the Atlantic region actually rose from 7.5 per cent in 1969 to 9.0 per cent in 1972; during the same period in Nova Scotia it went from 5.4 per cent to 7.5 per cent.[31]

A more direct distortion of DREE's plans for targeted assistance to growth centres in disadvantaged regions was the extension of industrial assistance under the RDIA program to Montreal. By all accounts this measure was forced upon the DREE minister by his cabinet colleagues. Marchand and Kent had been adamant that the regions designated for DREE assistance be sufficiently limited so as not to dilute the effectiveness of the program to help slow-growth regions.[32] To this end, if DREE were to spend less than 80 per cent of its budget in Eastern Quebec and the four Atlantic provinces, then it would be failing in its purpose.[33]

After the designation of the Montreal–Cornwall corridor as eligible for industrial incentives in the fall of 1970, Marchand was demonstrably unenthusiastic in his defence of the move before a Commons committee. He argued weakly that Montreal, in fact, could be classified as a 'regional problem.' However, when pushed on this seeming contradiction with earlier positions he had adopted, he readily admitted that he had to 'fight like hell' to ensure that the new Montreal incentive would be added to the Atlantic rates so as not to completely destroy the balance (areas in Quebec outside Montreal were *not* given the extra incentive, thus all but nullifying the utility of such incentives for redistributing growth within Quebec).[34] Even so, the newly designated region of Montreal generated a strong interest and a high number of applicants; DREE's industrial incentives quickly stimulated four and one-half times as much capital investment there, and created three times as many jobs, as for the whole of the Atlantic region for the same period![35]

There are two major reasons for this 'about-face' in DREE policy: first, the hostility of the Department of Finance to the 'distorting effects' of regional-development policies, and second, the October Crisis in 1970. Finance officials, who with other senior bureaucrats tended to view DREE as 'an illegitimate child surprisingly dumped on them by Trudeau,'[36] applied pressure against DREE's targeted assistance to chronically poor regions. Such assistance was viewed by Finance as nothing more than the diversion of potential growth from the most productive regions (especially when DREE programs operated in a period of slack growth).[37]

The real pressure on DREE to extend its program coverage to Montreal (thus offsetting incentives to locate on the periphery), however, came with the 'October Crisis.'[38] It produced an atmosphere in Ottawa, relates Kent, 'in which nobody was so keen on extending DREE programs to

Montreal as the Department of Finance.'[39] Priority-setting in the wake of the crisis became a vague search for programs that would aid 'national unity,' and regional-development expenditures were a handy tool in the battle against separatism.[40] That concern over Quebec at this time spilled over into regional-development policy generally is apparent in the growth of that province's share of DREE's budget from 12 per cent to 39 per cent in the first five years.[41]

In effect, Trudeau's articulation of regional development with 'national unity' can be seen to have benefited the Atlantic region in one sense by placing the issue at the centre of the governing coalition's political strategy and near the top of the formal agenda of the state. But as the French-English crisis deepened, it also became apparent that this articulation availed the government of a ready source of job-creating funds that could be easily diverted to Quebec. Regional development indeed had become part of the set of compromises that allowed state élites at the centre to accommodate political tensions within Canada; but which tensions?

Coterminous with these developments, a significant transfer of resources from centre to periphery in fact was taking place through changes in the field of social policy. The 1971 changes to the unemployment insurance program (UI) represent an outstanding example. The government had been considering a number of major social-policy proposals in order to make good on its electoral commitment to a 'just society,' and UI came to be seen as the best alternative. The changes – which were premised upon increasing affluence and an assumed absence of fiscal constraints – increased coverage, reduced entrance requirements, and increased benefits.[42] To an area of chronically high unemployment such as the Atlantic region, such a reform meant a sharp increase in the net flow of benefits into the region. Decisions to enrich other income security payments, such as family allowances and old-age security (OAS), also constituted positive contributions to increased per-capita incomes in the Atlantic region. Taken together such reforms transformed income security payments into an instrument of interregional redistribution roughly equal in importance to equalization grants.[43] But none of these policies had regional development per se, or even a decrease in regional disparities, as its primary objective. The inordinate benefits that accrued to economically lagging *regions* were incidental to the purposes of the programs. And while helping to maintain levels of consumption within such regions, they did nothing directly to augment those regions' productive facilities and capacities.

Thus, a decade after the Liberals came to power in Ottawa, a significant upgrading of the ability of periphery to provide a level of basic services and social infrastructure comparable to that of the centre had been made possible through intergovernmental transfer payments. Moreover, a measure of income redistribution between regions was encouraged by an expansion of national income-security programs. But national economic policy continued to be formulated without consideration of its detrimental effect on regional development. Achievement of the objective of the national economic policy as it was initially formulated was also impaired by its subordination to a political strategy dominated by an overweaning concern over Quebec nationalism. The cumulative effect of this particular articulation of national policies – with the need to alleviate chronic regional disparities clearly a subordinate priority – was the steady growth on the Atlantic periphery of 'regional dependence' rather than 'regional development,' as fiscal transfers from the federal government substituted for a genuine strengthening of the regional economy.[44] While this was not a result pursued as an *alternative* to regional development (that is, a deliberate, chosen policy outcome), it was a *consequence* of other national policies, given the failure of the state to design and implement an effective regional-development strategy for the Atlantic periphery.

Regional Development and the Debate over Industrial Strategy

If regional development was clearly a subordinate priority to Ottawa's management of the national economy, and DREE more or less available to be used as an instrument in the federalist-nationalist political struggle in Quebec, it was largely because of DREE's isolation within the federal bureaucracy, an isolation that was determined by the failure to articulate regional development with national economic and industrial policies. No comprehensive strategy linking together these various fields of state intervention in the economy was ever attempted. But without intersectoral co-ordination focused on common economic and industrial objectives for regions, that is, a regionally sensitive industrial strategy,[45] altering the basic industrial structure and long-term economic performance and prospects of the periphery would be next to impossible.

The act creating DREE specified the need for development planning and interdepartmental co-ordination if it was to achieve its objectives.[46] Major fiscal, transportation, employment, and resource-development strategies were formulated in such departments as Finance; Industry,

Trade and Commerce (ITC); Transport; Energy, Mines and Resources (EMR); Agriculture; and Fisheries and Oceans, making extensive consultations and joint undertakings with all these departments necessary if DREE were to fulfil its mandate. But there was a continual tension between DREE and other key departments, not least because of a lack of agreement on the advisability and desirability of DREE's ostensible objective: the decentralization of industry in Canada. In particular the Department of Finance continued to adhere to the position that the promotion of industrial development on the periphery through special incentives was misguided: it would sap resources from the centre, where they would be utilized more productively.[47] Similarly ITC, which served almost exclusively a central-Canadian business constituency, overwhelmingly supported through their assistance programs the preservation and even exacerbation of an industrial structure heavily concentrated in central Canada. Their passive rather than proactive policies ensured that industries on the periphery would continue to derive a minor, often minute, percentage of the industrial assistance dispensed by the department.[48] In effect, both Finance and ITC continued to be primarily concerned with the competitiveness of existing Canadian industry rather than its regional distribution. At the same time, certain other state élites, at both the bureaucratic and ministerial level, were becoming convinced that this passive approach to Canadian industry was no longer adequate to ensure future industrial competitiveness, and they were determined to place the idea of an industrial strategy on the formal agenda of the state.

That Canada's post-war economic and industrial orientation was coming under question at this point was largely the result of economic developments in the late 1960s and early 1970s.

Increasing materials costs, a low rate of innovation, relatively weak productivity increases, and high wage gains overflowing from a strong resource sector, combined with a high exchange rate for the Canadian dollar. The result was increasing unit costs, declining competitiveness and a declining share in world trade in finished goods ... The trade deficit in end products progressively worsened, creating balance of payments difficulties. These developments exposed systematic structural weaknesses in the manufacturing sector of the Canadian economy.[49]

This worrisome economic situation was fuelling a growing frustration on the part of some state élites with the lack of adequate medium- or long-range planning capability at senior levels. This perceived inadequacy inspired internal studies and reviews that were intended to map out strategies that would allow the government more political control over its formal agenda and a greater capacity to integrate and co-ordinate state actions to achieve certain objectives. This naturally raised interest and support in some quarters for an industrial strategy for Canada that would maximize benefits from the exploitation of natural resources and restructure secondary industry in Canada to heighten its international competitive position.[50] In January 1972, the prime minister let it be known that the cabinet was working on an industrial strategy. A few months later ITC minister Jean-Luc Pepin announced his hope that an industrial strategy would be brought forward in the fall, 'as a basis for consultation with the provinces, the private sector, and labour.'[51]

This push for greater co-ordination and long-range planning of the government's industrial and regional policies was not universal within the federal bureaucracy. It came primarily from the Planning and Priorities Secretariat of the Privy Council Office (PCO), with the ITC and its minister the main target of PCO's attempt to build a consensus on the need for an industrial strategy (or failing that at least a stronger core of cabinet support for the idea). A significant obstacle to this planning thrust emanating from the PCO was the still-dominant ideology within the senior civil service opposing state intervention to restructure Canadian industry. The PCO's advocacy of 'dirigiste' policies amounted to economic heresy for Finance and ITC officials who held more conservative views. The latter continued to support the rather crude de facto industrial strategy pursued by the Canadian state in the post-war era, with major dividends for central Canada. This strategy was based on a 'special relationship' with the United States and the U.S. economy. Simon Reisman, a prominent senior bureaucrat within the Canadian state, laid this out for the federal cabinet during the course of internal policy debates while Reisman served as deputy minister of finance (1970–4).

Canada, said Reisman, already had an industrial strategy. It was unarticulated and it was the only one really open to a nation in Canada's circumstances. Because of the location of primary markets, the strategy was centrist in its emphasis and focussed almost completely on the United States. There was very little Canadian policy could or should do, said Reisman, to alter these basic realities of economic geography. Instead Canada should promote the basic momentum of industrial strength in the Montreal–Windsor corridor, raising the peripheral regions up behind the centre. Given this, the notion of 'regional development' was essentially a kind of social policy ... To introduce issues of regional distribution into industrial development policy was to confuse social and economic policy.[52]

Behind Reisman's views was the full weight of a status quo supported by established bureaucratic-industry linkages. And as Riesman's discourse suggests, opposition was especially fierce to what was perceived as the proposed foisting of regional concerns – specifically the industrial under-development of the Atlantic periphery – onto departments other than DREE. Successive deputy ministers of ITC continued to share these views, as well as the finance department's more general reservations about meddling with industries. As a result, the rapid expansion of the federal government's industrial promotion and incentives programs, which took place in the 1970s, 'entirely escaped any horizontal policy coordination.'[53]

Internal divisions on this matter again became apparent during the 'Priorities Exercise' of 1975. Through the exercise the Priorities and Planning Secretariat of the PCO 'hoped to adapt the framework of major objectives and policy thrusts which had developed for the government's priorities during 1972–74, in order to plan the full mandate of the government.'[54] It was thought that the planning framework arrived at in this way would guide the allocation of resources by the government over a number of years. Departments were to submit assessments of how their existing policies and programs contributed to the government's priorities and how new departmental initiatives could do so. It would then be a relatively straightforward matter to reallocate and redirect departmental efforts, within existing resource levels, in light of the government's stated priorities. [55] One of the 'priority areas' memoranda subsequently submitted to cabinet by a core group of PCO and Treasury Board officials was National Industrial and Regional Development (NIRD), a document that proposed a radical break with past policies and procedures by attempting to marry *industrial strategy* to *regional development*.[56]

The Priorities Exercise as a whole proved disapppointing to the cabinet. Departmental responses to PCO requests proved completely inadequate to flesh out priority policy areas with tangible proposals. No single motif emerged that might provide some character and cohesion to government policy. As one observer put it, the memoranda to cabinet produced by the exercise succeeded only in 'disguising the woods by a too luxuriant display of trees.' The government had evidently set aside business while it waited for the 'big picture' to emerge from the Priorities Exercise, only to have that 'picture' itself turn out to be a mirage.[57]

Ultimately the Priorities Exercise, including the NIRD document, registered little effect on bureaucratic organization and policy development in Ottawa. Both fizzled and faded from view with the urgent and dramatic events in the fall of 1975, when John Turner resigned as minister of finance and the government soon after settled on the need to impose wage and price controls to combat rising inflation in Canada. Suffice it to say, in the 1968–75 period no overarching co-ordination and planning mechanism was ever devised by Ottawa and no comprehensive industrial strategy ever agreed upon. Instead, state élites were forced to back-pedal furiously from the premature pronouncements of 1971–2.[58]

Essentially, the failings of the federal government's regional-development policy cannot be understood apart from this larger lacuna in the realm of national industrial policy-making. Because regional development was never articulated with a national industrial policy with both sectoral and spatial implications, there could be no hope for the emergence of a coherent 'regional plan,' or of co-ordinated sectoral policies 'bent' to achieve particular objectives such as the promotion of a more diversified industrial structure on the periphery. In a sense, the parameters within which regional-development policies were formulated were the wrong ones (from the point of view of a program of regional industrialization). The set of political compromises at the national level, which determined the role to be played by DREE, permitted neither the necessary scope nor the requisite type of state intervention called for by the problem of regional economic disparities.

That DREE policies alone were inadequate to the task soon became apparent. After several years of DREE expenditures, little or no change was discernible in the relative size and mix of the Atlantic region's component industries. The region's industrial structure remained heavily weighted towards primary industries. Far from helping to alter this structure, DREE grants reflected it. Most new investments spurred by RDIA, for instance, were directed towards expansion of the existing industrial base. And, as noted by APEC, none of this 'new' investment was likely to be a source of future growth in job opportunities.[59] Under the special-areas agreements, the majority of DREE expenditures were devoted to highway construction (52 per cent), followed by schools (20 per cent), and municipal services such as sewer and water (17 per cent).[60] This pattern merely continued an earlier one of expenditures established by the ADB, and while valuable, there is no evidence that in and of themselves they were likely to attract new industry or spur the process of development in the region. As argued by APEC and others, this manner of proceeding was tantamount to putting the cart before the horse. Investment in infrastructure should logically have *followed* investment in directly productive activities, the latter inducing and making feasible the former. But neither the ADB nor DREE participated directly in such investment decisions and, of course, therein was the rub.

Reorganizing and Reorienting DREE: Phase I, 1972–5

The 1972 federal election placed new political pressures on the Liberals and 'helped along' the internal review of regional-development policies and programs recently begun by DREE. Considerable criticism had been directed at the federal government's regional-development effort during Trudeau's first mandate. Some of this criticism condemned particular instruments of DREE policy, such as the RDIA program.[61] Indeed, that program was one of the policy measures that provided the NDP with its successful 'corporate welfare bums' theme in the 1972 election.[62] But more general criticisms were also voiced concerning the structure of the department, its mode of operation, and its development strategy.

The results of the election – the Liberals received just two seats more than the Progressive Conservatives, with the NDP holding the balance of power – placed the Liberal government in a precarious position and focused its attention on tactics of parliamentary survival. The need to appease the NDP was reflected in a somewhat more interventionist and nationalist agenda during the two years of minority government that followed. DREE also went through a metamorphosis during this period, chiefly the decentralization of its organization and operations and the introduction of a new type of federal-provincial working agreement, the General Development Agreement (GDA). That agreement was intended to introduce greater 'flexibility' into DREE's operations and to improve federal-provincial co-operation in the field of regional development. DREE's reorganization also brought with it a broadened geographic and strategic focus. Now 'development opportunities' would be identified and exploited in every province. In effect, a new set of economic and political priorities had determined that DREE would cease being an agency with a mandate to eliminate regional disparities (primarily, although not exclusively, between Atlantic Canada and the rest of the country), and instead become a vehicle for delivering politically popular infrastructure projects and sectoral modernization programs to the provinces. One result of this shift was the gradual but steady growth of DREE spending in the West during the 1970s, both absolutely and as a percentage of total DREE expenditures, despite the fact that this was a period during which the resource-rich West was experiencing unparalleled economic prosperity.[63]

By 1974, then, the ambitions and optimistic mandate shouldered by

DREE in 1969 had all but disappeared from view. The regaining of a Liberal majority in the federal election of that year did nothing to change this direction in DREE's evolution, if anything confirming the government's new approach to regional development. Little attention was given to the issue in the campaign. The NDP attempted something of a repeat of 1972 by focusing on 'bad capitalists' who were ripping-off the system, and calling for a more just and equitable capitalism. The Liberals and the Tories took contrasting positions on the need for wage and price controls to dampen inflation, and this issue dominated the election. The structural weaknesses of an economy that produced high inflation went largely unmentioned and unaddressed, while the need for short-term crisis measures monopolized the public debate.[64] Unlike the 'national unity' and 'just society' concerns of 1968, however, this political discourse was not one with which 'regional development' could be easily or positively articulated.

Further evidence of the decline of regional development as a priority of state élites at the centre in the wake of the 1974 election was the granting of the cabinet portfolio to Marcel Lessard. The reins to what was originally to have been Ottawa's 'super department' were given over to a newcomer devoid of the status or clout of DREE's previous ministers, a further blow to the credibility of a department that was already not well accepted within the Ottawa 'system' even when its priority status with the prime minister and cabinet was much less suspect. The reorganization of DREE and the redefining of its role and mandate did assuage some of the department's critics. Provincial governments, in particular, had been highly critical of DREE in its original incarnation. For if interdepartmental co-ordination had proven unattainable simply through the ministerial representation afforded by DREE, neither was willing and active inter-governmental co-ordination a hallmark of the 1969–72 period. During these early years DREE's approach to federal-provincial relations generated considerable provincial hostility, and time and again the call was made by provincial representatives for a closer form of federal-provincial co-operation.[65] DREE operations during the early years were highly centralized. Both federal officials working 'in the field' and provincial governments were blocked from any significant input into DREE decision-making.[66] Anthony Careless has argued that this was, in fact, a conscious decision on the part of DREE, which was less concerned with federal-provincial co-operation than with federal visibility. And much of the 'blame' for this, according to Careless, lay with DREE's deputy minister Tom Kent.

Whether a visionary or anachronism, he [Tom Kent] personally had an important influence on Ottawa's policy, in removing the federal encouragement of provincial planning and even of operational coordination. His distaste for scattered decision-making, for excessive levels of planning or coordination, and for programs with intangible results, created successors to ARDA, ADA, and ADB which bore scant resemblance to the earlier styles of government. His practice consisted in deliberately by-passing the coordination apparatus at the provincial level (often created through earlier federal encouragement) to deal directly instead with provincial departments or the private sector of the provincial economy. Even the provincial departments usually had the choice only of accepting or rejecting federal packages.[67]

At the same time, Careless alludes to a broader political strategy behind DREE's manner of proceeding in these early years.

The control and direction of federal spending was a result of the growing desire at Ottawa to secure a greater visibility of federal policies. Along with the greater visibility which could be achieved by programs producing jobs, training labour, or building infrastructure, went a related effort to establish a new constituency of consumers of federal services greater than that comprised by provincial governments ... Ottawa sought a new constituency in the provinces – not their governments but their people – to combat the past habits of provincial regimes taking the full glory for joint expenditures under TVTA, ARDA, FRED and ADB ... In competing for the attention of the consumer and achieving greater efficiency in program design, finance, and delivery the federal government sought to remove intermediate and unnecessary levels that provided for a 'cooperative federalism' but did little for the delivery of service, except, as in the past, to obscure the federal component.[68]

Careless, then, offers both personality and federal political strategy as explanations for Ottawa's choosing to expand its own regional-development bureaucracy rather than initiating a major joint planning effort with the provinces.[69] But Careless's explanation says nothing of the effect on DREE operations of the stolid resistance on the part of most state élites at the centre to the design and implementation of any co-ordinated economic and industrial strategy, national or regional. This meant that DREE was forced to labour under a genuine insecurity and inability to engage in any comprehensive co-ordinated strategy of its own, let alone one that included the provinces.[70]

The simple fact remains that no regional plan, no provincial plan, and no effective urban government (for planning purposes) was ever brought into existence as part of the regional-development effort. Instead DREE plunged ahead not only without complete plans for the regions, but with unreformed and in many ways archaic governmental and administrative structures in place in the provinces that were to be the recipients of DREE programming. In lieu of any overall industrial strategy, DREE merely sought to encourage a greater 'economic regionalism' in the Atlantic provinces by enhancing the development of an 'urban core' in the geographical heart of the Maritimes. Ottawa would use federal monies to entice individual provinces to join in this approach.[71] Since almost all economic-development spending in the 'have not' provinces was done on a shared-cost basis, these provinces were more or less forced to participate in DREE-designed programs formulated without their input. In effect, provincial priorities in the economic-development field were being set by Ottawa.

The political hostility this approach earned for DREE between 1969 and 1972 hardly seems to have been worth the dubious promise it held for the development of the regional economy. In any event, the 1973–4 changes to DREE met provincial demands for a decentralization of the department's operations by shifting most of DREE's personnel and line functions to the provincial level. Programs would be formulated and implemented by DREE officers in the field working in collaboration with their provincial counterparts, an almost complete reversal of the situation that had existed previously. However, the reorganization made no provision for mechanisms of sectoral or interprovincial co-ordination. DREE was not granted any authority as an overarching co-ordinating agency; this continued to remain the exclusive preserve of the cabinet committees.[72] And while alternative means of soliciting the involvement of other departments in the formulation of DREE initiatives were implemented, these would be notoriously underutilized.[73]

Also affected by the reorganization was the federal commitment to the much-vaunted concept of 'growth centres' as the solution to the Atlantic region's economic ills. Certainly the DREE minister from the very inception of the approach was subjected to intense political pressure to abandon it and extend both the special areas to which infrastructure expenditure was to be funnelled and the designated regions eligible for industrial assistance under RDIA. Initially this pressure came from MPs representing depressed rural constituencies – many of whom were Liberal back-benchers – who feared that their constituents would be 'dealt out' of regional-development spending. Marchand argued in response that urban and industrial structures in the poorer provinces must first be put in place; later attention could be given to economically depressed rural areas.[74] Faced with continued pressure to extend coverage, Marchand defended the integrity of the program: 'the more you extend it [the special-areas program], the more you weaken it ... I know every day I received complaints and there are good cases ... but if we start extending it indefinitely it would become meaningless ... politically it is very difficult ... but anyhow this is the purpose of the program. We have to stick to our guns.'[75]

But provincial governments, too, were less than satisfied with DREE's decision to limit its assistance to the special areas, particularly with reference to highway construction. And on this point DREE did eventually give ground, agreeing to provide funds for highway construction outside the special areas in the case of New Brunswick, Nova Scotia, and Newfoundland.[76]

A partial federal retreat from DREE's early position, then, was made likely on political grounds. But there were also increasing doubts being expressed about the theoretical basis for the growth-centre approach. As a means of solving the problem of regional disparities the adoption of the concept had largely taken place in a vacuum as to its veracity, appropriateness, and applicability. As noted regional-planning specialist Benjamin Higgins has stated, 'perhaps never in the history of economic thought has so much government activity taken place and so much money been invested on the foundation of so confused a concept as the growth pole became in the late 1960's and early 1970's.'[77]

In fact, no sooner had the federal government embraced the concept than one of its early promoters, APEC, became sceptical about its usage. APEC argued that the central idea of 'agglomeration economies' embodied in the growth-centre approach did not explain how a centre arrived at the point where it had a clear advantage over other centres, nor did it adequately explain the dynamics of economic growth; it only explained why success in growth and development breeds more success.[78] For APEC, the deficiencies of the growth-centre concept as a theoretical base for the formulation of public policy and regional planning had become all too obvious.

Subsidiary agreements under GDA arrangements did not abandon the emphasis on growth centres, however, instead supplementing it with a continuation of ARDA programs aimed at rural resource industries. Labelled by DREE as the 'development opportunities' approach, government policy was now to address itself to 'potentials' and 'opportunities' rather than 'problems.' In practice this meant ignoring what was *not* present in periphery economies in favour of expanding and modernizing what was already there. Inevitably, the resulting programs and projects tended to reflect and replicate the existing industrial structure.[79] Thus, in the Atlantic region, primary industries would continue to be the chief recipients of DREE assistance, while infrastructure (and highway construction in particular) would continue to account for more than 50 per cent of DREE expenditures.[80]

DREE's early years demonstrated the functional futility of high levels of expenditure without a comprehensive framework that could integrate the efforts of a number of federal departments, not to mention the political hostility, and thus impediments, that bypassing provincial governments would incur. The 1973–4 review and reorganization could address the second of these, but it could not come to terms with the first. Adrift without policy, direction, or purpose, and detached from the programs and pursuits of other federal departments, in its internal review DREE was bound to respond to the strongest political pressures and choose the path of least resistance. Effectively there was no other frame of reference for DREE since the department and its role was defined and redefined, organized and reorganized, within a broader context shaped by the political and economic strategies employed by state élites at the centre.

Party, Bureaucracy, and Planning, 1968–75

The economic situation in Canada on the eve of the government's imposition of wage and price controls in the fall of 1975 was not good. Unemployment was high and rising (it had reached 7.1 per cent by 1975), and so was the inflation rate, which was running at 10.8 per cent in 1975–5.[81] The balance-of-payments position of the country was also deteriorating, dropping from a surplus of $96 million in 1973 to a deficit of $5 billion in 1975.[82] The situation was made worse by Canada's high degree of dependence on foreign-based multinationals. In the 1950s, U.S. direct investment made a contribution to Canada's capital needs of $1.2 billion. This became a deficit in the 1960s, and from 1968 to 1975 the difference between income remitted to U.S. parent corporations and new capital inflow to Canada increased to $6.6 billion.[83] Moreover, an end to major oil exports to the United States quickly revealed the country's severe overreliance on imported manufactured goods. An Organization for Economic Cooperation and Development (OECD) study found Canada to have the highest manufacturing wages in the world in the mid-1970s while productivity remained low. Hardly surprising, then, was the shrinking proportion of Canada's labour force engaged in manufacturing: it decreased by 5 per cent between 1966 and 1976.[84]

Surveying the situation as it stood in the mid-1970s, Brodie and Jenson conclude that in the increasing international competition among oligopolistic corporations, Canada was no longer an attractive site for investment in labour-intensive manufacturing industries. With wage demands tied to double-digit inflation, Canadian-made goods were simply too expensive to compete on international markets.[85] The reaction of the Canadian government was to impose mandatory wage and price controls. Explaining that controls involved 'nothing less than a wrenching adjustment of our expectations – an adjustment of our national lifestyle to our means,'[86] Prime Minister Trudeau established the Anti-Inflation Board (AIB) and wage increases were held well below the inflation rate, effectively reducing real incomes. In addition, all the major economic tools at the government's disposal – discretionary fiscal policy, monetary policy, and mandatory wage and price controls – were applied to the fight against inflation.[87] This compounded an economic downturn that, as always, was more severe on the periphery than at the centre. For example, manufacturing employment in the Atlantic region declined by over 7 per cent between 1974 and 1976 compared with a drop of less than 3 per cent in Ontario.[88]

Canada's deteriorating economic situation, then, brought new concerns to the forefront of the state agenda and new priorities for economic and industrial policy-makers. As the 1970s progressed, attention was clearly shifting towards the problems of the industrial heartland and their implications for Canadian competitiveness internationally. In the process regional development was pushed to the margins of Ottawa's horizons. Moreover, the revival and resuscitation of regional policy as a priority area for state intervention was unlikely unless it was incorporated into an overall economic and industrial strategy formulated to address the structural problems of the Canadian economy.

The imposition of controls in 1975 was a watershed for regional development as an issue in Canadian politics and as a field of state policy. Controls put debates within the government over an industrial strategy on hold, and brought an abrupt end to bureaucratic exercises aimed at establishing a 'planning framework' for policy development. Having been paralysed by internal disagreements within the bureaucracy, the government overcame its inertia only with the onset of crisis conditions, and then its response was of such a nature as to merely postpone the need to clarify its policy direction, in the interim pushing down the real income of workers. 'From that point [the imposition of controls] on, Trudeau and his government found themselves doing exactly what the ill-fated and politically costly priorities exercise had been designed to avoid: they were reduced to stumbling along without a plan, racing to catch up with events, improvising desperately.'[89]

This represented the nadir of the technocratic approach to policy-making that the 'Trudeauite' reformers had sought to establish in the 1968–72 period. In the face of entrenched bureaucratic and political opposition, a viable administrative framework for state planning had failed to materialize, and now controls had put an end to the last and most comprehensive of their planning initiatives. That this battle remained a bureaucratic one in large part explains its outcome. According to Phidd and Doern, the Trudeau government rarely faced the fact 'that the political meaning of co-ordination can only be contemplated when one acknowledges that such co-ordination involves in part the temporary victory of one or two ... objectives over other values and objectives, the use of one or more instruments over other instruments, and the relative triumph of one department over another and of one or more ministers over others.'[90]

Richard French has similarly argued in his study of federal government decision-making processes during this period that 'planning cannot create political conviction ... If planning systems ran at cross-purposes, it was because no sufficient ministerial consensus in support of any particular one existed. Without political conviction based on popular perceptions, the planning enterprise is like a hothouse plant, with bright flowers and no roots.'[91]

French goes further to assert that comprehensive national planning based on a popular mandate must necessarily be preceded by a change in the approach of the major parties, at least to the extent that their brokerage traditions and broad-gauge 'rolling compromise' political strategies are set aside for 'narrower' and more truly distinct party platforms. Planning would then presumably no longer be reverted to as a *substitute* for policy, but more properly an *instrument* of policy. 'No amount of [technical] sophistication can compensate for a political system predicated on personality rather than policy.'[92]

Parties in Canada have not been proficient at developing and sustaining policy thrusts. An important reason for this lack of proficiency has to do with the structure of power within Canada's major parties. Political strategy has remained the prerogative of a party élite intent upon the acquisition and maintenance of political power and sensitive to the pressures exerted by corporate interests, the media, and public-opinion polls.[93] This has supported the continuation of traditional brokerage politics and political strategy: the politicians mouth vague generalities and make the right symbolic gestures such that the party might represent, for as long as possible, all things to all people. Coherent policies were encumbrances that endangered electoral success, and were thus to be avoided. In the passage that follows Senator Keith Davey recites the traditional wisdom of a 'winning' party strategy in Canada.

The traditional strength of the Liberal Party has been that we spanned so much of the centre of the stage that we forced the Tories away out to our right and we forced the New Democrats away out to our left, and so this is a party that at one and the same time can contain Ross Thatcher and Walter Gordon; we've managed, to some extent, to make the cities think we are for them and to make the country think we are for them and even to be the party of labour and of big business at the same time – that's been a neat trick.[94]

While the Liberals were busy performing this trick, with varying degrees of success, in five consecutive elections (1963, 1965, 1968, 1972, 1974), the other parties were virtually barred from power. The NDP was confined to western Canada and a small Ontario base of support, while the Conservatives were crippled by their weakness in Quebec. In both cases the formula for Liberal electoral success pre-empted the rise of their opponents: the quasi–social democratic and mildly nationalist policy agenda pursued by the Liberals during this period siphoned-off potential support for the NDP, while French Canada and the issue of English-French relations were well staked-out by the Liberals (yet again) in the mid-1960s. With the Quebec electorate in the 1970s increasingly polarized by the federalist-nationalist struggle, the Liberals succeeded in all-but-monopolizing the federalist side of the debate, in the process becoming more or less synonymous with the notion of 'French power' in Ottawa. The NDP was never able to register on the Quebec electorate and the Conservatives struggled to win two seats there in 1972 and three in 1974.[95]

The Conservatives were also riven by factional conflicts and policy divisions. With regard to the latter, internal dissension over the party's official acceptance of bilingualism did nothing to improve the party's standing among French Canadians. The need for party leader Robert Stanfield to engage in a continual process of 'consensus-building' on policy – both as part of the attempt to 'paper over' major cracks within his caucus and in an effort to redirect the causus's energies away from factional disputes revolving around the leadership issue – produced vague, unclear policy statements that were difficult to translate into specific proposals (and if and when they were, always threatened to fracture the fragile edifice of party unity).[96]

So the Liberals were destined to remain in power throughout this period. And on certain issues the party did gradually piece together a distinct party position and construct a more or less viable long-term political alliance supportive of its position. This was certainly true with regard to French-English relations and related constitutional issues. The composition of the party's leadership, and the nature of its base of support and appeal to the electorate, gradually took the party beyond traditional brokerage politics on these matters. But no similar process occurred with regard to the elucidation of new strategies and options for industrial and regional development. Instead, continuing internal divisions among state and party élites on these matters produced only inertia, indecision, and paralysis.

On the Periphery: The Provincial State and the Development Function

During the Stanfield period in Nova Scotia (1956–67), the provincial and federal governments per se were indirectly involved, if involved at all, in planning and managing the process of economic development on the periphery. In IEL, APEC, and VEPB Stanfield and his cabinet looked to the province's indigenous business élite and to vehicles of business-government collaboration to find ways and means of replacing the province's declining industrial sector, especially coal-mining. A heavy reliance on private-sector actors and agencies to analyse development problems, put together strategies, and manage development spending kept the provincial state itself relatively small and both technically and managerially understaffed in the development field.

A number of factors that emerged in the latter part of the 1960s – the DOSCO crisis, IEL imbroglios, the evident irrelevance and impracticality of the experimental consultative/planning process, an end to the relative peace of the province's labour scene, not to mention movement by the federal government towards more concerted and systematic intervention in the development field – dramatically altered this situation. These events demanded a change in the capacities of the provincial-state apparatus concomitant with the more direct and broadened development role now thrust upon the provincial state, as well as a certain distancing of policy-making from the direct influence of the province's business élite (stated otherwise, an increase in the relative autonomy of the provincial state).

What occurred at the end of the decade was the demise of provincial innovations of the Stanfield era, such as IEL and VEPB, and in their stead an expanded role for state bureaucracies and corporations: DREE, DEVCO, SYSCO, and the provincial Department of Development. This appearance on the scene of a new set of institutional actors reflected a shift in the role assumed by the state in the development field. The Stanfield government's approach – which relied on a 'business knows best' philosophy and the opening of lines of communication and consultation between the government and socio-economic producer groups in the province (especially and primarily business) – was eclipsed by more direct state involvement in the crisis-ridden sectors of the provincial economy. Moreover, the inauguration of DREE in 1969 increased the importance of intergovernmental relations to provincial development policy. It gave greater prominence to an intergovernmental dynamic of conflict, co-operation, and consultation premised upon federal guidance and pre-dominance in policy and program design, and to negotiation over the flow of material blessings (in the form of grants, incentives, and infrastructure expenditures) from Ottawa to the periphery.

This period of transition was abetted by the election of a new Liberal government in Nova Scotia. In 1967, Stanfield was succeeded as premier of Nova Scotia by G.I. (Ike) Smith. When Smith went to the Nova Scotia electorate three years later, the results created an unprecedented situation in Nova Scotia politics: the Liberals under Gerald Regan took twenty-three seats on 46 per cent of the vote; the Tories, twenty-one seats on 47 per cent of the vote; the NDP under new leader Jeremy Akerman momentarily held the balance of power with two seats on 7 per cent of the vote. The Liberals benefited from a major shift of voter support in Metropolitan Halifax, where they had been all but shut out in the two previous elections. They were further aided by a minor renaissance in NDP fortunes premised upon a reconcentration of support for that party in the environs of the troubled coal and steel industries. These shifts enabled the Liberals to squeak out a narrow victory and form their first provincial government in fourteen years.

While in the previous two elections the Liberals had managed to capture only four and six seats, respectively, between 1967 and 1970 Regan was able to score political points with his criticism of the government's management of the province's economic development, charging that poor co-ordination of responsible agencies 'had inhibited the preparation and application of a well-planned development strategy and had weakened the government's capacity to properly assess development proposals.'[97] He was especially critical of the operations of IEL. In a policy address setting the tone for the Liberal campaign in 1970, Regan promised a more 'rational and scientific approach' to economic development, including a single department of economic growth to end the confusion of agencies working on industrial development. Presenting themselves in this way as 'the party of the problem-solving technocrats,' the Liberals one-upped a Conservative government that had prided itself on its achievements in the industrial development field.[98] Other major issues in the campaign damaging to the government were the mounting industrial-relations problems in the province and the acute housing shortage in Halifax.[99]

The Liberals election victory in 1970 was unexpected and the party came to power without a clearly definable base of social and political support. The Conservatives under Stanfield and Smith had long nurtured a close association with the province's business élite. Regan presented a younger, more modern, and technocratic face to the Nova Scotia electorate in 1970, but he and his party had not devised a coherent program for change. And while the new government did act on its pre-election promises in the field of development policy – downgrading the role of IEL and abolishing the Department of Trade and Industry to make way for the new provincial Department of Development – the results of this particular episode of state restructuring would be something less than what was promised. Indeed, the shallowness of the Liberal critique of Tory policies and the lack of an alternative development strategy would produce years of policy drift and a poor government performance in development planning, while initiative and leadership in the field of development policy would be yielded to DREE.

The IEL: The Demise of 'Let's Make a Deal'

Throughout the 1960s Nova Scotia continued to rely on its Crown corporation Industrial Estates Limited (IEL) to attract secondary manufacturing to the province in order to replace jobs disappearing in a modernizing and mechanizing primary sector and a declining industrial sector. And in the buoyant, expansionary economy of the mid-1960s, IEL was able to make a series of announcements about new factories to be located in the province. At a time when coal and steel industries in Nova Scotia had moved from gradual decline to grave crisis, and out-migration was bleeding the periphery of its young workers, such announcements accorded IEL a high profile and resulted in a favourable public perception. The provincial government, meanwhile, was able to bask in the political sunshine that radiated from IEL's successes. But a number of débâcles in the later 1960s altered this positive public image and IEL's status of grace with the provincial government; by 1970, its performance had become a factor in the demise of its political founders.

The worst of IEL's industrial imbroglios involved Clairtone Sound Corporation and Deuterium of Canada Limited (DCL). The first was a 'high-flying' stereo-equipment manufacturer led by two young promoters. Its relocation to Nova Scotia from Ontario was heralded as a major 'coup' for IEL, but a number of ill-advised and overly ambitious decisions left IEL as the major shareholder in a company that piled up net losses in 1967 of $6.7 million. Such losses continued until Clairtone's foreclosure sale in 1972, by which time the government's financial obligations totalled $26 million.[100]

An even greater fiasco, however, was IEL's involvement with DCL and its Glace Bay, Nova Scotia, heavy-water plant. The episode is emblematic of a number of flaws and weaknesses in the Nova Scotia government's approach to industrial development: the attraction of the megaproject with unrealistic expectations of an industrial 'ripple effect'; inadequate bureaucratic state capacity and expertise for purposes of negotiation, planning, and assessment of project proposals; and federally imposed constraints that left the province financially vulnerable.

The contract for the production of heavy water for Atomic Energy of Canada Limited (AECL) – Canada's Crown corporation responsible for producing and marketing the CANDU nuclear reactor – was given to DCL in 1963, after a prolonged cabinet struggle in Ottawa about who should get the contract and where the plant should be located. Stanfield had worked hard to land the plant for Nova Scotia, with support from within the federal cabinet from Pickersgill, MacEachen, and Pearson. A great deal of hype surrounded the announcement of a Cape Breton site for the plant. There would only be about two hundred permanent jobs associated with the completed facility, but there were reputed to be two thousand construction jobs involved. And more important, the provincial government argued that heavy-water production would attract a host of allied industries to Nova Scotia.[101] It was to be, according to Ike Smith, 'a keystone type of technology' that 'held the promise of becoming the cornerstone for the economic development of Cape Breton.'[102]

The major federal condition on the awarding of the contract was that the company had to be Canadian-owned, and DCL was, at this time, the creation of American scientist-promoter Jerome Spevak. To abide by the Government of Canada's provisions, the Province of Nova Scotia, through IEL, purchased a 51 per cent stake in DCL. At the same time Nova Scotia was required to expand its power-generation facilities near the proposed site at a cost of $12.5 million in order to provide the necessary steam to the new heavy-water plant. The province had acquired a technology about which it knew nothing; it began construction in 1964 but produced not a drop of heavy water until 1976 (by which time it was owned by AECL), and began with a $30 million price-tag but ultimately cost $250 million, $135 million of which was invested by the province.[103]

From the beginning DCL was not a project that IEL's corporate management wanted, or even felt confident they could handle. It was 'dumped' on IEL out of necessity because the provincial government had none of the requisite negotiating or management expertise within the ranks of its own bureaucracy. It appears that at the time IEL represented the full extent of the Nova Scotia government's expertise and capacity in the area of industrial promotion and development.[104] In the case of DCL, clearly, in the words of Dalton Camp, 'the reach exceeded the grasp.'[105]

Ironically, IEL's greatest success – enticing Michelin Tire to Nova Scotia – came just at the high point of the DCL fiasco in 1969. The French multinational has since become one of the largest private employers in the province. Its decision to locate in Nova Scotia came after lengthy negotiations with IEL, and enraged Quebec, which was also negotiating with the corporation and fully expected to be chosen by Michelin. It has been argued elsewhere that the decision not to go to Quebec was largely a product of the corporation's paternalism and fanatical anti-unionism. For its North American operations it chose Nova Scotia and South Carolina, locations where it surmised it could count on paying relatively low wages to a passive, non-unionized work-force. This assessment of Michelin's motives appears to have been borne out by subsequent events.[106] None the less, there can be no doubt that Michelin had a huge impact on Nova Scotia's relative performance in the manufacturing sector. In terms of employment and value-added, Nova Scotia outstripped the national average for the period 1961–75. However, without Michelin Tire, which accounted for over half the employment growth in Nova Scotia manufacturing during the years 1971–5, Nova Scotia's performance in manufacturing would have ranked below every province in Canada except Quebec.[107]

The Michelin success, however, could not shelter IEL from a number of criticisms regarding its role as a development agency. The corporation operated virtually without guide-lines or any type of industrial strategy. Instead, 'the ideas of successive managers, ministers, and boards of directors could determine its directions.'[108] There were also no criteria of assessment put forth by either the government or IEL itself, 'and evaluation of its performance has depended more on political than economic factors.'[109] Generally speaking, whereas IEL's ad hoc, promotion-oriented approach may have been good politics (when it worked), it was, according to APEC, bad development strategy and practice. Relying on personal contact and the judgment of the businessmen on IEL's board was not a sound method of assessing and screening potential clients. Up to 1972 fully one-third of IEL-sponsored relocations had failed.[110] Moreover, before 1970 IEL demonstrated little concern for the development of indigenous entrepreneurship and enterprise. Its ratio of financing was ten to one, outside to local! Its focus remained relatively narrow, concentrating on large, secondary-manufacturing enterprises with a mature product line – in most cases not enterprises likely to experience significant growth.[111]

IEL was not disbanded by the new Liberal government in 1970, but there was a change in its composition and methods. Thereafter the corporation assumed a significantly reduced role in the Nova Scotia government's overall development effort. It was taken out of the hands of prominent Nova Scotia businessman, and its public profile was lowered. In the same year the Department of Development was created as the provincial counterpart to DREE, and together these government departments substantially supplanted the role IEL had been playing in Nova Scotia.

Voluntary Planning: Outside Looking In

Yet another development agency of the Stanfield era to undergo substantial revision after 1970 was the Voluntary Economic Planning Board (VEPB). Voluntary planning in Nova Scotia, it should be recalled, was a technique that the provincial government adapted from British and French examples in the early 1960s. While completely without the power of sanctions (on either the private sector or the government), the technique was primarily intended to open up communication between government and private-sector actors (particularly business) in various sectors of the economy as an aid to policy-making. Its first and only 'plan,' released in 1966, was roundly criticized as a shopping-list of all the wants of every sector. No public body was ever designated the task of reviewing and assessing the plan. Indeed, there was no planning and co-ordinating mechanism within the provincial state that could have undertaken such a review and overseen the plan's implementation, a state of affairs senior officials within the provincial bureaucracy hostile to the concept of economic planning sought to maintain.[112] Just as salient was the emerging coal-and-steel crisis in 1966–7, which pushed the planning process into the background. Indeed, VEPB itself spent almost all its energies between 1966 and 1968 on the coal-and-steel problem.

Needless to say, VEPB's first (and only) plan quickly sank from public view and expired. By the end of the 1960s, earlier participants in voluntary planning's grass-roots planning exercise had become dissatisfied and disaffected, and withdrew their active support. On the verge of expiration in the late 1960s, the board was carried on as a 'bootstrap' operation by a number of 'concerned persons,' even though after 1967 there was no public acknowledgment or strategy of support for the organization on the part of the government.[113] Quite simply, the political and economic conditions that compelled and supported corporatist-type arrangements elsewhere were absent in Nova Scotia (as shown in the experience of the JLMSC).

With the election of a new government in 1970, a reassessment of the board's role was undertaken and it was decided that entrusting the board with the design of an economic plan for the province was an unrealistic objective. Instead the new Voluntary Planning Board (VPB) would limit itself to promoting a more active participation by the private sector in the process of development planning in the broad sense. Primarily, it would seek to perform a supportive function for interest groups aimed at facilitating the identification of development problems by the private sector and involving that sector in the analysis of government planning and policy proposals to deal with these problems. With this revised mandate the board's technical staff – the economists attached to the VPB – could be dispensed with, allowing the board to consider and present problems 'as perceived by the volunteers,' unencumbered by the expert but inhibiting views of state-employed 'technicians.'[114]

In the 1970s, then, voluntary planning was turned away from its initial aspirations to play a quasi-corporatist role in Nova Scotia politics to become a much more modest vehicle of interest representation within the new Department of Development. This is not to say, however, that its representation would subsequently reflect the broad range of societal interests. In particular, organized labour was not represented on the board; on the contrary, it had become openly hostile to the VPB. While the management of the board attributed this hostility to an unwillingness on the part of labour 'to involve itself in a forum which includes all elements of society and the resultant need for compromise,'[115] various positions adopted by the board in the early 1970s were certain not to endear it to organized labour. In October 1973, for example, the board presented its *Report on Manpower Planning and Unemployment* to the provincial government. The report dealt mainly with 'the negative effects of the overly permissive unemployment insurance programme (UIC) and the potential of effective manpower training. The report recommended a much more selective UIC programme and greater emphasis toward training more closely to the needs of industry.'[116] The report advocated a qualification period of at least six months, rather than ten weeks, to 'stabilize' the work-force. In October 1975, the board also went on record as strongly supporting the imposition of wage and price controls in order to 'set the stage for the return to a situation of less government presence in a relatively highly productive business community.'[117] It can be surmised, therefore, that in the 1970s the VPB became primarily a small-business lobby concerned with the impact of government policies and proposals on various sectors of the economy. Gone was the pretence of working towards on overall economic-development plan arrived at through the efforts of all the affected parties.

The Department of Development: The Dynamic of Dependent Federalism

Within the Nova Scotia government, the introduction of a nascent co-ordinating, planning, and policy-making mechanism in the field of development occurred almost simultaneously with deliberations and debates at the federal level over the structure and function of the proposed federal regional-development agency eventually to emerge as DREE. In 1969 a cabinet committee on planning and programs was formed, supported by a powerful secretariat under L.E. Poetschke, a former senior bureaucrat in ARDA. As related by Careless, Premier G.I. Smith had grown disenchanted with Nova Scotia's performance at federal-provincial meetings and was impressed with a brief by Poetschke to the cabinet in 1968 that criticized the rigid sectoral framework within which both the federal and provincial bureaucracies were organized, when in fact important economic and social problems overlapped several sectors. Poetschke argued that, because governments relied on departmental advice, they were limited in their understanding of the causes of poverty and underdevelopment; what was needed instead was an effective mechanism for determining long-term and broad policy for cabinet that could transcend the limitations of sectoral or jurisdictional solutions. Planning energies could then be directed towards a problem, opportunity, or area, rather than to traditional jurisdictions.

He [Poetschke] argued that public works constituted subsidies to an out-of-date economic, social, and political system in the Maritimes ... that regional economic disparities arose more from a lack of skill and poor labour force participation than from a lack of infrastructure ... Poetschke and the Secretariat stressed the improvement of procedures and methods rather than the extension of public works or passive industrial incentives as essential prerequisites to specific development projects. *New machinery* would enable assessment of long-term economic trends and the development of broad policy to affect major changes in the direction and integration of operating agencies to implement these programs.[118]

Poetschke, then, brought the developmental technocrat's perspective to Nova Scotia. The objective was to end highly fragmented departmental approaches to common problems, and the method was the secretariat's collaboration with departments in the identification of problems and in the formulation and administration of programs. The secretariat would introduce a whole new systems approach to which departments were expected to reorient themselves.

In practice, the new secretariat, comprised largely of hand-picked, out-of-province experts outside of regular civil-service categories and guide-lines, ruffled virtually everyone's feathers, provincial and federal. Provincial line departments in the three Maritime provinces preferred the sectoral over a spatial or problem-solving approach which, one thing, left responsibility with a co-ordinating agency such as the secretariat and offered a potential challenge to the line department's field of responsibility and expertise.[119] In general, this produced a core of resistance to increased planning capacity that often found sympathy with provincial cabinet members distrustful of planners and resentful of the restrictions planning imposed on partisan political decision-making.[120] In addition, proposed federal projects tended to be met by an alternative set of provincially designed projects, each set within different planning frameworks and requiring different inputs from the other level of government.

A breakdown in interdepartmental and intergovernmental co-operation was therefore not long in coming; nor was the end to Nova Scotia's fledgling technocratic 'super-agency.' Within two months of the Conservative government's defeat in 1970 and only a year after its introduction, the secretariat was disbanded and its staff dismissed.[121]

Besides doing away with the secretariat, the new Liberal government in Nova Scotia also disbanded the Department of Trade and Industry. In place of both it created the Department of Development. The department 'was perceived to have a distinct coordinative role. This assumption of central agency characteristics was one of the main reasons that a new organizational structure had been introduced.'[122] Further, the department would administer the province's economic-development policies, co-ordinate the development activities of the department with those of other departments, maintain liaison with the Government of Canada and federal departments concerned with economic development, and conduct research and analysis on the provincial economy. It would provide staff support to the Canada/Nova Scotia Joint Planning Committee convened by DREE (and later to the Management Committee of the Canada/Nova Scotia General Development Agreement). It would participate in studies conducted under DREE's Special Areas Agreement, ARDA, and Strait of Canso Area Development.[123]

In practice, the co-ordinative role assigned to the new department was performed only weakly, if at all. A possible surrogate in this function whose star rose briefly after the Liberal return to power – the Cabinet Office, under the secretary to the cabinet – quickly suffered a fate similar to that of its Conservative forerunner.[124] As for the department's own policy role in the development field, Nova Scotia's development strategy and pattern of expenditures were determined primarily by federal-provincial agreements. Before 1973, the determining factor was the set of proposals forwarded by DREE; after the 1973–4 review the Canada–Nova Scotia Joint Management Committee composed of DREE and provincial officials appears to have become central to the formulation of development programs.

Besides some broadening of development spending, subsidiary agreements reached after 1974 would vary little from earlier established patterns set down by ARDA, ADB, and DREE's own 'growth centre' strategy. The designated 'growth centres' in Nova Scotia – Metropolitan Halifax and the Strait of Canso – would continue to be recipients of high levels of expenditure, especially the former. The rationale was set out by DREE in a 1973 document on provincial-development prospects. Metropolitan Halifax would serve a dual purpose to the region: it would provide a concentrated local market for products from the rest of the region and it would be a centre for high-order services. The Strait of Canso, in contrast, earned its special status on the strength of its natural advantages and a recent heavy-industry boom that had raised expectations of continuing private-sector investment in the area. (Nor did it hurt that the Strait was located in the federal riding represented by Allan J. MacEachen, the most senior federal cabinet minister from the Atlantic provinces.)

Another subsidiary agreement reached under GDA arrangements – the Industrial Development Subsidiary Agreement – reinforced the concept of geographically concentrated development spending by focusing its expenditures on industrial parks in five urban centres in a 'central corridor' running from Halifax to the New Brunswick border. This decision was supported by the observation that strong gains were made in this corridor in the 1970–5 period, and that development spending by governments should strive to 'reinforce growth patterns.'[125] These three subsidiary agreements (Metro, the Strait, Industrial Development) captured over $164 million, with $110 million of this total going to Metropolitan Halifax, 'clearly the centrepiece of the development strategy envisaged for the Atlantic economy.'[126] With visions of a new metropole diffusing growth to its surrounding hinterland dancing in their heads, the planners reasoned that 'what was good for Halifax was good for the whole province.' 'It is essential that the rate of development and growth in the metro area be sustained, not only to ensure continued prosperity for the residents of Halifax–Dartmouth but also to ensure the generation of the maximum possible benefits for the remaining parts of Nova Scotia and the Atlantic Region.'[127]

The other major area of expenditure was that of rural-resource development or, more precisely, support for the ongoing rationalization of rural resource industries in the province. Much of this expenditure (which in the first-generation agreements reached $140 million) was more or less a direct extension of earlier ARDA programming. Agriculture and forestry received most of the money. The amount allocated to mining was very small, and though Nova Scotia made numerous attempts to mount a fisheries subsidiary, the federal Department of Fisheries and Oceans with Romeo LeBlanc as minister steadfastly resisted what it perceived as an unwarranted intrusion into its exclusive jurisdiction.[128] Considered as a whole, federal-provincial development expenditures in the 1970s demonstrated a distinct preference for the most visible and the most passive (or, in DREE terms, 'non-coercive') types of expenditure, primarily infrastructure and capital improvements. While formal strategy documents during this period repeatedly paid homage to the importance of training, technology transfer, management, marketing, and distribution, when it came down to allocating resources only a tiny portion was set aside for the development of 'people' as opposed to 'things.'[129]

In a sense, the policies of the federal and provincial development bureaucracies succeeded in their objective (whether their contribution was spurious or not). Economic growth in Nova Scotia throughout the 1970s *did* concentrate primarily in Metropolitan Halifax. It did not, however, produce the diffuse economic benefits for the rest of the province that the framers of the Canada/Nova Scotia Subsidiary Agreements claimed it would. Instead, as acknowledged by DREE, there was an increasing degree of income and growth disparity *within* the province and the Atlantic region as a whole.[130] In areas such as Cape Breton and eastern Nova Scotia, economic conditions actually worsened as the 1970s progressed. From the perspective of the residents of these locales, it was becoming increasingly difficult to discern the benefits of development strategy and planning by the state.

The Strait of Canso: Vision and Reality

Besides Metropolitan Halifax, the only other Nova Scotia locale that had been designated by DREE as a major growth centre was the Strait of Canso subregion, including the towns of Port Hawkesbury and Mulgrave. The reason for this designation was the perceived potential of the area's ice-free deep-water harbour formed by the completion in 1955 of the Canso Causeway linking Cape Breton with mainland Nova Scotia. In 1961–2 the Swedish multinational Stora Kopperberg had established a pulp mill at the site. In 1969 the corporation decided to double the plant's pulp capacity and add newsprint production to the operation. Coincidentally, Gulf oil announced that it would build an oil refinery at the Strait to process Venezuelan and Middle East crude for sale to customers in eastern Canada. In addition, Canadian General Electric (CGE), which in anticipation of its construction of a heavy-water plant to supply Canada's nuclear-power industry had been testing water samples from across Canada, selected the Strait of Canso as the best location. As part of the project, the Nova Scotia Power Commission would build a thermal power station adjacent to the new CGE heavy-water plant.[131]

In the space of a few short years the Strait of Canso took on the appearance of a significant pole of industrial development, which both federal and provincial governments seized on as an indication of much greater things to come. Projections were made that the population of the Town of Port Hawkesbury alone would grow from 2,000 in the mid-1960s to 30,000 by the end of the century. A major petrochemical complex was foreseen, with announcements to this effect 'just around the corner.'

The numerous problems that subsequently attended this surge of industrial investment at the Strait are revealing of the character of state priorities in the development field and the poverty of development planning in Nova Scotia in the 1968–75 period. To begin, it is clear that development policies and programs at the Strait were narrowly focused on industrial growth and, more particularly, on the needs of capital. Industrial infrastructure and subsidies to capital absorbed state attention and resources to the virtual exclusion of social and environmental concerns, with the end result that the people of the area were forced to bear a high social cost for questionable economic benefits. Because the nature of the industries to which governments were making their appeals to locate at the Strait were highly capital-intensive, requiring huge front-end capital costs and large, temporary construction work-forces, but a relatively small number of long-term jobs and few if any linkages to the local economy or spin-offs in the form of associated or feeder industries,[132] the result for the Strait area was chaotic: a rapid increase in the local population that put tremendous strains on the provision of adequate housing, schools, medical care, and other essential services. Living costs, local taxes, and rents rose precipitously.[133] Moreover, the people of the small community of Point Tupper were placed in immediate and long-term danger because of their sudden proximity to industrial pollutants, hazardous wastes, and potential industrial accidents that would impact directly upon them.[134]

The glaring absence of effective development planning by governments stands out as the chief cause of this confused and strained situation. Co-ordination and planning were lacking within the provincial state itself, between province and municipalities, and among the affected municipalities. On the one hand, the provincial government supported the designation of the Strait as a 'growth centre' and actively pursued and contributed to the new investment that created the boom conditions there; on the other hand, the same provincial state denied the affected municipalities the special assistance they needed to cope with the situation. While the new industries themselves were lavished with attention, municipal infrastructure and social services remained wholly inadequate to meet increased demands. As the problems dragged on, local officials and residents became increasingly frustrated and resentful at 'a catalogue of decisions perpetuated by provincial agencies with little reference to one another or to the community.'[135]

The provincial government proved similarly inept at overcoming the parochial rivalries and jealousies of the several local municipalities that were resisting proposals for a common strategy or regional-planning authority to co-ordinate development at the Strait. After its election, the Regan government quickly abandoned such a project in the face of this municipal resistance. A. Paul Pross has explained this display of provincial deference in terms of political calculation and cowardice: unsure of its own political-support base the government shrank from taking the lead in any municipal reorganization for development purposes.[136] This government response occurred again after the Royal Commission on Education, Public Services, and Provincial-Municipal Relations (the Graham Commission) submitted its report to the provincial government in 1974 – encountering municipal opposition to the commission's recommendations for reforms, the Regan government refused to act on them.[137]

While problems with Strait area development were exacerbated by the administrative and political weakness of the Nova Scotia government, there were also atrociously poor industrial relations, major cost overruns, and little relief from high levels of local unemployment despite the construction boom. Labour unrest at the Strait became a major cause for concern for the state in 1969–70. In 1970 there were 13 official strikes during which a total of 74,860 person-days were lost, 18.8 per cent of the Canadian total for that year for the construction industry. There were also 24 unofficial or 'wildcat' strikes, 80 per cent of all wildcats in the province in 1970. This state of affairs was partly attributable to poor project management and a 'cost-plus' contract system, but the composition of the work-force was also a factor. Fully 60 per cent of the construction workers at the Strait were former miners laid off after the DEVCO take-over of the mines. These former miners brought with them a strong sense of solidarity, a deep suspicion of management, and a resistance to close supervision. A related problem was that many local unemployed found themselves shut out of job-hiring at the Strait, unable to get access to union membership controlled in the mining districts. Indeed, because of the surfeit of former miners retrained in the construction trades and the nature of the new industries locating at the Strait, local unemployment remained at high levels before, during, and after the construction boom. Only the pulp-and-paper mill derived a high proportion of its employee requirements from the indigenous work-force of the area. This situation fuelled the resentment and frustration of local workers and created a good deal of hostility towards 'outsiders,' unions, and strikes.[138]

Provincial state élites responded to this situation in 1969 with the Royal Commission on Industrial Relations in the Construction Industry (the Woods Commission).[139] The continuation of problems also led to apologies and warnings from the politicians. Thus, in November 1971, MacEachen admitted that the haphazard development at the Strait had deprived the people of the area of any influence or control over events, and that this situation had to be addressed. (It would not be for a number of years.) At the same time, he warned that the area would have to drastically improve its image if it wanted to attract 'the second stage of industrial development which the region so desperately needs. Low productivity, haphazard decision-making, inflated costs and unfair hiring practices are all serious barriers to renewed investment in the area.'[140] Finally, a belated federal-provincial planning agreement on the Strait was reached, committing both governments to an expenditure of funds to ensure the creation and implementation of a regional planning authority.[141]

By the time the federal and provincial governments had 'gotten their act together' at the Strait, its economic prospects had so dimmed as to make any new co-ordinating agency largely irrelevant. Gerald Regan's repeated promises concerning the imminent arrival of a petrochemical complex were never fulfilled, and in light of conditions at the Strait his reference to developments there as making over Nova Scotians into the 'New Phoenicians' became a bitter joke.[142] In the end the 'inducements' offered by the state were inadequate and inappropriate; further industrial development at the Strait depended upon circumstances and events – such as the development of commercial quantities of nearby offshore oil and gas – that would be determined on the basis of considerations far removed from the mere absence or presence of the requisite infrastructure at a particular location. Ultimately, the industrial vision and development strategy that lay behind the designation of the Strait of Canso as a 'growth centre' were chimeras, premised as they were on a role for the state that was strictly complementary to anticipated large-scale private-sector investment decisions that never materialized.

DEVCO and SYSCO: The Cape Breton Problem

DEVCO

On 30 March 1968, the Government of Canada, through its Crown corporation DEVCO, took possession of DOSCO's Cape Breton coal-mines and sundry facilities, and began the attempt to fulfil its legislated mandate:

[To] reorganize and rehabilitate the coal mining ... undertakings ... and to conduct coal mining and related operations in the Sydney coalfield on a basis consistent with efficient mining practice ... [To] promote and assist, either alone or in conjunction with any person or the Government of Canada or of Nova Scotia or any agency of either of such governments, the financing and development of industry on the Island of Cape Breton to provide employment outside the coal-producing industry and to broaden the base of the economy of the Island.[143]

In acting as the attending physician over the death of coal-mining in Nova Scotia, it was expected that DEVCO would 'take into account progress in providing employment outside the coal producing industry and in broadening the base of the economy of Cape Breton Island.'[144] The act specified that the functions of DEVCO's coal division and industrial-development division were to be kept completely separate, each with its own vice-president, budget, financial statements, and grants from government. There was to be no financial switching between divisions. An initial grant of $25 million was extended for the rehabilitation and operation of the mines, and $20 million for industrial development (with another $10 million from the Nova Scotia government).

In his review of the role and performance of the Cape Breton Development Corporation, Roy George stresses that, from the beginning, DEVCO was given a 'free hand'; that guide-lines and obligations placed upon it by the federal government were minimal; that the provincial government contributed $10 million, then 'washed its hand' of the task of promoting new industry in Cape Breton; that the municipalities and unions were passive, co-operative, and 'non-obstructive'; that DEVCO, in effect, was free to run coal operations and promote industry pretty well as it saw fit. It could lend money at any interest rate it deemed appropriate and, after 1970, it could guarantee a loan for up to $100 million; it could take on an equity position in a company or enterprise; it could buy, lease, or improve land; in fact, it was permitted to 'do all such other things as the Corporation deems incidental or conducive to the attainment of its objects in relation to the Industrial Development Division.'[145]

But the 'free hand' that George presents in a positive light in his review of DEVCO can also be viewed in another light: no real guide-lines or constraints imposed by the federal government, the province, the municipalities, or even the unions (within conventional limits) also meant no industrial or development strategy within which DEVCO could situate its activities. No guide-lines meant no plan, no supporting framework for DEVCO initiatives, and no intergovernmental or intersectoral policy co-ordination with the objective of promoting and supporting a more diversified economic base on the periphery. By and large, DEVCO was on its own.

After assuming control of the mines in 1968, DEVCO management immediately began scaling back production and employment in the mines and offering grants and subsidies to attract footloose industries. The objective was to reduce employment in the mines to between 2,000 and 3,000 workers by 1973, from a total of more than 6,000 at the end of 1968; production was to be scaled back to 2 million tons from 3.1 million tons over the same period. In the event, of the four mines DEVCO inherited, two were closed and, soon after, a third abandoned as a result of a fire. Employment was run down to 3,500 by 1973, while production declines exceeded estimates and plunged to about 1 million tons.

A policy change in 1972 altered this initial trajectory for coal-mining in Cape Breton. The run-down in output was stopped, while a decision was taken to end by 1974 DEVCO's Pre-Retirement Leave Plan and the ban on hiring. Two new mines – Lingan and Prince – were opened and a large-scale program of renovation and mechanization was initiated. Finally, in order to raise the social status of employment in the mines and provide an incentive to higher productivity a deliberate policy of elevating miners' wages and fringe benefits to the level of steelworkers was introduced.[146] By 1978–9 only one old mine would remain (No. 26) while two new mines would be in production; output would reach 2.6 million tons, employment would rise to 4,300, and output per man-shift (OMS) – after some six years and $100 million of investment – would reach 5 tons, a figure comparable to OMS in deep mines in other countries.[147]

In its industrial-development efforts there was also a similar shift of policy after the first few years. Between 1968 and 1971 DEVCO entered the competition for footloose secondary industry, using its stock of grants and loans to overmatch the attractions offered by competing sites. By 1971, the initial $30 million industrial-development fund was exhausted and additional annual amounts had to be secured from Parliament. (The total reached $72 million by March 1979.) However, by mid-decade there was little to show for the $30 million expended over the initial three to four years of DEVCO's efforts at industrial promotion. Of nine projects entered into between 1968 and 1970, only two survived, one of which didn't seek or need a Crown corporation such as DEVCO to entice it in the first place.[148] Many foreign-controlled assembly operations, having received generous hand-outs from DEVCO, ceased operations only a short period after arriving. On the whole, George describes this period of DEVCO's history as 'a woeful failure.'[149]

DEVCO's approach changed dramatically after Tom Kent, the former deputy minister of DREE, took over stewardship of the Crown corporation in 1971. Thereafter DEVCO ceased the 'mug's game' of trying to entice foreign-controlled industries to locate a branch operation on the Island. Instead it implemented a strategy of fostering small 'grass-roots' enterprises, industries linked to Cape Breton's resource base, and services – especially the improvement of tourist facilities and support for handicrafts and 'specialty products.' New projects during this period were conceived mainly by DEVCO staff, which under Kent gradually became composed predominantly of local residents.[150] Kent also instituted more rigorous feasibility and cost-benefit analyses of proposals.[151] This change in direction led to a range of primary, secondary, and service activities that individually were modest contributors to the employment rolls but impressive in their diversity and apparent appropriateness for Cape Breton circumstances. And, as noted by George, most of these ventures were still in operation at the time of his writing in the early 1980s.[152]

Underlying this change of direction was a realization that if development of the expensive imported variety wouldn't 'take' in the Cape Breton environment, efforts would have to be made to foster a home-grown variety. The analysis of the obstacles preventing such development from succeeding identified one key missing element in the local economy: entrepreneurship. The large coal and steel conglomerates that had dominated the Island's economy in the past had inhibited local entrepreneurship. DEVCO would correct that by assuming the role of entrepreneur itself and by nurturing local residents willing to start businesses in areas that DEVCO officials thought most appropriate to local circumstances (e.g., activities linked to the Island's resource base) and therefore most likely to succeed.[153] Success with this strategy required that DEVCO adopt an 'open posture' towards the community, and so efforts were made to solicit ideas for possible projects from the Island's residents while financial aid and management advice were proffered to a local clientele. 'Harmonious relations' were cultivated with the province and the municipalities, including the occasional joint project and DEVCO support for municipal initiatives.[154]

Yet, by itself, this change of direction on DEVCO's part was not enough to reverse the economic prospects of the Island. Kent has argued that such an approach could really succeed only in an overall economic environment that was supportive of such initiatives, especially a buoyant national economy and non-restrictive national economic policies. In addition, other important actors, agencies, and structures on the periphery – such as other federal departments, the province, and municipalities – had to be involved with the effort and capable of formulating and implementing appropriate policies. But this was not the case. Moreover, without direction, guide-lines, or supportive structures within which to operate, DEVCO's policies could be easily overturned with the arrival of new management or subtle changes in the mandate conferred on the corporation by the governing coalition at the centre. Thus, it is Kent's opinion that the corporation's effort to create and sustain small-scale 'grass-roots' economic activities has not been continued in the years since his departure in 1976.[155]

Even if Kent's small-scale, 'grass-roots' strategy of development was a modest success on its own terms (as argued by George), it was an approach particularly suited to rural development. The enhancement and diversification of primary-sector activities in the sparsely populated rural areas, even if undertaken in combination with an expansion of tourism-related economic activity, could not by itself stabilize and revitalize Cape Breton's economy. Such a strategy would have had to occur in conjunction with the renewal of Cape Breton's urban, industrial base if there was to be any long-term, substantive improvement in the Island's economic prospects. And here the fate of the steel industry on the Island was crucial. In Kent's opinion, while the concept of DEVCO may have been unique and full of potential for addressing the problems of the regional economy, that concept 'was really cut down at the knees with the second stage of the DOSCO crisis ... The federal government refused to have anything to do with the steel problem ... with very serious ill-effects on the way that problem was handled.'[156]

SYSCO

When Premier G.I. Smith announced on 23 November 1967 that the Province of Nova Scotia would purchase DOSCO's Cape Breton steel-works and maintain operations until at least April 1969, he also made it abundantly clear how uncomfortable his government was with the notion of being in the steel business, and he stressed that the measure merely allowed the province to buy time to examine the steelworks and give prospective buyers the necessary information. As for much-needed capital improvements to the plant, Smith stated that his government was interested only in short-term operation of the facilities.[157] In response to Smith's announcement, the president of the Steelworkers' Union called on the federal government to provide the necessary funds to rehabilitate the plant. Above all, the workers had had enough of private ownership. They were adamantly opposed to any reprivatization scheme as part of the steel plant's future.[158]

Over the next two to three years the new management of the now publicly owned Sydney Steel Corporation (SYSCO) made a concious decision to maximize production and profits while running down plant. And the corporation did surprisingly well in production, sales, and the profit-loss column. A number of factors worked in SYSCO's favour in the late 1960s: a rising demand for steel, which gave SYSCO a role as a residual supplier in central Canada; the decision by SIDBEC (the Quebec Crown corporation created from the purchase of Hawker-Siddeley's Contrecoeur facilities) to supply from Sydney for one year; the high level of output and the wage restraint exercised by the workers; and a secure supply of coke over two years at a low fixed price through arrangements worked out with DEVCO. So pleased was the provincial government with SYSCO's performance that it announced plans for a self-financing $84 million modernization program.[159]

This initial turn-around in the fortunes of steel-making in Nova Scotia, however, was short-lived. By 1972 the factors contributing to SYSCO's early success had reversed themselves and the corporation's fortunes declined accordingly. The steel plant once again became uncompetitive and redundant in central-Canadian steel markets; SIDBEC cancelled its contract; the steel workers ceased 'biting the bullet' and went on strike; and management's heavy hand and 'scorched earth' policy after 1967 came home to roost. A new Liberal government in Halifax reacted by putting the modernization of the aged Sydney facilities on hold and commissioning a 1973 study on the future of steel-making in Nova Scotia.[160]

By 1974, Premier Gerald Regan was pursuing a bold new strategy with regard to SYSCO. Regan now had designs on a new, large, internationally competitive steel complex for Cape Breton, to be financed and run by an international consortium of steel producers and the province. The CAN-STEEL mega-project was an attempt to use production and marketing linkages to step into international markets, rather than rely on a very shaky future as residual supplier to central Canada, or alternatively to narrow SYSCO's focus and 'down-size' its operations to match the needs of the small regional market.

The CANSTEEL Corporation was established by provincial statute in March 1975, with Regan as chairman.[161] Its aim was to do the preliminary work and promote the concept of a large new integrated steel complex on Cape Breton Island and to negotiate the participation of private investors in the project. It would then review and determine the future role of SYSCO within the new complex and advise the provincial government on subsequent decisions to modernize or expand the Sydney plant within this context. Within nine months a site had been selected and a consortium of European, American, and Canadian steel-makers brought together. Only a year later, in its second annual report, the corporation's directors expressed regret at the unfortunate downturn in the world steel industry that was creating uncertainty among steel-producers. Markets and prices were depressed; the Japanese were invading world steel markets; energy costs were high and increasing; the European steel industry was operating at half its capacity. Under such circumstances, 'no private company could afford the high risk of building major new steel capacity.' A decision on CANSTEEL would have to be delayed indefinitely.[162]

CANSTEEL would finally be declared dead by a new provincial government in 1978, leaving SYSCO to shoulder a growing burden of mounting deficits and too-long–forestalled modernization needs. The federal government was not innocent in this débâcle of grandiose vision; its prevarication on an investment commitment to SYSCO after the 1967 take-over greatly hindered the chances for mapping out and implementing a viable future for the Sydney plant. Fundamentally, at no time did Ottawa alter its view of steel operations in Cape Breton: 'SYSCO was a welfare employer and not a serious commercial steel producer.' It was treated as such by the federal government when it came to the question of extending federal loans and grants, or approval for SYSCO development plans.[163] In effect, while DREE was proclaiming the need to foster industrial growth centres as the centre-piece of its regional-development policy, the federal government had all but written off the only significant industrial complex in the region. As a result, steel-making in Nova Scotia would be brought precariously close to an ignomious end, with a corresponding reduction in security and life prospects for the people of Sydney and industrial Cape Breton, and to some extent the whole of eastern Nova Scotia.

Conclusion

In 1968 Pierre Trudeau made regional development a prominent item on the agenda he planned to pursue as prime minister. It was an issue that fit well with the new Liberal leader's 'national unity' discourse and with a political project aimed at bringing about a recentralization (or at least a stemming of the decentralization) of political power in Canada and the transformation of what was perceived to be a chaotic federal government into a much more efficient planning and decision-making mechanism. Reflecting the new government's more technocratic bent, the new regional-development policy heavily emphasized planning, co-ordination, and adjustment. It also shifted the focus from infrastructure improvements in rural areas to assistance to industry to locate in designated urban 'growth poles' within the Atlantic region.

The drawbacks to this new federal initiative in the regional-development field were apparent from the outset. The articulation of regional development with straightforwardly political and technocratic goals rather than economic and industrial goals handicapped the effective performance of a regional-development function in a number of ways. It led to the exclusion of provincial-government participation in regional policy-making, a potentially debilitating design, given the nature of Canadian federalism and the policy field in question. It also strongly suggested that regional development would be co-opted into political strategies largely unrelated to its ostensible purpose: the reduction of regional disparities through the enhancement of economic-development processes in clearly disadvantaged or lagging regions, primarily Atlantic Canada. Moreover, by ignoring the need to co-ordinate the new regional policy with national economic and industrial policies, the former could hardly have been expected to succeed. The discursive emphasis on planning and co-ordination remained just that; no effective structure or strategy was ever devised within the federal government to operationalize these policy goals. The federal bureaucracy and Liberal cabinet remained sharply divided on the need for, or wisdom of, a comprehensive strategy that would co-ordinate economic, industrial, and regional policies, leading eventually to governmental inertia, indecision, and paralysis in these policy fields.

Left without an overall 'game plan' linked to a national vision or strategy, DREE attempted to impose on the Atlantic region a pattern of development spending consistent with an under-theorized 'growth centre' approach, in the process gaining the political enmity of the provinces and the rural MPs whose constituencies were being left out of the action. Such adverse reaction to DREE contributed to the government's poor showing in the 1972 election and acted as a catalyst in a subsequent reorganization and reorientation that signalled the effective abandonment of DREE's original mandate – unattainable in any case, given the department's mode of insertion into the federal bureaucracy and the balance of political forces at the centre – in favour of a much more limited role, to be carried out in close association with individual provinces. No longer at the forefront of the government's political strategies and policy priorities, the department and its regional-development function were shunted to the margins of the state agenda, simultaneously relegating the Atlantic periphery and its concerns to a more customary position on the fringes of the federal government's horizons.

All this is not to say that the state reduced its overall presence in the economy of the Atlantic periphery. On the contrary, an ever-greater amount of public resources found their way there. Increases in equalization payments, income security expenditures, and intergovernmental fiscal transfers for health, education, and social services considerably expanded the size and influence of the public sector in the regional economy. This massive increase in welfare-state expenditures transformed the social composition of the periphery by vastly increasing the size of the public-sector work-force and enlarging an urban middle class of managers, technicians, professionals, and white-collar workers generally. In Nova Scotia, Metropolitan Halifax – its economy based on governmental, defence, financial, health-care, and educational institutions – benefited enormously from this trend. Other areas of the province, more dependent upon declining heavy industries or primary-sector activities that were rapidly shedding labour, did less well. In these locales a growing number of unemployed and impoverished were becoming more dependent on temporary or seasonal job-creation programs and social-welfare payments. The problem in such areas was to stabilize the existing employment base while diversifying the local economy to provide a broader range of income-earning opportunities. Did state policies adequately address this development conundrum? In the context of relentless capitalist competition, stabilizing the employment base in rural areas dependent on primary-sector activities meant rationalization and modernization schemes to increase efficiency and productivity. Regional-development programs in agriculture and forestry had this as their primary objective. But it could be only one part of a broader rural-development strategy, since, alone, modernization schemes also tended to exacerbate employment problems.

State policies with regard to areas suffering from dependence upon declining industries were more problematic. In Nova Scotia DEVCO and SYSCO were state responses to a crisis situation in Nova Scotia's coal and steel industries, which underpinned the economy of eastern Nova Scotia. The onset of the crisis itself was in part the result of an earlier unwillingness on the part of the state to do more than subsidize DOSCO through grants and subventions. By the mid-1960s coal and steel operations had been allowed to deteriorate badly in relation to industrial competitors, and finally DOSCO announced an end to its Nova Scotia operations. The subsequent nationalizations divided the assets of what had been an integrated industrial complex between federal and provincial governments. Thereafter, provincial mismanagement and fiscal weakness, and federal hedging and scepticism regarding steel-making in Nova Scotia, undercut the chances for success of any planned rehabilitation of facilities. Given the destabilization and uncertainty of the existing employment base this situation induced, DEVCO's pursuit of a more diversified economy for Cape Breton – premised initially upon a disastrous policy of give-aways to footloose industries and then on an insufficient strategy of stimulating rural-based economic activities – could not hope to accomplish its objectives. If the state mismanaged the problem of industrial Cape Breton and left it to fester, the effect of development policies elsewhere in Nova Scotia was to heighten contradictions and disparities within the provincial economy. The growth-centre approach adopted by DREE directed expenditures to areas that already had relatively high growth rates. This self-serving and opportunistic strategy had the 'beneficial' quality of allowing state élites to associate themselves and their policies with 'success' without having to demonstrate the extent to which state policies were actually responsible for this success. Conversely, problem areas that were declining or economically stagnant could be justifiably ignored, thus side-stepping the risk (or certainty) of policy failure. The result in development terms, of course, was to worsen regional disparities within the province itself, revealing the hollowness of planners' assurances that what was good for the growth centres was good for everyone.[164]

Finally, regional-development planning and policy, such as it was, remained heavily dependent on private economic power. This influenced policy and program design such that the interests of private capital were served first and foremost. It also made the state's attempt to counter the spatial development patterns brought about in the first instance by the operation of the market subject to corporate investment decisions that were in the last instance determined by that very mechanism: a somewhat self-defeating cycle. Not surprisingly, those industries that were *already* located on the periphery as a matter of choice (primarily resource-based) became the chief recipients and prime beneficiaries of the state's industrial incentives and infrastructure expenditures, leaving the industrial structure of the periphery unchanged.

As we have seen, then, prior to 1975 the orientation of state élites at the centre towards the economic problems of the Atlantic periphery was rooted in the Liberal party's 1960s social-welfare policy agenda. Regional policies and programs were both sheltered and limited by the underlying policy compromises made necessary by the social and political composition of the Liberal governments of this period. This welfarist approach to the periphery was increasingly supplemented, and to some extent displaced, by a more technocratic reformist approach that, through the use of various measures, aimed to expand and diversify private-sector economic activity and restructure the economy of the periphery so as to lessen its dependence on subsidies. However, this new strategy never became the *primary* response of state élites at the centre to the development conundrums posed by the Atlantic periphery; it remained limited and ad hoc in its application because of the failure of state élites to arrive at a new set of policy compromises that would permit the development and implementation of a full-blown regional industrial strategy (a logical and necessary prerequisite for comprehensive regional planning). The upshot for regional development policy was its isolation from national economic and industrial policies. DREE's developmental technocrats, unable to carry out their new approach within the context of a co-ordinated state effort guided by a comprehensive regional plan, could not succeed in altering the basic industrial structure of the periphery, and therefore the fundamental basis for ongoing regional economic disparities between centre and periphery.

The 1968–75 period also offers a good example of the pitfalls of leaving policy development to the 'experts' in the bureaucracy, a common outcome of party politics in Canada. It would appear to be highly unlikely that new policy directions will 'emerge' from bureaucratic overviews of existing departmental priorities and policies; nor is it probable that a 'consensus' on policy will be reached by merely aggregating and distilling the internally generated opinions of the various departments of the bureaucracy. Yet this is precisely what the government hoped for from the 1974–5 *priorities exercise*. It should have come as no surprise that bureaucratic élites would opt for the status quo, given the shared interests of line departments and the clientele served by their programs, and in light of the unwillingness of most of the upper echelons of the federal bureaucracy to seriously contemplate or countenance a more interventionist, proactive, or 'dirigiste' role for the state in the economy. Thus, when Trudeau, shortly after the imposition of controls, attempted to begin a public debate on industrial strategy, corporatism, state intervention, and in general the future role of government in the economy, the sharp and hostile business reaction might have been predicted. Needless to say, upon gauging reaction to Trudeau's comments, the prime minister's political advisers recommended that no more be said on the subject. [165]

As for the Nova Scotia government, after 1970 its development role became deeply enmeshed with, and therefore shared in the failure of, federal policies. This state of affairs was ensured by the political and economic impact of a number of industrial crises and imbroglios in the later 1960s that were either left unincorporated, or else were directly precipitated by the development strategies and agencies of the Stanfield era. The DOSCO crisis and the heavy-water and Clairtone fiascos forced an unwilling provincial state to undertake direct intervention when and where it did not want to or plan to, and for which it was wholly unprepared and ill-equipped in terms of strategic, organizational, technical, and fiscal resources. The collapse of the Stanfield approach, however, was not replaced with any new policy direction at the provincial level, but instead with a vague and shallow technocratic appeal that slipped easily into dependence on federal initiatives and expenditures, and compliance with federal policies.

The provincial state during this period was plagued by poor policy co-ordination and development planning. As with state élites at the centre, there was strong resistance within the provincial-state apparatus to any internal restructuring of its agencies and operations away from a traditional narrow client focus towards a comprehensive spatial-development approach. Since DREE was without the backing of a comprehensive regional strategy or the mechanism for a co-ordinated federal effort, the general tendency was for discrete agreements to be reached with provincial line departments – and later through joint committees of federal and provincial officials – that likewise remained unencumbered by the strictures or guide-lines that would have been conferred by a comprehensive development strategy at the provincial level.

But provincial incapacities in this regard must also be traced to party and electoral politics in Nova Scotia. The demise of the development agencies and approaches associated with the Stanfield era did not give way to an alternative development strategy under the Regan government, largely because that government failed to engage in the construction of a viable political alliance around any such alternative, instead remaining satisfied with downgrading the former government's approach and substituting for it a vision of grandiose megaprojects as the source of future prosperity for Nova Scotians. Such projects offered the enticing prospect of the intervention of large-scale private capital with its huge investment potential to solve the province's development problems. While in part a politics of escapism and diversion, this way of proceeding also permitted the premier to pursue a personal agenda that skirted his government's administrative and political weaknesses, thus obviating the need for significant internal reforms. The failure of this development (and political) strategy was ordained by the onset of recessionary conditions in the mid-1970s, which produced sharply diminished interest on the part of large-scale monopoly capital in investments of this nature on the Atlantic periphery.

Ironically, the rising stock of resource commodities – and particularly the energy staple – would not only keep Regan's vision of energy-related megaprojects alive, but, with a new energy crisis looming, make them increasingly central to the politics of regional development.

8 The Demise of a National Policy: The Reconstitution of Regional Development, 1976–84

Opposition within the federal state to dealing with regional development as a priority problem intricately bound up with national economic and industrial policy – and therefore requiring a coherent and long-term development strategy – so narrowed the state response to the problem, and so limited the co-ordination of state policies towards the goal of reducing regional disparities, that little overall effect was discernible as the result of state programs in the regional-development field. Within a relatively few years, the initial vision of what the state should and could do in terms of a regional-development function had withered on the bureaucratic vine, starved of sustenance and support by the state apparatus within which it was encased. As a result the gains and concessions won for residents of the periphery through the creation of corporations and agencies such as DEVCO, SYSCO, and DREE in fact turned out to be quite modest when considered from the perspective of what was actually necessary if the state was to play an effective development role on the periphery. That this shortcoming was in fact recognized by state élites charged with the management of this policy field is suggested by the various strategic shifts and agency restructurings that occurred during the 1968–75 period. This is not to say, however, that the substance of the changes made to state structures and policies was directly related to, or functionally congruent with the needs and exigencies of economic development on the periphery. Rather, these changes were shaped by the clash of interests over state policy, both without and within the state.

In retrospect, it is now apparent that the mid-1970s was a watershed period in which fundamental realignments and adjustments were occurring internationally and within Canada. The appearance of stagflation in the industrialized nations at this time eroded Keynesian assumptions about the potential for unlimited, stable growth achieved through proper state management of the economy. A simultaneous fate befell the notion of a continuously growing pie available for redistribution to lagging regions. In these new circumstances state élites in Canada sought to assess the nature of the change that was taking place internationally and its policy implications for the domestic economy. Needless to say, these broader economic changes, and the ensuing process of redefining the proper role for the state in the economy and restructuring its intervention, necessarily impinged upon regional development, both as an issue and as a policy field. The upshot was that if the state as constituted was incompatible with the performance of a regional-development function as originally conceived, and the governing coalition could not resolve itself upon the necessity, or even the desirability, of effectively addressing this incompatibility of structure and function so as to attain the normative policy goal of regional development, then the issue and policy field itself would have to be reconstructed and the mandate for state activity in this area redefined. In short, normative policy goals would be brought into closer conformity with the reality of state performance in this area.

National Politics and the Federal Retreat from Regional Development, 1976–9

What Role for the State after Controls?

As noted previously, the imposition of wage and price controls in the fall of 1975 shunted aside the results of the priorities exercise undertaken by the PCO in 1974–5, and along with it the National Industrial and Regional Development (NIRD) memorandum, that was one of the sixteen priority areas outlined in the so-called big picture that was the object of the exercise. As a result, departmental policies and programs, including those of DREE, largely went on as before, but within a more constrained fiscal milieu. In fact, wage and price controls did nothing more than offer a 'breathing space' to state élites within which the impact of recent events and developments could be considered and strategies for the post-controls period plotted. In 1976 a document entitled 'The Way Ahead' emerged from the 'DM'-10' committee of deputy ministers formed for the purposes of economic co-ordination during the controls period. (A year later a philosophically similar position paper on post-incomes control society – 'Agenda for Cooperation' – was released.) While 'The Way Ahead' professed to seek a middle ground between economic efficiency and social justice, at the very least it represented in its thinking a 'strategic retreat' from what it perceived as the social-policy thrust of the 1965–75 period. It suggested that the concern with inequality would henceforth have to be more integrated with the pursuit of economic goals, and that this should be accomplished in policy terms after a process of public consultation aimed at the formation of a consensus on policy direction.[1] A greater role for the state itself was played down; reminiscent of the 'you're not getting older' line of product pitch, the new credo for Ottawa would be 'doing less, but doing it better.' In the wake of controls, a shift in the set of compromises that underpinned state policies appeared to be under way. 'Regional development' would have to be redefined accordingly.

Soon after 'The Way Ahead' the government revitalized the Interdepartmental Committee on Trade and Industrial Policy (ICTIP), which included the deputy ministers of all economic departments. Chaired by ITC deputy minister Gordon Osbaldeston, ICTIP was given a mandate to link Canada's commercial policy with an industrial-policy thrust made urgent by the increasing evident weakness of the country's manufacturing sector. At the same time Osbaldeston and ITC officials were also working closely with their minister, Jean Chrétien, in developing a sectoral strategy for ITC. This strategy led to 'Enterprise '77,' a consultative exercise involving interviews with 5,000 industrial firms about their 'needs,' followed by a memorandum to cabinet proposing the inauguration of twenty-three sectoral task forces as the 'centre-piece' of a new industrial-development thrust.[2] After extensive intergovernmental consultations were held on the matter, committees composed of representatives of management, labour, academics, and governments were convened, the first part of a two-phase operation (the Tier 1 and Tier 2 committees) aimed at producing a comprehensive report and recommendations on new policy initiatives in the area of industrial development.[3] After the expenditure of much effort, however, the exercise produced no consensus among the relevant groups on what should be done.[4]

State actions such as these expressed the growing concern of state élites with the health and structure of Canadian industry, the needs of business in a more inhospitable, international economy, and the Liberal government's search for the most 'suitable' and 'efficient' role for the state after wage and price controls. In addition, the growing influence of neo-conservative criticism of the growth of government led to the adoption of a more restrictive fiscal regime. After making a political commitment to restraint at the 1978 Bonn economic summit, Trudeau without prior consultation with cabinet colleagues announced that his government would institute a Draconian budget cut of $2 billion.[5] The throne speech and budget that followed Trudeau's announcement referred to 'laying the basis for future growth' and continued with the theme of neo-conservative restraint.[6]

As a result of all these pressures, a new central agency was inaugurated in November 1978: the Board of Economic Development Ministers (BEDM), to be supported by the new Ministry of State for Economic Development (MSED). The task of the BEDM was to identify 'the most appropriate means by which the Government of Canada may have a beneficial influence on the development of industries and regional economies in Canada.' It was also to oversee 'the integration of programs and activities providing direct support to industry including their coordination with other policies and programs.'[7] The newly appointed president of the BEDM, Robert Andras, described his modest role this way: 'It will be my role, and my Ministry's, working with the Board, to review and advise upon the spending of resources, from the departments involved, in the areas of enterprise development, employment, regional expansion, resource industries, and research and development.'[8]

The BEDM was operative for only a few months before an election brought a new government to power. But its creation suggests that both economic and fiscal circumstances were inciting experiments on the part of state élites into some means or mechanism to co-ordinate state policies in related areas and combine this function with the regulation of state expenditures. However, whether the intention was simply to get 'the biggest bang for their buck,' as one minister put it, or to develop a more effective kind of 'fire-fighting' (the rescue of plants or industries in trouble), as asserted by Richard French, a co-ordinated industrial strategy with both sectoral and regional components does not appear to have been envisaged as an objective or even a possibility.[9]

Reorienting DREE, Phase II: The Lessard Review

It is apparent that the shifting focus of concern within the government between 1976 and 1978 had some resonance within DREE. Just as regional development had not been immune to the priorities of national economic policy at the beginning of the decade, so DREE now assumed a reduced and reshaped profile within the context of a new state agenda in the latter half of the 1970s: the need for expenditure restraint and increased productivity and economic efficiency as a means of reining in inflation and restoring the competitiveness of Canadian industry abroad. Thus, in its 1978 annual report, DREE reserved its greatest expression of concern for the vulnerability of a number of Quebec industries to increasing competition from abroad and 'the apparent softness of the Ontario economy.' In light of these new developments, it was felt that a full-scale review of DREE policies and programs was necessary: 'another stage in the evolution of regional development policy.'[10]

While the 1973 departmental review undertaken by DREE had been motivated and shaped by the need to alleviate federal-provincial tensions by allowing for a greater variety of DREE activities within individual provinces as well as throughout the country, and through closer intergovernmental co-operation in formulating and administering DREE programs, the 1978 review reflected DREE's decreasing emphasis on policies addressing inequality between regions and the higher priority accorded by the department to the need for Canadian industry to be competitive internationally (the traditional concern of the departments of Finance and Industry). The review sized up the situation in this way: the resource-rich West was prospering (thanks to high commodity prices in the 1970s); the relative poverty of Atlantic Canada was virtually unchanged (a state of affairs the authors of the review characterized as 'seemingly impermeable to government policy'); the industrial heartland in Quebec and Ontario was experiencing problems. Quebec industries were facing difficult structural problems and were badly in need of rationalization and modernization. The province was plagued by high unemployment, poor productivity, lack of investment, and the decline of the Montreal urban area. Nor could Ontario's growth any longer be taken for granted. High energy costs and the westward movement of investment capital were weakening the province's economic performance, and a weakened Ontario was 'a matter of national concern ... [with] negative implications for the whole country.' These problems of industrial adjustment had to be met and overcome. In particular, the Ontario government's attempts to stimulate its slow-growth areas now had to be replaced by conscious attention to the overall development of that province.[11]

DREE's caution to the government of Ontario is revealing: in effect, the federal agency given the mandate to reduce regional disparities in Canada was admonishing a provincial government for directing scarce resources to this end when more important economic matters demanded its attention! It appears that in the late 1970s DREE was indeed in the process of adopting a significantly altered perception of its own role. The review recommended that thenceforth DREE should be highly selective in its support programs, tying them to specific investment opportunities that proffered strong potential for growth and employment. The DREE minister was in agreement with the review. Lessard categorically stated that his department was not 'a welfare agency,' and that its efforts in each region would be directed to nurturing 'those areas and prospects with the best potential for development.'[12] Over time, the vast untapped economic potential in lagging regions (optimistically described in numerous DREE background papers) would produce self-sustaining regional economies. Having been armoured in this way by his own bureaucrats with 'the "no cost" myth,'[13] Lessard approved the departmental review and informed his fellow cabinet ministers that DREE would seek to adjust its programs in accordance with it. In early 1979 a new legislative package based on the review was submitted to cabinet for approval, but it was decided to delay any new policy directions until after the upcoming general election.[14]

Besides such changes in DREE's official understanding of its own role and mode of operation, there was also a revival at this time of the department's role as a player in the federal government's struggle against Quebec separatism. With rising unemployment in Quebec in 1976, Montreal-area MPs were pressing the DREE minister to again designate that city under DREE's industrial incentive program. But resistance within cabinet to the redesignation of Montreal was considerable, with fundamental questions posed about DREE's mandate and its role in alleviating regional disparities. This resistance broke down, however, in the wake of the outcome of the November 1976 Quebec provincial election. With the separatist Parti Québécois in power in Quebec, Lessard, aided by the support of seven Montreal-area cabinet ministers, was able to win concurrence on the need to once more designate Montreal under the RDIA program.[15] The result was the same as in 1970: a sharp increase in the share of DREE expenditures going to Quebec at the expense of the Atlantic region.[16]

Other 'Regional' Policies

If DREE was 'changing its stripes' and redefining its role so as to downplay the need to redress regional inequalities in favour of the renewal of Canada's industrial heartland, it was also apparent that the federal government's regional policy was less and less predicated upon DREE expenditures and activities per se. A declining share of the federal budget was being allocated to DREE as the 1970s progressed (from 2 per cent per annum in 1970–1 to 1 per cent in 1980–1).[17] In 1977, a federal program that did not involve DREE at all – investment tax credits with higher rates earmarked for economically depressed regions – was announced. And in the November 1978 budget, an employment tax credit was introduced.[18] Of course, the federal government's social programs continued to be enormously important. Lithwick has estimated that in 1977–8 alone the 'regional' component of the Unemployment Insurance program (UI) delivered $900 million in benefits to individuals in the five easternmost provinces, an amount 80 per cent larger than DREE's entire budget for that year.[19]

The importance to the region of UI can be gauged from the reaction of Atlantic region MPs to government attempts in the fall of 1978 to tighten up eligibility requirements for the program, with the ostensible purpose of lessening 'abuse of the system.' Bill C-14 would have rendered thousands of seasonally employed workers in Atlantic Canada ineligible for benefits. The reaction of the Atlantic caucuses of both the governing Liberals and the opposition Progressive Conservatives was to launch an intense lobbying effort within their respective parties against the changes. When employment minister Bud Cullen remained unswayed, and Atlantic region MPs met with resistance within the Liberal and Conservative caucuses from central-Canadian and Western MPs, they threatened to break party ranks on the issue. In the end, all party leaders in Parliament accepted the need for changes to the legislation to allow for regionally varied requirements for UI eligibility. When interviewed later about their stand, both the Liberal and Conservative members from the Atlantic region admitted that such an impressive show of solidarity in pursuing an issue to 'the brink' – as they had done on Bill C-14 – effectively could be done only very rarely, and only on issues of critical importance to their constituents![20]

There is good reason to argue, then, that DREE was not the federal government's main response to the problem of uneven regional development. The real pillars of regional policy remained the equalization payments that made possible the similar provision of basic public services in every province, and the social-welfare and income-security programs that had become essential to the Atlantic region's economy. In his study of the impact of the welfare state on Canadian federalism, Keith Banting stressed this point:

Transferring responsibility for welfare to the federal government does not necessarily produce programs that are more redistributive between income classes, but it does transform income security into a powerful instrument of redistribution between regions ... National income security programs redistribute inter-regionally because greater proportions of elderly, unemployed and needy people, and children, are found in some regions, and because revenues to finance those programs are raised disproportionately from different regions. The resulting net inter-regional redistribution through income security is equal to, or greater than that achieved through the more publicized system of equalization grants, and income security payments have become a critical part of the standard of living and the general economy in poor regions ... *The income security programs of the federal government represent a compromise, not only between high-income and low-income Canadians, but also between those of high- and low-income regions* [emphasis added].[21]

As an indication of a popular awareness of this reality within the poorer regions of the country, Banting cites studies that show that, as a group, individuals in Atlantic Canada and Quebec are more supportive of social welfare programs than are other Canadians.[22] Certainly, the stand taken by Atlantic region MPs on Bill C-14 illustrates an awareness on the part of the periphery's political representatives of the essential nature of the 'compromise' inherent in the operation of income-security programs, a point undoubtedly driven home to political élites at the centre during this episode, and tacitly acknowledged by them in their decision to relent on the issue.

The Political Alternatives to the Liberals

What were the strategic alternatives to this approach to regional development in the late 1970s? The Conservative party after Stanfield (who resigned as party leader in 1976 and was replaced by Joe Clark) was quickly gravitating to the 'new conservatism' that identified the big, interventionist state as the source of Canada's economic malaise. The solution proffered was a return to free enterprise, 'down-sized' government, and a stiff dose of fiscal restraint. During the 1976 leadership race and convention, the party was widely portrayed in the media as split between a moderate left and a radical right. George Perlin's study of the convention delegates suggests that the shift to a moderately progressive populism that accompanied Diefenbaker's rise in 1957–8 had become by the mid-1970s a conservative populism, one distinctly hostile to federal-government intervention, referred to by some as 'Liberal statism,' and much more favourably disposed towards the further decentralization of power to the provinces. Perlin's analysis of the leadership candidates' positions suggests that on these essentials there was no ideological split within the party: both the 'Red Tory' and 'right wing' candidates in 1976 were in general agreement on the need to significantly reduce the role of the central state in the economy.[23]

Certainly the Conservatives under Joe Clark were in favour of less government intervention in the economy, the privatization of many Crown corporations, and the reduction of government deficits, and on these matters they were in the mainstream of neo-conservative thinking. Moreover, this advocacy of a smaller, less interventionist government in Ottawa was articulated with a vision of federalism that extolled the virtues of regional diversity and a greater decentralization of power to the provinces (also a rallying cry of conservatives in the United States).[24] This general ideological predilection in favour of 'less government,' however, did not translate into a clearly articulated alternative in the field of regional development policy. Throughout the 1979 election campaign that brought the Progressive Conservatives briefly to power, Clark insisted that 'the fight against regional disparity will be central to our policy as it is central to the Progressive Conservatives' concept of national unity.' Notwithstanding this commitment to the goal of reducing regional disparities, the new DREE minister in the Clark government would not be included in the inner cabinet where decisions on priorities would be taken.[25]

Though somewhat more enthusiastic in their adherence to the popular tenets of economic conservatism, the Conservatives remained a brokerage party like the Liberals, with weak internal policy-formation processes and an inclination to 'fudge' on issues as much as possible so as to remain inoffensive to as broad a swath of the electorate as possible. In the 1979 election they used the general theme of 'time for a change' and sought to focus public attention on the Liberal record. In addition, numerous segments of the population were targeted and individual policies designed to appeal to them.[26] The results of the 1979 election gave the Conservatives a rather weak mandate, however; they garnered only 36 per cent of the vote, with little representation in Quebec and no significant gains in the Atlantic provinces. It was sufficient, none the less, to win them a minority government, though one fated to be among the shortest in Canadian history.

As for the NDP, the imposition of wage controls in 1975 suddenly made that party again relevant to organized labour in Canada. Certainly it set in motion a period of strategic rethinking on labour's part that would lead to a strengthening of ties – at the élite level – between the NDP and the

Canadian Labour Congress (CLC). Labour's response to the imposition of controls was initially protest, followed by a tentative movement towards tripartism, and then, after internal resistance towards the latter orientation, a closer relationship with the NDP and a more concerted effort to enhance that party's electoral fortunes.[27] However, it seems that the executive decision to do more to draw union votes into the NDP by using 'top-down mobilizational techniques' bore little fruit in the 1979 election. The NDP increased its popular vote, but only by 2.7 per cent over 1974, and it actually lost two seats in the industrial core of Ontario.[28] Once again the party's electoral strategy was aimed at broadening its appeal to accommodate all voters dissatisfied with the government. Its vision of a mixed economy where public ownership would be used as a 'tool' by the state, and its emphasis on 'cooperation, contact, and negotiation ... between public and private sectors in industrial planning,'[29] differed little in its essentials from the then-current Liberal government's approach. This demonstrated just how close to the mainstream Canada's 'democratic socialist' party had moved, and how little it had to offer in terms of an imaginative, innovative, socialist alternative to the major parties.

Energy Megaprojects and the Reorganization for Economic Development, 1980–4

The Liberal Phoenix and the NEP

The fate of the Clark government has been well documented by Jeffrey Simpson in *Discipline of Power*. Image problem's and Clark's determination to follow through on a host of ill-considered election promises placed the government in trouble soon after the election. In particular, the government's energy policy – which tilted sharply towards the interests of the producing provinces and the private sector – proved a minefield for the government. Carrying through this policy orientation proved extremely difficult. Agreement could not be reached with the main producing province, Alberta, on a taxation and revenue regime, while another Conservative government in Ontario remained adamantly opposed to any sharp increase in oil prices as well as to other aspects of the government's energy policy (such as the privatization of the state oil company, Petro-Canada).[30] Before winter a second 'energy crisis' brought on by the Iranian Revolution had further jacked-up world oil prices and raised to a fever pitch public concern about such issues as security of supply, prices, and the need for greater domestic control over Canada's energy resources.

By the time the Clark government was set to bring down its first budget in December 1979, it was badly trailing the Liberals in the public-opinion polls. Then, in an unlikely sequence of events, the government was defeated in the House and Pierre Trudeau revoked his retirement announcement and led the Liberals into the subsequent winter election. As had not been the case in 1979, energy policy was a key issue in the 1980 campaign.[31] And as so often had been the case in the past, the political discourse was once again being shaped along regional lines. The Conservatives were branded as sell-outs to Alberta's Premier Lougheed; in contrast, the Liberals presented themselves as protectors of the 'Canadian national interest.' In this way the politics of energy became a structured contest between the national interest and the selfish demands of regionalism. With the political right neatly conjoined with the regions, the stage was set for a political realignment that pitted a regionalist right against a nationalist centre-left coalition, a situation highly favourable to the Liberals.[32] They were returned to power with a comfortable majority, though their elimination as a major party in western Canada was confirmed and reinforced.

During its period in opposition, the Liberal caucus had renewed its seemingly interminable debate over economic and industrial strategy, but this time the debate was egged on by the perception that the party had erred in drifting too far to the right in the late 1970s. This perception found reflection in the nationalist and interventionist agenda adopted by the Liberals in the 1980 election campaign. In Trudeau's most important policy speech of the campaign, he laid out the basic ingredients of what would later become the National Energy Program (NEP). In addition to commitments to expand the role of Petro-Canada and to bring about greater Canadian ownership and control of the energy sector, Trudeau also asserted that energy would become part of a larger economic strategy and the core of any industrial or regional-development approach. This assertion was reinforced in the throne speech that followed the election.[33] In October 1980, the NEP was introduced in Parliament. Among its provisions were a number of items of immediate and direct relevance to the Atlantic region, the site of significant new finds of offshore oil and gas.

The *Canada Oil and Gas Act* was designed to accelerate the development of frontier oil and gas resources. It also reserved a 25 per cent interest for the Crown in all permits and licences, required 50 per cent Canadian ownership to obtain a production licence, and gave the federal government authority over the timing and pace of development and issues such as procurement. The *Petroleum Incentives Program* (PIP), what energy minister Marc Lalonde referred to as 'the richest fiscal incentives in the world,' replaced depletion allowances with cash grants tied to Canadian ownership for exploration costs – up to 80 per cent on Canada Lands in the North and offshore and 35 per cent in the provinces. An extension of the gas-pipeline system to be known as the *Trans-Quebec Maritimes pipeline* (TQM) would carry western gas to Quebec City and the Maritimes.[34]

Obviously the NEP had far-reaching consequences for the level of economic activity on the Atlantic periphery. Moreover, its economic impact would not be limited to the sudden influx of petro-dollars associated with an expanded exploration program. As explained by the deputy minister of finance shortly after the NEP's introduction, the government's energy policy also tied in with the construction of a broader economic and industrial agenda, 'the core of the state's approach to economic revitalization.'[35] In 1980–1, a major and multidimensional policy initiative was under way in Ottawa. Its effects would soon become manifest in the field of regional-development policy, as well as in the strategies, both political and economic, of provincial state élites on the periphery.

The Megaproject Strategy

In the summer and fall of 1980, two contending positions on economic and industrial strategy were vying for the approval of the federal cabinet. One proposal from Industry minister Herb Gray advocated the expansion of FIRA's authority to allow it to actively monitor and regulate the performance of foreign-owned subsidiaries in Canada as a means of improving the research and development capacities and export capability of the Canadian manufacturing sector. A much less interventionist policy paper prepared by economic development minister Bud Olsen favoured instead the traditional emphasis on exploiting Canada's bounty in natural resources, an alluring alternative (once again) given the favourable terms of trade at the beginning of the 1980s for resource commodities.[36]

It was the latter perspective that was reflected in the NEP and later in the statement on economic-development strategy that accompanied the November 1981 budget.[37] The NEP signalled the importance accorded by the government to the energy sector, and its intention to use oil and gas exploration and development as a lever to 'rebalance' fiscal, economic, and ultimately political power in Canada between governments and

within the private sector (mainly to the detriment of the western producing provinces and foreign-owned oil corporations).[38] In the strategy
document accompanying the budget (*Economic Development for Canada
in the* 1980's), the government asserted that natural resources would be
the engine of growth for Canada in the 1980s and that the process and
pace of resource-led development could be managed so as to derive
maximum economic benefits, including increased manufacturing to
supply the equipment needed for the exploitation of natural resources.
The government's intention was to harness these industrial benefits for
the purpose of aiding and abetting regional and industrial development.
In effect, the federal government was proposing to 'back into' an industrial strategy from the supply side.

At the beginning of the 1980s, the Liberal strategy had much to
commend it. The government assumed that the shift in the terms of
international trade that had increased the price of resource products
relative to manufactured goods was not a temporary phenomenon. Moreover, the proposed energy megaprojects within Canada had a favourable
geographical distribution, and so would lend themselves as instruments
for furthering regional-development goals. By allowing the government
to neatly conflate the demands of regional and industrial development,
the megaproject strategy had solved a major policy conundrum that had
plagued Ottawa for more than a decade. It also opened the way for a
major reorganization of regional-development structures and policies.

The Demise of DREE

Prior to the Liberal defeat in 1979, it appears that DREE had gradually
become even more of a pariah within the federal state apparatus than it
had been during the early years of its operation. By the late 1970s
hostility towards DREE originated not only with those bureaucratic élites
who were opposed to the very concept of a DREE, but also with political
élites at the federal level who were increasingly resentful of the lack of
political credit for federal expenditures on DREE programming that was
being delivered exclusively by the provinces, as well as with others
frustrated at being shut out of what had become a highly bureaucratized
process of decision-making. The origins of these complaints can be
discerned in the program design and delivery arrangements in place since
1974.

The General Development Agreement format, which was the centre-
piece of the 1973–4 departmental reorganization, removed the action of

program formulation and implementation from federal to provincial offices. At the same time most of the decision-making about DREE's role and activities was removed from 'political' to 'administrative' hands; that is, to joint committees made up of DREE and provincial development officials. The obligatory references to the reduction of regional disparities would surface from time to time in the rhetoric of the politicians, and provisions would be made for interdepartmental involvement and co-operation, but in reality these were little more than gestures, largely devoid of substantive content. Fundamentally, it was teams of bureaucrats working at the provincial level that now controlled the process of designing and implementing regional-development agreements. Therefore, earlier notions of *regional* development were now all but discarded for practical purposes; the focus of DREE programs after 1974 would be synonymous with the narrower but more politically palatable notion of *provincial* development. There would be nary a hint of regional planning or interprovincial co-ordination under GDA agreements. Only bilateral committees of officials existed, assuring that all agreements would be provincial in focus and in scope.[39]

The GDA arrangements had been shaped in the aftermath of the 1972 election by a chastened and contrite Trudeau government that had endured sharp and sustained criticism from the provinces regarding what they perceived as a unilateralist DREE barely tolerant of provincial sensibilities or jurisdictional rights – an approach, the provinces argued, that was not in keeping with the previous operation of federal regional-development programs or with the general tenets and principles of co-operative federalism. In subsequent years, however, a separatist government would come to power in Quebec, relations between the western provinces and Ottawa would become increasingly embittered as a result of disagreements over resource regulation and taxation, and the two orders of government would become entangled in a sustained struggle over constitutional reform. By the end of the decade, the climate of federal-provincial relations was markedly more hostile and competitive than it had been at the beginning of the decade. Within this context, the provincial focus and provincially controlled delivery mechanism of DREE programs under the GDA formula were increasingly irksome to federal-government ministers and officials who saw no political credit accruing to Ottawa whatsoever for DREE expenditures.[40]

A second problem with the GDA format was the extent of bureaucratic dominance over decision-making and the resulting restrictions on access to information for politicians and public. Under the GDA, DREE provincial officers and their provincial-government counterparts had almost complete control over program formulation and implementation. According to Donald Savoie, who undertook a detailed study of the operation of the Canada/New Brunswick GDA, the involvement of the DREE minister was usually limited to briefing notes on politically sensitive agreements (after a joint management committee had decided on the project); provincial cabinet ministers would get in on the process after the broad outlines of projects had been agreed upon, but were generally of the opinion that the process diluted their departmental authority; and MPs, MLAs, and interest groups were shut out of the process – as a rule they were neither invited to submit representations nor consulted on their opinions during formulation (thus clearing the way for the bureaucrats to engage in 'serious' planning).[41] Attempts to side-step the GDA bureaucracy by making representations through cabinet ministers' offices – a tactic often used to get around bureaucratic bottlenecks, in particular by government MPs and MLAs – met with little success.[42]

In the case of DREE after 1974, then, 'decentralization' could not be equated with a more democratic or somehow less bureaucratic process. And while this was a situation with which DREE and provincial bureaucrats were quite content, it ultimately eroded political accountability, routinized initiatives into familiar patterns, and increasingly annoyed politicians and other interests who desired greater input into decision-making, or simply more access to information. 'Freezing out' the political process made DREE more unpopular; it invited charges that the department had become 'an expensive, inefficient and secretive bureaucracy' that ought to be dismantled.[43]

After the Liberals were returned to power in 1980, the new DREE minister, Pierre de Bané, called for a major policy review. De Bane was a harsh critic of DREE as it was constituted in 1980. He publicly informed his cabinet colleagues of the need for its complete overhaul, including a much greater injection of federal funds if there were to be any reasonable expectations of DREE's alleviating regional disparities. He even publically rebuked finance minister Allan MacEachen for holding down DREE's budget to what De Bane considered an unacceptably low level.[44]

De Bane's vision for DREE and his understanding of the department's mandate contrasted sharply with the vision of his Liberal predecessor in the portfolio. Indeed, the new minister's re-emphasis on the department's role in alleviating regional disparities between the poorest and most well-off of regions was much closer to the view of DREE expressed by Trudeau in the late 1960s than to the role the department had actually been playing in the intervening years. When De Bane rejected the internal review submitted to him by his own department because of its status quo orientation, he was declaring that he would not be satisfied with marginal changes and improvements. Indeed, shortly thereafter he appealed directly to the prime minister, requesting a complete review of federal policy on regional development. His assertion that DREE had been a failure because of its 'inability to muster a concerted federal effort in promoting regional development' led him to the conclusion that a much stronger DREE was needed.[45]

The obvious personal commitment to a reformed and reinvigorated DREE exhibited by De Bane was admirable, but, in the final analysis, it seems highly unlikely that the minister's exertions alone, no matter how impressive, could have significantly strengthened DREE within the federal bureaucracy or even retrieved its original mandate. In any case, wider developments within the federal government in 1981 relating to the construction of a national economic and industrial strategy for Canada were already determining a different fate for DREE.

The Reorganization for Economic Development and its Critics

On 12 January 1982, Prime Minister Trudeau announced the 'Reorganization for Economic Development.' According to Trudeau, the reorganization would provide a government-wide focus on regional economic development by giving all economic departments a more direct role to play in regional policy. This focus was to be facilitated by the dissolution of DREE and the addition of its regional-policy and co-ordination functions to those of MSED to create the Ministry of State for Economic and Regional Development (MSERD). The ministry's regional role would be to ensure that national programs were appropriately shaped to achieve specific economic-development objectives in each region. MSERD would also be responsible for developing a new set of development agreements to replace the GDA.[46]

Besides MSERD, the Department of Regional Industrial Expansion (DRIE) was created through the amalgamation of most of DREE's program functions and ITC's domestic responsibilities for industry, tourism, and small business. The new department would integrate DREE's regional and ITC's sectoral expertise. The expectation of the government was that DRIE would work closely with MSERD to ensure that Canada derived the maximum industrial benefits from major projects as well as administer the various ITC and DREE programs.[47]

Like two heavenly bodies that are briefly in position to produce an eclipse, a unique opportunity had evidently presented itself for this combination of industrial- and regional-development strategies to occur. The prime minister's announcement took note of this: 'The traditional Canadian economic balance between have and have not provinces is shifting, largely under the impetus of present and forecast resource developments in the West and offshore of the Atlantic provinces. For the first time in our history every region of the country, and not just those that have been traditionally well-off, is faced with major opportunities for development.'[48]

Atlantic Canada was expected to enjoy a decade of solid growth. The new regional strategy was to 'build on that strength.'[49] Notably, there was nothing in the prime minister's statement about regional disparities, a further indication that 'regional development' had taken on a new meaning in the federal lexicon in light of altered economic and political circumstances.

The initial reaction in the Atlantic region to the dismantling of DREE was one of alarm. Provincial premiers, in particular, were left seething at the sudden end to a federal agency that they had come to look upon as their own. The intention of the move was well understood: Ottawa wanted a higher profile in the region, more political credit for money spent, and greater control over economic and industrial policy.[50] Given that the provinces had been relatively content with the GDA format, their reaction to the demise of DREE was understandable. DREE's abolition had removed a crucial source of discretionary economic spending that had made it possible for these governments at least to contemplate the development of independent industrial strategies. Now they would be much more closely tied to Ottawa's apron-strings.

In the aftermath of DREE's demise, however, there was also a more realistic and critical assessment of the agency's overall failure. APEC undertook an analysis of the reorganization that was anything but laudatory regarding DREE's record. It had operated without goals and with an increasingly smaller share of the federal budget. Even worse, the proportion of this declining budget devoted to the Atlantic provinces declined steadily from 53 per cent in 1970–1 to 36 per cent in 1980–1. Its industrial incentive program, the RDIA, had served the Atlantic region poorly. In 1980–1, only 15.2 per cent of the total estimated amount of incentive funding went to companies in the Atlantic provinces, and a disproportionately larger number of these grants went to support industries that supplied low-paying and low-skilled jobs than in other parts of Canada.[51]

In other words, the national effort to do something about regional development had not been great. DREE never had mounted a coherent attack on disparities, or even developed a strategy to do so. The results, then (no discernible improvement between 1970 and 1981 in the relative position of the Atlantic provinces in terms of unemployment statistics, participation rates, and per-capita incomes), were scarcely surprising. What limited improvement had occurred in the regional economy during this period APEC attributed primarily to equalization payments and other federal transfers.[52]

Concurrently with the release of APEC's assessment of the reorganization, the Senate Committee on National Finance released its report, *Government Policy and Regional Development*. Like APEC, the senators were generally favourable towards the GDA arrangements as an effective instrument for promoting intergovernmental co-ordination, and recommended that the federal government solve its 'political recognition' problem within the context of the GDA format. Similarly, they were highly sceptical of the new economic strategy underlying the reorganization. They pointed out that the megaprojects on which the strategy rested involved 'enormous risks, are dependent on developments in international markets, and are very sensitive to minute changes in efficiency and costs.' The 'lumpiness' of the projects was another concern. There would be a great deal of initial activity followed by a drastic tapering off. For the least-developed regions, megaprojects were unlikely to promote much long-term employment.[53] As for the bureaucratic restructuring that accompanied the enunciation of this new economic strategy, it harboured real dangers for the least developed regions. It was crucial that MSERD not duplicate the errors of past policies and pay particular attention to the needs of these regions.

As DREE discovered, a political system generates enormous pressures to extend the boundaries of programs that generate cash flow. As a result, DREE ended up including more than half the geographic area of the country in the designated areas, and the purpose became hopelessly diluted. But without DREE to argue the case for the least developed regions, it becomes very important that MSERD designate specific regions of the country that most require, and that could benefit from, special industrial assistance programs.[54]

The senate committee stressed the fate of what it termed the 'least developed' regions because of what it perceived as a change in the way the government was using the term 'regional.' In the opinion of the senators, the term was clearly *not* being used to refer to the least-developed regions within provinces. They were also concerned about the lack of any mention of 'disparities' in the announcements and documents surrounding the reorganization. This omission left the distressing impression that the cause of the least-developed regions would be inadequately represented within the government. 'The Ministers heading MSERD and DRIE both have divided responsibilities and the regional emphasis placed in the government's announcement shows a strong concern for securing credit for federal initiatives of all kinds in the provinces ... The Committee regrets the decision to submerge DREE in DRIE because it removes the one voice in Cabinet committed to the development of the least developed regions ... MSERD may not face the same pressure to focus on regional disparities.'[55]

This seemed particularly likely given the government's new emphasis on megaprojects. The implication was that the fall-out from these projects would be sufficient to look after the least-developed regions. Neither was DRIE likely to devote attention to the areas of the country most in need. Granting responsibility to one department both for programs having a sectoral thrust and for those with a regional objective would lead only to the resolution of potential conflicts at the bureaucratic level rather than the cabinet level. The likely outcome was that the regional mandate would lose out 'while assistance flows to the industrial sectors and regions of the country that appear to offer the best prospects for growth and development.'[56]

As events transpired, the critics of the megaprojects strategy and the reorganization that followed proved quite prescient. Because the federal government's resource-based, export-oriented strategy was extremely dependent upon factors beyond Canada's control, it stalled almost as soon as it was announced as official government policy. A severe international recession in the early 1980s meant falling demand, slowed economic growth, the collapse of the oil-price bubble, and sharp cut-backs in the private sector's planned investments. The recession killed the major tar-sands projects in Western Canada and made the development of other frontier exploration sites less promising and attractive to the oil companies. In any event, related assumptions regarding the ability of Canadian capital to successfully capture backward and forward linkages to megaproject investments were tenuous at best. A weak Canadian capital-goods sector, the legacy of Canada's branch-plant status, and Canada's failure to persuade major trading partners to reduce tariffs on upgraded raw materials posed serious obstacles to the achievement of the federal government's optimistic scenario. Moreover, there was little incentive for multinational corporations to change the locale of their resource processing from foreign sites to Canadian ones, particularly given Canada's comparatively high wage economy.[57]

The collapse of the underlying economic strategy for the reorganization made it little more than a bureaucratic reshuffling that did nothing to promote regional development. The abolition of DREE and the incorporation of its functions into DRIE had less to do with regional development per se than with political control: it was motivated by a political strategy on the part of state élites at the centre to gain greater political credit for Ottawa's regional expenditures and to recapture the initiative in the regional-development policy field.[58] It was assumed that the much-vaunted megaprojects would take care of the substance of Ottawa's new policy thrust in this field.

The replacement for the GDA, the Economic and Regional Development Agreement (ERDA), differed from its predecessor primarily in its stress on direct delivery of programs by the federal government. The actual agreements themselves, however, were strikingly similar to GDA forerunners. In Nova Scotia, the three subsidiary agreements under the Canada/Nova Scotia ERDA signed in 1984 were on the Strait of Canso (wharf construction, all-weather highway), minerals (continuing along the lines of earlier GDA subsidiary agreements in this area), and a planning agreement (modelled on GDA arrangements).[59] With unemployment rates in the Atlantic provinces in the 1980s the worst in fifty years, the federal government had little to offer the region but more of the same.

Nova Scotia Economy and Politics, 1976–84

Economic Stagnation and the 1978 Election

While the Nova Scotia economy performed well in the early 1970s, stagnant economic conditions prevailed in the province between 1975 and 1978. The unemployment rate rose to 9.6 per cent in 1976 and 10.8 per cent in 1977, a level at which it remained throughout 1978 and 1979 (compared to a national level of 8.4 per cent). The *primary sector* – agriculture, forestry, the fishery, mining – showed some slight decline in terms of its contribution to both real domestic product and employment during the decade.[60]

More significant to the performance of the provincial economy, however, was the virtual halt after 1975 in the growth of the *public sector*. In the 1960s and early 1970s expanding employment in this sector had been the engine of growth in Nova Scotia and the other Atlantic provinces. In this context the clamp-down on government expenditures and the growth of the public sector, which began around mid-decade, hit especially hard on the periphery.

Manufacturing also stagnated after 1975. During the first half of the 1970s, there had been a steady increase in output largely because of Michelin. But the right prospect of a major expansion and diversification of Nova Scotia's manufacturing sector in the 1970s was not fulfilled. Instead there was a sharp reduction in manufacturing's share of total capital investment in Nova Scotia from the 20 to 30 per cent range in the early 1970s to 8 to 12 per cent in the later 1970s.[61] Moreover, linkages were not developing within the manufacturing sector. The level of inter-industry demand for manufactured products within the province re-mained virtually constant from 1960 to 1975, with almost no change in the top employers of the manufacturing work-force during this period.[62] An assessment made by DREE in 1979 was not encouraging. 'The results of the analysis show the manufacturing sector has not become the "engine of growth" for the provincial economy. The economy's growth has not achieved sufficient linkages and diversification to achieve income and employment levels equivalent to national averages.'[63]

Increasingly it was apparent that Nova Scotia's pursuit of large, labour-intensive secondary-manufacturing firms, a development strategy that yielded at best some modest success in the 1960s, was clearly and perhaps irrevocably removed as a viable option for the province in the altered environment of the late 1970s and early 1980s. There were not likely to be more Michelins. Meanwhile the continued importance to the provincial economy of resource-based, low value-added industries – in the context of slumping world demand, rising energy costs, and the structural weakness of supply constraints – left the province's economic and indus-trial base vulnerable and the economic future for Nova Scotians clouded.

The slumping Nova Scotia economy and the failed visions of industrial renewal offered by Premier Regan and his Liberal government in Nova Scotia eventually brought electoral defeat. In the 1978 provincial election the Liberals managed to retain their traditional rural strongholds in southwestern and eastern Nova Scotia, but lost most of their Halifax seats to the Conservatives. The final results more or less reversed the standing of the two major parties in the legislature and brought the Progressive Conservatives back to power after an eight-year interregnum, this time with John Buchanan as premier. The alternative to the Liberals and Conservatives, the Nova Scotia NDP, improved its vote share marginally in 1978 to 15 per cent; it also added an extra seat to its meagre total to give the party four seats, all of which were located in industrial Cape Breton. The election results were a bitter disappointment to NDP party leader Jeremy Akerman. Not since the founding of the Nova Scotia CCF in 1938 had the party of the democratic-socialist left in Nova Scotia been able to achieve any real success beyond industrial Cape Breton. Yet the party organization had always been characterized by a certain antipathy between the party executive headquartered in Halifax and its electoral stronghold in Cape Breton, a rift that was to widen considerably in the aftermath of the 1978 election.[64] In the 1940s and 1950s the CCF unquestionably had been the party of Cape Breton miners and steelworkers, by and large led and manned by its representatives. But the founding of the NDP in 1962 brought changes to this established arrangement, with Halifax-based academics and professionals playing a much more important role thereafter in party organization and leadership. While this change-over did not produce any tangible electoral gains outside Cape Breton, it did coincide with the decline of the party's traditional electoral strength in that area. Subsequent developments within the party confirmed and worsened the geographic split, which, to make matters worse, overlay what has alternately been described as an academic/worker or white-collar/blue-collar division within the party.[65] Too, the basis of financial support for the party appears to have been exceedingly slim during these years, heavily reliant throughout the 1960s and 1970s upon the support of two wealthy Halifax businessmen.[66]

The election of Jeremy Akerman as leader of the Nova Scotia NDP in an acrimonious 1968 convention (by four votes over the preferred candidate of the Halifax executive)[67] was the beginning of an electoral comeback in Cape Breton, but also what appear to have been interminable power struggles and personal antagonisms within the provincial party. According to Paul MacEwan, MLA for Cape Breton Nova and a vocal supporter of Akerman, the NDP leader was continually at loggerheads with the party executive and their Halifax supporters on policy, on strategy and tactics, and on caucus-party relations.[68] Finally, in May 1980, Akerman announced his resignation from the provincial leadership of the NDP and his seat in the Legislature to accept a post as executive director of intergovernmental affairs for the Buchanan government. The sudden departure of the NDP leader also brought to a head the festering enmity between MacEwan and party officials. After MacEwan lashed out at his antagonists with the public accusation that 'Trotskyites' had in-filtrated party ranks, he was expelled as a party member.[69]

The Akerman-MacEwan fiasco badly damaged the credibility of the NDP, at least in the short term. Moreover, in the period between the 1978 election and Akerman's resignation, grass-roots party organization had been allowed to deteriorate. To complicate matters, the new leader chosen by the party – Alexa McDonough – was without a seat in the Legislature and was forced to endure the unrelenting attacks of MacEwan and others for being a 'millionaire socialist.'[70] At the beginning of the 1980s, then, the electoral prospects for Nova Scotia's political alternative on the Left were less than encouraging.

The Department of Development, 1976–81

Economic conditions in the second half of the 1970s appear to have given pause to provincial economic strategists and planners and led to a recon-sideration of the appropriateness of various development models for Nova Scotia. The Nova Scotia Department of Development, unsettled by the onset of stagflation and amidst growing concern as to the adequacy of the department's structure and programs, conducted its first major inter-nal review in 1976. The result of the review was the emergence, on 1 January 1977, of what the department described as 'a more clearly defined, mission-oriented organization.'[71] The departmental reorganiza-tion reflected a greater emphasis on program delivery to small and medium-sized businesses as part of a major shift in development strategy towards support for the province's small-business sector, rather than the past practice of 'merely relying on attracting major investment projects that would hopefully have a spin-off effect on the small business community.'[72]

The 1978 election of the Buchanan government gave further impetus to this bureaucratic rethinking of provincial development policy. In a 1979 review of the strenghts and weaknesses of the provincial economy leading up to the release of a Green Paper on economic development strategy, past government policies were given short shrift. The traditional empha-sis placed on the development of the province's natural resources was considered as 'useful in permitting a society to gain time ... [but] neither a necessary nor a sufficient condition of development.'[73] Large production gains in future in provincial agriculture, forestry, and mining were seen as highly unlikely. Even the future prospects for offshore oil and gas were 'clouded by the lack of exploration success to date.' Clearly, resources per se were not a basis for further economic development in the province.

The document also questioned the frequently cited need for capital that underlay government policies and programs designed to attract capital to the province by offering to subsidize investment costs. Nova Scotia's capital stock was thought to be more than adequate. But, 'like natural resources, capital resources alone are an insufficient condition of development.'[74] Also rejected was the notion that the province's industrial and urban structure was somehow an obstacle to progress, and that policies designed to alter this fact would significantly spur industrial development. 'It is by no means clear that advantages to rural living such as life style and access to income in kind do not offset the disadvantages. In many respects, industrial and urban structure is a legacy of disparity and, therefore, as much an effect as a cause. If this is so the prospects for direct intervention are modest.'[75]

The 'indisputable' conclusion reached was that future development hinged on Nova Scotia's 'human resources': on indigenous skills, ideas, and capital. No amount of tinkering with structure or spatial distribution and no quantity of capital or natural resources could make up for the misuse or underdevelopment of the human resource. And this, it was argued, was the root of the province's economic problems: 'attitudes towards change, toward new technology and modern management, and perhaps ultimately, the failure to recognize people as the most important resource.'[76]

To a large extent this perspective was that reflected in the department's 1980 Green Paper, *Towards an Economic Development Strategy for Nova Scotia*. The Green Paper admitted that in the past the province had largely followed the structure of federal programs. As a result, development programs and structures had evolved 'less as a conscious response to policy decisions than as a response to actions of other jurisdictions ... programs evolved quite independently of, and as a substitute for policy.' This manner of proceeding 'had failed to set in motion a sustained development process in Nova Scotia.'[77] It called for a new direction in the 1980s. The emphases of past programs – natural resource upgrading, capital works, subsidization of existing enterprise – had to be supressed in favour of a new emphasis on people, skills, and productivity. In particular, development policy would have to address the following areas: government/business/labour relations, management skills, innovation, restructuring, and marketing, especially the extension of marketing assistance to small local enterprises. In general, a much greater investment in human skills was required.[78]

Ironically, while the province's development bureaucrats were busy designing a 'new direction' in development policy based on their reading of past errors and failures, a glaring lack of commitment to both the spirit and the content of the new approach was apparent at the political level. Thus, of the five federal-provincial development agreements signed in 1980–1, four were patently of the type criticized by the Green Paper.[79] Most contrary to the strategy advocated by the Green Paper was a $56 million grant to the French multinational Michelin to expand tire production in Nova Scotia;[80] this was not only because it directed government assistance away from those areas emphasized by the Green Paper, but also and most tellingly because of the events leading up to Michelin's decision to proceed with a further investment in Nova Scotia.

Industrial Relations and Development Strategy

From the point of its election in 1978, the Buchanan government demonstrated a markedly different attitude towards organized labour in the province than had the prior Conservative administrations of Robert Stanfield and Ike Smith. The most glaring example of this was the so-called Michelin Bill enacted in the last days of December 1979. The bill – which regulated the certification process within industries having multiple plants in the province (thereby retroactively setting aside an application for certification of the United Rubber Workers as the bargaining agent for employees at Michelin's Granton plant) – was anti-union and directly served the interests of the Michelin Corporation. It embittered what had been a relatively stable labour-relations climate in Nova Scotia and led to the break-up of the Joint Labour-Management Study Committee (JLMSC). Moreover, the government's willingness to design and pass such legislation in the first year of its term of office was indicative of the general philosophy that the Buchanan government would adopt towards organized labour in the province.

The JLMSC was, in fact, consulted by the government on the legislation that it planned to introduce in the spring of 1979. The minister of labour provided a copy of the proposed bill to executive members of the committee, and informed them of its purpose (preventing the United Rubber Workers from organizing Michelin's Granton plant). The JLMSC considered the matter throughout the summer of 1979, submitting its report to the minister in the fall. The economic rationale that had been given by the government for the bill – that it would promote full employment by broadening the collective-bargaining base – was rejected, and the JLMSC stated its opposition to the practice of amending the Trade Union Act 'for the purpose of making it into a major vehicle for industrial development in the province.'[81]

However, while the JLMSC formally rejected the proposed legislation, the management caucus within the JLMSC did put forward for discussion an amendment that had a similar intent to the Michelin Bill, but made the legislation applicable only to the Michelin company. The response of the labour caucus was that both the original legislation and the amended version constituted an attack on one of the fundamental compromises that had served as the corner-stone of the committee's work: 'that both management and labour recognize the right of all workers to organize for collective bargaining and recognize the contribution that organized labour can make to the economy.' When the management caucus of the JLMSC could not reach agreement on opposition to the legislation, and no compromise took shape, the labour members resigned 'en bloc.' This move was followed by a general condemnation of the government by the Nova Scotia Federation of Labour (NSFL) and the withdrawal of labour representatives from advisory and consultative boards. None the less, there was no indication from the government that it was ready to change its policies or to patch up its relationship with the NSFL.[82]

Shortly after the introduction of the Michelin Bill, the Michelin Tire Corporation announced that it would construct a third manufacturing facility in the province. It chose a predominantly agricultural area of the province with no previous history of union activity as the site for the new plant. For its part the provincial government announced that Michelin would receive a $56 million contribution towards construction and start-up costs under the Canada/Nova Scotia GDA.

There can be no doubt that by deciding to act at the behest of a multinational corporation over and against the strong objection of the JLMSC, the provincial government was turning its back on the basic principles that had been enunciated some eighteen years earlier in the MacKinnon report on industrial relations in the province. But the Michelin bill also revealed the cracks within the JLMSC and the limitations of the tripartite process as represented by that agency's operation. The failure in the late 1960s to move beyond a relatively narrow definition of the committee's role, or to bring about the formation at the provincial level of a more inclusive and representative employers' association, left the process highly vulnerable to changes of government or to the intrusion of external actors opposed to the committee's philosophy. When a large multinational corporation decided to utilize its considerable bargaining power for purposes directly contrary to the values and objectives of an agency ostensibly representative of indigenous capital and labour, both government and at least some elements of business were willing to sacrifice a 'good relationship' with labour for the promise of further investment and jobs.

In fact, the provincial government made known its determination to proceed even if there had been unanimous business and labour opposition to the legislation. The simple fact of the matter was that good labour relations demonstrably had not produced the requisite investment to ensure high levels of employment in the province. In the end it was this regional reality that gave Michelin its leverage over the government, and as well enabled the government to justify to the Nova Scotia electorate with little difficulty its departure from the path of 'labour peace' in order to accomplish the 'greater good' of job creation.

Energy Policy and Development Strategy

If the Buchanan government was drawn away from the 'human resource' development model advocated by its own development bureaucracy by the siren call of large-scale manufacturing, it was also increasingly diverted by the prospects in the 1980s of a resource-based development strategy, especially energy-related resources. Once again this displaced the focal point of provincial development policy away from the Green Paper's particular emphases towards the centrality of negotiations with state élites at the centre and with multinational oil corporations over such matters as jurisdiction, revenue-sharing, incentives, resource management and regulation, royalties and taxation, and other concerns linked to the anticipated impact on the province of huge investments of capital in energy-related megaprojects.

Prior to 1979, there was little planning and muted enthusiasm in the Atlantic provinces regarding offshore oil and gas. Gerald Regan had promoted the notion of a bounty of offshore oil and gas waiting to be discovered and exploited, but results had been disappointing. None the less, in 1977 the Trudeau government had offered to Nova Scotia a revenue-sharing and management formula should the development of offshore hydrocarbons become a reality. Provincial participation in resource management under the formula would have been limited to one vote on a six-member Maritime Offshore Resources Board.[83] The federal government was also actively encouraging and subsidizing the Maritime provinces to reduce by various means their dependence on imported oil (the price of which was subsidized by the federal government).[84] In this connection, it sought to act as marriage broker (including the offer of a dowry) in getting the three Maritime provinces to set up a regional energy corporation – the Maritime Energy Corporation (MEC) – which would plan and fund the development of major energy projects within the region, such as Fundy tidal power and nuclear power, as well as participate in the TQM gas pipeline and offshore mineral development.[85]

Both these federal initiatives (the 1977 offshore agreement and the MEC) envisaged and promoted regional bodies that would undertake a common regional approach to energy questions. Both foundered on provincial resistance to the imposition of this regional mould onto the design and implementation of provincial energy policy. Trudeau's proposal on the offshore was repudiated by Nova Scotia shortly after the election of the Buchanan government in 1978.[86] And the MEC, despite the offer of federal money and the prospect of easier financing for large-scale energy projects, stumbled on the question of cost-sharing and the CANDU nuclear-power station being constructed at Point Lepreau, New Brunswick.[87] Nova Scotia and PEI, both reluctant to become involved in Lepreau, eventually decided to pursue different strategies based on their own respective energy resources. By October 1980, the corporation was dead and New Brunswick was left with a billion-dollar reactor and a power surplus.[88]

The Hibernia and Venture offshore oil and gas discoveries in 1979 no doubt stiffened the Buchanan government's resolve to develop an energy policy based on provincially owned resources. The discoveries certainly increased the significance of the offshore in the province's own assessment of its development prospects, a perception that was further encouraged in the fall of 1979 when the Clark government, in stark contrast to the previous administration in Ottawa, pledged itself to recognition of the province's right to full ownership and control of the offshore, 'as if the resource were on land.'[89] Thus, the province was launched seriously into the task of developing a policy framework for the development of the offshore and its integration into provincial economic-development strategy.[90]

The return of the Trudeau Liberals to power in February 1980 once more put the federal and provincial governments at loggerheads on the ownership and management issue and forced the province to contest its claim to jurisdiction – a claim that it wanted entrenched through either a constitutional amendment or a boundary adjustment.[91] The province staked out its position – and confirmed the growing profile of the offshore on the Buchanan government's agenda – with the passage of the Nova Scotia Petroleum Resources Act (PRA), the establishment of a Petroleum Information Centre within the Department of Development, and the release, in July 1980, of *Offshore Oil and Gas: A Chance for Nova Scotians*. In order to ensure that Nova Scotia would cash in on this chance for prosperity, the PRA asserted the province's right to the resource, provided for a revenue-sharing regime, made provision for provincial participation in production, and signalled the province's intention to adopt a local preference policy in employment and the supply of goods and services. The experience of Alberta was not lost on provincial planners. 'Energy developments could give Nova Scotians the financial resources to attack deeply rooted economic problems, in much the same way as royalty incomes have given Alberta the capabilities to support organizations such as the Alberta Opportunity Company. The real importance of oil and gas lies in the extent to which it can be used to stimulate development elsewhere in the economy because, inevitably, the resource runs out.'[92]

Exploiting the energy staple, it appears, was beginning to cast a long shadow over the development strategy of state élites in Nova Scotia. That it was also eminently 'saleable' politically became apparent when Buchanan unexpectedly called a provincial election in the summer of 1981, claiming the need for a mandate in the ongoing negotiations over the offshore then taking place with the federal government. Halfway through a Conservative campaign that was noticeably long on Nova Scotia boosterism and short on policy substance, Buchanan made the triumphant announcement that the Trudeau government had guaranteed the province all revenues from offshore oil and gas finds. The premier confidently predicted that all other outstanding issues relating to the offshore would now be quickly settled, with a full agreement in place before year's end.[93]

Other reasons were apparent, however, for the early election call. A poll had suggested that the government was riding a wave of public optimism and popularity in the summer of 1981, while the opposition was in obvious difficulties. The Liberals had only recently lost their leader (the former premier) to federal politics and the Trudeau cabinet. The New Democrats were still reeling from the Akerman-MacEwan affair. Given these opposition instabilities and the buoyancy of the public mood thanks to the 'impending prosperity' associated with offshore exploration and development, the election was all but decided from the outset.[94] This was so despite the government's alienation of organized labour and its 'behind the scenes' role in a number of ongoing strikes at the time of the election.[95] The election results gave the Conservatives a landslide victory while reducing the Liberals to their lowest-ever vote total in provincial history (31 per cent). Although the NDP managed to increase its vote share from 15 to 18 per cent, it suffered the loss of all four of its Cape Breton seats. Ironically, the party finally made its long-awaited breakthrough on the mainland, with McDonough winning in her Halifax riding.

The Provincial Response to the Megaproject Strategy

While the Nova Scotia government along with those of the other Atlantic provinces criticized the demise of DREE in 1982, this criticism was muted by the material implications for the Nova Scotia economy of the federal government's megaproject strategy. The NEP and the Reorganization for Economic Development provided the policy framework and the fiscal incentives for a massive subsidization of offshore exploration activity in Atlantic Canada and plans for a state-administered funnelling of related economic and industrial benefits to Canadian companies. Private capital, provincial governments, and regional development agencies (both public and private) were thus encouraged to focus their attention on the bounty to be reaped from the exploration and development of offshore gas and oil.

One consequence of the sudden prospect of a surge of offshore activity was intense and highly conflictual negotiations – between the federal government, on the one hand, and the governments of Newfoundland and Nova Scotia, on the other – over the ownership and management of these same offshore resources. However, while the Newfoundland-Ottawa negotiations dragged on and became increasingly embittered, Nova Scotia took advantage of the situation to sign an agreement with the federal government, in March 1982, providing for joint management and revenue-sharing, but with built-in federal predominance.[96] This agreement allowed the province to 'get the jump' on Newfoundland in attracting exploration activity and energy-related businesses to Nova Scotia and was also consistent with the Buchanan government's strategy of pursuing a 'soft line' with business, aimed at encouraging private capital to invest in Nova Scotia as its regional base of operations.[97] The success of such tactics in securing for Halifax at least a temporary ascendance in offshore-related business and construction activity was evident in that city's overt prosperity in comparison with the less conspicuous rise of Newfoundland's capital city, St John's.[98]

The development 'hype' surrounding energy megaprojects in Atlantic Canada was reinforced by both government and private-sector reports. Though exuding optimism regarding the general outlook for the future of the regional economy in terms of investment and growth, these reports also sounded a note of caution regarding the concrete benefits likely to accrue from the development of the offshore. Thus, in a 1982 assessment, the Nova Scotia government pointedly noted that the bulk of employment creation would be in construction, with a high demand for temporary housing and services, while long-term industrial and manufacturing benefits were played down.[99] Other private-sector analyses of major projects slated for the Atlantic provinces predicted that, relative to the size of the economies involved, the Atlantic region would lead the nation in major capital projects between 1983 and 1995 in terms of jobs created and total capital investment. Like the government reports, the private-sector analyses cautioned against North Sea–type expectations from such megaprojects, noting that most of the employment generated would be in the construction phase, with only a small amount of impact in the manufacturing sectors of the respective provinces.[100]

APEC argued that megaprojects could serve as a basis for a more diversified provincial economy only if government and local business could combine to take deliberate action to capture project benefits. The difficulties and disadvantages suffered by local firms in the competition for a piece of the action were seen to be insurmountable *unless* joint-venture arrangements could be worked out and governments in the region employed policies aimed at maximizing regional content.[101] The effectiveness of government provisions with regard to these policies was therefore crucial. That such was, in fact, the hoped-for outcome (if not the projected strategy) of the Nova Scotia government was made clear by members of the provincial cabinet at the 1984 Canadian Offshore Resources Exhibition in Halifax, where they strongly indicated their desire for more than 'temporary benefits' for the provincial economy from offshore development. The projected scenario was that Nova Scotia companies would be able to reap long-term benefits from supply, fabrication, and production activities through partnerships and joint ventures, thereby allowing for the transfer of skills and technology to local firms, which would then provide the basis for effective competition in the world market.[102] Apparently the provincial government was eyeing a role for itself in negotiating the terms of a 'shotgun' alliance between local and multinational capital in fields of activity related to the offshore play.

The impact of the megaproject strategy was also felt within the province's development bureaucracy. Between 1981 and 1984 the emphasis moved away from small business and towards 'major investment fields,' and particularly the offshore oil and gas industry. In 1980, the Department of Development had its organizational structure reviewed for a second time, 'to determine changes needed to capitalize on present and future development opportunities.'[103] The resulting reorganization created a new departmental division, the Industrial Development Division. Its allotted tasks were fourfold: to develop new export markets, to maximize benefits to Nova Scotia from resource megaprojects, to assist local firms to increase their level of exports, and finally to increase the number of firms locating in the province. The Industrial Benefits Office was created out of the existing Petroleum Information Centre and transferred to the new division, as was the Market Development Centre and Industrial Promotions (formerly carried out by IEL).[104] This re-organization would seem to indicate the extent to which provincial development policy had come to focus on the opportunities afforded by the megaproject strategy and, related to this, the pumping-up of provincial exports. Notably, the goal of attracting secondary manufacturing firms to the province, formerly the overriding thrust and centre-piece of provincial development strategy, was much less of a preoccupation in the early 1980s.

The world energy crisis, fortuitous discoveries of evidence of offshore hydrocarbons, national policies in the fields of energy and industrial and regional development, and numerous public- and private-sector projections, all led the Nova Scotia government to enthusiastically attach its development policies to the megaproject strategy. But in doing so the provincial government was accepting not only assumptions about the potential of megaprojects to act as an engine of growth and industrial development on the periphery, but that this potential would in fact be realized. All, of course, was premised on large-scale offshore developments that kept receding into the future, the arrangements of which continued to be the subject of renegotiation between governments and corporate capital.[105] Most telling on the plans, hopes, and expectations of the Nova Scotia government and regional business engaged in offshore-related activities, however, was a shift in the economic and political conditions that all along supported the strategy. With world oil prices softening as the 1980s progressed, the likely profitability of offshore development became ever more questionable. Reserves in Nova Scotia's Venture gas field were not 'proven up' in test drilling, and disappointing results added fuel to speculation that development would be indefinitely delayed.

By the fall of 1984, the bloom was beginning to fade on the offshore rose. That this was having its effect on provincial development planners is evidenced by the government's return after a four-year hiatus to the process of developing a more autonomous provincial-development strategy. In 1984 *Building Competitiveness: A White Paper on Economic Development* was released. In it the provincial government criticized the 1982 Reorganization for Economic Development for not living up to the promises made for it. Federal departments had not taken on a more regional perspective in their policies since the inauguration of DRIE and MSERD, and federal-provincial consultation on economic issues had only been made more difficult by the changes.[106] The implication of this failure of federal regional-development policy was that the province would be forced to rely more on its own resources and its own development strategy and policies.

Although offshore activity drew a mention in the White Paper as 'a springboard for a stronger overall provincial economy' to be realized by the provincial government's commitment to 'increasing the share of offshore-related activity that accrues to local firms and labour,' the overwhelming thrust of the document was away from the resource-based, export-oriented strategy that had been the predominant focus since 1980. The White Paper pointed out that the growth in world trade in the 1980s had not been in natural resources, but in manufactured goods. Moreover, it recognized that changes had occurred in the structure of economic activity that indicated that the production of services had displaced the production of goods as the basis for future growth and development.[107] In order to enhance the province's development prospects in future, then, the provincial economy had to be reoriented in this direction and away from its heavy dependence on resource-based exports.[108]

The governing philosophy of the *Building Competitiveness* was the 'lean and mean' competitive credo that appears to have become predominant in business and government circles during the recession of the early 1980s. The main strategy proposed for state intervention was to aid 'firms and individuals to strengthen their competitive ability and performance,' to be achieved through government measures aimed at 'enhancing human resource strengths' (for example, improving management skills, making available a venture-capital fund, and improving employee training and tying it more closely to market requirements), and 'improving the business environment' (by, for example, contracting out government services). The government would also try to promote a larger market for local business through a public-sector purchasing policy that would give preference to Nova Scotia suppliers.[109] While employment creation was the ultimate goal of the province's development policies, it was considered to be only a symptom of the level and type of economic activity, and the province was 'determined to avoid any temptation to concentrate on addressing symptoms ... enhanced competitiveness is the target.'[110]

While the White Paper suggests that the provincial state had come down from its offshore 'high,' the Buchanan government nevertheless found it useful to parlay one more time the promise of major offshore developments that were 'just around the corner' into a third provincial election victory. Of course, it was of some benefit to the government that the election call came hard on the heels of a massive Conservative election win at the national level in the fall of 1984, while the scent of strong popular resentment towards the Liberal party still hung fresh in the electoral air. Predictably, in November 1984, the Conservatives swept forty-two of the province's fifty-two seats. The Liberals were reduced to a scattered six seats; they also became the third choice in Metropolitan Halifax, where the NDP had substantially improved its showing. The dividends for the NDP from an increased vote total in the province's main urban centre were minimal: one additional seat in Halifax plus a surprise win in a mainland rural riding. The party was again shut out in its former stronghold of industrial Cape Breton, a result in no small part attributable to competition for the labour vote from former NDP MLA Paul MacEwan's newly formed Cape Breton Labour Party.

A New Mandate and Negotiating Survival: DEVCO and SYSCO in the 1980s

DEVCO

During its history, the nature of DEVCO's 'rescue mission' in Cape Breton altered radically. At the beginning of the 1970s its primary task was to phase out coal-mining and to replace it with a diversified economic base. By mid-decade the initial strategy adopted to accomplish this – using financial inducements to attract footloose secondary manufacturing – had fallen flat and out of favour, while the notion of totally scrapping coal-mining was replaced by a limited modernization program in the mines. Between 1976 and 1978, the value of coal production doubled, with a stable work-force of 3,000 (down from 6,600 in 1966).[111]

The shift in development strategy towards reliance on the energy staple as the 'engine of growth' on the Atlantic periphery during a period of high and rising oil prices reverberated as well through the strategies and policies of the federal agency responsible for development in Cape Breton. Speculation and planning regarding billion-dollar energy mega-projects placed Cape Breton's huge but expensive undersea coal reserves in a new light; suddenly coal-mining on the Island once more appeared to be an economically viable proposition. By 1980, the 'coal strategy' was taking on considerable momentum in DEVCO planning. Not only the expansion of coal-mining itself, but coal-related industrial developments on the Island such as coal liquefaction and the production of synthetic fuels, became central to the development scenarios of DEVCO officials.[112]

Of course, there were problems with the rebirth of 'King Coal' as the key element in DEVCO's overall development strategy. Where transportation, domestic heating, and steel-making once provided ample and diversified markets for Nova Scotia coal, in the 1980s DEVCO was heavily reliant on the Nova Scotia Power Corporation (NSPC) and its oil-substitution program in thermal-power generation, selling 60 to 70 per cent of its coal production to NSPC. Finding other markets for a doubling or tripling of coal production depended on a continued rise in world fossil-fuel prices, as well as the realization of other coal-related megaprojects using expensive and untried technology. Reliance on the NSPC also created problems for DEVCO since this market had been secured only through DEVCO's agreement to a long-term contract at prices that had quickly been made outdated both by oil-price rises and by operating costs. Yet the NSPC refused to consider any renegotiation of the contract, a position encouraged by a provincial-government chary about the political costs of a rise in electricity rates.

As a result of these constraints, DEVCO began to incur large deficits. Its attempt to limit costs by keeping wages down produced the first major strike in the mines since 1947. The result was the loss of twelve weeks' production and the further deterioration of DEVCO's balance sheet.[113] Then the collapse of oil prices brought a price drop for the coal that DEVCO sold on world markets – from $90 per ton in 1982 to $75 ton in 1984.[114] By the end of 1983 mounting DEVCO losses led DRIE minister Ed Lumley to place a moratorium on DEVCO's expansion plans pending a renegotiation of the NSPC contract and a review of DEVCO management and operations.[115]

Then, in April 1984, a disastrous fire killed one miner and force DEVCO to permanently seal one of its three active mines, throwing 1,200 miners out of work. The disaster did have a catalysing affect on federal and provincial politicians. Negotiations between DEVCO and the NSPC, which had been stalled, were quickly concluded with agreement on a 40 per cent increase in coal prices. And before another month had lapsed, the federal DRIE minister announced that the moratorium on funding had ended, and that $324 million had been approved for mine development.[116]

As events unfolded, however, it became clear that there was a price to pay for this commitment of development funds for DEVCO's coal-mining operations. In the wake of DRIE's review of DEVCO, a new chairman, Joe Shannon, was appointed with a mandate to reorient the corporation along more business-like lines. A series of management dismissals followed, a cost-cutting campaign was launched (which included the axeing of a number of money-losing but cherished operations set up under Kent's 'small is beautiful' presidency in the mid-1970s, and a management drive was put on to improve productivity in the mines.[117] Coal operations, it was announced, would be placed on a sound commercial basis through 'improved financial performance, increased production, the establishment of management accountability and the restoration of confidence with government, employees, community and the general public so that continuing investment in the industry can be financially justified.'[118].

Shannon also brought a new philosophy to DEVCO's role as a development agency. A key problem, he surmised, was the lack of definition of the corporation's role: 'The corporation is almost indefinable ... It is as if the corporation has its hands in almost everything imaginable. And what we're supposed to be doing in Cape Breton depends on who you talk to.'[119] Of course, this problem's origins can be located in the long-term failure of the federal government to situate DEVCO within an overall regional-development strategy or plan. Left to its own devices as *the* federal response to the Cape Breton problem, corporation policies and activities remained ill-supported, undefined, and unfocused. According to Kent, 'Government was never clear how DEVCO should work in Cape Breton ... Part of the corporation's mandate was to enlighten the Government on the nature and extent of Cape Breton's economic problems and experiment with regional development.'[120]

In 1984, almost twenty years after DEVCO had been established by the federal government, its dismal failure to fulfil its mandate of putting the economy of Cape Breton Island on a stable footing was all too obvious. The general economic situation on the Island had deteriorated noticeably, even from its poor state in the previous decade. The official unemployment rate for the Cape Breton subregion stood at 19.6 per cent, compared to a 13.2 per cent provincial average. And with the participation rate on the Island only 48.3 per cent, as compared to a provincial average of 57.3 per cent (and a Halifax-area figure of around 70 per cent), wide-spread underemployment was evident as well.[121]

Apparently, DEVCO's new management decided at this point that the 'experiment' was indeed a failure and should be brought to an end. Since the late 1960s the key instrument utilized by DEVCO to promote the Island's economic diversification was the corporation's Industrial Development Division (IDD). But DEVCO had remained primarily a coal corporation, with IDD allocated only 4 per cent of its budget and 5 per cent of its employees. Yet even this level of commitment was too much for Shannon, who announced cuts in IDD staff and a full review of its activities to determine its future as part of DEVCO operations.[122] Some months later, both Shannon and his newly appointed vice-president, Len MacNeil, indicated in public statements that DEVCO would cease to perform any 'entrepreneurial' role itself in favour of 'tangible and technical support' to private-sector enterprises that had the potential to be stable over the long term. This statement was accompanied by a caution that such businesses would have to become 'vibrantly competitive' if they were to expect continued DEVCO assistance.[123]

These changes suggest that the point of the 1984 review was to give birth to a more market-oriented DEVCO less concerned with social goals or its general responsibility for the economic welfare of Cape Breton Island. As had occurred with DREE, the corporation's mandate was adjusted to reflect the reconstitution of federal regional development policy, a key feature of which was the government's general retreat from any active attempt to bring about a significant reduction in regional disparities.

SYSCO

The deflation of the CANSTEEL megaproject in 1975–6 left the fate of a neglected SYSCO in limbo. In 1976–7, losses at the plant increased sharply, with even higher losses of $1 million per week projected for 1977–8. The situation was obviously spiralling out of control, raising the possibility of a full shut-down caused either by the mounting losses or by equipment failure in the run-down plant. Finally, in December 1977, DREE and the government of Nova Scotia signed an interim agreement on SYSCO to carry out immediate maintenance and repairs while options were examined and a business plan developed. The agreement made provision for the expenditure of $19.5 million for capital works and business planning, an amount characterized by then SYSCO president

Tom Kent as totally insufficient to meet SYSCO's needs, nothing more than a short-term delaying or holding action at best.[124]

In 1979, a task force on SYSCO made up of senior bureaucrats within the Nova Scotia government submitted its report to the Policy Board of the Nova Scotia cabinet. The report noted that the minor changes made at the plant since 1967 had not resulted in any significant deviation from the trend towards the decline of steel operations in Sydney. The plant was using antiquated and to some extent, as the result of partial modernization, incompatible production systems. Maintenance and upkeep had been poor: a total of some $110 million had been spent since 1971 on replacement or maintenance to safeguard productive capacity when some $540 million would have been the normal allotment set aside 'by an average competitive company of comparable size.' SYSCO also had a poor record of industrial relations and poor-quality management.[125] To say the least, the task force was condemnatory of past practices and operations at SYSCO.

In reviewing the costs and benefits of alternative plans for SYSCO, the report concluded that the options of 'full rehabilitation' and 'basic oxygen' steel-making would produce the greatest benefits to the Nova Scotia economy in terms of employment and integrated industrial activity in Cape Breton (coal-mining, coke production, electrical generation, steel-making), but that these options were also extremely expensive, and would almost surely run large deficits upon completion. For these reasons both options were rejected by the task force. Simply improving the plant's antiquated 'open hearth' operations, although likely to maintain current employment levels at the plant, was not considered to be a final answer for SYSCO, and was therefore emphatically rejected. The option that was favoured was the installation at SYSCO of 'electric arc' furnaces, a relatively low-capital-cost method of producing small quantities of steel without the use of coke or molten iron (i.e., a non-integrated or 'mini-steel plant'). Although this option promised much smaller economic benefits than those to be reaped from other options in terms of employment, export sales, and industry linkages, it would mean a smaller, more manageable, and less crisis-prone company, with a minimum reliance on foreign markets and the least requirements for ongoing government support.[126]

The conclusion and recommendation of the task force, then, was that a much smaller SYSCO, employing at most 900 workers (rather than the 3,000 on the payroll in 1979), was the best option for the province. This strategy could not properly be considered a 'development' one as far as the stimulation of the provincial economy was concerned. Rather, it was a 'protective' strategy, safeguarding what would otherwise be totally lost. Added to this recommendation was a provision that modernization should proceed only if negotiations with the federal government on a cost-sharing formula were concluded to the province's satisfaction, with closure the only realistic alternative. Finally, the primary objective at the end of the process should be to deliver a saleable plant to non-government owners and management.[127]

Subsequent events suggest that the recommendations of the task force were overridden at the cabinet level for political reasons. During the 1980 federal election campaign, all parties promised financial aid to revive SYSCO, and in 1981 a $96 million development agreement for SYSCO modernization – phase I of a $350 million plant rehabilitation that would maintain SYSCO as an integrated steel producer – was announced.[128] Phase II of the plan was contingent on the outcome of a further study in which the technology of production would have to be chosen. This study (undertaken by Bailey Hoogovens Canada) recommended that modernization proceed, using basic-oxygen steel-making technology. Within months of this recommendation, however, Ottawa was witholding modernization funds, pending a review by DRIE of 'certain aspects' of the plan. SYSCO management's response was to announce further lay-offs at the plant.[129] The commissioning of yet another study in 1983 (by Hatch Associates) to check the results of the first resulted in a counter-recommendation for a smaller, less expensive, non-integrated electric-arc operation.[130]

The conflicting recommendations of various studies fuelled the disagreement raging within and between federal and provincial governments over the shape of SYSCO's future. The Steelworkers Union and local politicians (municipal, provincial, and federal) were unanimous in their rejection of the electric-arc option because of its adverse employment impact. Premier Buchanan continued publicly to voice solidarity with this position, while remaining unclear as to his own government's preference. Meanwhile, phase I of the modernization – which included a $40 million blast furnace that presumed the continued operation of an integrated steel mill at Sydney – proceeded apace.[131]

The protracted stalemate over SYSCO created by bureaucratic vetoes and political gamesmanship kept the situation thoroughly muddied and allowed the workers and the general public little substantive knowledge of the details and consequences of the various strategies and options under consideration, instead feeding them a diet of rumours, denials, and vague pronouncements regarding the need for further reviews, assessments, or studies to confirm or elaborate upon SYSCO's business plan. In the interim, employment dropped steadily from 3,000 to 2,000, to 1,200, and SYSCO's annual orders for rails – the one product it now produced – narrowed to Canadian National (CN) and occasional Third World purchases obtained through the intervention of the Canadian International Development Agency (CIDA).[132]

In 1981, SYSCO's future as an integrated steel producer had appeared secure. But as the Canadian economy went into a severe recession and the federal government's megaproject strategy faded, intergovernmental negotiations on SYSCO modernization stalled, and federal financial commitments to the project became subject to re-evaluation. SYSCO clearly was not, nor had it ever been, a major element in either government's economic-development strategy. As a result its history as a Crown corporation became a sad litany of plant mismanagement and government irresponsibility towards the maintenance and renewal of productive capacity. The adverse consequences for ailing industry on the periphery of poor development planning, political vacillation, indecision, and governmental stalemate have seldom been so clear.

The Determinants of State Intervention: Crisis and Restructuring in the Fishery

In many ways the fishing industry in the Atlantic region has always been unique. Its importance is often underestimated. More than a quarter of the region's people live in small fishing communities, 'at least half of which have essentially single-sector economies, with fishing and processing plant employment occupying 30 per cent or more of the labour force.' In 1981, the fishery accounted for 17 per cent of all employment and value-added in Nova Scotia's commodity-producing industries, and 32 per cent of its exports.[133]

Capital

In the years leading up to the Canadian government's declaration of an exclusive two-hundred-mile fishing zone effective 1 January 1977, the fishery was subject to a growing crisis. The growth of capital in the 1960s had augmented the size of the Canadian trawler fleet, while competition between domestic and international fleets for fish stocks was growing. Between 1964 and 1974, offshore trawlers considerably expanded their operations in areas traditionally occupied by the inshore/nearshore sector.[134] One result of this increased competition was a drastic decline of the inshore fishery in the early 1970s, especially in Newfoundland. But the slump in catches also hit the large companies, which experienced major losses in 1974.[135] A shift in stock ownership occurred within the corporate sector that, by 1977, saw one family, the Nickersons, gain control of the largest corporation, National Sea. A year later, National Sea's stock was worth six times what Nickerson had paid for it. In the two years following the declaration of the two-hundred-mile limit the five largest fish companies in Atlantic Canada doubled their asset base to $400 million, dispensing some $45 million during this period in dividends to shareholders.[136] They also borrowed extensively from banks and provincial governments to finance their expansion.[137]

But while the volume and value of the resource increased steadily after 1977, other factors were conspiring against continuing profits for the large fishing companies. By 1981 high fuel costs, high interest rates, high inventories, and poor markets were threatening all the major companies with bankruptcy. In the summer of 1981, eighteen processing plants and trawler operations were closed down in Atlantic Canada, throwing 4,000 people out of work. The crisis prompted the federal minister of fisheries, Romeo LeBlanc, to start talking in earnest about the possibility of a nationalized deep-sea fleet and a powerful government marketing agency.[138] However, the eventual resolution of the growing financial crisis of big capital in the fishery would develop somewhat different contours.

Labour

While the growth of capital and capitalist social relations of production in the fishery reflects developments in other primary sectors in the Atlantic region in the post-war period, the fishery departs from the norm when employment trends are considered. In agriculture, forestry, and mining, rationalization and mechanization had steadily reduced the size of the labour force. But in the fishery employment has fluctuated, depending upon the state of the industry. Between 1974 and 1981, the number of licensed fishermen in the Atlantic fishery increased by some 45 per cent (to 53,500) and the number of processing facilities by 35 per cent (to 700). Both labour and capital were subject to seasonal variables, however, with labour underemployed and capital underutilized in the off-peak season.[139]

In Newfoundland the provincial government passed legislation in 1971 granting bargaining rights to all fishermen (inshore and offshore), thus providing the legal base for the eventual emergence of a single dominant union: the Newfoundland Fish, Food, and Allied Workers Union (NFFAWU). Inshore fishermen in the Maritimes, however, continued to be denied state-sanctioned bargaining rights, although such denial did not prevent a union from developing. In 1977 the Maritime Fishermen's Union (MFU) was started by Acadian fishermen in New Brunswick, spreading in the next few years to Nova Scotia and PEI. Finally, in 1982, the New Brunswick government passed Bill 25, officially recognizing the MFU and giving it 'enough strength to test the waters.' Crucial to the MFU's future progress, however, was organizing Nova Scotia, and the union received financial support in this endeavour from the NFFAWU. Even in its New Brunswick base, however, the union didn't gain application of the Rand formula (compulsory check-off of dues) and, by the mid-1980s, it was very much in debt. For its part, the NFFAWU began making inroads into Nova Scotia, pushing a complacent CBRT (which had been accorded voluntary recognition as representative for trawler crew on National Sea and Nickerson vessels following the 1971 Canso strike) into its own organizational drive.[140]

The other key producer association to arise during this period was the Eastern Fishermen's Federation (EFF), formed in 1979 at the behest of then fisheries minister Romeo LeBlanc. One year later, thirteen separate associations had been brought together under this umbrella association. The EFF was designed as a lobbying group, 'meant to give voice to the diverse Atlantic groups.' After an initial meteoric rise, the loose alliance was shaken by conflicts 'linked to EFF's involvement in over-the-side sales and processor-like activities plus the rising strength of the MFU which has been its constant opponent.' Fundamentally, however, the EFF continued to draw support on the strength of its political role, for to many fishermen, not without justification, 'the fishing industry is all politics, run by government.' Naturally this view creates desire for an influential voice, 'where it really counts – in government decision-making.'[141]

The State

In January 1982, the federal government appointed a task force on Atlantic fisheries headed by Michael Kirby to investigate the troubled industry. The report of the Kirby task force made sixty recommendations on needed changes to the organization and operation of the Atlantic fishery. Taken as a whole, the report was arguing for a regime of state-orchestrated supply-and-demand management. One of the most important changes advocated by Kirby and subsequently implemented by the government was the introduction of quasi-property rights in the form of 'enterprise allocations' or saleable individualized quotas, accompanied by strict limitations on catch potential. The aim was to reward the efficient and provide the inefficient with a financially rewarding exit from the fishery. The objective was simple: 'a gradual rationalization similar to what has occurred in agriculture.'[142]

With regard to the near-bankrupt fish processors, the report identified the crisis for the highly capitalized and volume-oriented large companies as acute.[143] In contrast to the large processors, the smaller independent processors were better equipped to withstand falling margins and rising interest rates. Running on a seasonal basis, and supplied by independent inshore fishermen, these operators could take advantage of the assumption of risk embodied in their supplier's ownership of boats and gear, as well as the ability to exploit subregional conditions of labour surplus.[144] The task force therefore concerned itself with the financial restructuring of the five large processors in the region, whose combined debt had reached $300 million by 1983.[145]

The solution recommended by the task force to the financial crisis of the large companies (which together dominated the Atlantic fishery) was a rationalization of their operations and an infusion of funds. Subsequently a federal negotiating team (which included fisheries minister Pierre de Bané and Kirby himself) entered negotiations with the major debt-holders – the Bank of Nova Scotia and the provinces of Nova Scotia and Newfoundland. The results were quite different for Newfoundland and Nova Scotia: a state-owned corporation in the former, and a new large private company in the latter. This outcome was determined by a number of factors, most important among them the differing relative strengths of capital and organized labour in the fishery in the two provinces and the bargaining strategies and goals adopted by the respective provincial governments.

That the outcome of the negotiations over the future of the 'big five' companies would be different in the two provinces was not immediately apparent as the federal negotiators went about their task. After a search of capital markets had failed to uncover a private-sector saviour, an equity investment by government was accepted as the only solution, and in the fall of 1983 the federal government was poised to consolidate all five companies into one huge state-owned company.[146]

The Newfoundland negotiations were concluded first. There was little overt opposition to a public-sector solution to the problems of Newfoundland's large fish companies, and a great deal of support for something akin to this outcome from the NFFAWU. Most of the manoeuvring in the actual negotiations involved the Newfoundland government's attempt to seize the opportunity offered by the crisis to gain greater influence over the fishery, and its refusal to accept the federal view that certain redundant fish plants would have to be closed as one result of the restructuring.

The Nova Scotia negotiations that followed were strikingly different, with the Buchanan government staunchly opposed to any federal takeover and quite willing to let the firms in question go into bankruptcy so as to allow the pieces to be picked up by the private sector. This opposition to the federal proposal was not just indicative of an ideological preference on the part of the Buchanan government for a private-sector solution (although it was that as well). It was also a case of the Nova Scotia government being wary of the political influence Newfoundland might wield over a single federal Crown corporation dominating the Atlantic fishery. The Newfoundland government was demanding that fish caught in Newfoundland waters be caught and processed by Newfoundlanders: a direct threat to an important segment of the Nova Scotia offshore fleet. The government also feared that the fishery's commercial viability would be 'sacrificed to the exigencies of the "welfare fishery." '[147]

The Buchanan government found support for its negotiating position from big capital, independent processors, and the prosperous small-boat fishery of southwest Nova Scotia. The last named feared that the federal government would abuse its allocative authority and give favoured treatment to its own firm. But despite these sources of support, the province had nothing in the way of a counter-offer to the federal plan. Its only gambit was to keep the fish companies out of Ottawa's hands until private-sector investors could be found. In this delaying ploy it was aided by divisions within the federal cabinet. The Nova Scotia ministers – MacEachen and Regan – were rumoured not to be in favour of the 'one big state-owned company' proposal; the former minister of fisheries, Romeo LeBlanc, was resentful because his own views had been passed over; and even on the federal negotiating team Kirby and de Bané were at odds on some matters.[148]

Despite this less-than-united federal front, a tentative agreement was reached with the Nova Scotia government on federal terms. With the introduction of the bill in Parliament, however, opposition to the proposal in Nova Scotia was inflamed, and both provincial MLAs and Nova

Scotia MPs came under increased political pressure. At this point revelations of a secret agreement made between the federal government and the Bank of Nova Scotia came to light, which seemed to indicate that favoured treatment would be given to the bank and that Ottawa would eventually have a controlling interest in the new company. This situation gave the provincial government a reason to renege on what was now looking like a very unpopular agreement. At the same time the premier, his fisheries minister, and a representative of the Royal Bank were meeting with the representative of a group of minority shareholders in National Sea (shareholders who also happened to be among the wealthiest families in Atlantic Canada). The federal government and the Bank of Nova Scotia were subsequently approached with a refinancing scheme, and after initial rejection and further negotiation, an agreement was reached on a 'private sector solution.' Scotia Investments – composed of the Jodrey, Sobey, and Morrow interests – would control 47 per cent of the company; the federal government, 20 per cent; the Bank of Nova Scotia, 14 per cent; and a private float, 19 per cent.[149]

In 1984, two huge companies – National Sea and Fishery Products International – exercised dominance over the Atlantic fishery, where five companies had previously. Both companies were vertically integrated, seeking to synchronize harvesting and processing with resource availability and market management. In the 1980s the federal government became a crucial overseer in the fishery. Its role in the management of supply and its resource-allocation decisions – which confer property rights on individuals and firms – have placed it at the centre of competitive and often intense struggles between provinces, among firms and fishermen, between the inshore and offshore sectors, and increasingly between factions within the inshore sector itself as it becomes more differentiated internally between 'sheep' and 'wolves in sheep's clothing.' With its broad responsibility for – and increased involvement in – the fishery, it is to be expected that the federal government will continue to respond (though not necessarily equitably) to the demands of various groups, reflecting in its decisions and actions the effects of diverse class struggles within the fishery over state structures and policies.

Conclusion

In more than one sense the shift in economic conditions beginning in the mid-1970s and the state response to the problems this created for the Canadian economy can be viewed as a watershed for regional development policy. It put on hold debates within the upper reaches of the state over the need for an industrial strategy, or at least more comprehensive planning and co-ordination of the various fields of state policy. It marked the shift towards increasing concern with the state of the national economy, and in particular the international competitiveness of central-Canadian manufacturing. It began a period of expenditure restraint, monetarism, and public-sector hiring freezes that had a direct and harmful impact on the economic welfare of the Atlantic periphery. And, finally, it undermined development strategies, such as that pursued by the Nova Scotia government, that relied upon expansionary economic conditions supportive of state attempts to entice large secondary manufacturers or capital-intensive resource-processing enterprises to locate on the periphery.

After 1975, political and fiscal pressures on the state mounted for the curtailment and restructuring of state intervention on the periphery in line with the broader political and economic strategies of state élites. Economic conditions and the state response to those conditions were in fact forcing changes in the political discourse and state agenda in such a way as to lower the priority accorded the issue of regional disparities and narrow the space for regional demands at the centre (even as state policies to cope with the exigencies of stagflation, recessionary conditions, and/or a growing fiscal crisis exacerbated those disparities).

Such pressures on state élites at the centre, however, did not always translate successfully into new policies. Thus, attempts to cut back on UI transfers to the periphery foundered on the concerted bi-partisan opposition of Atlantic-region politicians,indicating the centrality of such transfers to the set of policy compromises underlying the political integration of the Atlantic periphery. Regional-development policies, however, were another matter. Such expenditures were reduced in relative terms. They were also redirected away from addressing regional inequalities or disparities towards sectoral adjustment and modernization, not only or even primarily in the Atlantic region, but also and to an increasing degree in the Montreal area and the Western provinces.

In the 1980s the reconstitution of regional development policy was hastened by its incorporation into a sectoral economic strategy rooted in the prospect of energy megaprojects on the periphery. This new policy thrust had its origins in a Liberal agenda shaped by constitutional and intergovernmental struggles that were brought to a head by the Quebec referendum and the energy crisis. The subsequent reorganization of state structures and policies to accommodate the federal government's new political and economic strategies resulted in a further derogation of the goal of eliminating regional disparities. Combining the regional mandate of DREE with the sectoral mandate of Industry did not produce a viable regional industrial strategy; the regional 'tail' was unlikely to end up wagging the sectoral 'dog.' And the strategy itself, a basket in which a fair number of government eggs had been deposited, was balanced precariously, and ultimately erroneously, on a number of fragile assumptions about Canadian resources and international markets. The passing of the specific historical conjuncture that had made plausible such assumptions left state élites at the centre without a viable response to the dramatic worsening of regional disparities in Canada that accompanied the 1982 recession and the regionally uneven recovery that followed.

The implications of these events for the nature and scope of state intervention in the field of regional development were not only evident in the activities of DRIE (which, in lieu of energy megaprojects on which to feed, fell back on the standard programs and formulas previously employed by DREE). They were also manifested in developments at DEVCO, where a long-term federal commitment to mine development was accompanied by a decision by newly appointed management to de-emphasize the corporation's industrial-development activities. With unemployment in Cape Breton in the 20 to 25 per cent range, DEVCO appeared ready to retreat from its mandate to oversee the diversification of Cape Breton's economic base; in future it planned to concern itself primarily if not exclusively with the task of becoming a profitable mining operation.

As for SYSCO, after its status as an integrated steel mill was ostensibly secured by federal-provincial agreement in 1981 (just prior to the onset of the recession), a review subsequently undertaken by DRIE led to the imposition of fresh conditions on further federal aid that would have had the effect of either closing the ageing facility or reducing it to a mini-steel plant. From that point on a politics of state-managed 'down-sizing' – in terms of both concrete industrial shrinkage and the paring down of local expectations – was in play, punctuated by repeated cuts in work-force and production levels at SYSCO and a seemingly interminable process of political bargaining and gamesmanship between the province and the federal government.

On the periphery the megaproject strategy produced a predictable result. In Nova Scotia the Buchanan government seized on the prospect of offshore development and made it the centre-piece of provincial-development strategy. There were, in fact, some immediate benefits to be had for the provincial economy, especially new economic activity related to the increased pace of offshore exploration. However, almost all the benefits were limited to the province's capital and largest urban centre. None the less, the growing enthusiasm of the provincial government for the megaproject strategy elicited widespread public support on the basis of the government's projections of the economic prosperity that would attend the start of such projects. From the beginning such claims were always far in excess of the actual benefits likely to accrue from the projects. Still, it was a relatively easy matter for the Buchanan government to continue to wax enthusiastic about offshore prospects, and even to restructure its development bureaucracy in readiness for the windfall, given the fact that the federal treasury was 'footing the bill' for continued offshore activity.

The 1982 recession also pushed the fishery's recently expanded corporate sector into a financial crisis that made some sort of concerted state intervention necessary if a disastrous collapse was to be forestalled. The result was twofold: state regulations aimed at further limiting and controlling access to the available resource (with the expectation that this would rationalize the inshore fishery and increase its productivity by squeezing out less-efficient operators) and the reorganization of the corporate sector into two super-companies that were provided with new financing, guaranteed access to a major portion of the total allowable catch (TAC) on the Atlantic seaboard, and a mandate to rationalize corporate fishing and processing operations. The thrust of this particular episode of state intervention appears to have been finally to place the fishing industry on a footing not unlike those of other resource-based industries, with a similar development trajectory more and more likely: further rationalization, mechanization, and productivity increases, accompanied over the long term by higher average wages and profits in the corporate sector but an overall reduction in employment levels brought on by a decline in the numbers of small operators. In Nova Scotia, primarily because of the determination of provincial state élites to limit the reach of Ottawa's direct control over the fishery, the new regime would continue to allow a large portion of the control over industrial restructuring, as well as the economic benefits derived therefrom, to remain in the hands of a prominent group of indigenous corporate capitalists.

In general, state élites on the periphery during the period under consideration attempted to articulate concerns and deploy their resources vis-à-vis state élites at the centre in such a way as to consolidate popular support for various strategies, aims, and positions formulated at the provincial level. It can be surmised, however, that the development principles inherent in strategies formulated *at the bureaucratic level* on the periphery did not always or necessarily correspond to the ideological and policy predilections of *the government*, a fact revealed in the growing dichotomy between the formal strategy advocated by the Nova Scotia Department of Development and the situational and short-term responses of the Buchanan government. Moreover, the concrete interests served by that government's policies were often obscured through the use of a provincialist rhetoric that always placed the government's actions in the context of 'getting the best deal for Nova Scotians' or protecting and promoting 'the provincial interest.' This discourse was used to generate public support for a number of government actions that either clearly advantaged particular interests while prejudicing or ignoring others, or else remained poorly articulated and unclear in their long-term implications.

In this connection the Michelin Bill, and the GDA subsidiary agreement on Michelin that followed, placed restrictions on the rights of workers while further securing the power, control, and profits of corporate capital in the province. Similarly, in the case of the fishery, provincialism was used effectively to raise fears among prosperous small-boat fishermen and small capital in the fishery that further domination of the fishery by state élites at the centre would not be in their best interests. This tactic substantially buttressed support for the government's position that the ownership of Nova Scotia's fishing assets was best left in the hands of Nova Scotia's capitalist élite. Finally, in regard to SYSCO, the Buchanan government could publicly adopt a position popular with local unions and politicians while refusing to be drawn into 'too expensive' a proposition. Again, the federal government could be posed as the central obstacle to SYSCO's rehabilitation, and political pressure could be brought to bear on state élites at the centre by portraying the fate of SYSCO as a test of the federal government's commitment to regional development. Thus, the provincial government could garner public support for its position even as negotiations stalled and steel-making operations were cut back. After 1982 the all-too-evident failure of the Trudeau government's economic-development strategy contributed to the rapid decline of Liberal political fortunes. The severity of the recession allowed the federal Conservative opposition to portray the Liberal government's nationalist, interventionist agenda as being at the root of Canada's economic difficulties, with a return to the free market offering the best, indeed the *only*, viable solution. The inefficiency of Crown corporations and government involvement in the economy was a repeated theme in Conservative criticism, with such 'boondoggles' as the continued operation of Cape Breton's two heavy-water plants (despite the absence of a market for their product) singled out as a case in point.[150] At the same time, the Conservatives could effectively argue that, despite such policies, the Atlantic region was farther behind in 1984 than it had been when Trudeau had come to office sixteen years earlier.[151] Indeed, the fact that Atlantic Canada's relative economic position actually deteriorated after DREE was replaced by DRIE in 1982 was used as a basis for laudatory remarks by Tory MPs from Atlantic Canada about the virtues of DREE and criticism of its dismantling as a blatantly political move designed to promote 'Liberal pork-barrelling.'[152] Incredibly, the last Trudeau government actually succeeded in giving credence to such criticisms; a badly flawed and ineffective DREE was suddenly transformed into a relatively attractive development agency that was unworthy of the fate it had suffered.

Well-intentioned or not, over two decades the policies of successive Liberal governments had done much to confuse and discredit the whole concept of 'regional development.' It was left poorly defined as a field of state intervention and highly vulnerable politically, and in the wake of the Liberals' electoral defeat in 1984, all too easily 'written off' by proponents of the virtues of the market and free enterprise as relatively impervious to state intervention and therefore a waste of public resources.[153]

9   The State, Politics, and Centre-Periphery Relations

To understand the magnitude and character of deterministic elements was for him [H.A. Innis] to establish the margin, invariably narrow, in which men were free to make their own history.[1]

This study has addressed a number of questions relating to regional development as a political issue and a policy field. How has the issue of regional development been 'constructed,' debated, and promoted to the state agenda? How has it been related to other major issues on that agenda? How has it been fitted into partisan political strategies? What explains the character of state policies and the pattern of development on the periphery that has been promoted or encouraged? What kind of concessions or gains for the periphery could be extracted through the political mechanisms linking centre and periphery? And what has been the impact of state policies in terms of the general economic welfare of the periphery?

Considering the case of Nova Scotia, its worsening economic situation in the inter-war period created sharp fiscal constraints on the provincial government at the same time that it spurred demands for public monies to ease social hardship and aid economic development. Within a national economic structure that left the province (indeed the whole Atlantic region) in a position of marginality, and that was impervious to adjustment through purely local efforts and actions, political forces in the province sought to secure regional advantage through Ottawa. Thus, it became necessary to alter the attitude of the federal government towards the plight of the Atlantic periphery. To this end, regional representatives articulated Maritime grievances and demands to successive federal governments with the aim of obtaining concessions in national policies and/or a more direct involvement on the part of the federal state in the promotion of regional development. What concessions, if any, and what form of federal intervention, if any, became the subject of a bargaining process, the outcome of which for the peripheral Maritimes was attendant upon a host of factors and conditions. The decision to embrace a policy of reducing regional disparities and effect a change in the regional distribution of economic growth was taken only when economic, political, ideological, and institutional factors tipped the balance of power within the federal state in the direction of such a compromise.

Political forces on the periphery, then, succeeded in gaining the attention of policy-makers to the extent that the issue of regional development was placed on the state agenda. But subsequent state policies were shaped by political, ideological, and organizational factors beyond the control of the periphery. Elites there used what resources were made available to them, in the process adapting to the priorities and strategies of their counterparts at the centre. The alternative – contesting the pattern of national policy through the elaboration of autonomous provincial or regional strategies – was for peripheral élites highly problematic as a course of action, given the meagre resources at hand and the structural constraints imposed by federal policies. And, as demonstrated by the experience of DEVCO, freedom to design and pursue autonomous development strategies at the local or regional level meant little without national policies supportive of those efforts.

Would a national industrial strategy sensitive to the problems of regional development once and for all have solved the problem? Given the evident pressures on state agencies to follow rather than compensate for 'free market' logic and to structure regional-development incentives accordingly, this strategy seems highly unlikely to have been the solution. However, an industrial strategy might have widened the parameters for regional policy-making (from overtly discouraging a greater geographic dispersion of economic activity to actively promoting it in certain sectors). And, given the political will, significant results might have been attained in those public-sector activities not explicitly tied to the operation of market forces (e.g., the growth of government employment through decentralization of government operations and increased defence-related spending in depressed regions). Nevertheless, it appears that as long as the parameters for state intervention were determined by an economy that was capitalistically structured, state policies would remain tied to the logic of that economy, and by extension to interests and needs (those of the dominant fractions of capital) that were seldom congruent with those of periphery residents.

The political economy of the Atlantic periphery is unique in its historical particularity. But it is not without resemblance to the experience of other peripheries within the industrialized capitalist democracies. There is some indication that deeper insights are to be gained about this particular case through the elaboration of certain points of theory about centre-periphery relations in general. A broad theoretical treatment of state, economy, and politics follows, informed by revelations derived from the foregoing study.

A Capitalist State: State Intervention in the Economy

Various theorists have attempted to establish the nature of the broad relationship between the 'economic' and the 'political' in capitalist democracies. Central to much of this work have been the dual concepts of 'relative autonomy' and 'structural constraints.' It has been variously argued that the 'managers' of the capitalist state, while sharing some common characteristics, interests, and objectives with the capitalist class in general, and while subject to the structural constraints imposed by a capitalistically structured economy, nevertheless have a 'relative autonomy' vis-à-vis capital that stems from the separation of the economic and the political in these societies.[2] The state is not, in fact cannot be, confined to the narrow rationality of the accumulating capitalist. Its concern must be with continued overall stability and growth for the whole (which includes, of course, 'capital' as a whole), and the often conflicting and competing demands of specific elements of capital upon the state must be balanced by this overall concern. The importance of preserving the welfare of capital in general, however, goes beyond its mere consideration as one of many actors and social forces in capitalist democracies. The maintenance and expansion of the state itself and its activities depend upon a process of accumulation that, in a capitalist society, is beyond its power to organize. Thus, every occupant of state power is given an interest in promoting those conditions most conducive to continuing accumulation on an ever-widening scale.[3] This *institutional self-interest* of the state in accumulation is conditioned by the fact that the state is denied the power to control the flow of those resources which are nevertheless indispensable for the exercise of state power. Although the agents of accumulation are not particularly interested in "using" the power of the state, state actors must be interested – for the sake of their own power – in guaranteeing and safeguarding a "healthy" accumulation process.'[4]

It should be understood that state intervention in the economy is inevitable and essential for the continued stability and expansion of the accumulation process. Even in the current period of neo-conservatism (more properly called 'neo-liberalism') the state does not cease to intervene; rather its intervention is *restructured*. The state remains central to the process of capitalist development because the dynamics of the capitalist modes of production are such that the conditions for accumulation are continually subject to change, and since the process itself is not a linear one, there is a tendency towards the build-up within the economy of dilemmas and contradictions.[5] In and of themselves, these do not necessarily imply any automatic breakdown of the capitalist mode of production. Their destructive potential can be controlled and/or kept latent through various adaptive mechanisms of the system, including and perhaps most important of all *the state* itself. It provides the institutional means for controlling, reconciling, and overcoming these problems (even if temporarily). It is the one actor or agency within capitalist society which has sufficient autonomy and authority to intervene in order to counteract them.[6]

Thus, the state is obliged to exercise a managerial and supervisory role over an economy that assigns its seminal role to private capital and thus grants to that social class that owns and controls capital a structurally privileged position within capitalist society. This is the true meaning of the term 'capitalist state.' The term does not mean that certain or all capitalists rule directly at the political level. Rather, to paraphrase Panitch, it means that the state's role primarily entails maintaining the social conditions for economic growth and the reproduction of classes in a way consistent with the dynamics of a capitalist economy.[7]

The state, however, does not inherently possess knowledge of the most appropriate response to the needs, problems, and crises of the economy in any particular conjuncture that would allow it to act, reflex fashion, to secure the requisite changes and conditions (this despite the fact of vastly increased organizational, analytical, and general problem-identifying and -solving capacities in advanced capitalist states). There can be no guarantee that state interventions that are subsequently undertaken with the objective of promoting, maintaining, or restoring the process of accumulation will automatically produce the desired results and culminate in a rationalized capitalism. There is no automatic correspondence here between intentions and effects. In Fred Block's words, 'they [state managers] grope towards effective action as best they can within existing political constraints and with available economic theories.'[8] In effect, Block is arguing that the functionality of state policies and processes to the accumulation process should be considered as essentially problematic, which means that the implications of state policies for the accumulation process cannot be predetermined theoretically. Instead they are subject to empirical investigation and assessment.

There do appear to be some basic strategies that state élites can employ in their attempts to reconcile the divergent structural conditions of the capitalist state (i.e., private production, taxation constraints, accumulation, and democratic legitimation) and thus assure continued accumulation and legitimation. Offe and Ronge have identified three such strategies. The first of these is the 'classical' strategy of *inaction*: hoping for the operation of the self-corrective mechanism of the market. Second, the *subsidized protection of values*, or the 'welfare state' strategy, may be adopted. This strategy involves a situation where those owners of labour power and capital who can no longer participate in exchange relationships are 'artificially' maintained by granting them income from sources other than the sale of value. The last strategy, and the one of most recent vintage, is what Offe and Ronge have termed *administrative recommodification*, whereby the state attempts to create politically conditions under which legal and economic subjects can function as commodities. That is, the state implements policies designed to enhance the 'saleability' and 'adaptability' of labour power (through education, training, and regional mobility) and manufactured goods (through research and development, trans-national integration of markets, etc.). It may also encourage a process of rationalization and modernization in those industries, regions, and labour markets that find themselves subjected to increasing market pressures.[9]

All three of the above state strategies have been apparent in the response of the Canadian state to uneven regional development. However, the general pattern has not been one whereby state élites utilize one of these strategies to the exclusion of the others. Rather, there appears to have been a cumulative process whereby a greater emphasis has been given, in successive historical periods, to each of the above-mentioned strategies. Thus, greater, more systematic state intervention in the economy has been the rule since the 1960s, while inaction as a solution to economic problems and crises no longer appears to be a viable strategy for state élites (despite neo-conservative political rhetoric extolling the virtues of the unfettered market). This imperative to intervene is particularly apparent when the role of the state in the field of regional development is considered.

How have state élites justified and rationalized this changing pattern of state intervention in the economy of the periphery? In his innovative and perceptive study of centre-periphery relations in Italy and France, Sidney Tarrow identified three distinct 'models of moral hegemony' or 'ideologies' that informed the discourse of policy élites at the centre in their orientation towards the periphery.

The first of these ideologies, *fostering formal equality*, emphasized equality of access to the law, education, and mobility. Most typical of pre–welfare state liberal capitalism, it defended the legitimacy of material outcomes determined by the operation of the market, whether this applied to individuals or to regions. It tended to offer a narrowly defined equality to citizens and allocated to the individual the responsibility for his/her own material failure or success.

The second ideology, *distributing welfare*, legitimized the distribution of benefits to the periphery to compensate for the market's extractions. Its rise was closely associated with the crisis of 'laissez-faire' capitalism during the Depression years and the Keynesian solution to this crisis, and with the post –Second World War era of economic growth and prosperity, ever-expanding tax revenues, and redistributive public expenditures on social programs. In such circumstances, distributing welfare became a viable and attractive moral option for state élites.

The third ideology, *imposing technocratic reform*, sought to apply the standards of efficiency, market concentration, and competitiveness to the periphery. Its increasing influence on state élites in more recent times can be placed within the context of an important, qualitatively different role for the state in advanced capitalist societies. Lowered trade barriers and increasing international competition has made the restructuring of national economies imperative for state élites at the centre, while fiscal crisis has placed pressure on the growth of welfare expenditures. This pressure led to a redirection of state expenditures to productive activities, with corresponding limits placed on redistribution. Less-developed or lagging regions came to be viewed not only as welfare recipients, but as a serious 'drag' on the national economy.[10]

Each of the above ideologies was used to support the creation, maintenance, and/or reform of particular state structures, policies, and decision-making processes, and each conflicted 'more or less sharply with the values and interests of the periphery.'[11] All remained within the logic of the capitalist economy, but each carried its own implications for various social groupings on the periphery. Viewed within the Canadian context, policies that increased the flow of welfare expenditures to the periphery (e.g., regionalized unemployment-insurance criteria) were of direct benefit to certain subordinate groups, such as inshore fishermen in Atlantic Canada. However, policies aimed at increasing the productivity of industry on the periphery (e.g., supporting modernization schemes) directly benefited capital by enhancing profitability and competitiveness, often at the cost of jobs.

It is no coincidence that the centre-periphery ideologies cited by Tarrow seem to fit within the basic strategies utilized by state élites for dealing with malfunctions or crises in the operation of the capitalist economy; the discourses that govern centre-periphery relations generally surface within the broader context of strategies for dealing with the problems of a capitalist economy and for securing continued accumulation and legitimation. By and large the latter determine the ideological parameters of state policy towards the periphery. And it is within these parameters that official representatives of the periphery, and political forces on the periphery in general, must attempt to articulate their concerns and demands so as to win gains and concessions and stimulate a reshaping of state policies in a way more favourable to their interests.

Parties, Groups, and Bureaucracies: The Balance of Power

Which of the aforementioned strategies for dealing with actual or anticipated economic obstacles, crises, or disruptions – *inaction, subsidized protection*, or *administrative recommodification* – finds expression in state policies depends in large part upon the appearance of particular material pre-conditions within the economy that yield particular 'demands and exigencies.' Yet the simple appearance of such material pre-conditions does not itself determine the manner, timing, or scope of state intervention to 'maintain the commodity form.' Rather, such things will be determined primarily in the realm of *politics*.

As previously argued, the state must promote capital accumulation. But it does so within a framework of containing and mediating relations among the various fractions of capital and between the subordinate and dominant classes. And in performing this role, the state is *not* the preserve of one class but a 'field of political struggle.' The capitalist class remains structurally privileged, based on 'the capitalist's structural position as investor and organizer of production on which all other classes and the state are dependent.'[12] But the strength of subordinate classes (classes other than the capitalist class) is also relevant to any assessment of the balance of forces.

It follows from this that the state will be influenced and constrained by the democratic basis of socio-political relations in these societies. To quote Adam Przeworski:

The indeterminancy inherent in a democratic system constitutes for all the opportunity to realize some of their material interests. Democracy is a social mechanism by which anyone as a citizen can express claims to goods and services which have expanded because a part of the societal product was withheld in the past from the immediate producers. While as immediate producers, wage-earners have no institutional claim to the product, as citizens they can process such claims through the democratic system. Moreover, again as citizens as distinguished from immediate producers, they can intervene in the very organization of production and allocation of profit ... The opportunity is limited but nonetheless real ... [I]t is the only one that is organized, the only one that is available collectively.[13]

Free elections and competition between political parties to determine who wins formal control of the state act as both a source of autonomy for the state (through the legitimacy it gains to act in the interests of society as a whole) and a restraining or moderating factor on its actions. The electoral imperative, however, is only one source of popular influence on state actions. Democratic political institutions also provide other (more direct) channels of access to the state's decision-making apparatuses – channels that are formally made available to non-capitalist as well as capitalist interests.[14]

In this way, expressions of the balance of power among socio-political forces will be reflected within the party system (and within the parties themselves); among state élites, functionaries and analysts; and through the representations of individuals, groups, and classes who attempt to impress upon the state and its political leadership the importance and relevance of their interests in state policy-making. While reorganization and change in state forms and policies may find their impetus in crises or problems in the economy, the state's recognition and handling of these crises and problems is mediated by 'politics,' and the direction and scope of state policy will be limited and shaped by the changing balance of forces engaged in the struggle over policy, and the discursive content of their respective appeals.

Parties and the Representation of Periphery Interests

As previously noted, while the maintenance and expansion of the state and its activities depend upon a process of accumulation that, in a capitalist society at least, is beyond its power to organize, it is *electoral competition between political parties* that determines who gains formal political control over the state, thus creating the potential for state policies to be influenced by political discourses and shifts in the balance of power among various social forces.

Political competition and conflict suffuse capitalist democracies. The party system constitutes the most significant institutional manifestation of this competition, though by no means the only one. Parties mobilize and organize popular and electoral support behind them in their quest for political power. As such they constitute an obvious and readily available mechanism of representation for the expression and mediation of regional interests. But what role have political parties actually played in the Maritimes? How significant, for instance, has the historical absence of a viable third-party alternative in the region been? Does this mean that Maritime politics can be safely labelled as 'conservative' and 'deferential'?[15] Have regional political élites 'sold out,' placing party unity ahead of regional interests?[16] Has the region's potential political power somehow been 'frittered away' in the process, or has it been realized and used constructively? And if so, to what end?

Answering these questions requires an adequate theoretical understanding of the role of political parties in capitalist democracies. To begin, it is a mistake to do as so often has been done and simplistically arrange parties 'along ideological or policy dimensions of "left" or "right" and then hypothetically assign classes to them in a bifurcated fashion.'[17] Such is not characteristic of vote-seeking parties in capitalist democracies that seek to contain within themselves a broad spectrum of the social relations in a society. Subordinate class interests and demands will find expression and mediation *within* traditional bourgeois parties, as well as in 'radical' working-class or producer-based parties. (And this, too, is revealing of the balance of class forces.) At the same time, this responsiveness to the demands of subordinate groups often will tend to be rather limited and symbolic, and generally speaking tied to perceptions of a potential electoral pay-off. 'Political parties constantly sort through the issues, championing some and ignoring others, in order to gain electoral advantage.' According to Janine Brodie, such behaviour on the part of party élites is especially evident in Canada, 'where the ideological differences between the two major parties are minimal and the electorate is volatile.'

In Canada, the major parties act as 'brokers' of a variety of social interests; they must recreate their electoral coalitions at each election. The absence of hard and fast party loyalties in the electorate encourages our parties to be conservative and expedient. They compete for the same voters, so they will not take innovative positions that might alienate significant numbers of voters. But they are also expedient: they become overnight champions of specific groups whose support promises tangible electoral gains.'[18]

This striving for political ascendance, the attempt to subsume diverse and often antagonistic interests under the political leadership of a single party, gives parties a key ideological role. Parties mobilize and organize popular and electoral support behind them in their quest for political power. To this end they employ political strategies that utilize a particular *discourse*[19] with the aim of resolving the abstract problem of conflicts between particular interests and the general interest. This strategic, discursive, and programmatic competition can result in the introduction of new discursive elements, or indeed, in particular conjunctures, may lead to the effective replacement of the dominant discourse by a competing one. At the very least, a dialectic of strategy-programs is likely to stimulate a 'cross-fertilization' process, whereby new elements are adopted into the strategy-programs of political parties as part of the effort to undercut the competition.[20]

Through their use of language and symbols, then, political parties structure electoral competition and shape political conflict.[21] In an oligopolistic party system this structuring and shaping tends to exert a restrictive effect on the political discourse. The acquisition of political power necessarily involves this ideological terrain, which is the main field for political conflict and competition. The ability to sustain the dominance of a discourse favourable to its interests is thus an important measure of the political and ideological power of a class, and any significant change in the balance of class forces must also register itself in this sphere.[22]

With regard to centre-periphery relations, the dominant discourse utilized by élites at the centre will act to limit the range of policy options considered to be available, based on the consequences drawn out of such a discourse, thus shaping responses to the problems and demands of the periphery. A change in the discourse used at the centre can open 'space' for the voicing of demands that had not previously found a receptive ideological framework, and as a result were submerged or inhibited. It can lead to a redefinition of the problems of the periphery and suggest possible new solutions.[23]

In their attitude towards the periphery, what determines the discourse(s) of national party élites? Certainly, political factors and conditions such as how closely those élites are linked with dominant economic groups, and the degree of integration with peripheral social groupings, are likely to produce a set of élites that are more or less sensitive to the problems and demands of the periphery. Regardless, from the point of view of the tactics of political survival and success, broad-based political support for a governing coalition at the centre could make the support of the periphery (and its interests) expendable. Conversely, the instability of political, and especially partisan, alignments at the centre can revalue the political support of the periphery and thus the need to make concessions to periphery demands.[24]

However exploitative or sensitive the attitudes of political élites at the centre towards the periphery, it should also be remembered that any incorporation of periphery demands by élites at the centre takes place within the context of broader political strategies that can be focused upon such diverse objectives as military success, social reform, political stability, national unity, moral regeneration, or any number of broad issues relating to civil society and the state.[25] And, as we have seen, once in power political and bureaucratic élites must always concern themselves with accumulation, and the non-economic aspects of a strategy for acquiring and/or maintaining political power exist in a mutually conditioning relationship with particular economic-growth models. Thus, while there is certainly room for dissociation and inconsistency, if not contradiction, between the two, those who manage the state or seek to manage the state must ultimately organize the necessary compromises and concessions that will make them compatible. State policy towards the periphery will necessarily be formulated within this broader setting, and the 'margin of manoeuvre' for political forces on the periphery to win gains and concessions from the centre will vary accordingly.

From Politics to Policy

The constraints and influences of politics discussed above must be filtered through a particular set of political institutions and state structures, and these exert their own influence on the balance of power between various social and regional groupings. Properly understood, state institutions and policies 'are no more than long-lasting legal resolutions of historically specific conflicts among classes and groups ... states are social structures which reflect the distribution of resources, organization, and support – in short, of power – among classes and other groups at given points in time. These structures, once created, usually pattern political life for many years – specifically, until power is significantly redistributed, at which time new conflicts arise to cause change.'[26]

In the Canadian case, assessing the role of the state apparatus itself in centre-periphery relations – the design and functioning of the institutions of the Canadian state – requires that some consideration be given to bureaucratic and policy-making structures.

To begin, the capacities of bureaucratic structures at particular historical conjunctures can exert some independent effect on centre-periphery relations. The extent of this effect will vary with specifically political histories and the prior development of state structures. The latter, of course, will have implications for the capacity for state intervention in economies and societies at any given time.[27] An expansion in the resources and capabilities of the bureaucracy, for example, opens possibilities for influence and action that might otherwise be inconceivable. Thus the growth of the federal bureaucracy during the Depression and war years provided the administrative and planning capacity for the expanded management role of the state in the post-war period. With the increased popularity of a Keynesian discourse within the upper echelons of the state and the greater autonomy and influence granted bureaucrats by the demands imposed by the war and post-war reconstruction, social-welfare programs were designed and implemented that brought about a significant increase in the allocation of resources (though not a significant redistribution of wealth) to poorer social classes and regions.[28] The adoption of the Keynesian management function and the attendant growth of resources under state control also created a more general capability for intervention in the economy, including if necessary the addressing of regional problems.

Claus Offe has argued that the increased scope and changing quality of the state's intervention in economic decision-making since the Second World War has forced it to establish a 'balance' or 'reciprocity' between its accumulation function, which relates to the accumulation process and its dynamics, and its own internal structure and modes of policy production.[29] Every time the state deals with a problem in its environment, it is forced simultaneously to deal with the problem of its own internal organization (i.e., its appropriateness and adequacy for dealing with the problem at hand). According to Offe, existing state structures and modes of decision-making constitute a major impediment to attaining the necessary reciprocity between the internal organization of the state and any new functions it may seek to perform.

Offe is chiefly referring here to the problems created for modern technocratic planners by the earlier bureaucratization patterns of the state apparatus. Those patterns resulted from the need for the formal and substantive co-ordination of state activities in various spheres. As these proliferated, public bureaucracies became professionalized and organized around a functionalist administrative structure. While this structure imparted an important formal unity to the state, enabling it to carry out administrative and regulative functions with some degree of rationality and efficiency, it has since become a source of problems for the goal of overall planning and direction in state activities to be attained through the creation of some synthetic policy instrument that could imbue the decision-making and administrative process with certain overall values (for instance administrative rationality or economic productivity). Divided as state bureaucracies in their policy and planning functions between hoards of ministries, autonomous agencies, career hierarchies, etc., and in light of the tighter linkages that bind particular departments and agencies to the interests of their client groups than those that exist within the bureaucracy as a whole, overall co-ordination has proved to be extremely difficult.[30]

Of course, Offe's observations, while perceptive, tend to obscure the important fact that attaining 'reciprocity' between state function and structure is pre-eminently a *political* problem, rather than an administrative or technical one. Overcoming or altering prevailing opinions, attitudes, and values within the state is a crucial part of this process. And because change of this sort inevitably embodies differential costs and benefits for various classes in society and client groups of the bureaucracy, it also presages a shift in the interests served by the state.

As noted earlier, states are social structures that reflect the distribution of power in society among various groups, usually over long periods of time. With regard to regional development, a political commitment to address the problem did not alter the fact that, with corporate and financial power and industrial activity concentrated in central Canada, the interests of peripheral regions tended to be 'frozen out' of an essentially sector-oriented administrative structure.[31] Attempts to increase periphery access to bureaucratic and policy-making processes required a reorganization of bureaucratic structures and priorities (and/or the creation of new ones).[32] But this process, common in recent times to most Western capitalist democracies, has largely been one in which regional planning bodies simply have been added alongside, or inside, existing structures, and not substituted for them. The position of these bodies in relation to established administrative institutions has therefore remained ambiguous. Rather than striving for co-ordination through a genuine co-operation between sectors, the tendency has been to expand the scope of responsibilities of each. The outright substitution or subordination of one group of officials by another has been strongly resisted. As a result attempts at regional planning have everywhere tended to stall in the face of determined resistance within the state itself; 'substantive policy integration has been more apparent than real, consisting for the most part of the juxtaposition of sectoral policies.'[33] This planning failure reveals something fundamental about the nature of the state and its relation to social forces. As asserted by M. Watson:

Planning has failed to break down sectoralization in policy-making because it cannot effectively challenge the existing balance of forces in society. The attempt to limit and control the variability of departmental interests inherent in the integration approach really involves, at bottom, the impossible task of regulating the complex of societal interests, with their own separate power bases. What this means is that *planning cannot be a successfully neutral, 'rational' activity*, harmoniously elaborating the 'optimum' development. *The planners have either to choose an alliance or fall back on incremental adjustment simply in response to short-run party and group pressures.* The planning experience is, indeed, at the most fundamental level of relationships, a further illustration that the state is not apart from society, least of all above it, but in it and, as such, the object as well as the subject of many, if not today most, of the great pressures that traverse society [emphasis added].[34]

The obstacles and pitfalls facing technocratic attempts to impose a rational design on state activities, then, are considerable; the state itself is mined with those very societal contradictions and interest conflicts that state planning, co-ordination, and harmonization exercises are intended to diminish or overcome. The state becomes a field of political struggle, and its internal structures will tend to reflect the differential ability of various political and social forces to shape the state apparatus and voice specific demands for state action, whether or not this exerts a distorting effect on the rational intervention of the state to secure maximum efficiency and economic growth. Adjustments to state structures and policies are made as part of the response of state élites to new demands, conflicts, and tensions given rise to by shifts in the distribution of power in society. At the same time, the need to avoid alienation of the structurally privileged capitalist class, which holds the key to economic growth, has remained of paramount concern.

The manner in which changing societal relations of power gain reflection in state structure and policies, while continuing to be subject to 'management' by state élites within a continuing overall hegemony accorded to the capitalist class, has been theorized by Rianne Mahon:

the effect of class conflict on the state apparatuses can be understood as the constitution of the various branches and organs of the state as 'representatives' of the interests of the classes and class fractions present in a social formation. These institutional sites within the state, in turn, act as the means through which the state is able to 'hear' and formulate a response to the issues arising out of inter- and intra-class conflict. Yet just as the relations amongst these forces are unequal, so too does the quality and form of their representation within the state vary; the structure of representation is *unequal*.[35]

In this way Mahon links the development of the state administrative apparatus to the problems associated with maintenance of the 'unstable equilibrium of compromise' that underpins a particular pattern of class domination and capital accumulation. This is a process whereby state representatives translate the demands of particular forces within the state. However, these representatives are not free to formulate and implement the response they deem appropriate to manifestations of instability, 'especially when this procedure involves new initiatives.' Instead, their case is argued within the wider policy network, giving rise to a bargaining process that may or may not result in 'the formulation of new compromises and institutions through which to implement them.' *Political tensions are in this manner translated into administrative problems.* 'Politics' is transformed into 'policy.' As noted by Mahon, 'such adjustments within the structure of representation are necessary in fact, if the state is to be able to work out new patterns of policy compromise.'[36]

What Mahon does not address in her theorization of the 'unequal structure of representation' is the role of party and electoral politics. As previously discussed, partisan political competition demands that parties employ political strategies that make use of particular discourses. The 'shaping' of political conflict that results will determine in broad terms the agenda of whatever coalition of political élites assumes formal control of the state apparatus. In this manner political energy and direction can be injected into the government's supervision of the bureaucracy and the policy-formation process. In this way space for new policy initiatives and altered policy-formation processes can be created through political intervention. But such initiatives will stall or be blunted by the bureaucracy if they are bereft of substantive content, or if they remain oblivious to, or poorly articulated with related policy fields.

The Case of Atlantic Canada

Federal regional-development efforts in Atlantic Cananda typified both weaknesses. Regional demands regarding the appropriate strategy of state intervention to promote economic development on the periphery were shaped primarily by a business-government alliance working closely to promote regional development as an issue at the national level and to develop it as a field of state intervention at the provincial level. However, the ability of periphery élites to shape the response of national state élites to the problem was limited. Some congruence of interest existed with some elements within the state élite at the centre, providing the basis for rather shaky vertical alliances between centre and periphery on this matter. But the extent of congruence varied, depending in large part upon the composition of the state élite and the strategies and discourses employed by them, factors in turn shaped by particular bases of political support as well as the demands and exigencies of managing the national economy and polity.

Arguments for change in the kind of functions performed by the national state, or for that matter the manner in which functions were being performed, occurred within a wider policy network that removed from the representatives of *particular* interests the exclusive power to formulate and implement responses to new demands made upon the state. Thus, regional representatives within the state apparatus and those bureaucrats in favour of an expanded regional-development function for the federal government could make the case for regional policy, but ultimately could not control the manner in which the problem was defined and placed on the state agenda. Instead such aspects of the problem were determined by a number of forces shaping the response of state élites to the politicization of regional disparities, In the event, regional development came to be attached in a haphazard fashion to other state strategies and priorities, significantly distorting and reducing the potential impact of this field of state policy on the spatial distribution of economic activity in Canada.

The potential role for the central state apparatus in regional development, then, has in various ways been constrained. But within such constraints, gains and concessions for the periphery have always been possible. Material concessions to Nova Scotia, and more generally the Atlantic region, have been forthcoming, whether in the form of freight-rate adjustments, coal subsidies, military spending, regionally specific criteria for unemployment benefits, or simply support for infrastructure projects.

Of course, other more individualized benefits have been more or less continuously derived from the patronage bestowed by the party system. In this way *clientism* succeeded in creating a 'vertical alliance' of sorts that bound together local, regional, and national political élites while simultaneously cementing the support of numerous other individuals within the subordinate classes. But clientism alone, though prominent, seldom constituted a *sufficient* system of concessions to subordinate class interests. And with changes to the economic, social, and political landscape on the periphery in the post–Second World War period (for the periphery was stagnant only in a relative sense), the importance and significance of clientism and individualized patronage was gradually reduced as a basis for winning and keeping political support there.

In particular, business élites on the Atlantic periphery in the post-war era became increasingly dissatisfied with the economic state of affairs, and as a result new kinds of vertical alliances began to take shape, replete with the promise of direct government involvement to bolster the economic prospects of the periphery. In the process state élites were drawn more deeply and directly into the economic problems of the periphery. 'Regional development' became the rallying cry for business and government élites on the periphery. It was also an issue that solidified the pre-eminent political position accorded to business interests on the periphery since it generated a political discourse that incorporated the interests of all classes under the banner of 'region.' Such was the case even though the kinds of action generally called for by periphery élites would directly privilege and benefit primarily business – through grants, tax incentives, and other incentives that underwrote the cost of doing business.

All classes, of course, had an interest in expanded economic and industrial activity on the periphery, but the manner in which this was achieved, and the mode and scope of state intervention towards this end, determined the socially allocative range of regional-development policies (i.e., the extent of the 'spread effect' within the periphery community engendered by state actions). If subordinate classes on the Atlantic periphery have *for the most part* appeared to be 'silent' regarding the appropriate strategies and actions the state should adopt in the field of regional development, it has been because the representation of their interests – in discursive terms if nothing else – was 'rolled into' the struggle for 'region.' And leadership in this struggle – including the power to define the issue and determine the policy field – was commandeered by an alliance of business and government élites on the periphery and their supporting cast of agencies.

Does this suggest that the interests of subordinate classes on the periphery have been ignored? The politics of regional development as examined herein might appear to confirm that, for the most part, this, in fact, has been the case. To some extent this impression is a function of the foregoing study's focus on state and political élites. In and of itself, this study is revealing of the nature of subordinate-class power and the representation of subordinate-class interests in Nova Scotia – and more broadly in Canadian – politics. Federal and provincial political élites have been the key actors who on behalf of the periphery have mediated centre-periphery relations, interpreting and incorporating the interests of residents of the periphery in their representations and deliberations.

But beyond this tendency for political élites on the periphery to assume the mantle of guardians of 'the regional interest' is the question of the manner in which that interest has been defined. In the case of Nova Scotia, the process of defining the regional interest has largely been determined by the collaborative efforts of a provincial state–regional business alliance. Other classes have had their interests defined as congruent with the interests of regional business and dependent upon the satisfaction of such interests. In other words, subordinate classes for the most part have had a ghostly presence in regional representations, implicitly present as junior partners often spoken for but seldom speaking for themselves. This does not mean that subordinate class interests are not represented, but rather that they are represented precisely as *subordinate-class* interests, not as a hegemonic interest.

As argued by Tarrow, 'regionalism as ideology,' on the one hand, generally disguises the policy goal of capitalist concentration on the periphery; on the other, it has provided a range of symbols useful in struggles to defend the social and economic space that constitutes the periphery by extracting policy compromises from state élites at the centre, in the process turning domination into hegemony, 'understanding the latter, as Gramsci did, to include both domination *and* consensus.'[37]

Thus, regional-development policies have supported rationalization and capitalist concentration in agriculture, forestry, mining, and fishing; they have promoted large-scale capital-intensive projects in manufacturing and processing; they have favoured the spatial concentration of commercial and industrial activities in growth 'poles' or 'corridors.' Such policies have been designed to provide inordinate benefits to the capitalist class on the periphery, whether regional or multinational in character. As well, they have supported the trend towards widening spatial disparities on the periphery itself. However, the same discourse of regionalism that has elicited this response from state policy-makers has also provided the range of symbols that have been used to convince state élites at the centre to extend the equalization formula, to grant support (however reluctantly) to Nova Scotia's declining coal and steel industries, to launch innovative local development agencies and job-creation projects, and to introduce and maintain regionalized criteria for unemployment-insurance benefits. In other words, regionalism has proved useful as an ideology within which to formulate and legitimate periphery demands. And concessions won in this way from state élites at the centre have served to reaffirm the political salience and appeal of this ideology for residents of the periphery.

A Federal State: The Dialectic of Functionalism and Territoriality

It is through the territorial units they live in that men organize their relations with the state, reconcile or fight out conflicts of interest, and attempt to adapt politically to wider social pressures. Through these same units, central governments distribute grants and services, organize consent, and, when forced to do so, offer correctives to the pressures of economy and society. Thus, how central governments and their territorial subunits are linked politically is not only a problem of inter-governmental relations but also one of managing the class and interest conflicts of modern societies.[38]

The institutional division of a federal system into territorial jurisdictions reinforces the conflictual tendencies – but may also reinforce, in an untidy but generally flexible manner, tendencies to resolve conflicts, through institutionalized channels for playing off functional and territorial interests.[39]

As Tarrow and Whitaker suggest in the above quotations, the role of politics and the state in determining the pattern and pace of development on the periphery will also be shaped by the nature of the institutional setting and the political arrangements that link centre and periphery. Indeed, one of the more notable aspects of advanced capitalist societies has been the continued salience of the territorial cleavage and territorial units of representation.

This proposition is not self-evident, although it may seem to be. Since the beginning of the industrial revolution there has been a trend towards the direct functional representation of organized interests at the apex of the capitalist state. This trend also became more pronounced with the rise of a state that privileges the distinct representation of functional interests in contrast to the classical liberal democracy of an earlier time in which these interests were largely channelled through parliamentary representatives. This general trend has spawned scholarly arguments that territorial representation has declined and will continue to decline vis-à-vis functional representation. Underlying many of these arguments has been the assumption that 'changes in the focusses of representation follow the curve of the modernization process in substituting functional for territorial cleavages as the major axis of politics and forcing demands upwards to the summit of the political system where they are dealt with by technocratic elites in contact with the national representatives of functional groups and parties.'[40]

The relationship between economic modernization and the increasing salience of functional politics occurs as the result of the formation of coalitions by functional interests to influence the actions of government. Moreover, 'in the age of technocratic politics, the core of political pressure and policy proposals moves to within government and its associated circles of professionals and technically trained cadres. New functional clientele groups arise which cut across the levels of government and the traditional governmental system.'[41]

This process leads to increased centralization and increased governmental response to functional interests at the expense of the territorial representation of national parliaments and territorial subunits of the national government.[42]

However, despite the prognostications of numerous theorists of pluralist modernization or corporatism, increasing functional interdependence has not led to the decline or suppression of other factors such as class conflict or centre-periphery tensions. Indeed, based on his examination of centre-periphery relations in Italy and France, Tarrow claims quite the opposite: that as the migration of functional conflicts to the summit of the political system has eroded the role and effectiveness of national parliaments, citizens have turned more and more not to functional representation, but to the territorial institutions around them, reinforcing the territorial dimension in representation.[43] The result is that a new equilibrium of sorts is established between policy centralization and territorial representation. *In effect, the new centralism has created a new localism or regionalism that clings to institutional arrangements premised upon territoriality and uses them to resist the trend to increasing functionalism and centralism.*

In the case of Canada, federalism reinforces and accentuates this phenomenon. Constitutionally both the federal and provincial governments have important powers and jurisdictions, with parallel political executives, state bureaucracies, representative institutions, courts, and police. Moreover, the growth of state activities since the end of the Second World War has taken place at both levels of government, increasing the need for the state to devise means of intergovernmental co-ordination and co-operation and rather byzantine financial arrangements. This situation has developed because, as the scope of state activities has increased, so too have the degree of overlap and blurring between federal and provincial powers and responsibilities. Through its spending power and other means the federal government has vastly expanded its area of concern within the provinces, while, on their part, provincial governments have, in reflex fashion, extended their own expenditures and jurisdictional scope. The resulting need for co-ordination of state activities, expenditures, and interventions of various sorts has led to a wide range of federal-provincial agreements and cost-sharing arrangements that have provided the focus for both co-operation and conflict.[44]

The changing nature and role of the federal-state system in Canada has also served to escalate pressures on the traditional mode of political integration of the subordinate provincial jurisdictions by the central government through the mechanism of national political parties. In Canada, this has historically taken the form of a system of 'ministerialism' that has revolved around the formation and role of federal cabinets. Reg Whitaker has described it as a political device that

places a premium on the regional representativeness of the executive [encouraging] the emergence of regional power-brokers as key Cabinet ministers, who thus play a double role as administrators and as political leaders of regions ... In the absence of strong class bases to national politics [such] cadre-ministerialist party organization rests most comfortably on what can loosely be called a patron-client model. The regional discontinuities of the country lend themselves to a clientelist type of politics in which one sees vertical integration of subcultures and horizontal accommodation among the elites generated by these subcultures. So long as politics revolves mainly around questions of patronage and regional bargaining, ministerialism fits in well with the needs of the party as an organization.[45]

The problem for the practitioners of ministerialism is that as the forces of industrialism and urbanism, and events such as depressions and world wars, have made their impact on the central government in Canada, its attention has been irresistibly drawn to wider problems that demand universalist, bureaucratic solutions. Under the pressure of such external forces, Whitaker argues, *ministerialist* government exhibits a tendency to become *administrative* government and 'politics' turns into 'bureaucracy.' In the past, this tendency has proved to be an impediment to the political health of the governing party, which loses sight of its role as an electoral as well as an administrative organization.

Whitaker's analysis attempts to explain the declining effectiveness of ministerialism as a means of politically integrating Canada's disparate regions, a pre-eminent problem in the history of the Canadian state. But while it is true that individuals in all regions of the country increasingly became clients of a state bureaucracy, it would not be as accurate to say that at the same time they ceased being clients of a political patron or party apparatus or that the latter no longer provided a form of highly valued political linkage to the centre. Instead, the extent to which the party system was displaced as the predominant mode of political integration of the periphery varied across Canada.

In the Maritimes, parties and political élites have continued to retain a greater semblance of their traditional role of using their influence to acquire resources from the centre to distribute on the periphery, propping up party organization and cementing political support in the process. Not that this practice has precluded the growth of formal bureaucratic linkages and transfers as the predominant channel for confronting and resolving tensions in centre-periphery relations, but politics *in all its forms* takes on greater import in regions where the market falls short in performing its distributive function. And despite, indeed in part because of, the modernization of economy and state in the Maritimes, the need for resources from the centre in addition to 'normal' bureaucratic or statutory transfers has remained great – a state of affairs that has fostered an inordinate dependence upon the effective use of political mechanisms to win concessions and acquire resources from the centre as a supplement to, or substitute for, market allocations.

Ministerialism and the party system, then, have continued to play an important role in acquiring resources from the centre to distribute on the Atlantic periphery because political forces in their struggles seize upon and utilize existing structures; they adapt what exists. And what has continued to exist in the Maritimes is sufficient bases of support for both major parties for a modicum of regional representation within the governing party and federal cabinet normally to have been guaranteed. Only twice – in 1925 and again in 1968 – has the Maritimes failed to return to the ranks of the government caucus a contingent that approximated or exceeded the region's percentage share of members in the House of Commons.[46]

In combination, the Maritimes' dependent economic status and the virtually uninterrupted predominance of the traditional two-party system in the region have provided the conditions for a particular role for the party system and political élites in centre-periphery relations. In turn, this has contributed to the shaping of a set of political attitudes and a mode of political behaviour that shows up as evidence in the various cultural explanations for the region's politics. (Thus, intense partisanship has indeed been encouraged, but a partisanship that is more *entrepreneurial* than *militant*. And while a certain *cynicism* about the political process has been perpetuated, it has occurred without undermining a continued rationale for extensive *political involvement* in traditional party politics.)[47] In short, cause and effect often have been confused in explanations for Maritime politics based on political culture. The argument presented here is that it has been the historical role of political institutions in the region that has shaped the political culture, rather than vice versa. And while changes to economy and state may have eroded the basis for traditional clientist politics within the region, continuing relations of external dependence have ensured that the role of parties and political élites in the region has not been completely recast; if they now play a less-central role than they once did, in its essentials it is not an unfamiliar one.

Recalling Tarrow's observations on centre-periphery relations, political system dynamics in Canada *do* appear to have encouraged a certain 'dialectic of functionality and territoriality.' The new centralism associated with the migration of functional conflicts to the summit of the political system in fact has been offset by a new localism associated with the reinforcement and reinvigoration of territorially based representation. Expanded allocations and expenditures originating with state élites at the centre have not eclipsed state structures and capacities on the periphery; in some ways they have buttressed them. And residents of the

Maritimes have turned to territorially bound political institutions and élites as a means of countering and mediating the debilitating effects engendered by a centralizing state and a market-determined marginality.

Intergovernmental and intraparty arrangements do provide a pipeline of sorts for the periphery to ameliorate the domination of the centre. Concessions have been derived and some demands have been acted upon. Federalism has offered regional power groupings the *potential* for greater leverage over the design and implementation of those state policies that apply to the periphery. It has also offered the opportunity and incentive to political parties to become brokers of centre-periphery policy allocation through the exercise of partisan political exchange. In this way both formal and informal patterns of political representation and administrative linkage between centre and periphery have continued to be central to the question of whether governments and groups on the periphery can utilize political links to the centre to their advantage, or whether these are used to make more complete the political and economic domination of the centre over the periphery.

Conclusion

The case of Nova Scotia, and the Atlantic region of which it is a part, offers some insights into the more general fate of peripheral or underdeveloped regions within national social formations. These regional interests are bound up with national struggles over economic-growth models and political hegemony. Indeed, the very constitution of the periphery through its economic and political subordination to the centre is an outcome of these struggles. One should be wary, however, about making assumptions about the role of the state in creating or preserving spatial inequalities in the capital-accumulation process, or, indeed, the political effects of such inequalities. With regard to the historical evolution of the political economy of Nova Scotia, the role of the state has not been unequivocally 'good' or 'bad' for provincial residents. But politics has always been integral to the process of shaping, countering, and ameliorating the impact of market forces. Success in utilizing this avenue of adjustment has been dependent upon the 'space' for regional concerns and demands accorded by the predominant strategy adopted by state élites at the centre towards the economy, which in turn has been a function of the balance of political forces in particular historical conjunctures.

State intervention has also depended upon élite assessments of the threat posed by regional inequalities to continued capital accumulation and political stability, and thus the ramifications for state élites should they choose *not* to intervene. In lieu of a perceived threat to the economic vitality of the centre and/or to the continued existence of the government itself, the pressure for anything more than symbolic state intervention on the periphery has been much attenuated. In this situation stricken regions have been unable to secure any dismantling or redesigning of a policy framework that continued to be operative and viable at the centre, and supported by all those groups that continued to be privileged by it.

This is not to say that concessions and remedial measures were not provoked by regional political forces as a result of their ability to organize an effective political campaign for state intervention to address the regional problem, one that mobilized regional political forces as well as available allies and support groups. Such a campaign succeeded in pre-cipitating certain state actions out of a fear on the part of state élites of the political consequences of not doing so and as the result of the successful linkages that were made between the regional interests at stake and the broader concerns of state élites at the centre. But *fundamental* change in the economic status of the periphery was not achieved. Such change was premised upon, at the very least, a shift in the dominant economic-growth model. But within such constraints, the simple ability of political forces on the periphery to gain concessions and tilt state policies more in their favour, to ameliorate their subordination and marginally improve their long-term development prospects – in effect, to exploit what 'margin of manoeuvre' existed for them – has played and will continue to play some role in determining the future of the periphery.

State élites have always mediated the process of capital accumulation and the uneven regional development that has accompanied it. They have done so within a framework of containing and brokering relations among the various fractions of capital and between the dominant and subordi-nate classes. This mediation has made the role of the state contingent not only upon the demands and exigencies of a capitalistically structured economy, but also upon the changing balance of socio-political forces in society. The former has provided *the material base for politics and state policy-making*, generating a shifting pattern of economic and socio-political pressures and constraints to which state élites have been forced to respond. State policy towards the periphery has been shaped in a general way by such structural constraints. However, the manner, timing, and scope of direct state intervention to address problems of develop-ment on the periphery (or for that matter its conscious non-intervention) have been more immediately determined by factors and conditions expressive of *the balance of socio-political forces in particular historical conjunctures*: the social base, strategies, and discourses of political élites both at the centre and on the periphery; the availability to the periphery of external allies and their strategic posture (what Tarrow has referred to as the 'political opportunity structure' for the periphery);[48] and the bureaucratic structures and ideologies that have constrained and influenced state élites.

Taken together, the above-mentioned factors – encompassing the broad effects of both structure and human agency – have yielded a varying 'margin of manoeuvre' at the centre that has been more or less restrictive, and thus more or less exploitative, vis-à-vis the periphery. The opportunities for political forces on the periphery to win gains and concessions from the state, for the successful posing of their demands (and indeed the very nature of these demands), has been affected accordingly. Thus, the future of the periphery remains tied to developments at the centre, and to the emergence of a set of social and political arrangements reflective of a radical change in the balance of socio-political forces and concomitantly in the dominant strategies and discourses employed by state élites.

Notes

Introduction

1 Tarrow, 'Regional Policy, Ideology and Peripheral Defense: The Fos-sur-mer,' 118
2 Royal Commission on Maritime Claims (Duncan Commission), 1926
3 Atlantic Provinces Economic Council, *The Atlantic Vision – 1990*, 16
4 See Sacouman, 'The "Peripheral" Maritimes and Canada-Wide Marxist Political Economy'; Bickerton, 'Underdevelopment and Social Movements in Atlantic Canada: A Critique'; Clow, 'Politics and Uneven Capitalist Development: The Maritime Challenge to the Study of Canadian Political Economy.'
5 APEC, *Seventh Annual Review: The Atlantic Economy*, 8
6 Williams, *Not for Export: Toward a Political Economy of Canada's Arrested Industrialization*, 173
7 Macridis and Brown, *Comparative Politics*, 14
8 See Kuusisto and Williams, 'Social Expenses and Regional Underdevelopment.'
9 Ibid., 266–7
10 Kent, 'The Brief Rise and Early Decline of Regional Development,' 121

Chapter 1

1 Forbes, 'In Search of a Post-Confederation Maritime Historiography 1900–1967'
2 Ibid., 48–50
3 The following interpretation is largely drawn from the insightful discussion of the literature on Maritime underdevelopment to be found in Clow, 'The Overthrow of Orthodoxy: The New Literature on Maritime Under-development'; and 'Politics and Uneven Capitalist Development: The

Maritime Challenge to the Study of Canadian Political Economy.'
4 Fay and Innis, 'The Maritime Provinces'
5 Saunders, *The Economic History of the Maritime Provinces*
6 Innis, *Essays in Canadian Economic History*, Mary Q. Innis, ed.
7 Mackintosh, 'Economic Factors in Canadian History'
8 Saunders, *Economic History*
9 Ibid., 35
10 Careless, 'Aspects of Metropolitanism in Atlantic Canada'
11 Rawlyk, 'The Maritimes and the Canadian Community'
12 George, *A Leader and a Laggard: Manufacturing Industry in Nova Scotia, Quebec and Ontario*
13 Young, 'Teaching and Research in Maritime Politics: Old Stereotypes and New Directions,' 157
14 Ibid., 159
15 For the most recent example, see Adamson and Stewart, 'Politics in the Mysterious East.'
16 Tarrow, *Between Center and Periphery: Grassroots Politicians in Italy and France*, 20
17 Ibid.
18 Kierstead, *The Theory of Economic Change*, 269–81
19 Woodfine, 'Canada's Atlantic Provinces: A Study in Regional Economic Retardation'
20 See Kuttner, 'The Poverty of Economics.'
21 For an application of such an analysis to the Maritimes, see Courchene, 'Avenues of Adjustment: The Transfer System and Regional Disparities.'
22 Ibid.
23 Alexander, 'Development and Dependence in Newfoundland, 1880–1970,' 16
24 For examples of the application of such explanations and analyses to the economic problems of the Maritimes, see the Royal Commission on Canada's Economic Prospects, *Final Report*, 1957, 401; Graham, *Fiscal Adjustment and Economic Development: A Case Study of Nova Scotia*; George, *A Leader and a Laggard*; Economic Council of Canada, *Living Together: A Study of Regional Disparities*.
25 Weaver and Gunton, 'From Drought Assistance to Mega-Projects: Fifty Years of Regional Theory and Policy in Canada,' 10–11
26 Poetschke, 'Regional Planning for Depressed Rural Areas: The Canadian Experience'
27 Allain and Cote, 'The State and Regional Development Organisations: A Comparative Analysis of Citizen Participation in Quebec and New Brunswick 1960–1980'; see also Gagnon, *Developpement Regional, Etat, et Groupes Populaires*
28 For example, for 'inside' criticism, see Higgins, 'Social Aspects of Regional Planning.'

29 Veltmeyer, 'A Central Issue in Dependency Theory,' 198
30 For a review of the world system model and the role it posits for the dependent state, see Carnoy, *The State and Political Theory*, 185–92.
31 Hechter, *Internal Colonialism: The Celtic Fringe in British National Development 1536–1966*, 33–4
32 Veltmeyer, 'A Central Issue,' 200
33 Ibid., 203
34 Tarrow, *Between Center*, 24
35 Acheson, 'The National Policy and the Industrialization of the Maritimes'
36 T.W. Acheson, 'The Maritimes and "Empire Canda,"' 101
37 Forbes, 'Misguided Symmetry: The Destruction of Regional Transportation Policy for the Maritimes'
38 Sacouman, 'The "Peripheral" Maritimes and Canada-Wide Marxist Political Economy'
39 Clow, 'Politics and Uneven Development,' 120
40 Barrett, 'Perspectives on Dependency and Underdevelopment in the Atlantic Region,' 274
41 Ibid., 277
42 Archibald, 'Atlantic Regional Underdevelopment and Socialism'
43 Frank, *Latin America: Underdevelopment or Revolution*, 9–10
44 Veltmeyer, 'The Underdevelopment of Atlantic Canada'; 'The Capitalist Underdevelopment of Atlantic Canada'
45 Veltmeyer, 'The Underdevelopment of Atlantic Canada,' 96
46 Veltmeyer, 'A Central Issue,' 201
47 Barrett, 'Perspectives on Dependency,' 280
48 See Brym, 'Political Conservatism in Atlantic Canada,' 59–79; Sacouman, 'Semi-Proletarianization and Rural Underdevelopment in the Maritimes.'
49 See Kuusisto and Williams, 'Social Expenses and Regional Underdevelopment.'
50 Tarrow, *Between Center*, 26
51 Barrett, 'Perspectives on Dependency,' 282
52 Brym, 'Political Conservatism,' 64–5
53 See Bickerton, 'Underdevelopment and Social Movements in Atlantic Canada: A Critique'; Fairley, 'The "Metaphysics" of Dualism and the Development of Capitalism in the Fishing Industry in Newfoundland,' and 'The Struggle for Capitalism in the Fishing Industry of Newfoundland,'
54 Clow, 'Politics and Uneven Development,' 133–4
55 'The argument presented here is that capitalist development should be perceived as the social project of the bourgeoisie, not a process governed by the automatic capitalist "laws of motion" ... It [further] argues that politics and federal policies have tended at least to intensify and calcify the regional effects of capital concentration and centralization.' Ibid., 136
56 Jenson, 'Gender and Reproduction: Or Babies and the State'

57 Panitch, 'Dependency and Class in Canadian Political Economy,' 11–12
58 Ibid., 13
59 Ibid., 18
60 On 'issue expansion' as a strategy of dissident or subordinate political groups, see Cobb and Elder, *Participation in American Politics: The Dynamics of Agenda-Building*, 49.
61 The formal agenda of the state refers here to the active consideration of an issue by the political leadership leading to a decision to take some action to resolve or address the issue. Mahon, 'Toward a Marxist Analysis of Issue Formation,' 16; Mahon, *Textiles*, 27
62 Jane Jenson defines the concept of political discourse as, 'the universe of socially-constructed meaning resulting from political struggle. Within this universe, the parameters of political action are established by the process of limiting a set of actors accorded the status of legitimate participants; the range of issues considered within the realm of political debate; the policy alternatives considered feasible for implementation; and finally, the alliance strategies available for achieving change.' Jenson, 'Gender and Reproduction,' 25–6
63 On the basis of his own study of centre-periphery relations in Italy and France, Tarrow warns that politicians representing the local economic élite can divert even the most socially distributive policies to the benefit of those with greater social power. Tarrow, *Between Center*, 41
64 Brym, 'Political Conservatism in Atlantic Canada,' 61, 63, 64, 73, 79. A 'catch-22' is implicit within the direct association posited by Brym between the future political possibilities of subordinate classes and an increase in the latter's structural and organizational capacities. For, with regard to the further industrialization that would provide the structural basis for this change, Brym argues that the process of 'capitalist underdevelopment' continually and necessarily starves the region of the requisite capital investment. Thus, an impasse is reached. Yet economic stagnation has *not* been a permanent feature of the Maritime landscape. In an uneven and irregular fashion the expansion and extension of capitalist social relations of production – in agriculture, forestry, fishing, mining, manufacturing, services – has been proceeding, simultaneously altering the material basis for politics in the region.
65 Brodie and Jenson, 'The Party System,' 225–6
66 Ibid., 225

Chapter 2

1 Muise, 'The Federal Election of 1867 in Nova Scotia: An Economic Interpretation'; Tennyson, 'Another Look at Confederation: A Case Study of Cape Breton'

2 Gordon, 'The Trawler Question in the United Kingdom and Canada,' 119–23
3 This was true for obvious reasons. The capital required was much greater and technical expertise played a much larger role. Large corporations were quickly consolidated after the 1887 'iron tariff' guaranteed a stable market for potential output, gaining control over the major manufactories and coal and iron-ore supplies. Acheson, 'The National Policy and the Industrialization of the Maritimes, 1880–1910'
4 Ibid., 6
5 Forbes, *Maritime Rights: The Maritime Rights Movement*, 61
6 McCallum, *Unequal Beginnings: Agriculture and Economic Development in Quebec and Ontario Until 1870*, 110
7 Acheson, 'The National Policy,' 3
8 Frost, 'The "Nationalization" of the Bank of Nova Scotia, 1880–1910'
9 Acheson, 'The National Policy,' 15–19; 'The Social Origins of Canadian Industrialism: A Study in the Structure of Entrepreneurship,' 84–94; 'The Maritimes and Empire Canada,' 95
10 Alexander, 'Economic Growth in the Atlantic Region, 1880–1940,' 67
11 Ibid., 54
12 Traves, *The State and Enterprise: Canadian Manufacturers and the Federal Government 1917–1931*, 6
13 Hobsbawm, *Industry and Empire*; Landes, *The Unbound Prometheus: Technological Change and Industrial Development in Europe from 1750 to the Present*, 231–358
14 Williams, *Not For Export: Toward a Political Economy of Canada's Arrested Industrialization*, 27–9
15 Laxer, 'The Political Economy of Aborted Development: The Canadian Case,' 95. Laxer classifies Canada, along with Italy, Japan, and Sweden, as a 'late follower,' a country that experienced its period of industrial 'take-off' not long after this process had already been completed in Britain and the second group of industrializers – Germany, France, and the United States.
16 Dominion Bureau of Statistics, *The Maritime Provinces Since Confederation*, 5, 32
17 Ibid., 66
18 Alexander, 'Economic Growth,' 63. In 1911, pulp production represented only 7 per cent of lumber output; this rose to 55 per cent by 1926, and by the mid-1930s pulp-and-paper production had overtaken a depressed lumber sector.
19 Ibid., 66
20 Laxer, 'Aborted Development,' 78–84
21 Frank, 'The Cape Breton Coal Industry and the Rise and Fall of the British Empire Steel Corporation,' 77

22 Forbes, *Maritime Rights*, 26, 49, 63–4
23 Traves, *State and Enterprise*, 7–11
24 Saunders, *The Economic History of the Maritime Provinces*, 85
25 Forbes, *Maritime Rights*, 61–3
26 Ibid., 65
27 Alexander, 'Economic Growth,' 67, 70
28 Forbes, *Maritime Rights*, 55
29 Ibid., 55–6
30 Ibid., 66–7
31 Alexander, 'Economic Growth,' 71
32 Forbes, *Maritime Rights*, 77
33 Ibid., 64
34 English, *The Decline of Politics: The Conservatives and the Party System 1901–1920*, 50
35 Ibid., 87
36 Ibid., 85
37 Ibid., 74
38 Forbes, *Maritime Rights*, 25
39 Ibid., 69
40 Ibid., 22–3. As noted by Forbes, Maritime politicians themselves were partly responsible for creating this image of the ICR in the first place, through their internecine battles and partisan attacks over the years on the issue of its management and operation.
41 Ibid., 20–1
42 Forbes, 'Never The Twain Did Meet: Prairie-Maritime Relations 1910–27'
43 Armstrong, 'The Politics of Federalism: Ontario's Relations with the Federal Government 1896–1941,' 444–9, 469–71
44 Forbes, *Maritime Rights*, 27. New Brunswicker Sir George Foster, Minister of Trade and Commerce throughout the Borden years, sat as a member for a Toronto constituency from 1904 onward.
45 Ibid., 28
46 Ibid., 67–9
47 Ibid., 68
48 Ibid., 23
49 Ibid., 25
50 Ibid., 40–3; Brodie and Jenson, *Crisis, Challenge and Change: Party and Class in Canada*, 139–42
51 Rawlyk, 'The Farmer-Labour Movement and the Failure of Socialism in Nova Scotia'
52 Forbes, *Maritime Rights*, 96–101
53 Ibid., 108
54 Ibid., 87
55 Ibid., 88–95; Brodie and Jenson, *Crisis, Challenge and Change*, 139–42

56 Forbes, *Maritime Rights*, 94
57 Ibid., 88, 98–9, 117
58 Macgillvary, 'Military Aid to the Civil Power: The Cape Breton Experience in the 1920's'
59 Forbes, *Maritime Rights*, 130–4, 157
60 Frank, 'Cape Breton Coal,' 79
61 These were resolutions passed by UMW delegates at a provincial labour convention. This suggests a high degree of left-wing militancy at this time within the elected leadership. Forbes, *Maritime Rights*, 42, 59
62 Ibid., 60
63 Ibid., 120
64 Mellor, *The Company Store: James Bryson McLachlan and the Cape Breton Coal Miners* 1900–1925; MacEwan, *Miners and Steelworkers*, 124, 131
65 MacEwan, ibid., 74, 124
66 Ibid., 92–8, 103–4
67 Ibid., 133; Mellor, *The Company Store*, 202, 296
68 Mellor, ibid., 207–8
69 Frank, 'Cape Breton Coal,' 124–5
70 Forbes, *Maritime Rights*, 185
71 Saunders, *Economic History*, 45
72 Forbes, *Maritime Rights*, 47, 112
73 Ibid., 55–6
74 Ibid., 183
75 Ibid., 162
76 Ibid., 164–8
77 Ibid., 160–1
78 Ibid., 173–5
79 Ibid., 176
80 Ibid., 180
81 Ibid., 180–1
82 Ibid., 189–90
83 Grant, 'Population Shifts in the Maritimes', 282–94
84 Forbes, *Maritime Rights*, 148
85 Ibid., 187
86 Armstrong, 'The Politics of Federalism,' 444–9, 469–71
87 Neatby, *William Lyon MacKenzie King: Volume Three* 1932–39: The Prism of Unity, 150, 156, 161

Chapter 3

1 Kierstead, *The Economic Effects of the War on the Maritime Provinces of Canada*, 98–9
2 In the fishing industry the most notable examples of this were the Anti-

gonish Movement co-operatives, which emerged after the MacLean Commission had urged the development of co-operatives among inshore fishermen. In the forest industry, 'co-operative organization' generally took the form of woodlot owners' associations.

3 Forbes, 'The Rise and Fall of the Conservative Party in the Provincial Politics of Nova Scotia 1922–33,' 144

4 Saunders, *The Economic History of the Maritime Provinces*, 48, 63. Actually, some areas and product groups did fairly well during the Depression. However, the sector remained dominated by the small, unspecialized semi-subsistence farm, a situation reinforced by the flow of labour back into the agricultural sector occasioned by the Depression. Saunders, *Studies in the Economy of the Maritime Provinces*, 237–8; Lattimer, 'Agriculture,' 157, 164

5 Saunders, ibid., 62, 65

6 Ibid., 50

7 Kierstead, *Economic Effects of the War*, 98–9. 'Small holdings' in this instance are considered to be less than 1,000 acres.

8 Saunders, *Economic History*, 81

9 Royal Commission of Provincial Economic Inquiry (Jones Commission), *Complementary Report*, 148–9

10 Saunders, *Economic History*, 73

11 Lounsbury, *Secondary Manufacturing in the Atlantic Provinces*, 33. The Depression-era expansion of manufacturing linked to wood-using industries is largely attributable to the growth of pulp-and-paper production.

12 Jones Commission, *Complementary Report*, 140

13 Saunders, *Economic History*, 68

14 Ibid., 70

15 Ibid., tables 28 and 30, 128–30

16 Ibid., 45–6

17 Ibid., 71

18 Ibid.

19 Ibid., 49. The average number of persons engaged in primary fishing operations in the Maritime provinces rose from 28,000 in 1925, to 30,000 in 1929, to 35,600 in 1938.

20 Barrett, 'Development and Underdevelopment and the Rise of Trade Unionism in the Fishing Industry of Nova Scotia 1900–1950,' 6, 21–30, 37–8, 110; Parks, *The Economy of the Atlantic Provinces 1940–1958*, 50–1

21 Royal Commission on Canada's Economic Prospects (Gordon Commission), *Report*, 123–5; Barrett, 'Development and Underdevelopment,' 92–4

22 Barrett, 'Development and Underdevelopment,'

23 Ibid., 96–7, 100

24 Ibid., 105–7, 118–22

25 Ibid., 51–2, 122

26 Coady, *The Man From Margaree: Writings and Speeches of M.M. Coady*
27 The strongest agricultural co-operative in the inter-war period – the United Fruit Company Cooperative – was based in Nova Scotia's prosperous Annapolis Valley. See MacPherson, *Each for All: A History of the Cooperative Movement in Canada, 1900–1945*, 100.
28 Baum, *Catholics and Canadian Socialism*, 189–90; MacInnis, 'Clerics, Fishermen, Farmers, and Workers: The Antigonish Movement and Identity in Eastern Nova Scotia,' *passim*.
29 Coady, *Man From Margaree*, 95–107
30 Baum, *Catholics*, 193, 196, 202–4
31 Coady, *Man From Margaree*, 132; MacInnis, 'Clerics,' 430
32 MacPherson, *Democracy in Alberta: Social Credit and the Party System*, 45–6
33 Panitch, 'Corporatism in Canada?,' 58
34 MacPherson, *Each for All*, 169
35 Ibid., 22
36 Ibid., 82
37 Forbes, 'Rise and Fall,' 13
38 Ibid., 4–5
39 On the neglect of the Maritimes by the King government between 1921 and 1925, see Neatby, *William Lyon MacKenzie King 1924–32: The Lonely Heights*, 12.
40 The widening rift within the Farmer-Labour camp allowed the Conservatives, through conciliatory gestures and promises, to entice at least two Farmer-Labour MLAs to run as Conservatives in the next provincial election. Forbes, 'Rise and Fall,' 30
41 Ibid., 52
42 Ibid., 10–12
43 Forbes, *Maritime Rights: The Maritime Rights Movement 1919–1927*, 130–7
44 MacEwan, *Miners and Steelworkers: Labour in Cape Breton*; Beck, 'The Party System in Nova Scotia: Tradition and Conservatism,' 187, 189
45 MacEwan, *Miners and Steelworkers*, 145–6
46 Forbes, 'Rise and Fall,' 79–80
47 This occurred despite the attempts of the Liberal party to rehabilitate its poor labour image with promises of old-age pensions, an eight-hour workday for miners and steelworkers, and increased benefits under the Workmen's Compensation Act. Ibid., 121
48 Ibid., 109–10
49 Ibid., 102; Forbes, *Maritime Rights*, 147
50 Lounsbury, *Secondary Manufacturing*, 23; Saunders, *Economic History*, *passim*. Between 1926 and 1929 output in secondary manufacturing rose 34 per cent and employment jumped 26 per cent. These increases are misleading, however, when one considers the very low levels of produc-

tion and employment at mid-decade, and the fact that almost all the increase in secondary manufacturing in the later 1920s was attributable to a recovery in steel and transportation equipment (primarily rail cars).

51 Policy changes or promises that were put on hold included old-age pensions for Nova Scotians, a department of labour, and a sharp reduction in expenditures on public works, notably highway construction. Forbes, 'Rise and Fall,' 112, 141, 146; Provincial Secretary's Papers (referred to hereafter as PS Papers), Nova Scotia Public Archives, RG-7, vol. 231, F5–10. Letter from the federal minister of labour to the Nova Scotia premier.

52 Forbes, 'Rise and Fall,' 157; MacEwan, *Miners and Steelworkers*, 169–84. The latter schism was one that forced the provincial government to take sides, negating not only the likelihood of a solid bloc of labour support for the Conservatives, but also the influence of organized labour in the province as a potentially determinant voting bloc in many constituencies.

53 Forbes, 'Rise and Fall,' 184–92

54 Ibid., 162

55 Ibid., 166; Hawkins, *The Life and Times of Angus L. Macdonald*

56 Forbes, 'Rise and Fall,' 168–9

57 Hawkins, *Life and Times*, 171–3

58 Royal Commission of Provincial Economic Inquiry (Jones Commission), *Report*, 7

59 Jones Commission, *Submission of the Government of Nova Scotia*, 119

60 Ibid., 161–95

61 Jones Commission, *Report*, 43, 49

62 Ibid., 31–3

63 Ibid., 63–6

64 Ibid., 71

65 Ibid., 75–6

66 Ibid., 84

67 Ibid., 87

68 Ibid., 90, 93, 96

69 Ibid., 91–5, 224

70 Jones Commission, *Complementary Report* (H.A. Innis), 156

71 Ibid.

72 Ibid., 220

73 Ibid., 221

74 Beck, *The Government of Nova Scotia*, 222–4

75 During the eight-year period 1930–7 capital outlay on highways was four times as great as total expenditures by all levels of government in the province on direct relief. Royal Commission on Dominion-Provincial Relations (Rowell-Sirois Commission), *Report*, Book I: 'Canada 1867–1939,' 65

76 Saunders, *Economic History*, 44–51, 73, 82; Hawkins, *Life and Times*, 184

77 PS Papers, vol. 231, F8–7. Dominion-Provincial Conference, 1935, Minutes of the Committee on Unemployment Relief

78 Hawkins, *Life and Times*, 183

79 MacEwan, *Miners and Steelworkers*, 202–5

80 Ibid., 182–9

81 Armstrong, 'The Politics of Canadian Federalism: Ontario's Relations with the Federal Government 1896–1941,' 444–9

82 Ibid., 463, 471. Prime Minister King was no more concerned or sympathetic. He referred to the pleas of P.E.I.'s Premier Saunders for a larger subsidy as 'a terrible piece of mendicancy, unworthy of manhood.' Quoted in Forbes, *Maritime Rights*, 186

83 Armstrong, 'Politics of Canadian Federalism,'

84 Ibid., 463

85 Forbes, 'Rise and Fall,' 112, 141

86 Armstrong, 'Politics of Federalism,' 502, 506. The dominion's growing frustration with the situation, however, and perhaps too the mounting pressure on Ottawa to do something about it, became evident at a similar conference the next year when the meetings broke up after Bennett's ranting attack on provincial wastefulness and extravagence.

87 Neatby, *William Lyon MacKenzie King: Volume Three* 1932–39 'The Prism of Unity', 150

88 Ibid., 130

89 Dominion-Provincial Conference, 1935, *Proceedings*. The Judicial Committee of the Privy Council would eventually rule the package of legislation Bennett called his 'New Deal' as *ultra vires* and therefore invalid.

90 PS Papers, vol. 231, F5–2. Dominion-Provincial Conference, 1935, Minutes of the Sub-conference on Financial Questions. It appears that unemployment relief was not the most important of these for reasons already cited. In fact, Nova Scotia adopted the position at the 1935 conference that the responsibility for relief should be left with the municipality, with provincial supervision. See PS Papers, vol. 231, F8–7. Minutes of the Committee on Unemployment Relief.

91 Neatby, *WLMK: Vol. Three*, 151, 156

92 Royal Commission on Financial Arrangements Between the Dominion and the Maritime Provinces

93 Neatby, *WLMK: Vol. Three*, 156

94 Ibid., 161

95 Granatstein, *The Ottawa Men: The Civil Service Mandarins* 1935–1957, 56–61

96 Neatby, *WLMK: Vol. Three*, 157

97 Ibid., 255–7. Granatstein, *The Ottawa Men*, 156–7

98 Rowell-Sirois Commission, *Submission of the Government of Nova Scotia*, 144–5

99 Armstrong, 'The Politics of Federalism,' 569–72
100 Rowell-Sirois Commission, *Report*, Book II: 15, 20–2, 78–9
101 Armstrong, 'The Politics of Federalism,' 572

Chapter 4

1 Royal Commission on Provincial Development and Rehabilitation (referred to hereafter as Dawson Commission) *Report*, 58.
2 Ibid., 46–7
3 Kierstead, *The Impact of the War on the Maritime Economy*, 24–5
4 Graham, *Fiscal Adjustment and Economic Development: A Case Study of Nova Scotia*, table IV, 25. These calculations include a rise in the relative position of the region during the 1943–6 period that was all but wiped out by a sharp downturn for the period 1946–8.
5 Parks, *The Economy of the Atlantic Provinces* 1940–1958, 11.
6 Department of Labour, *Employment and Manpower Utilization in Nova Scotia* 1950 to 1960
7 Fletcher, *Post-War Agriculture Trends in the Atlantic Provinces*, 19
8 Parks, *The Economy*, 67
9 Howland, *Some Regional Aspects of Canada's Economic Development*, chart X, 178
10 Fletcher, *Post-War Agriculture*, 12
11 *Financial Post*, 'The Maritimes: A Feature Report,' 15 June 1957, 50
12 Fletcher, *Post-War Agriculture*, 37
13 Ibid., 43–7. A simple change in the census definition of farms in 1961 (adding $50 in goods sold as a criterion for farm status) statistically eliminated 30.4 per cent of all Atlantic region farms, as compared to 12 per cent in Quebec and 4.8 per cent in Ontario. This outlines the considerable degree to which subsistence and part-time agriculture remained prevalent in the Atlantic provinces.
14 Ibid., 51–2
15 Ibid., 81, 92
16 Ibid., 64–5. Morse, 'Agriculture in the Maritime Provinces,' 477
17 *Financial Post*, 'The Maritimes,' 50
18 Royal Commission on Canada's Economic Prospects (referred to hereafter as Gordon Commission), *Submission of the Government of Nova Scotia*, October 1955, 11; Special Senate Committee on Land Use in Canada, *Proceedings*, 28 February 1957, 85–92
19 Gordon Commission, *Preliminary Report*, 102; Gordon Commission, *Report*, 407
20 Graham, *Fiscal Adjustment*, 112
21 Fletcher, *Post-War Agriculture*, 23
22 Parks, *The Economy*, 26–8

23 Ibid., 39–45
24 Howland, *Some Regional Aspects*, 181
25 Department of Labour, *Employment*, 9
26 Pepin, *Life and Poverty in the Maritimes*, 204–6
27 Wilbur, 'Maritimes: Planned Underdevelopment,' 15
28 Department of Labour, *Employment*, 10
29 Gordon Commission, *Submission of the Government of N.S.*, 15–16
30 Gordon Commssion, *Report*, 406–7
31 Barrett, 'Development and Underdevelopment and the Rise of Trade Unionism in the Fishing Industry of Nova Scotia, 1900–1950,' 123
32 Ibid., 125
33 Ibid., 126; Gordon Commission, *Report*, 127
34 Barrett, 'Development and Underdevelopment,' 132–4
35 Jansen, 'Regional Socio-Economic Development: The Case of Fishing in Atlantic Canada,' 245
36 Gordon Commission, *Report*, 187
37 *Financial Post*, 'The Maritimes,' 50
38 Parks, 'The Economy,' 52–3. In current values
39 Howland, *Some Regional*, 179
40 Gordon Commission, *Report*, 187–8
41 Barrett, 'Development and Underdevelopment,' 179
42 Clement, *The Struggle to Organize: Resistance in Canada's Fishery*, 23, 74.
43 The Canadian union movement attempted to purge itself of those unions that were less than squeaky clean in this regard. See Lazarus, *Years of Hard Labour*, 49–51; Abella, *Nationalism, Communism, and Canadian Labour*; Penner, *The Canadian Left*. With regard to the Canadian Seaman's Union, the federal cabinet itself was involved in its destruction, having invited in a U.S.–based international, the Seaman's Internatinal Union (SIU), led by the notorious Hal Banks. See the CBC Television documentary *Canada's Sweetheart* (1985). The CCF leadership fought the communists at every turn throughout the 1930s and 1940s, only to suffer by dint of association with things 'socialist.'
44 Barrett, 'Development and Underdevelopment,' 206–7
45 Department of Trade and Industry, *A Brief Review of the Fisheries of Nova Scotia*, 40, 45–7
46 Angus L. Macdonald Papers (hereafter referred to as ALM papers). Nova Scotia Public Archives. MG2/914. Letter from H. Connolly to A.L. Macdonald, 16 and 28 October 1947
47 Parks, *The Economy*, 20
48 Royal Commission on Coal (referred to hereafter as Rand Commission), *Report*, 1
49 Ibid., 18
50 MacEwan, *Miners and Steelworkers*, 275

51 Ibid., 285–7
52 Rand Commission, *Report*, 2
53 Gordon Commission, *Report*, 409
54 Ibid., 18–19. The Gordon Commission's own study on the Nova Scotia coal industry anticipated a further decline to seven thousand miners before completion of the mechanization program.
55 Rand Commission, *Report*, 7. The work-force in West Virginia dropped from 117,000 to 40,000 in ten years, yet production levels actually increased. Higher Nova Scotia production costs meant that the average cost at pit-head for Nova Scotia coal was $10.72 per ton as against U.S. costs ranging from $3.60 to $5.33 per ton. Average output per man in U.S. mines was 11 tons and rising, as against 2.66 tons in Nova Scotia in the 1950s. Rand, ibid., 17; Gordon, *Report*, 409
56 Rand, *Report*, 10
57 Ibid., 33, 38, 44, 47, 49
58 Parks, *The Economy*, 76
59 MacEwan, *Miners and Steelworkers*, 257–8
60 Voluntary Planning Board, *Annual Report*, 1967
61 MacEwan, *Miners and Steelworkers*, 261, 265
62 Graham, *Fiscal Adjustment*, table VII, 29
63 Parks, *The Economy*, 79–80. Iron and steel and transportation equipment continued to dominate Nova Scotia's post-war manufacturing sector.
64 Lounsbury, *Secondary Manufacturing in the Atlantic Provinces*, 36
65 Ibid., 45–6
66 Ibid., 58
67 Ibid., 88–9
68 Parks, *The Economy*, 104, 107, table LIV
69 Department of Labour, *Employment*, 6
70 Graham, *Fiscal Adjustment*, 110
71 Department of Labour, *Employment*, 8, 12
72 Ibid., 10
73 Nova Scotia Voluntary Planning Board, *Report on Progress*, 36
74 In identifying the 'source' of the region's relatively impoverished state, the commissioners noted that the disparity between the Atlantic region and the other six provinces in Canada would be reduced by from 37 to 15 per cent if metropolitan areas alone were considered.
75 Gordon Commission, *Report*, 410–13
76 Parks, *The Economy*; Graham, *Fiscal Adjustment*; Cairncross, *Economic Development and the Atlantic Provinces*
77 Parks, *The Economy*, 147–9
78 Graham, *Fiscal Adjustment*, 139–40
79 A.K. Cairncross as quoted in ibid., 141
80 As evidenced by the public outcry in the Atlantic provinces at those Gor-

don Commission recommendations that appeared to imply the need for a modern-day highland clearances

81 Howland, *Some Regional Aspects*, 190–1
82 Parks, *The Economy*, 139, 141
83 Pickersgill, *The MacKenzie King Record Vol. 1*, 466
84 See Lewis, *The Good Fight: Political Memoirs* 1909–1958, 292–3; Whitaker, *The Government Party*, 147–8
85 Whitaker, *The Government Party*, 147–8
86 Neatby, *William Lyon MacKenzie King: Volume Three:* 1932–1939 'The Prism of Unity,' 239, 255, 257; Granatstein, *The Ottawa Men: The Civil Service Mandarins* 1935–1957, 156–8
87 Granatstein, *Canada's War: The Politics of the MacKenzie King Government* 1939–1945: see chapter 7, 'Public Welfare and Party Benefit.'
88 See Lewis, *The Good Fight*, chapters 12–14
89 David Lewis, national secretary of the CCF at the time, remembers his surprise at the UMW decision, and his complete lack of knowledge about the Maritimes and District 26 of the UMW. Believing their example would be widely and quickly followed, Lewis was careful to work out organizational and constitutional details for affiliation. One of his concerns was to keep communist 'infiltration' of the party to a minimum through specially designed constitutional provisions. Lewis, *The Good Fight*, 153–4
90 See Lewis, *The Good Fight*, chapter 13, 'Post-Mortems.'
91 Brodie and Jenson, *Crisis, Challenge, and Change: Party and Class in Canada*, 204
92 Dawson Commission, *Report*, 57
93 Ibid., 58, 59, 65, 66, 72
94 Kierstead, *The Impact of the War*, 28
95 ALM Papers, MG2/898: Report of the Executive of the Cape Breton Committee for Full Employment, 14 December 1945; letter from the United Mine Workers to H. Connolly, Minister of Industry, 15 December 1945; proposed legislation presented to Premier A.L. Macdonald by the Nova Scotia Federation of Labour, February 1946
96 ALM Papers, MG2/898: letter to A.L. Macdonald from R.M. Dawson, 27 March 1946
97 Ibid., letter to Hon. T.A. Crerar, 18 January 1946
98 Ibid., letter to H.A. Innis, 18 January 1946
99 Ibid., letters exchanged between A.L. Macdonald and J.A. Corry, January and February 1946. This concern that Nova Scotia had to 'beef-up' its bureaucratic capacities had been earlier argued by Innis (1934) and Dawson (1944) in their respective royal commisison reports to the Nova Scotia government, but it was a recommendation that Macdonald resisted, not surprisingly in light of his seeming aversion to larger bureaucracies.
100 Ibid., letter to A.L. Macdonald, 17 January 1946

101 Ibid., letter to A.L. Macdonald, 13 February 1946
102 ALM Papers, MG2/899A/ F339, F343
103 Ibid., MG2/899A/ F3–27
104 Ibid., MG2/899A/ F4–12
105 Ibid., MG2/899A/ F3–28, p. 8
106 Ibid., MG2/899A/ F4–12
107 Ibid., MG2/899A/ F3–28, p. 4
108 Ibid., MG2/899A/ F3–28, p. 3
109 Dominion-Provincial Conference, 1946, Nova Scotia Submission and Plenary Discussion, 316–17
110 ALM papers, MG2/898: letters exchanged between Drew and A.L. Macdonald, 18 August, 20 September, 27 December 1946; notes on a conversation between Drew and Macdonald at Toronto, 5 February 1947
111 Ibid., MG2/899A/ F4–12: Summary of Proceedings of Economic Committee by L.E. Peverill (Nova Scotia's representative), p. 4
112 MacKinnon, *The Life of a Party: The History of the Liberal Party in Prince Edward Island*
113 ALM papers, MG2/899A: letters from King to Drew, 10 October 1946 and King to Manning, 14 October 1946
114 Ibid., MG2/899A: letter to Grant Dexter, 14 December 1946
115 Ibid., MG2/899A: letters to A.L. Macdonald, 11 and 21 February 1947;letters from A.L. Macdonald to Winters, 14 February 1947. Winters even attempted to argue that old-age pensions and family allowances had sweetened the deal for Nova Scotia relative to some wealthier provinces, but when this succeeded only in provoking an angry response from Macdonald, he resorted to a simple statement of support for the dominion position, while assuring Macdonald that caucus members would do all in their power to sell the deal to Nova Scotians.
116 Ibid., MG2/899A: letter to Drew, 10 May 1947
117 Wolfe, 'Economic Growth and Foreign Investment: A Perspective on Canadian Economic Policy 1945–57'
118 See Ray, 'The Location of U.S. Manufacturing Subsidiaries in Canada'
119 Bothwell, *War Into Peace: C.D. Howe as Minister of Reconstruction*, 14–17. The 'public works shelf' refers to the large-scale program of public works that was thought to be ready and waiting should the need arise. Exactly the type of state intervention advocated at the time by Dawson, Nova Scotia unions, and the CCF, it was never put into effect.
120 Ibid., 19
121 ALM Papers, MG2/933: letter to A.L. Macdonald, 5 February 1948
122 Camp, *Gentlemen, Players and Politicians*, 7
123 ALM papers, MG2/946/F32–1/24. The 'autocratic' attitude of the dominion government towards the attempts by the Maritime premiers (in alliance with some other provinces) to have the decision overturned, or at least

postponed, infuriated the Nova Scotia premier, and led him to warn of an impending rise in anti-Ottawa, regionalist sentiment should this method of dealing with Maritime grievances continue. MG2/933/27–3/18

124 Ibid., MG2/933/F27–3/69 and 86. The complaints of the Maritimes about freight-rate increases eventually resulted in another royal commission (the Turgeon Commission, 1951). The appeal of regional representatives, however, was met with a terse statement that the MFRA was a 'once and for all' measure that had performed 'all the functions for which it was designed.' Forbes, 'Misguided Symmetry: The Destruction of a Regional Transportation Policy for the Maritimes,' 76

125 ALM Papers, MG2/933/27–3/18: letter to Alex Johnson, 12 April 1948; MG2/946/F32–1/24: correspondence exchanged with Rand Matheson and Maritime Board of Trade Transportation Commission; MBTTC submission to Turgeon Commission

126 Forbes, 'Misguided Symmetry,' 76

127 Federal-Provincial Conference, 1950, *Proceedings*, 6

128 Atlantic Provinces Economic Council, *Defence Expenditures and the Economy of the Atlantic Provinces*, passim

129 Green, *Against the Tide: The Story of the Canadian Seamen's Union*, 214

130 Ibid., 210

131 Ibid., 205

132 Ibid., 286

133 Ibid., 210

134 Hawkins, *The Life and Times of Angus L. Macdonald*, 179, 242

135 ALM Papers, MG2/952/F21–1/5: memo to H. Connolly, 15 May 1950; Nova Scotia, Budget Address, 7 March 1952, 12. It should be recalled that in the 1930s the Jones Commission had strongly argued the case for complete provincial control over Nova Scotia's fishery because of federal neglect.

136 For example see MG2/914: letter from Connolly to A.L. Macdonald, 28 May 1947; letter from Connolly to Manager of Annapolis Valley Wood Products, 23 April 1947

137 Bruce, *Frank Sobey: The Man and the Empire*, 245

138 ALM Papers, MG2/898: letter from R.M. Dawson to A.L. Macdonald, 27 March 1946

139 Beck, *The Government of Nova Scotia*, 208–19

140 Ibid., 222–4

141 Ibid., 224

142 Gordon Commission, *Submission of the Government of Nova Scotia*, 31

143 Federal-Provincial Conference, 1955, *Proceedings*, 26

144 Ibid., 48

145 Ibid., 15

146 Federal-Provincial Conference, 1955; Preparatory Committee for the Federal-Provincial Conference, unpublished Minutes

147 Federal-Provincial Conference, 1955, *Proceedings*, 13
148 Ibid., 52; Preliminary Meeting, 29–30
149 Pickersgill, *My Years with Louis St. Laurent: A Political Memoir*, 309
150 Ibid., 310
151 Federal-Provincial Conference, 1957, *Proceedings*, 29–30
152 Ibid., 32

Chapter 5

1 Margaret S. Conrad, 'George Nowlan and the Conservative Party in the Annapolis Valley, Nova Scotia, 1925–1965,' 187
2 Ibid., 308–9
3 Ibid., 311
4 Ibid., Beck, *Pendulum of Power*, 241–90
5 Conrad, 'George Nowlan,' 353–6
6 Camp, *Gentlemen, Players, and Politicians*, 126
7 Ibid., 151
8 Ibid., 172
9 Ibid., 221
10 Ibid., 229
11 MacEwan, *Miners and Steelworkers*, 289–90, 301–2
12 Stevens, *Stanfield*, 108
13 Beck, *The Government of Nova Scotia*, 158–70
14 Camp, *Gentlemen*, 213
15 Ibid., 212
16 See Brym, 'Political Conservatism in Atlantic Canada,' 59–80
17 The four Atlantic provinces named council appointees to attend the first meeting. Nova Scotia's appointees were Gordon Elman, president of Elman Motors Ltd; L.A. Forsyth, president of Dominion Steel and Coal Corp., C.J. Morrow, president of National Sea Products Ltd. *Maritime Merchant* (March 1964), 4
18 Ganong, 'APEC – Its Beginning and Meaning,' 15–19
19 R.W. Ganong, vice-president, Ganong Bros.; C.J. Morrow, president, National Sea Products; E.D. Brown, general manager, National Gypsum; R.E. Tweedledale, asst. chief engineer, New Brunswick Electric Power Corp.; W.D. Melvin, Royal Bank supervisor
20 Mann, 'Atlantic Provinces Economic Council'
21 *Maritime Merchant* (March 1964), 1, 20
22 Camp, *Gentlemen*, 217
23 Ibid., 216–18
24 Stevens, *Stanfield*, 128–9; Bruce, *Frank Sobey: The Man and the Empire*
25 Bruce, *Frank Sobey*, 247–8. 'By deliberate intent, we have created a company which will speak for itself which will operate independently of gov-

ernment direction and interference ... Finally, and I would like to emphasize this, the government will permit the company to operate as an autonomous corporation.' Stanfield as quoted in Bruce, ibid., 254

26 Ibid., 251–3

27 *Atlantic Advocate* (January 1959), 33

28 Bruce, *Frank Sobey*, 254. IEL would also finance up to 60 per cent of a client's cost of equipment, and arrange tax concessions from municipalities. It would eventually also come to take equity positions in some client industries, a change of practice that would prove to be very damaging and costly to the agency.

29 Ibid., 246

30 *Atlantic Advocate* (January 1965), 16

31 Sobey was given the go-ahead to acquire land for an industrial park and to solicit industry, a portent of things to come when, as president of IEL, he was able to attract several major new industries for Pictou County. Bruce, *Frank Sobey*, 244

32 Ibid., 262

33 Ibid., 287

34 Ibid., 257–9. In many ways, this provincial Crown corporation was a forerunner of the federal Cape Breton Development Corporation (DEVCO), set up in 1966 as the federal response to DOSCO's announcement that it would cease coal-mining entirely in Nova Scotia.

35 Members of the advisory board included: J.S.D. Tory, Toronto-based merger-master; Henry Borden, Toronto, president of Brazilian Traction, Light and Power; Charles Gasvie, prominent Montreal lawyer and former president of the St Lawrence Seaway Authority; K.M. Sedgewick, Montreal investment councillor and executive vice-president of W.C. Pitfield; Ross MacLeod, vice-president, New York Life Insurance; Alfred C. Fuller, Chairman, Fuller Brush Co. All except Tory, who was the son of a Nova Scotian, were Nova Scotians by birth. Bruce, *Frank Sobey*, 269–70

36 *Financial Post*, 26 June 1965, 57. A major selling feature employed by IEL was that Nova Scotia wages averaged 45 per cent below U.S. levels.

37 *Canadian Business*, August 1965, 36, 39, 40. Given IEL's preferences for this corporate profile, it is interesting to note that as of 1965, sixteen Nova Scotian firms had taken advantage of IEL's incentives, as had eleven foreign firms, and only nine non-Nova Scotia Canadian firms.

38 By 1964 IEL had thirty-six clients. By 1967, in many ways its high point, IEL had spent more than $75 million to aid investors from eight countries in settling or expanding in Nova Scotia. Directly and indirectly, the Nova Scotia government claimed it had created 9,000 jobs. IEL-assisted plants produced fish, fibreglas, paper boxes, aluminum cans, boats, glue, cement, rugs, sweaters, industrial belting, electronic equipment, flour, envelopes, and automobiles. Bruce *Frank Sobey*, 266

39 See Stevens, *Stanfield*, on Clairtone and Deuterium of Canada Ltd; Mathias, *Forced Growth*
40 In particular, the anti-union legislation passed by Nova Scotia governments as part of a deal with Michelin Tire Corporation, a French multinational that is now the largest private-sector employer in Nova Scotia, has soured labour relations in the province considerably. See Belliveau and de Marsh, 'The Five-Legged Sheep: Michelin Tire in Nova Scotia.'
41 See Harry Bruce's discussion of some of these charges against IEL. Bruce, *Frank Sobey*, 241–319
42 This criticism has been levelled by Roy George, among others. See George, *The Life and Times of Industrial Estates Ltd.*
43 Stevens, *Stanfield*, 155–6; Bruce, *Frank Sobey*, 299–300
44 Smith, 'What Can Aid Maritimes?' 46
45 Mann, 'An overall planning scheme is a must for the Atlantic Provinces,' 9
46 Ibid.
47 Mills, 'Voluntary Economic Planning in Nova Scotia,' 162
48 Ibid., 161. And, of course, the provincial government on its part would not be compelled to adopt VEPB plans.
49 *Canadian Business*, August 1965, 50. According to *Canadian Business* magazine, such an exercise was, in itself, 'no mean achievement.'
50 Mills, 'Voluntary,' 164
51 *Canadian Business*, August 1965, 76
52 Nova Scotia, Fact-Finding Body on Labour Legislation, *Report*, 19, 27
53 Henson, 'The Nova Scotia Labour-Management Agreements,' 95
54 Ibid., 97
55 Ibid., 100
56 Ibid., 116, 122
57 Ibid., 99
58 Ibid., 109
59 Ibid., 118
60 Ibid., 119–21
61 Meisel, *The Canadian General Election of 1957*, 18–19
62 Perlin, *The Tory Syndrome*, 54
63 Meisel, *Canadian General Election*, 25
64 *Tory Syndrome*, 54; Peter C. Newman, *Renegade in Power: The Diefenbaker Years*, 45–6
65 Camp, *Gentlemen*, 241
66 Meisel, *Canadian General Election*, 25–7
67 Ibid., 43
68 Camp, *Gentlemen*, 329–30
69 Meisel, *Canadian General Election*, 75
70 *Financial Post*, 15 June 1957. A cabinet committee looking into the latter had not yet reported.

71 Meisel, *Canadian General Election*, 11. The contrast with the 'old' Conservative party, which usually occupied itself with expressions of grave concern over a rise in expenditures, must have been startling, not least to the Liberals.
72 Ibid., 9–12
73 In the first year of the equalization formula's operation, Nova Scotia received only $26.4 million in payments, as opposed to the $23.3 million it would have received in any event under the 1952–7 tax-rental agreement – a very modest $3 million gain.
74 Stanfield also made a pitch for federal co-operation in examining and responding to the findings of the Nova Scotia Royal Commission on Rural Credit, which strongly recommended a change in farm lending policies in Nova Scotia. In particular, Stanfield pointed out the unsuitability for Nova Scotia of the Canadian Farm Loan Board's credit policy, which catered to farms of large acreage. Dominion-Provincial Conference, 1957, *Proceedings*, 27, 30, 33, 36
75 Ibid., 32
76 Whelan, 'Public Policy and Regional Development: The Experience of the Atlantic Provinces,' 113–17
77 MacNutt, 'The Atlantic Revolution,' 13
78 Wardell, 'Atlantic Premiers and APEC Meet at St. John's,' 12
79 Dominion-Provincial Conference, 1957, 41
80 *Chronicle Herald* (Halifax), 5 March 1959, 1
81 Ibid., 6 March 1959
82 Ibid
83 Dominion-Provincial Conference, 1960, *Proceedings*, 25–7 July 1960, 37–8
84 In 1929, total dominion payments to the provinces represented 4 per cent of dominion revenues and 9 per cent of provincial revenues; in 1960–1 they constituted 14 per cent of federal revenues and 36 per cent of all provincial revenues – 68 per cent of all Nova Scotia revenues! Graham, *Fiscal Adjustment*, 42
85 Dominion-Provincial Conference, 1960, 41–2
86 Ibid., 43–5
87 Ibid., 10–12
88 Ibid., 25–30. Only 21 per cent of Nova Scotia revenues under Diefenbaker's revised formula would be 'equalized' – less than the 30 per cent coverage cited by Stanfield at the 1957 Dominion-Provincial Conference.
89 Conrad, 'George Nowlan,' 418
90 *Maritime Merchant* (July 1961), 3
91 Careless, *Initiative and Response: The Adaptation of Canadian Federalism to Regional Economic Development*, 74–7
92 Ibid.

93 Ibid., 109–15
94 Burbridge, 'The Atlantic Development Board and Atlantic Regional Development,' 26
95 Regenstrief, *The Diefenbaker Interlude: Parties and Voting in Canada*, 52
96 ALM Papers. MG2/933/27–3/18. Letter from Chubby Power to Macdonald; MG2/964/F31–2/7. Letter from Macdonald to Senator T.A. Crerar; exchange of letters with Alex Johnston, February, March, April 1947. See also Camp, *Gentlemen*, 7
97 Smith, *Gentle Patriot: A Political Biography of Walter Gordon*, 33–44
98 For example, see Halifax senator John A. Macdonald's suggestions to G.C. Marler, chairman of the Resolutions Committee of the National Liberal Convention. Liberal Party of Canada Papers (LPC Papers), National Convention, 1958, Policy Resolutions MG28/IV–3, vol. 879
99 Smith, *Gentle Patriot*, 76
100 Ibid.
101 Lamontagne, 'Growth. Price Stability and the Problem of Unemployment,' 6, 12
102 Kent, 'Towards a Philosophy of Social Security'
103 National Liberal Rally, 1961. Resolution submitted to the NLR policy committee by the subcommittee on the Atlantic provinces. LPC Papers, vol. 891
104 Smith, *The Regional Decline of a National Party: Liberals on the Prairies*, 93
105 See Smith, *Gentle Patriot* and *Regional Decline*; and Wearing, *The L-Shaped Party: The Liberal Party of Canada, 1958–1980*.

Chapter 6

1 Wolfe, 'The State and Economic Policy in Canada, 1968–1975,' table 1, 259
2 Atlantic Provinces Economic Council (APEC), *Fourth Annual Review*, 7
3 Ibid., 64–5
4 Ibid., 11
5 APEC, *Atlantic Canada Today*, 112
6 APEC, *First Annual Review*, 10
7 APEC, *Fourth Annual Review*, 9
8 APEC, *Statistical Review*, A–7
9 APEC, *First Annual Review*, 8
10 APEC, *Atlantic Canada Today*, 56–7, 74
11 Veltmeyer, 'The Capitalist Underdevelopment of Atlantic Canada,' 28
12 APEC, *Atlantic Canada Today*, 80
13 Nova Scotia, Department of Lands and Forests, Ext. Note #66, 'Forestry Incentives for Increased Fibre Production in Nova Scotia' (March 1970); see also DREE, 'Summaries of Federal-Provincial General Development

Agreements and Currently Active Subsidiary Agreements.'

14 Clement, *The Struggle to Organize: Resistence in Canada's Fishery*, 88–9, 122

15 Darrah and Belland, 'The Canso Fishermen's Strike 1970–71'

16 Ibid.; Clement, *Struggle to Organize*, 105–9

17 APEC, *Atlantic Canada Today*, 77

18 APEC, *First Annual Review*, 8

19 APEC, *Fourth Annual Review*, 61

20 Ibid., 11

21 APEC, *Atlantic Canada Today*, 86

22 Ibid., 74

23 APEC, *Statistical Review*, B6

24 Conrad, 'George Nowlan and the Conservative Party in the Annapolis Valley, Nova Scotia 1925–65,' 478

25 Beck, *Pendulum of Power: Canada's Federal Elections*, 357

26 William Woodfine as quoted in *Maritime Merchant* (November 1963)

27 Interview with Tom Kent, 3 September 1985

28 Granatstein, *The Ottawa Men: The Civil Service Manderins, 1935–1957*, 267–73

29 McCall-Newman, *Grits: An Intimate Portrait of the Liberal Party*, 43

30 Ibid., 45, 47. While apparently never an economic nationalist in cabinet discussions, he did espouse 'progressive' Liberal policies in areas such as regional disparities and medicare. The latter, however, were more acceptable to Gordon's opponents than were his ideas on repatriating the Canadian economy.

31 Ibid., 45–9; Smith, *Gentle Patriot: A Political Biography of Walter Gordon*, 260–8

32 Careless, *Initiative and Response: The Adaption of Canadian Federalism to Regional Economic Development*, 114

33 Ibid.

34 Mackaay, 'Canadian Regionalism: The Atlantic Development Board: a case study,' 56

35 Careless, *Initiative*, 114

36 Mackaay, 'Canadian Regionalism,' 41–2, 50–1; Bruce, *Frank Sobey: The Man and the Empire*, 281. After Sobey left the board in 1967, he joined a growing chorus in the Atlantic region calling for the removal of the board from Ottawa to the region.

37 Mackaay, 'Canadian Regionalism,' 32–4, appendix 1

38 Atlantic Development Board, *Annual Report*, 1968–9, 28

39 Weeks, 'The Atlantic Provinces: A Case Study,' 80

40 *Financial Post*, 26 June 1965, 46

41 APEC, *First Annual Review*, 66–7

42 Careless, *Initiative*, 118–19

43 Interview with Robert Stanfield, *The Monetary Times*, August 1965
44 Kent interview
45 *Monetary Times*, August 1965, 27. Designated area benefits, in the form of a tax holiday and liberal depreciation rates, and later a 25 per cent capital grant, applied to seven of Nova Scotia's twelve National Employment Service areas before the federal government's revision of the definition of designated areas. The latter made all of Nova Scotia except Halifax County eligible for these benefits. *Canadian Business*, August 1965, 45
46 *Monetary Times*, August 1965, 27
47 *Financial Post*, 28 June 1965, 46. While unpopular with business élites in those areas left out of APEC's scenario (e.g., APEC's suggestions brought howls of protest from the New Glasgow Chamber or Commerce), this approach appeared to have Stanfield's tacit support.
48 In its *First Annual Review* this 'softening' was evident. However, the agency still warned about disincentives to mobility *within* a province or region, and urged that development areas contain at least one growth centre. APEC, *First Annual Review*, 67
49 Kent interview
50 Brewis, 'Regional Development in Canada in Historical Perspective,' 222
51 Report of the Department of Industry, 1965, 18
52 J.E. Hodgetts as quoted in Mahon, 'Canadian Public Policy: The Unequal Structure of Representation,' 180
53 Mahon gleaned this explanation from an interview with Lance Howie. Ibid., 181
54 Klaus Stegemann in his study of Canadian adjustment assistance policy, as quoted in Mahon, ibid., 182
55 French, *How Ottawa Decides: Planning and Industrial Policy-Making 1968–1984*, 109
56 Drury was one of the right-wing business representatives in cabinet and generally conducted himself accordingly. Reisman, later deputy minister of finance, was a believer in 'the basic realities of economic geography' and thought Canada should concentrate on promoting the basic momentum of industrial strength in the Montreal–Windsor corridor. 'Regional development' was at best a kind of social policy. See ibid., 114
57 Poetschke, 'Regional Planning for Depressed Rural Areas – The Canadian Experience,' 10
58 Buckley and Tihoranyi, 'Canadian Policies for Rural Adjustment: A Summary of Conclusions,' 148–9
59 Poetschke, 'Regional Planning,' 10
60 APEC, *First Annual Review*, 67
61 Kent interview. See also Banting, *The Welfare State and Canadian Federalism*, 11–13, 94

62 Kent interview
63 Poetschke, 'Regional Planning,' 19
64 Ibid.
65 See, for example, Tom Kent on the P.E.I. Development Plan. House of Commons, Standing Committee on Regional Development, 22 April 1970, 4
66 Poetschke, 'ARDA and Poverty: Lessons in Regional Planning,' 41
67 Ibid., 44–7
68 Poetschke, 'Regional Planning,' 11–12
69 A *plan* has been defined as 'a well organized and logically ordered set of statements forming a coherent discourse' comprising five categories of statements: 'a / the state of nature; b / the future states of nature; c / the socio-economic rules of the game; d / the goals pursued; e / the actions to be taken.' *Planning* is 'the process through which the plan is implemented.' Brewis and Paquet, 'Regional Development and Planning in Canada: An Exploratory Essay,' 128. *Regional planning* could mean a number of things: planning for a region as a separate economy (with the implication that some authority has the necessary regulatory and fiscal powers for the geographic unit in question); testing the consistency of regional plans with each other and with the national plan (with the aggregation of regional plans adding up to an overall allocation of land, labour, and capital for the economy as a whole); or merely putting 'space tags' on projects within the national plan, in order to ensure the best possible location of industry while reducing gaps in productivity and income in various regions of the country. Of necessity, it was the last of these to which Canada's nascent regional-development technocracy aspired, and to those working in the field the ostensible objective was clear: to maximize spread effects among regions, while reducing regional gaps, in large part by overcoming the tendency for the productivity of 'leading' and 'lagging' sectors to pull farther and farther apart. Higgins, 'The Concept of Regional Planning,' 168, 173
70 Tom Kent as quoted in Paul Phillips, *Regional Disparities*, 91
71 Aaron Wildavsky as quoted in Simeon, 'Studying Public Policy,' 554. The point being made by Wildavsky is that the efficiency criterion used by state planners assumes the current distribution (of values, norms, institutions, patterns of power, etc.) is valid. As a result, the fact of different people having different preferences cannot be given due consideration.
72 Poetschke, 'ARDA and Poverty,' 40
73 This point is made in Wilson, *Financial Assistance with Regional Development*, 67.
74 Buckley and Tihoranyi, 'Canadian Policies,' 151, 155; Brewis and Pacquet, 'Regional Development,' 141
75 Under the TVTA program the division of expenditures within capital con-

struction, and between youth and adult training, as well as criteria for success, was left in provincial hands. Careless, *Initiative and Response*, 55, 69, 81. Federal contributions under the program were approaching the $600-million mark at the end of 1966. Statement by the Rt Hon. L.B. Pearson, Conference on Financing Higher Education, 24–6 October 1966

76 Statement by the Hon. Jean Marchand, ibid.

77 APEC, *First Annual Review*, 74

78 Careless, *Initiative*, 66

79 Brewis and Pacquet, 'Regional Development,' 154

80 Buckley and Tihoranyi, 'Canadian Policies,' 151–3

81 Brewis and Pacquet, 'Regional Development,' 126, 160

82 The Hon. Maurice Sauvé, minister of forestry and rural development, as quoted in APEC, *First Annual Review*, 63

83 Careless, *Initiative*, 126; French, *How Ottawa Decides*

84 Higgins, 'The Concept,' 175

85 Careless, *Initiative*, 131

86 E.P. Weeks, executive director, ADB, 'The Atlantic Provinces,' 77

87 Ian MacKeigan, chairman of the ADB and member of the board of the ECC in 1965, acknowledged the 'ad hoc' basis on which the ADB had been proceeding since its inception, while expressing optimism about its long-awaited planning program. 'We got going originally on an ad hoc basis hoping that our efforts would eventually fit into an overall plan ... We progressed more on faith than on a scientific basis. We are getting actively into the plan now, however. We've started out with five economists to form our new planning division. We believe we're going to make the first attempt on this continent to produce a comprehensive economic plan for a region.' *Monetary Times*, August 1965, 21

88 Weeks, 'The Atlantic Provinces,' 84

89 Walton, 'Atlantic Development: An Appraisal,' 65, 69

90 See the above discussion of the bureaucratic obstacles faced by the ADB, and the key role of Pickersgill in salvaging the agency (if also transforming its role and function).

91 Tupper, 'Public Enterprise as Social Welfare: The Case of the Cape Breton Development Corporation,' 534

92 MacEwan, *Miners and Steelworkers: Labour in Cape Breton*, 337. DOSCO's share of Canadian ingot capacity had shrunk from 22.6 per cent in 1944 to 11 per cent in 1964.

93 *Canadian Business*, June 1960, 46

94 *Atlantic Advocate*, January 1962, 15

95 DOSCO management let it be known that according to their estimates semi-finished steel could be produced at their steel-making facilities in Montreal and purchased from other sources at prices significantly lower than the delivered costs of Sydney steel at Contrecoeur. *Chronicle Herald*

(Halifax), 14 October 1967, 1–2
96 MacEwan, *Miners and Steelworkers*, 336–7; Webb, 'The DOSCO Crisis: Some Political Aspects of a Regional-Economic Problem,' 45
97 Address of E.A. Manson, former Nova Scotia minister of trade and industry, Special Session of the Nova Scotia legislature, 4 December 1967
98 MacIntosh, 'Turmoil in the Nova Scotia NDP, 1968–80,' 12
99 MacEwan, *Miners and Steelworkers*, 327
100 Ibid., 332–3
101 Ibid., 334; Tupper, 'Public Enterprise,' 539
102 Kent interview
103 The Hon. A.J. MacEachen as quoted in Tupper, 'Public Enterprise,' 540
104 Ibid., 542. An NDP motion in the House of Commons on 27 June 1967, calling for nationalization of DOSCO's steel-making facilities, was defeated.
105 MacEwan, *Miners and Steelworkers*, 338, 345, 347
106 Kent interview
107 Canada, *Debates and Proceedings*, House of Commons, Vol. III, 27th Parliament, 3157–8
108 Various articles in the *Chronicle Herald*, October-December 1967
109 Webb, 'The DOSCO Crisis,' 45–6
110 MacEwan, *Miners and Steelworkers*, 348; Webb, 'The DOSCO Crisis,' 90; *Chronicle Herald*, 15, 18, 20 November 1967
111 MacEwan, *Miners and Steelworkers*, 348; Webb, 'The DOSCO Crisis,' 92–102, 106–7

Chapter 7

1 Atlantic Province Economic Council (APEC), *Fifth Annual Review*, 14–15
2 Constitutional Conference, Ottawa, First Meeting, February 1968. *Proceedings*, 79, 105, 143
3 Brodie and Jenson, *Crisis, Challenge and Change: Party and Class in Canada*, 290
4 Pierre Trudeau as quoted in APEC, *Fifth Annual Review*, 15
5 Pierre Trudeau as quoted in *Atlantic Advocate*, vol. 59, no. 7 (March 1969), 13, 16
6 Radwanski, *Trudeau*, 155
7 Ibid., 145
8 Ibid., 146–7
9 Ibid., 162
10 Ibid., 158
11 Ibid., 159–60
12 Economic Council of Canada (EEC), *Third Annual Review*, 1966, 265
13 APEC, *Sixth Annual Review*, 7–8. In the Atlantic region APEC was making similar arguments.

14 Savoie, *Regional Economic Development: Canada's Search for Solutions*, 30
15 Ibid., 31
16 Ibid., 31–2
17 Savoie, *Federal-Provincial Collaboration: The Canada-New Brunswick General Development Agreement*, 15–16
18 Savoie, *Regional Economic Development*, 33
19 Canada, *Debates of the House of Commons*, 20 March 1969, 6900
20 P.E. Trudeau, 'The Expansion of the Atlantic Economy,' 16
21 APEC, *Sixth Annual Review*, 7–8
22 Savoie, *Regional Economic Development*, 40
23 Trudeau, 'The Expansion,' 15
24 Marchand, 'Notes for an Address by the Rt. Hon. Jean Marchand, Minister of Regional Economic Expansion, at the Conference of the Community Planning Assoc. of Canada, St. John's, Nfld.,' 15 September 1969, 3–4
25 Ibid., 6–7
26 Wolfe, 'The State and Economic Policy in Canada, 1968–1975,' 260–3
27 Ibid., 266–8; Radwanski, *Trudeau*, 248
28 Radwanski, *Trudeau*, 247–9
29 Kent interview
30 Radwanski, *Trudeau*, 247
31 APEC, *Statistical Review*, A8; Statistics Canada, *The Labour Force*, Catalogue no. 71–001. This compared to a nation-wide increase during this period from 4.7 to 6.3 per cent.
32 APEC, *Statistical Review*, 39–40
33 Canada, House of Commons, Standing Committee on Regional Development, *Minutes and Proceedings*, 15 April 1970, 3:62
34 Careless, *Initiative and Response*, 133
35 Savoie, *Regional Economic Development*, 41. The figures were $225 million and 14,000 jobs for the Montreal region versus $48 million and 5,000 for Atlantic Canada.
36 Kent interview
37 Careless, *Initiative and Response*, 132
38 The 'October Crisis' refers to the events of October 1970, when British high commissioner James Cross and Quebec cabinet minister Pierre Laporte were kidnapped (and Laporte murdered) by an extremist separatist group, the Front de Libération du Québec (FLQ). The ensuing national panic created an atmosphere in which there was widespread public support for the federal government's restriction of civil liberties and deployment of the army under the War Measures Act.
39 Kent interview. It was at this point, says Kent, that he resolved to leave Ottawa, believing that DREE's role and mandate was being undermined and distorted.

40 Doern, 'Priorities and Priority-Setting in the Trudeau Era,' 73
41 Lithwick, 'Regional Policy: The Embodiment of Contradictions,' 137
42 Pal, 'Revision and Retreat: Canadian Unemployment Insurance'
43 Banting, *The Welfare State and Canadian Federalism*, 97–100
44 One way of gauging the growth of regional dependence is to compare the relative dependence of Nova Scotians on government transfer payments with Canada's. There was a conspicuous rise, from 103 per cent of the Canadian average in 1971 to 112 per cent in 1973, before it fell to 110 per cent in 1977. DREE, *Economic Development Prospects in Nova Scotia*, 10
45 An industrial strategy has been defined by the Economic Council of Canada as 'an integrated set of complementary measures embodying both strategic economic and industrial objectives.' This definition presents a planning and a political problem for the state because it implies political choice of overriding criteria, 'within which the competing claims of different sectors will be rationalized. It also implies the identification by ministers of dominant concerns to which policies and programs conceived within the parochial context of a given sector must be bent.' French, *How Ottawa Decides*, 87
46 DREE, *Annual Report* 1970–71
47 Careless, *Initiative and Response*, 132; French, *How Ottawa Decides*, 114
48 Tupper, *Public Money in the Private Sector*, 13–19; Phidd and Doern, 'Politics and Management'
49 Ibid., 95
50 Ibid., 96
51 Ibid., 105
52 Ibid., 114
53 Ibid., 110–11
54 French, *How Ottawa Decides*, 78
55 Ibid., 77–8
56 Ibid., 117
57 Ibid., 78–83
58 Ibid., 108
59 APEC, *Fifth Annual Review*, 46, 72
60 Ibid., 31–2
61 See APEC, *Fifth Annual Review*, 99–100; Chodos, 'The Business of Jean Marchand in Business'; Springate, 'Regional Development Incentive Grants and Private Investment in Canada'
62 See Lewis, *Louder Voices: The Corporate Welfare Bums.*
63 DREE, *Department Profile*, 40
64 Brodie and Jenson, *Crisis, Challenge and Change*, 287
65 Savoie, *Regional Economic Development*, 43
66 Savoie, *Federal-Provincial Collaboration*, 18
67 Careless, *Initiative and Response*, 168

68 Ibid., 177–8
69 Ibid., 89
70 The ideal form for such co-operation, according to APEC, would see each province and municipality devote many man-hours to analysing, assisting, and negotiating with DREE and mobilizing the provincial and municipal resources required for each negotiated project. This would allow provinces and municipalities to retain some control over developments occurring within their jurisdiction, while fitting DREE proposals into pre-assembled development plans for the municipal, provincial, and regional levels. APEC, *Fifth Annual Review*, 88
71 Savoie, *Federal-Provincial Collaboration*, 15–16, 22
72 Savoie, *Regional Economic Development*, 52
73 Ibid., 57. Provisions were made for DREE conferences in the Atlantic region at which federal departments could discuss Ottawa's efforts at promoting regional economic growth. These were invariably poorly attended by other departments, if they were attended at all. An elaborate computerized information system was developed to alert other DREE offices and relevant federal agencies when a new initiative was being contemplated, so that they too could contribute to its development. But this would be notoriously underutilized.
74 Savoie, *Regional Economic Development*, 34
75 Jean Marchand, 'Notes for an Address by the Rt. Hon. Jean Marchand, Minister of Regional Economic Expansion, at the Annual General Meeting of the Quebec Chamber of Commerce in Sherbrooke, Quebec,' 18 September 1970
76 Savoie, *Regional Economic Development*, 37
77 Ibid., 118
78 APEC, *Sixth Annual Review*, 16
79 Savoie, *Federal-Provincial Collaboration*, 40–3
80 Savoie, *Regional Economic Development*, 55
81 Wolfe, 'State and Economic Policy,' 259
82 Brodie and Jenson, *Crisis, Challenge and Change*, 267
83 Wolfe, 'State and Economic Policy,' 280
84 Brodie and Jenson, *Crisis, Challenge and Change*, 265
85 Ibid., 269
86 Ibid.
87 Wolfe, 'State and Economic Policy,' 281–2
88 DREE, Discussion Paper, 'Canadian Manufacturing Prospects from A Regional Prospective,' 1978
89 Radwanski, *Trudeau*, 304
90 Phidd and Doern as quoted in French, *How Ottawa Decides: Planning and Industrial Policy-Making 1968–1984*, 153
91 French, *How Ottawa Decides*, 153

92 Ibid., 156. The conclusion is little different from that reached by John Porter in 1965 when he despaired of the conservative tone and obsession with unity/discord dialogue of Canadian party politics ever giving way to a more 'creative politics.' See Porter, *The Vertical Mosaic*, 366–76.

93 Clarkson, 'Democracy in the Liberal Party'

94 As quoted in Radwanski, *Trudeau*, 305

95 Brodie and Jenson, *Crisis, Challenge and Change*, 290–3; Clarke, Jenson, Leduc, and Pammett, *Absent Mandate: The Politics of Discontent in Canada*, 82–3

96 Perlin, *The Tory Syndrome*, 108–29

97 Pross, *Planning and Development: A Case of Two Nova Scotia Communities*, 81

98 *Chronicle Herald* (Halifax), 14 October 1970; Aucoin, 'The 1970 Nova Scotia Provincial Election: Some observations on recent party performance and electoral support,' 29

99 Aucoin, 'The 1970 Provincial Election,' 28–9

100 Bruce, *Frank Sobey: The Man and the Empire*, 296–9

101 MacEwan, *Miners and Steelworkers: Labour in Cape Breton*, 324–5

102 Stevens, *Stanfield*, 149–50

103 Bruce, *Frank Sobey*, 306; Mathias, *Forced Growth*, 122. Ironically, the 'permanency' of these jobs was to last no more than ten years (from the mid-1970s to the mid-1980s).

104 Bruce, *Frank Sobey*, 302–3. In turn, IEL was heavily dependent upon the expertise and judgment of one individual, Halifax accountant Harold Egan, who died suddenly in June 1968.

105 As quoted in Stevens, *Stanfield*, 156

106 Belliveau and de Marsh, 'The Five-Legged Sheep: Michelin Tire in Nova Scotia.' The Michelin case was not the start of a pattern in Nova Scotia. No other major multinational manufacturer followed Michelin's example and chose Nova Scotia as a relatively low-wage, non-union North American production site. Whether because of the direct competition of the sunbelt in the United States, or the more attractive option of other Third World locales, in the decade and a half following Michelin's arrival the strategy of promoting Nova Scotia as an attractive site for export-oriented manufacturing has not proved to be an effective path of reindustrialization for the province.

107 Nova Scotia, Department of Development, *Sector Profiles* (1979)

108 APEC, *Seventh Annual Review*, 25–31

109 Ibid., 31

110 Ibid., 44, 45, 61. Between 1957 and 1972 IEL spent $200 million ($47.2 million of which went to Clairtone and DCL).

111 Ibid., 72, 73. APEC favoured better industrial intelligence and the systematic application of a set of criteria to proposals.

112 *Province of Nova Scotia Voluntary Planning: A Review and Annual Report* (1975), 6–8
113 Ibid., 52
114 Ibid., 14
115 Ibid., 48
116 Ibid., 43
117 Ibid.
118 Careless, *Initiative and Response*, 148–9
119 Ibid., 150–2; Savoie, *Federal-Provincial Collaboration*, 83
120 Pross, *Planning and Development*, 84–5; Savoie, *Federal-Provincial Collaboration*, 40, 104
121 Careless, *Initiative and Response*, 149–51
122 Boswell and Gillis, 'The Story of the Department of Development, Province of Nova Scotia,' 15
123 Nova Scotia, Department of Development, Annual Reports, 1972, 1977
124 Pross, *Planning and Development*, 85
125 Cleland, 'The General Development Agreement and Provincial Economic Development,' 166–7
126 Ibid., 167
127 DREE, *Summaries of Federal-Provincial General Development Agreements and Currently Active Subsidiary Agreements*, 44
128 Cleland, 'General Development Agreement,' 171
129 Ibid., 170–1
130 DREE, 'Climate for Development: Atlantic Region,' 14–15. Between 1971 and 1976, income disparity between the 'central corridor' in Nova Scotia and the rest of the province advanced from 31 to 37 per cent.
131 Payn, 'An Industrial Revolution for Cape Breton,' 30
132 Foote, *The Case of Port Hawkesbury*, 71; Pross, *Planning and Development*, 41
133 The completed Gulf refinery, for instance, had a payroll much smaller than one Cape Breton coal-mine could generate. Neither heavy-water nor oil refining generated any significant linkages or spin-off industry for the local area. Newton, 'What is happening in Cape Breton?,' 28
134 Because of the location of industries at the Strait, eventually these people would be forced by the government to relocate; similarly the site for a much-needed new hospital was finally designated by the provincial government, after considerable political wrangling, for a location far removed from the community it was intended to serve.
135 Pross, *Planning and Development*, 87–8
136 Ibid., 68–9
137 See Higgins, 'Canada: New Brunswick and Nova Scotia.'
138 Foote, *Port Hawkesbury*, 69–71, 166. This fuelled local frustration and

resentment and created a good deal of hostility towards 'outsiders,' unions, and strikes.

139 Antoft, 'Harnessing Confrontation: A Review of the Nova Scotia Joint Labour-Management Study Committee 1962–79'

140 *Chronicle Herald* (Halifax), 20 November 1971, 21

141 In 1976 the Strait of Canso Development Office was inaugurated and given the mandate to 'take a leadership role in the development of the Strait of Canso.' It would ensure that the overall interests of the region were being met by the bevy of departments, agencies, and other groups concerned. Nova Scotia, Department of Development, 'A Plan of Organization for the Strait of Canso Development Office,' 7–12

142 Dyck, *Provincial Politics in Canada*, 120

143 From the DEVCO act, as quoted in George, 'Cape Breton Development Corporation,' 368.

144 From the DEVCO act, ibid., 369

145 From the DEVCO act, ibid., 370

146 George, 'Cape Breton,' 369–72

147 Ibid., 378. OMS reached eight tons in the highly mechanized Lingan operation.

148 Doyle, 'DEVCO's Island in the Sun,' passim

149 George, 'Cape Breton,' 369–72. Some of these footloose industries were Hustler Products of California, General Instrument of Canada, and Rand Electronics. DEVCO also contributed to an aid package for the multinational giant Gulf Oil (for wharf construction at the Strait of Canso), an expenditure of scarce funds that would seem to be difficult to justify.

150 Doyle, 'DEVCO's Island,' 39

151 George, 'Cape Breton,' 374

152 Ibid., 383

153 Doyle, 'DEVCO's Island,' 38; Kent interview

154 George, 'Cape Breton,' 376

155 Kent interview

156 Ibid.

157 See various articles on the provincial takeover in the *Chronicle-Herald* (Halifax), October–November 1967.

158 Ibid., 24 November 1967, 3

159 See Laux, 'Expanding the State: The International Relations of State-Owned Enterprises in Canada.'

160 Ibid.; Nova Scotia, Department of Development, *Steel-making Study*

161 A year later Kent, having moved from DEVCO to the presidency of SYSCO, would appear as a vice-chairman.

162 CANSTEEL Corporation, *First Annual Report*, 1976; *Second Annual Report*, 1977

163 Laux, 'Expanding the State,' 42. Based on quotes drawn from a joint industry-government report on steel.
164 Regional-development expenditures also gravitated disproportionately to the local bourgeoisie and other élites, contributing to the growth of class disparities within the region. See Gillespie and Kerr, *The Impact of Federal Regional Economic Expansion Policies on the Distribution of Income in Canada.*
165 Radwanski, *Trudeau,* 307

Chapter 8

1 French, *How Ottawa Decides,* 162
2 Ibid., 122
3 Ibid.
4 See Brown and Eastman, *The Limits of Consultation: A Debate Among Ottawa, The Provinces and the Private Sector on an Industrial Strategy*
5 Ibid., 123
6 Doern, 'Liberal Priorities 1982: The Limits of Scheming Virtuously,' 78–9
7 French, *How Ottawa Decides,* 124
8 Ibid., 125
9 Ibid., 128
10 Ibid., 62
11 Ibid., 63–4
12 DREE minister Marcel Lessard as quoted in Savoie, *Regional Economic Development: Canada's Search for Solutions,* 62
13 Savoie, 'The Continuing Struggle for a Regional Development Policy,' 145
14 Ibid., 66
15 Savoie, *Regional Economic Development,* 59–60. As part of the bargain to put the proposal to designate Montreal 'over the top' in cabinet, Lessard agreed to the possibility of designating yet other regions under the program, particularly northern British Columbia and eastern Ontario.
16 DREE, *Departmental Profile,* 40
17 Ibid., 140–2
18 Doern, 'Priorities,' 79; Lithwick, 'Regional Policy: The Embodiment of Contradictions,' 139–40
19 Lithwick, 'Regional Policy,' 140
20 McKinley, 'Regional Accommodation in Canada: The Atlantic Caucuses of the Liberal and Progressive Conservative Parties,' 28–9
21 Banting, *The Welfare State and Canadian Federalism,* 175–6
22 Ibid., 127–33. These findings hold even when income differences are held constant.
23 Perlin, *The Tory Syndrome,* 182–6
24 Simpson, *Discipline of Power,* 54–61

25 Savoie, *Regional Economic Development*, 66–7
26 Ibid., 64
27 Brodie and Jenson, *Crisis, Challenge and Change: Party and Class in Canada*, 276–8
28 Ibid., 278
29 Ibid., 289
30 Simpson, Discipline of Power, 179–80, 191–205
31 Clarke, Jenson, Leduc, and Pammett, *Absent Mandate*, 84
32 Milne, *Tug of War: Ottawa and the Provinces under Trudeau and Mulroney*, 79, 92, 94
33 Pratt, 'Energy: Roots of National Policy,' *Studies in Political Economy*, 30–1
34 Ibid., 35
35 Ibid., 37
36 Molot and Williams, 'The Political Economy of Continentalism,' 90
37 Canada, *Economic Development for Canada in the 1980's*
38 The report of the Major Projects Task Force in the summer of 1981 further confirmed the potential economic benefits attached to the huge projected investments in energy-related megaprojects in the 1980s. It also suggested the basis for a nationalist alliance between indigenous Canadian capital and organized labour that would be supportive of a program of Canadianization of the economy under federal leadership. S. Carr and S.R. Blair, co-chairs, *Major Projects Task Force*, 23 June 1981
39 Savoie, *Federal Provincial Collaboration: The Canada–New Brunswick General Development Agreement*, 66; *Regional Economic Development*, 50. DREE's regional offices, set up in conjunction with provincial offices, were there simply to provide staff support to the latter, and to conduct general economic analysis and research for their 'regions.'
40 Savoie, *Federal-Provincial Collaboration*, 119–20, 147
41 Ibid., 103–6; Savoie, 'Cooperative Federalism with Democracy,' 56–7
42 McKinley, 'Regional Accommodation,' 22–4
43 MacAllister, 'How to Re-Make DREE,' 42
44 Savoie, *Regional Economic Development*, 68–9
45 Ibid., 70–3. De Bane also took steps to answer some of the department's critics, particularly the charge that DREE expenditures served only to enhance the political profile of provincial governments, since it was they who delivered DREE programs. In Manitoba, PEI, and Quebec, DREE acted unilaterally to deliver new programs or negotiated a change in the project-delivery mechanism. One dividend of this federal offensive on GDA arrangements was a 25 per cent increase in DREE's budget in 1981–2, to be focused on needy areas.
46 Office of the Prime Minister, 'Reorganization for Economic Development'
47 Ibid., 2–3

48 Ibid., 3

49 Energy Minister Marc Lalonde as quoted in Savoie, *Regional Economic Development*, 77

50 *Globe and Mail*, 15 January 1982, 10. Needless to say, the new arrangements received a scathing review. Ottawa was accused of setting up a 'parallel government' in the region; the reorganization would accomplish nothing more than the creation of a 'bureaucratic jungle' that would discourage potential investors. All the premiers believed the changes would lead to a deterioration in federal-provincial relations.

51 APEC, *An Analysis of the Reorganization for Economic Development*, 13–15

52 Ibid., 19–24, 26. Just the same, APEC was not impressed with DREE's replacement, or with the return to a resource-based economic strategy for the region heralded by the federal government's emphasis on mega-projects, an approach that struck APEC as reminiscent of the 1950s vision of the Canadian economy embodied in the discredited recommendations of the Gordon Commission.

53 Senate Committee on National Finance, *Government Policy and Regional Development*, 51

54 Ibid., 12

55 Ibid., 72

56 Ibid., 72–5

57 Molot and Williams, 'Political Economy,' 101–2. The federal government's determination to counter this tendency through a strengthening of the Foreign Investment Review Agency (FIRA), and the creation of an Office of Industrial and Regional Benefits (OIRB) to improve access for Canadian manufacturers and service companies to opportunities generated by projects within the Canadian market, withered under American pressure. Plans to strengthen FIRA and broaden its mandate were shelved while Bill C-48 creating the OIRB was amended to read that Canadian companies should have 'a full and fair opportunity to participate *on a competitive basis* in the supply of goods and services used in that work program.' Moreover, as asserted by Clarkson, in the aftermath of a GATT ruling against Canada on this question, 'American officials remained on their guard lest the OIRB block U.S. suppliers with bureaucratic impediments.' Clarkson, *Canada and the Reagan Challenge*, 112

58 Savoie, *Regional Economic Development*, 87. That DRIE was in part a way of recentralizing the design and implementation of regional-development policy can be discerned in the new role for DRIE provincial offices, which became contact points and intelligence-gathering operations with little say in formulating policies and programs. Moreover, DRIE's Ottawa-region staff ratio was set at 6:4, compared to DREE's 3:7.

59 Ibid., 84

60 DREE, 'Economic Development Prospects in Nova Scotia,' 12; 'Strategic Regional Development Overview: Atlantic Region,' 5
61 DREE, 'Economic Development Prospects,' 16
62 Ibid., 32
63 Ibid., 35
64 Lewis, *The Good Fight: Political Memoirs 1909–1958*, 160
65 MacEwan, *Miners and Steelworkers*, 108
66 MacEwan, *The Akerman Years*, 46
67 Ibid., 45–9
68 Ibid., 66, 67, 94, 96, 108, 141, 166. Akerman favoured caucus supremacy over the party; he was primarily concerned with overcoming what he saw as the NDP's image of radicalism in the public's mind by presenting the NDP as the party of 'reason and common sense'; and he saw electoral success and the attainment of political power as the main objective, with 'party ideology' a secondary consideration. Moreover, MacEwan leaves the distinct impression that Akerman was largely unsympathetic to the emergent 'new social movements' such as women's issues and native rights, which were becoming prime topics of concern for the national party and for representatives of the Halifax wing of the provincial party.
69 *Chronicle-Herald*, 17 May 1980, 1–2
70 *Globe and Mail*, 20 October 1981, 10. McDonough's father is wealthy Halifax industrialist and long-time CCF–NDP supporter Lloyd Shaw.
71 Boswell and Gillis, 'The Story of the Department of Development, Province of Nova Scotia,' 16
72 Nova Scotia, Department of Development, *Annual Report 1977*, 7. In 1979 the Buchanan government added a new division to the department to oversee short-term job-creation projects, part of the government's response to stubbornly high unemployment levels in the province.
73 Nova Scotia, Department of Development, *Strengths and Weaknesses of the Nova Scotia Economy*, 106
74 Ibid., 108
75 Ibid., 109
76 Ibid.
77 Nova Scotia, Department of Development, *Towards an Economic Development Strategy for Nova Scotia*, 33–4
78 Ibid., 29–30, 32
79 The four – Panamax, Michelin, Sysco, and Pulp and Paper Modernization – fell into the spurned categories of capital works, resource upgrading, and subsidies to existing industry.
80 DREE, *Annual Report 1980–81*, 15
81 The written response of the committee was cited in Antoft, 'Harnessing Confrontation: A review of the Labour-Management Study Committee, 1962–79,' 113

82 Ibid., 113–14
83 Nova Scotia, Department of Mines and Energy (DME), *Offshore Oil and Gas: A Chance for Nova Scotians*, 27
84 In this connection DREE and Nova Scotia, in July 1978, signed a $25 million regional-development agreement on energy conservation designed to stimulate 'the production, installation, and servicing of energy conserving and renewable energy technologies.' DREE, *Development Agreements*, 44–6
85 *Chronicle-Herald*, 24 January 1978
86 DME, *Offshore*, 28
87 *Chronicle-Herald*, 20 December 1978
88 *Financial Post*, 18 February 1978; *Maclean's*, 6 October 1980, 38. New Brunswick disposed of its surplus through a long-term export contract with New England utilities.
89 DME, *Offshore*, 29
90 DREE remained more sanguine regarding the potential of Nova Scotia's offshore resources. In its December 1979 review, *Economic Development Prospects in Nova Scotia*, it played down the benefits to be expected from this sector in the short-to-medium term, while holding out hope for its long-term potential.
91 DME, *Offshore*, 30
92 Ibid., 21
93 *Globe and Mail*, 15 September 1981
94 *Globe and Mail*, 5 October 1981
95 In the summer of 1981, school-bus drivers, coal-miners, and hospital workers were all out on strike, and all attributed their bargaining problems in some way to the Buchanan government. McDonough strove to capitalize on this situation by structuring the NDP campaign around the government's anti-labour stand, but in the wake of the election she attributed the loss of at least one of the party's seats to the evident lack of support from striking workers. 'When I campaigned on the picket line there [industrial Cape Breton], some of them had the courtesy to remove their Tory buttons, others did not.' *Globe and Mail*, 20 October 1981, 10
96 *Globe and Mail*, 'Ottawa gets offshore control, most of money goes to N.S.,' 3 March 1982
97 *Globe and Mail*, 'Doing business in Nova Scotia,' 8 March 1982
98 *Citizen* (Ottawa), 'Battling Brian fading hero in Newfoundland,' 26 February 1983
99 *Globe and Mail*, 'Report outlines development strategies for natural gas fields in Nova Scotia,' 6 January 1982
100 *Globe and Mail*, 'APEC reports $35 worth of projects for region,' 9 May 1984; *Chronicle-Herald*, 'Major projects aimed at Atlantic provinces,' 9 November 1983. APEC reported $35 billion worth of major projects were

on stream for the Atlantic region, with oil and gas projects totalling 79 per cent of the projected spending.

101 APEC, *Atlantic Report*, 1 April 1983, and 1 April 1984
102 *Globe and Mail*, 'Nova Scotia makes offshore case clear,' 17 October 1984
103 Boswell and Gillis, 'The Story,' 25
104 Ibid., 27
105 *Chronicle-Herald*, 'Special incentives needed – Shell', 5 March 1985. The regulatory and taxation regime with regard to Nova Scotia's offshore gas, and thus the division of benefits between private capital and the public sector, was questioned by the multinationals. And tactics such as production delays and statements about the need for 'special incentives' were being increasingly employed to reduce any prospective royalty and taxation structure.
106 Nova Scotia, Department of Development, *Building Competitiveness: A White Paper on Economic Development*, 31
107 Ibid., 12
108 Ibid., 8–10
109 Ibid., 21–6
110 Ibid., 15
111 Nova Sotia, Department of Development, *Sector Profiles*, 7–9
112 DEVCO, *13th Annual Report*, 1981, 7; *Atlantic Insight*, January–February 1980, 22; September 1984, 47; *Globe and Mail*, 18 October 1981, B18; *Maclean's*, 26 September 1983, 38; *Chronicle-Herald*, 21 October 1983, 21. The sums being considered were huge: $330 million to open the first new mine, $2 billion to bring three new mines into production by 1993.
113 DEVCO, *Annual Report* 1982, 4
114 *Report on Business Magazine*, July–August 1985, 68
115 *Ottawa Citizen*, 7 November 1983, 5
116 *Atlantic Insight*, September 1984, 47
117 *Globe and Mail*, 16 November 1984, B3. Among the enterprises ditched at this time were Cape Breton Woollen Mills and Cape Breton Marine Farming.
118 *Chronicle-Herald*, 2 April 1985, 21
119 *Report on Business Magazine*, July–August 1985, 68
120 Ibid., 68–9
121 APEC, *Newsletter*, 28:1 (January 1984)
122 *Chronicle-Herald*, 15 November 1984, 33; *Globe and Mail*, 16 November 1984, B3.
123 *Chronicle-Herald*, 25 February 1985, 17; 16 May 1985, 1.
124 DREE, *Summaries*, 'Subsidiary Agreement on SYSCO'; Kent interview
125 Nova Scotia, Department of Development, 'Problems Related to the Sydney Steel Corporation: Recommended Courses of Action,' Report of a Task Force for the Policy Board, 15–18

126 Ibid., 45–50, 75, 106–8, 113–16
127 Ibid., 121–2, 126
128 *Chronicle-Herald*, 3 November 1982, 1
129 *Chronicle-Herald*, 6 November 1982, 2; 10 November 1982, 2.
130 *Chronicle-Herald*, 9 April 1985, 7
131 *Chronicle-Herald*, 10 November 1982, 2; 9 April 1985, 7; 15 June 1985, 21; 16 May 1985, 2.
132 *Chronicle-Herald*, 24 July 1985, 25; 1–8 November 1984. With such a slender customer base for one product, more than ever the situation was open to political opportunism. Six days before the provincial election in 1984, a federal cabinet minister from Nova Scotia announced that thenceforth CN would purchase its rails exclusively from SYSCO. Within eight days this was contradicted by another federal cabinet minister and finally retracted by the Nova Scotia minister.
133 Task Force on Atlantic Fisheries, *Navigating Troubled Waters: A New Policy for the Atlantic Fisheries*, 9, 14ff, 70. The industry is generally divided into inshore/nearshore and offshore sectors. In 1981, there were 17,000 inshore vessels providing fish to over 500 processing facilities. The offshore sector is dominated by corporate-owned trawlers landing fish at approximately 19 ports. In 1981 there were 150 trawlers in this sector accounting for 50 per cent of all groundfish landings.
134 Barrett and Davis, 'Floundering in Troubled Waters: The Political Economy of the Atlantic Fishery and the Task Force on Atlantic Fisheries,' 128
135 Task Force, 13
136 *Atlantic Insight*, October 1981, 22; *Globe and Mail*, 16 October 1986, B10
137 *Atlantic Insight*, October 1981, 25–6. The Nova Scotia government was criticized by its auditor-general for loaning $52 million to Nickerson without receiving a consolidated financial statement.
138 *Globe and Mail*, 29 August 1981, B20; 5 December 1981, 1
139 Task Force, 13
140 Clement, *The Struggle to Organize*, 108, 147–9, 152, 163. From the point of view of the NFFAWU, its 'raiding' in Nova Scotia was motivated by self-protection, since the positions adopted less aggressive CBRT was hurting the tough bargaining stances taken by the Newfoundland union. By 1983, the latter was representing more large-scale boat crew in Nova Scotia than the CBRT.
141 Ibid., 153, 157
142 Task Force, 227
143 Ibid., 109
144 Barrett and Davis, 'Floundering,' 132–3
145 *Financial Post*, 19 March 1983, 5. This debt was held primarily by the Bank of Nova Scotia, the government of Nova Scotia, and the government of Newfoundland.

146 *Globe and Mail*, 5 November 1983
147 Pross, 'The Fishery: Ali vs. Frazier,' 95–6
148 Ibid., 97–8
149 Ibid., 104
150 *The Citizen* (Ottawa), 9 February 1983, 60. While MacEachen was able to convince cabinet to keep the plants operating at a loss while the Liberals were in power, their closure was probably inevitable given the state of Canada's nuclear industry. In the first budget of the newly elected federal Conservative government in 1984, the immediate closure of the plants was announced, with the loss of seven hundred jobs. *Chronicle-Herald*, 10 February 1986, 7
151 Between 1969 and 1984 there was no improvement discernible in income disparity between the Atlantic provinces and the rest of Canada. And only 6 per cent of the jobs created in this period were in Atlantic Canada, leaving the unemployment ratio exactly the same in 1984 as in 1968 (one-and-a-half to one to the disadvantage of the Atlantic region). Moreover, in the interim the region had become more heavily dependent on government spending to sustain it, with the latter accounting for 72 to 89 per cent of gross provincial product in the four Atlantic provinces compared with 45 per cent nationally. *Charlottetown Guardian*, 6 June 1984, 'Poor a relative term in regional disparity'; *Chronicle-Herald*, 23 March 1985, 'Massive direct aid needed'
152 *Chronicle-Herald*, 18 May 1984, 'Atlantic region falling further behind'
153 A series of editorials on Cape Breton by Jeffrey Simpson in the *Globe and Mail*, 29 January–6 February 1986, is indicative of the recent attitude of the media in central Canada towards regional development. The post-1984 Conservative government itself adopted the general position that just about everything that could be done had been tried already and that their own initiative in the regional-development field – the Atlantic Canada Opportunities Agency (ACOA) – was to be, in the words of the prime minister, the 'last and best effort' to win the war of jobs in Atlantic Canada. Stewart McInnes, political minister for Nova Scotia in the federal cabinet, conceded that ACOA was 'the last chance of effecting a change in the region.' *The Citizen* (Ottawa), 8 June 1987, A4

Chapter 9

1 Berger, *The Writing of Canadian History*, 102
2 See the Miliband–Poulantzas debate in Blackburn, ed., *Ideology and Social Science*, 238–62
3 See Block, 'The Ruling Class Does Not Rule: Notes on the Marxist Theory of the State,' and Crouch, 'The State, Capital and Liberal Democracy.'

4 Offe and Ronge, 'Theses on the Theory of the State,' 120
5 *Dilemmas* refer to the incidence of opposing demands and conflicting pressures that have to be absorbed by a particular institutional setting; *contradictions* are tendencies inherent to a specific mode of production to destroy those very pre-conditions upon which its survival depends. The latter become manifest in situations where a collision occurs between the constituent pre-conditions and the results of a specific mode of production.
6 On this point major analytical controversies and divisions of opinion continue to occur, with liberal theorists allocating to the state the necessary autonomy and neutrality to perform this function effectively, while Marxist theorists posit the existence of systemic contradictions on the level of state activity itself that prevent the state from dealing successfully with the contradictions of the capitalist mode of production.
7 Panitch, 'Dependency and Class in Canadian Political Economy,' 24–5. Capital's privileged position does not preclude intervention by the state to capture and redistribute a share of the capitalists' profits, the generation of which the state has made possible through its maintenance of the framework for capitalist social relations of production.
8 Block, 'The Ruling Class,' 94
9 The policy instruments available to the state to achieve these ends range from regulations and financial incentives, to public infrastructure investment, to the introduction of schemes of joint decision-making and joint financing 'designed to force market partners to agree in an organized way upon conditions of mutually acceptable exchange outside the exchange process itself, so that the outcome is predictable for both sides.' Ibid., 123–5
10 Ibid., 28. Such state discourses should not be considered as mutually exclusive. While historically they have tended to correlate with specific periods in the development of the capitalist democracies, they continue to co-exist in the political realm. Their expression in state policies will reflect a varying balance and emphasis as alternate discursive and programmatic elements assert themselves in the considerations of state policy-makers and governing élites.
11 Tarrow, *Between Center and Periphery: Grassroots Politicians in Italy and France*, 33
12 Panitch, 'Elites, Classes and Power in Canada,' 242
13 Przeworski, *Capitalism and Social Democracy*, 143
14 Business will undertake an extensive mobilization of resources and at times engage in feverish activity in order to influence political decision-making processes through pressure groups, media, parties, personal contracts, etc.; they fear that they may not receive favourable treatment otherwise. See Lindblom, *Politics and Markets: The World's Political Economic Systems*.

15 Whitaker, *The Government Party: Organizing and Financing the Liberal Party of Canada 1930–1958*, 382.
16 Beck, 'The Party System in Nova Scotia: Tradition and Conservatism,' 183
17 Panitch, 'Elites, Classes, and Power,' 246–7
18 Brodie, *Women and Politics in Canada*, 125; see also Clarke, Jenson, Leduc, and Pammett, *Absent Mandate*, 10–16.
19 Discourse has to do with the formation of the 'social real' – through the use of concepts, symbols, images, etc., it renders social reality as rationalizable, transparent, and programmable. Programs follow from discourses, presupposing and articulating a knowledge of the field of reality upon which it is to intervene and/or which it is calculated to bring into being. Such programs also carry with them attendant technologies and techniques of power. The coherence of discourses, their unifying principle, is a particular vision or conception of society, one that generally predicates the welfare of society as a whole upon the interests of a particular class or classes. Thus, discourse has to do with power. It is a product of power, which in turn reinforces power in a circular relation. See Foucault, *Power/Knowledge: Selected Interviews and Other Writings*.
20 Ibid., 252
21 See Brodie and Jenson, *Crisis, Challenge and Change: Party and Class in Canada*, passim.
22 Once again see Lindblom, *Politics and Markets*, for a discussion of the incredible activity and expense on the part of business in the United states to control the political debate and value system in general.
23 This discussion is based on Jenson's elaboration of the concept of 'prevailing universe of political discourse' in Jenson, 'Gender and Reproduction: Or, Babies and the State,' 25–6.
24 Tarrow, 'Struggling to Reform: Social Movements and Policy Change During Cycles of Protest,' 28–31
25 Jessop, 'Accumulation Strategies, State Forms, and Hegemonic Projects,' 98
26 Brym, 'The Canadian Capitalist Class 1965–1985,' 15
27 See Skocpol and Weir, 'State Structures and Social Keynesianism: Response to the Great Depression in Sweden and the United States'; Evans, Rueschenmeyer, and Skocpol, eds., *Bringing the State Back In*.
28 For a discussion of the role of senior bureaucrats during this period see Granatstein, *The Ottawa Men: The Civil Service Mandarins 1935–1957*.
29 See Offe, 'The Theory of the Capitalist State and the Problem of Policy Formation.'
30 Tarrow, *Between Center*, 89–90
31 The ostensible reason for the creation of DREE was to ensure better co-ordination of dispersed regional-development programs and to give regional concerns a voice that they previously did not have at the cabinet

level. See Phidd and Doern, *The Politics and Management of Canadian Economic Policies,* 319.

32 Thus, the need to include other departments besides DREE in regional economic development was cited as the main reason for the Trudeau government's Reorganization for Economic Development in 1982. Office of the Prime Minister, 'Reorganization for Economic Development'

33 Watson, 'The Regional Dimension of Planning,' 466

34 Ibid., 466–7

35 Mahon, *The Politics of Industrial Re-structuring: Canadian Textiles,* 39

36 Ibid.

37 Tarrow, 'Regional Policy, Ideology and Peripheral Defence: The Fos-sur-mer,' 118

38 Tarrow, 'Introduction,' in Tarrow, Katzenstein, and Graziano, eds., *Territorial Politics in Industrial Nations,* 1–2

39 Whitaker, 'Federalism, Democracy and the Canadian Political Community,' 88

40 Tarrow, 'Introduction,' 5–6

41 Ibid., 7

42 In Canada, this process was seen to be occurring in the post–First World War period. See Corry, *The Growth of Government Activities Since Confederation.*

43 Tarrow, 'Introduction,' 3

44 See Young, Faucher, and Blais, 'The Concept of Province-Building: A Critique.'

45 Whitaker, *The Government Party: Organizing and Financing the Liberal Party of Canada 1930–1958,* 407.

46 Jackson, Jackson, and Baxter-Moore, *Politics in Canada,* 435

47 Simeon and Elkins, 'Regional Political Cultures in Canada,' passim

48 Tarrow, 'Struggling to Reform,' 26–34

Bibliography

Books, Articles, and Theses

Abella, I.M. *Nationalism, Communism, and Canadian Labour*. Toronto: University of Toronto Press 1973
Acheson, T.W. 'The Maritimes and Empire Canada.' In *Canada and the Burden of Unity*, ed. D.J. Bercuson. Toronto: Macmillan 1977
– 'The National Policy and the Industrialization of the Maritimes', *Acadiensis*, 1 (Spring 1972): 2–28
– 'The Social Origins of Canadian Industrialism: A Study in the Structure of Entrepreneurship.' PhD Thesis, University of Toronto 1971
Adamson, A., and I. Stewart. 'Politics in the Most Mysterious East.' In *Party Politics in Canada*, 5th ed. ed., H. Thorburn. Scarborough, Ont.: Prentice-Hall 1985
Alexander, David. 'Economic Growth in the Atlantic Region 1880–1940.' In *Eastern and Western Perspectives*, ed. D.J. Bercuson and P.A. Buckner. Toronto: University of Toronto Press 1981
– 'Development and Dependence in Newfoundland, 1880–1970.' In *Atlantic Canada and Confederation: Essays in Canadian Political Economy*. Toronto: University of Toronto Press 1983
– *Atlantic Canada and Confederation: Essays in Canadian Political Economy*. Toronto: University of Toronto Press 1983
– 'New Notions of Happiness: Nationalism, Regionalism, and Atlantic Canada.' *Journal of Canadian Studies*, Summer 1980: 29–42
Allain, G., and S. Côté. 'The State and Regional Development Organizations: A Comparative Analysis of Citizen Participation in Quebec and New Brunswick 1960–1980.' A paper presented to the annual meetings of the Canadian Sociology and Anthropology Association, University of British Columbia, 1–4 June 1983
Amin, Samir. *Unequal Development*. New York: Monthly Review Press 1976

Antoft, Kell. 'Harnessing Confrontation: A Review of the Nova Scotia Joint Labour-Management Study Committee 1962–79.' *Social Science Monograph Series, Vol. 4: Labour and Atlantic Canada*. Moncton: University of New Brunswick 1981

Archibald, Bruce. 'Atlantic Regional Underdevelopment and Socialism.' In *Essays of the Left*, ed. L. Lapierre. Toronto: McClelland and Stewart 1971

Armstrong, C. 'The Politics of Federalism: Ontario's Relations with the Federal Government, 1896–1941.' PhD Thesis, University of Toronto, 1972

Atlantic Provinces Economic Council (APEC). *Defence Expenditures and the Economy of the Atlantic Provinces*. Pamphlet No. 9. December 1965

– *Newsletter* 28:1 (January 1984)

– *First Annual Review: The Atlantic Economy*. Halifax: APEC, 1967

– *Second Annual Review: The Atlantic Economy*. Halifax: APEC 1968

– *Third Annual Review: The Atlantic Economy*. Halifax: APEC 1969

– *Fourth Annual Review: The Atlantic Economy*. Halifax: APEC 1970

– *Fifth Annual Review: The Atlantic Economy*. Halifax: APEC 1971

– *Sixth Annual Review: The Atlantic Economy*. Halifax: APEC 1972

– *Seventh Annual Review: The Atlantic Economy*. Halifax: APEC 1973

– *Atlantic Canada Today*. Halifax: APEC 1977

– *The Atlantic Vision – 1990*. Halifax: APEC 1979

– *Atlantic Report*, 1 April 1984

– *Atlantic Report*, 1 April 1983

– *An Analysis of Reorganization for Economic Development*. Halifax: APEC 1982

Aucoin, P. 'The 1970 Nova Scotia Provincial Election: Some Observations on Recent Party Performance and Electoral Support.' *Journal of Canadian Studies* 7, no. 3 (August 1972): 25–35

Baker, John F. 'The Underdevelopment of Atlantic Canada, 1867–1920: A Study of the Development of Capitalism.' MA Thesis, McMaster University 1977

Banting, K.G. *The Welfare State and Canadian Federalism*. Montreal: McGill-Queen's University Press 1982

Barrett, G., and A. Davis. 'Floundering in Troubled Waters: The Political Economy of the Atlantic Fishery and the Task Force on Atlantic Fisheries.' *Journal of Canadian Studies* 19, no. 1 (Spring 1984): 125–37

Barrett, L.G. 'Development and Underdevelopment and the Rise of Trade Unionism in the Fishing Industry, 1900–1950.' MA Thesis, Dalhousie University 1976

– 'Perspectives on Dependency and Underdevelopment in the Atlantic Region.' *Canadian Review of Sociology and Anthropology* 17, no. 3 (August 1980): 273–86

– 'Underdevelopment and Social Movements in the Fishing Industry of Nova Scotia.' In *Underdevelopment and Social Movements in Atlantic Canada*, ed.

R.J. Brym and R.J. Sacouman. Toronto: New Hogtown Press 1979
Baum, Gregory. *Catholics and Canadian Socialism*. Toronto: Lorimer 1980
Beck, J. Murray. *The Government of Nova Scotia*. Toronto: University of
   Toronto Press 1957
– *Pendulum of Power*. Scarborough, Ont.: Prentice-Hall 1968
– 'The Party System in Nova Scotia: Tradition and Conservatism.' In *Cana-
   dian Provincial Politics*, ed. M. Robin. Scarborough, Ont.: Prentice-Hall
   1972
Belliveau, M., and B. de Marsh. 'The Five-Legged Sheep: Michelin Tire in
   Nova Scotia.' *Round One*, nos. 8 and 9 (May and November 1977)
Bercuson, D.J., ed. *Canada and the Burden of Unity*. Toronto: Macmillan
   1977
Bercuson, D.J., and P.A. Buckner, eds. *Eastern and Western Perspectives*.
   Toronto: University of Toronto Press 1981
Berger, Carl. *The Writing of Canadian History*. Toronto: Oxford University
   Press 1976
Bickerton, James. 'Underdevelopment and Social Movements in Atlantic Can-
   ada: A Critique.' *Studies in Political Economy* 9 (Fall 1982): 191–202
Bickerton, James, and A.G. Gagnon. 'Regional Policy in Historical Perspec-
   tive: The Federal Role in Regional Economic Development.' *American Re-
   view of Canadian Studies* 14, no. 1 (Spring 1984): 72–92
Black, E.R. *Divided Loyalties*. Montreal: McGill-Queen's University Press
   1975
Blackburn, R., ed. *Ideology in Social Science*. London: Fontana Press 1972
Block, Fred. 'The Ruling Class Does Not Rule: Notes on the Marxist Theory
   of the State.' *Socialist Revolution* 7, no. 3 (May–June 1977): 6–28
Boadway, R., and F. Flatters. *Equalization in a Federal State: An Economic
   Analysis*. Ottawa: Minister of Supply and Services 1982
Boswell, F., and C. Gillis. 'The Story of the Department of Development,
   Province of Nova Scotia.' Nova Scotia Department of Development, 1983
Bothwell, Robert. *War into Peace: C.D. Howe as Minister of Reconstruction*.
   Toronto: University of Toronto Press 1979
– *C.D. Howe: A Biography*. Toronto: McClelland and Stewart 1979
Bourque, G. 'Class Nation, and the Parti Québécois.' *Studies in Political Econ-
   omy* 2 (Autumn 1979): 129–58
Brenner, Robert. 'The Origins of Capitalist Development: A Critique of Neo-
   Smithian Marxism.' *New Left Review*, 104 (July–August, 1977): 25–92
Brewis, T., and G. Paquet. 'Regional Development and Planning in Canada:
   An Exploratory Essay.' *Canadian Public Administration* 11, no. 2 (Summer
   1968): 123–62
Brewis, T.N. 'Regional Development in Canada in Historical Perspective.' In
   Regional Economic Policy: The Canadian Experience, ed. N.H. Lithwick.
   Toronto: McGraw-Hill Ryerson 1978

– *Regional Economic Policies in Canada*. Toronto: Macmillan 1979

Brodie, J. *Women and Politics in Canada*. Toronto: McGraw-Hill Ryerson 1985

Brodie, J., and J. Jenson. 'The Party System.' In *Canadian Politics in the 1980's*. 2nd ed., ed. M.S. Whittington and G. Williams. Toronto: Methuen 1984

– *Crisis, Challenge, and Change: Party and Class in Canada*. Toronto: Methuen 1980

Brooks, Rowena. 'Government Policies and Occupational Structure in New Brunswick.' MA Thesis, University of New Brunswick 1980

Brown, D., and J. Eastman. *The Limits of Consultation: A Debate among Ottawa, the Provinces and the Private Sector on an Industrial Strategy*. Ottawa: Science Council of Canada (May 1981)

Bruce, Harry. *Frank Sobey: The Man and the Empire*. Toronto: Macmillan 1985

– *R.A.: The Story of R.A. Jodrey Entrepreneur*. Toronto: McClelland and Stewart 1979

Brym, R.J. 'Political Conservatism in Atlantic Canada.' In *Underdevelopment and Social Movements in Atlantic Canada*, ed. R.J. Brym and R.J. Sacouman. Toronto: New Hogtown Press 1979

– 'The Canadian Capitalist Class 1965–1985.' In *The Structure of the Canadian Capitalist Class*, ed. R.J. Brym. Toronto: Garamond Press 1985

Buckley H., and E. Tihoranyi. 'Canadian Politics for Rural Adjustment: A Summary of Conclusions.' In *Social and Cultural Change in Canada*. Vol. 1, ed. W.E. Mann. Toronto: Copp Clark 1970

Buckley, Kenneth. 'The Role of Staple Industries in Canada's Economic Development.' *Journal of Economic History* 18, no. 4 (December 1958): 439–50

Burbridge, J.K. 'The Atlantic Development Board and Atlantic Regional Development.' MA Thesis, University of New Brunswick 1971

Cairncross, A.K. *Economic Development and the Atlantic Provinces*. Fredericton: Atlantic Provinces Research Board 1961

Cairns, Alan. 'The Electoral System and the Party System in Canada 1921–1965.' *Canadian Journal of Political Science* 1, no. 1 (1968): 56–80

– 'The Governments and Societies of Canadian Federalism.' *Canadian Journal of Political Science* 10, no. 4 (1977): 695–725

Camp, Dalton. *Gentlemen, Players and Politicians*. Toronto: McClelland and Stewart 1970

Cardoso, F.H. 'Associated-Dependent Development: Theoretical and Practical Implications.' In *Authoritarian Brazil*, ed. A. Stepan. New Haven: New Haven Press 1973

Careless, Anthony. *Initiative and Response: The Adaptation of Canadian Federalism to Regional Economic Development*. Montreal: McGill-Queen's University Press 1977

Careless, J.M.S. 'Aspects of Metropolitanism in Atlantic Canada.' In *Regionalism in the Canadian Community 1867–1967* ed. Mason Wade. Toronto: University of Toronto Press 1969

Carney, J., R. Hudson, and J. Lewis, eds. *Regions in Crisis: New Perspectives in European Regional Theory*. London: Croom-Helm 1980

Carnoy, M. *The State and Political Theory*. Princeton, NJ: Princeton University Press 1984

Castells, Manuel. *The Urban Question: A Marxist Approach*. Cambridge, Mass.: MIT Press 1977

Chodos, Robert. 'The Business of Jean Marchand in Business.' *The Last Post* 2 (July 1972): 34–46

Clarke, H.D., J. Jenson, L. Leduc, and J. Pammett. *Absent Mandate: The Politics of Discontent in Canada*. Toronto: Gage 1984

Clarkson, Stephen. 'Democracy in the Liberal Party.' In *Party Politics in Canada*. 4th ed., ed. H. Thornburn. Toronto: Gage 1984

– *Canada and the Reagan Challenge*. Toronto: James Lorimer and Co. 1982

Cleland, M. 'The General Development Agreement and Provincial Economic Development.' In *Governing Nova Scotia: Policies, Priorities and the 1984–85* Budget, ed. B. Jamieson. Halifax: Dalhousie School of Public Administration 1984

Clement, Wallace. *The Struggle to Organize: Resistance in Canada's Fishery*. Toronto: McClelland and Stewart 1986

– *Continental Corporate Power*. Toronto: McClelland and Stewart 1978

– 'A Political Economy of Regionalism in Canada.' In *Modernization and the Canadian State*, ed. D. Glenday, H. Guindon, and A. Turowetz. Toronto: Macmillan 1978

Clow, Michael. 'Politics and Uneven Capitalist Development: The Maritime Challenge to the Study of Canadian Political Economy.' *Studies in Political Economy* 14 (Summer 1984): 117–40

– 'The Overthrow of Orthodoxy: The New Literature on Maritime Underdevelopment.' Paper presented to the Atlantic Provinces Political Studies Association, College of Cape Breton, Sydney, NS, 16–18 October 1980

Coady, M.M. *The Man from Margaree: Writings and Speeches of M.M. Coady*, ed. A.F. Laidlaw. Toronto: McClelland and Stewart 1971

Cobb, R.W., and C.D. Elder. *Participation in American Politics: The Dynamics of Agenda-Building*. Boston: Allyn and Bacon 1972

Conrad, Margaret S. 'George Nowlan and the Conservative Party in the Annapolis Valley, Nova Scotia, 1925–69.' PhD Thesis, University of Toronto 1979

Copithorne, Lawrence. *Natural Resources and Regional Disparities*. Hull, PQ: Minister of Supply and Services 1979

Corry, J.A. *The Growth of Government Activities since Confederation*. Ottawa: Royal Commission on Dominion-Provincial Relations 1939

Courchene, T. 'Avenues of Adjustment: The Transfer System and Regional

Disparities.' In *Canadian Confederation at the Crossroads*, ed. M. Walker.
Vancouver: Fraser Institute 1978

Crouch, Colin, ed. *State and Economy in Contemporary Capitalism*. New
York: St. Martin's Press 1979

Darrah, L., and R. Belland. 'The Canso Fishermen's Strike, 1970–71.' In
Strikes in Nova Scotia, ed. C. Gilson. Windsor, NS: Lancelot Press 1986

Doern, G.B. 'Priorities and Priority-Setting in the Trudeau Era.' In *How Ottawa Spends 1983*, ed. G.B. Doern. Toronto: James Lorimer and Co. 1983

– 'Liberal Priorities 1982: The limits of Scheming Virtuously.' In *How Ottawa
Spends 1982*, ed. G.B. Doern. Toronto: James Lorimer and Co. 1982

Doyle, B. 'DEVCO's Island in the Sun.' *Atlantic Advocate*, June 1975, passim

Dyck, Rand. *Provincial Politics in Canada*. Scarborough, Ont.: Prentice-Hall
1986

Economic Council of Canada. *Third Annual Review*. Ottawa: Supply and Services 1966

– *Financing Confederation*. Ottawa: Minister of Supply and Services 1982

– *Living Together: A Study of Regional Disparities*. Ottawa: Minister of
Supply and Services 1977

English, J. *The Decline of Politics: The Conservatives and the Party System
1901–1920*. Toronto: University of Toronto Press 1977

Esping-Anderson, G., R. Friedland, and E.O. Wright. 'Class Struggle and the
Capitalist State.' *Kapitalistate* 4–5 (1976): 186–98

Evans, D., D. Rueschenmeyer, and T. Skocpol, eds. *Bringing the State Back
In*. Cambridge, Mass.: Harvard University Press 1985

Fairley, Bryant. 'The Struggle for Capitalism in the Fishing Industry of Newfoundland.' *Studies in Political Economy*. 17 (Summer 1985): 33–70

Fay, C.R., and H.A. Innis. 'The Maritime Provinces'. *The Cambridge History
of the British Empire*, Vol. 6. Cambridge: Cambridge University Press 1930

Fleming, Susan. 'The Growth-Centre Concept: Its Application in the Maritime
Provinces.' MA Thesis, University of New Brunswick 1979

Fletcher, R.K. *Post-War Agriculture Trends in the Atlantic Provinces*. Atlantic
Provinces Economic Council, Research Paper no. 3, 1966

Foote, R.L. *The Case of Port Hawkesbury*. Toronto: PMA Books 1979

Forbes, E.R. 'The Rise and Fall of the Conservative Party in the Provincial
Politics of Nova Scotia, 1922–33.' MA Thesis, Dalhousie University 1967

Forbes, Ernest. 'Misguided Symmetry: The Destruction of Regional Transportation Policy for the Maritimes.' In *Canada and the Burden of Unity*, ed.
D.J. Bercuson. Toronto: Macmillan 1977

– *The Maritime Rights Movement 1919–1927*. Montreal: McGill-Queen's University Press 1979

– 'In Search of a Post-Confederation Maritime Historiography 1900–1967.' In
Eastern and Western Perspectives, ed. D.J. Bercuson and P.A. Buckner.

Toronto: University of Toronto Press 1981
- 'Never the Twain Did Meet: Prairie-Maritime Relations 1910–27.' *Canadian Historical Review* 59, no. 1 (March 1978): 18–37
- 'Consolidating Disparity: The Maritimes and the Industrialization of Canada during the Second World War.' *Acadiensis*, Spring 1986: 3–27
Forster, Ben. 'The Coming of the National Policy: Business, Government, and the Tariff, 1877–79.' *Journal of Canadian Studies* 14, no. 3 (Fall 1979): 39–49
Foucault, Michel. *Power/Knowledge: Selected Interviews and Other Writings 1972–77*, ed. Colin Gordon. Brighton, Sussex: Harvester Press 1980
Frank, Andre Gunder. *Capitalism and Underdevelopment in Latin America*. New York: Monthly Review Press 1967
- *Latin America: Underdevelopment or Revolution*. New York: Monthly Review Press 1969
Frank, David. 'The Cape Breton Coal Industry and the Rise and Fall of the British Empire Steel Corporation.' *Acadiensis* 7, no. 1 (Autumn 1978): 3–34
French, Richard. *How Ottawa Decides: Planning and Industrial Policy-Making 1968–1984*. Toronto: James Lorimer and Co. 1984
Frobel, F., J. Heindricks, and O. Kreye. 'The World Market for Labour and the World Market for Industrial Sites.' *Journal of Economic Issues* 12, no. 4 (December 1978)
Frost, J.D. 'The "Nationalization" of the Bank of Nova Scotia, 1880–1910.' In *Industrialization and Underdevelopment in the Maritimes, 1880–1930*, ed. T.W. Acheson, D. Frank, and J.D. Frost. Toronto: Garamond Press 1985
Frost, James, 'Principles of Interest: The Bank of Nova Scotia and the Industrialization of the Maritimes 1880–1910.' MA Thesis, Queen's University, 1979
Gagnon, Alain-G. *Développement régional, état, et groupes populaires*. Hull, Quebec: Asticou 1985
Ganong, R. Whidden. 'APEC – Its Beginning and Meaning.' *Atlantic Advocate* 1 (September 1956)
Gelinas, A., ed. *Public Enterprise and the Public Interest*. Toronto: Institute of Public Administration of Canada 1978
George, R.E. *The Life and Times of Industrial Estates Ltd*. Halifax: Dalhousie Institute of Public Affairs 1974
- 'Fifteen Years of Regional Industrial Development Policy: A Case Study of Nova Scotia.' In *Merchant Shipping and Economic Development in Atlantic Canada*, ed. L.R. Fischer and E.W. Sager. St John's: Maritime History Group, Memorial University 1982
- 'The Cape Breton Development Corporation.' In *Public Corporations and Public Policy in Canada*, ed. A. Tupper and G.B. Doern. Montreal: IRPP 1981

- *A Leader and a Laggard: Manufacturing Industry in Nova Scotia, Quebec, and Ontario.* Toronto: University of Toronto Press 1970
Gillespie, W.I., and R. Kerr. *The Impact of Federal Regional Economic Expansion Policies on the Distribution of Income in Canada.* Ottawa: Minister of Supply and Services 1977
Gordon, H. Scott. 'The Trawler Question in the United Kingdom and Canada.' *Dalhousie Review* 31, no. 2 (Summer 1951): 117–27
Graham J.F. *Fiscal Adjustment and Economic Development: A Case Study of Nova Scotia.* Toronto: University of Toronto Press 1963
Granatstein, J.L. *Canada's War: The Politics of the MacKenzie King Government 1939–1945.* Toronto: Oxford University Press 1975
- *The Politics of Survival: The Conservative Party of Canada, 1939–45.* Toronto: University of Toronto Press 1967
- *The Ottawa Men: The Civil Service Mandarins 1935–1957.* Toronto: Oxford University Press 1982
Grant, J.W. 'Population Shifts in the Maritimes.' *Dalhousie Review* 18, no. 3 (October 1937): 282–94
Green, Jim. *Against the Tide: The Story of the Canadian Seamen's Union.* Toronto: Progress Books 1986
Haliburton, E.D. *My Years with Stanfield.* Windsor, NS: Lancelot Press 1972
Harvey, David. 'The Geography of Capitalist Accumulation.' *Antipode* 2, no. 2 (September 1975): 9–21
Hawkins, Jack. *The Life and Times of Angus L. Macdonald.* Windsor, NS: Lancelot Press 1969
Hazelton, R. 'Labour in Prince Edward Island: A Case Study.' In *Labour in Atlantic Canada*, ed. R. Chanteloup. St John: University of New Brunswick Press 1981
Hechter, Michael. *International Colonialism: The Celtic Fringe in British National Development 1536–1966.* Los Angeles: University of California Press 1975
Henson, G. 'The Nova Scotia Labour-Management Agreements.' *Industrial Relations* 24, no. 1 (January 1969)
Higgins, Benjamin. 'The Concept of Regional Planning.' *Canadian Public Administration* 9, no. 2 (June 1966): 158–76
- 'Social Aspects of Regional Planning.' In *Social Issues in Regional Policy and Regional Planning*, ed. A. Kuklinski. Paris: Mouton 1977
Higgins, D. 'Canada: New Brunswick and Nova Scotia.' In *International Handbook on Local Government Reorganization: Contemporary Developments*, ed. D.C. Rowat. Westport, Conn.: Greenwood Press 1980
Hirschman, A.O. *Strategy of Economic Development.* Binghampton, NY: Yale University Press 1958
Hobsbawm, E.J. *Industry and Empire.* Harmondsworth: Penguin 1969
Holland, Stuart. 'Regional Underdevelopment in a Developed Economy: The

Italian Case.' *Regional Studies* 5, no. 2 (July 1971): 71–90
– *Capital versus the Regions*. London: Macmillan 1976
Howland, R.D. *Regional Aspects of Canada's Economic Development*. Ottawa: Royal Commission on Canada's Economic Prospects 1958
Hymer, Stephen. 'The Multinational Corporation and the Law of Uneven Development.' In *International Firms and Modern Imperialism*, ed. H. Radice. Harmondsworth: Penguin 1975
Innis, H.A. *Essays in Canadian Economic History*, ed. Mary Q. Innis. Toronto: University of Toronto Press 1956
Jackson, R.J., D. Jackson, and N. Baxter-Moore. *Politics in Canada*. Scarborough, Ont.: Prentice-Hall 1986
Jansen, Janni. 'Regional Socio-economic Development: The Case of Fishing in Atlantic Canada.' Ph D Thesis, Rutgers University 1981
Jenkin, Michael. *The Challenge of Diversity: Industrial Policy in the Canadian Federation*. Science Council of Canada Background Study no. 50. Ottawa: Minister of Supply and Services 1983
– 'The Prospects for a New National Policy.' *Journal of Canadian Studies* 4, no. 3 (Fall 1979): 126–39
Jenson, Jane. 'Gender and Reproduction: Or Babies and the State.' *Studies in Political Economy* 20 (Summer 1986): 9–46
Jessop, Bob. 'Accumulation Strategies, State Forms and Hegemonic Projects.' *Kapitalistate* 10/11 (1983): 89–111
– *The Capitalist State*. Oxford: Martin Robertson 1982
Jones, Kenneth. 'Response to Regional Disparity in the Maritime Provinces, 1926–1942: A Study in Canadian Intergovernmental Relations.' MA Thesis, University of New Brunswick 1980
Kent, Tom. 'Towards a Philosophy of Social Security.' *Study Conference on National Problems*, Kingston, Ontario, 7 September 1960
– 'The Brief Rise and Early Decline of Regional Development.' *Acadiensis* 9, no. 2 (Autumn 1979): 120–4
Kierstead, B.S. *The Theory of Economic Change*. Toronto: 1948
– *The Economic Effects of the War on the Maritime Provinces of Canada*. Halifax: Dalhousie Institute of Public Affairs 1944
Kuklinski, Anton. *Social Issues in Regional Policy and Regional Planning*. The Hague: Mouton 1977
– ed. *Polarized Development in Regional Planning*. The Hague: Mouton 1974
Kuttner, R. 'The Poverty of Economics.' *The Atlantic* 255, no. 2 (February 1985): 74–84
Kuusisto, N., and R. Williams. 'Social Expenses and Regional Underdevelopment.' In *Inequality: Essays on the Political Economy of Social Welfare*, ed. A. Moscovitch and G. Drover. Toronto: University of Toronto Press 1981
Kwavnick, David. *Organized Labour and Pressure Politics*. Montreal: McGill-Queen's University Press 1972

Laclau, Ernesto. 'Feudalism and Capitalism in Latin America.' *New Left Review* 67 (May–June 1971): 19–38

Lamontagne, Maurice. 'Growth, Price Stability and the Problem of Unemployment.' *Study Conference on National Problems*, Kingston, Ontario, 7 September 1960

Landes, D.S. *The Unbound Prometheus: Technological Change and Industrial Development in Europe from 1750 to the Present.* Cambridge: Cambridge University Press 1969

Landry, J.M. 'L'administration provinciale dans la region-plan du nord-est du Nouveau Brunswick.' MA Thesis, Laval University 1980

Lattimer, J.H. 'Agriculture.' In B.S. Kierstead, *The Economic Effects of the War on the Maritime Provinces of Canada.* Halifax: Dalhousie Institute of Public Affairs 1944

Laux, J.K. 'Expanding the State: The International Relations of State-Owned Enterprises in Canada.' A paper delivered at the annual meeting of the American Political Science Association, New York, 3–6 September 1981

– 'Global Interdependence and State Intervention.' In *Canada's Foreign Policy: Analysis and Trends*, ed. B. Tomlin. Toronto: Methuen 1979

Laxer, G. 'The Political Economy of Aborted Development: The Canadian Case.' In *The Structure of the Canadian Capitalist Class*, ed. R.J. Brym. Toronto: Garamond Press 1985

Lazarus, M. *Years of Hard Labour.* Don Mills: Ontario Federation of Labour 1974

Levitt, Kari. *Silent Surrender.* Toronto: Macmillan 1970

Lewis, David. *Louder Voices: The Corporate Welfare Bums.* Toronto: Lewis and Samuel 1972

– *The Good Fight: Political Memoirs 1909–1958.* Toronto: Macmillan 1981

Lindblom, C.E. *Politics and Markets: The World's Political-Economic Systems.* New York: Basic Books 1977

Lithwick, N.H. 'Regional Policy: The Embodiment of Contradictions.' In *How Ottawa Spends 1982*, ed. G.B. Doern. Toronto: James Lorimer and Co. 1982

– *Regional Economic Policy: The Canadian Experience.* Toronto: McGraw-Hill Ryerson 1978

Lounsbury, F.E. *Secondary Manufacturing in the Atlantic Provinces.* Halifax: Atlantic Provinces Economic Council 1961

McAllister, Ian. 'How to Re-make DREE.' *Policy Options* 1, no. 1 (March 1980): 39–43

McCall-Newman, Christina. *Grits: An Intimate Portrait of the Liberal Party.* Toronto: Macmillan 1982

MacCallum, John. *Unequal Beginnings: Agriculture and Economic Development in Quebec and Ontario until 1870.* Toronto: University of Toronto Press 1980

MacDonald, L.R. 'Merchants against Industry: An Idea and Its Origins.' *Canadian Historical Review* 56 (1975): 263–81

MacEwan, Paul. *The Akerman Years*. Antigonish, NS: Formac 1980

– *Miners and Steelworkers: Labour in Cape Breton*. Toronto: Samuel Stevens Hakkert and Co. 1976

Macgill, Don. 'Military Aid to the Civil Power: The Cape Breton Experience in the 1920's.' In *Cape Breton Historical Essays*, ed. D. Macgillivray and B. Tennyson. Sydney, NS: College of Cape Breton Press 1980

Macgillivray, Don, and Brian Tennyson. *Cape Breton Historical Essays*. Sydney, NS: College of Cape Breton Press 1980

MacIntosh, P.S. 'Turmoil in the Nova Scotia NDP, 1968–80.' MA Thesis, Dalhousie University 1982

MacKaay, Carole. 'Canadian Regionalism: The Atlantic Development Board: A Case Study.' MA Thesis, McGill University 1969

McKinley, Cindy. 'Regional Accommodation in Canada: The Atlantic Caucuses of the Liberal and Progressive Conservative Parties.' A paper presented to a conference on Atlantic Political Development, Queen's University, Kingston, Ontario, 27–9 July 1981

MacKinnon, Frank. *The Life of a party: The History of the Liberal Party in Prince Edward Island*. Summerside, P.E.I.: Williams and Crue Ltd. 1973

MacKintosh, W.A. 'Economic Factors in Canadian History.' *Canadian Historical Review* 4 (1923): 12–25

McNutt, W.S. 'The Atlantic Revolution.' *Atlantic Advocate*, June 1957: 11–13

MacPherson, C.B. *Democracy in Alberta*. Toronto: University of Toronto Press 1962

MacPherson, Ian. *Each for All: A History of the Cooperative Movement in Canada, 1900–1945*. Ottawa: Carleton Library Series 1979

Macridis, R.C., and B.E. Brown. *Comparative Politics*. Homewood, Ill.: Dorsey Press 1977

Mahon, Rianne. 'Canadian Public Policy: The Unequal Structure of Representation.' In *The Canadian State: Political Economy and Political Power*, ed. L.V. Panitch. Toronto: University of Toronto Press 1977

– *The Politics of Industrial Restructuring: Canadian Textiles*. Toronto: University of Toronto Press 1984

– 'Toward a Marxist Analysis of Issue Formation.' A paper presented to a conference on Problem Recognition and the Setting of a Public Agenda, Department of Political Science, Carleton University, 6–8 April 1983

Mallory, James. *Social Credit and the Federal Power in Canada*. Toronto: University of Toronto Press 1954

Mann, O. Nelson. 'Atlantic Provinces Economic Council.' *Dalhousie Review* 35, no. 4 (Winter 1956): 309–22

– 'An Overall Planning Scheme Is a Must for the Atlantic Provinces.' *Financial Times*, 9 November 1964

Markusen, Ann. 'Regionalism and the Capitalist State: The Case of the United States.' *Kapitalistate* 7 (1978): 39–62

Massey, D., and R. Meegan. *The Anatomy of Job Loss*. London: Methuen 1982

Massey, Doreen. 'Towards a Critique of Industrial Location Theory.' London: Centre for Environmental Studies, Research Paper no. 5

– 'Regionalism: Some Current Issues.' *Capital and Class* 6 (Autumn 1978):106–25

Mathias, Philip. *Forced Growth*. Toronto: James, Lewis, and Samuel 1971

Matthews, Ralph. *The Creation of Regional Dependency*. Toronto: University of Toronto Press 1983

Maxwell, J., and C. Pestieau. *Economic Realities of Contemporary Confederation*. Montreal: C.D. Howe Research Institute 1980

Meisel, John. *The Canadian General Election of 1957*. Toronto: University of Toronto Press 1962

Mellor, J. *The Company Store: James Bryson MacLachlan and the Cape Breton Coal Miners 1900–1925*. Toronto: Doubleday 1983

Mills, J.R. 'Voluntary Economic Planning in Nova Scotia.' *Canadian Public Administration* 8, no. 2 (June 1965): 160–5

Milne, D. *Tug of War: Ottawa and the Provinces under Trudeau and Mulroney*. Toronto: James Lorimer and Co. 1986

Molot, M., and G. Williams. 'The Political Economy of Continentalism.' In *Canadian Politics in the 1980's*, 2nd ed., ed. M.S. Whittington and G. Williams. Toronto: Methuen 1984

Morse, Norman H. 'Agriculture in the Maritime Provinces.' *Dalhousie Review* 39, no. 4 (Winter 1959): 471–84

Muise, D.A. 'The Federal Election of 1867 in Nova Scotia: An Economic Interpretation.' In *Collections of the Nova Scotia Historical Society*. Halifax 1968

Murray, Robin. 'The Internationalization of Capital and the Nation State.' In *International Firms and Modern Imperialism*, ed. H. Radice. Harmondsworth: Penguin 1975

Myrdal, Gunnar. *Economic Theory and Underdeveloped Regions*. London: Gerald Duckworth 1957

Nairn, Tom. *The Break-up of Britain: Crisis and Neo-Nationalism*. London: New Left Books 1977

Naylor, Tom. *The History of Canadian Business 1867–1914*. 2 vols. Toronto: James Lorimer and Co. 1975

Neatby, H.B. *William Lyon MacKenzie King*, Vol. 2 1924–32: *The Lonely Heights*. Toronto: University of Toronto Press 1963

– *William Lyon MacKenzie King*, Vol. 3, *1932–39: The Prism of Unity*. Toronto: University of Toronto Press 1976

Nelles, H.V. *The Politics of Development: Forests, Mines and Hydro-electric Power in Ontario 1849–1941*. Toronto: Macmillan 1974

Newman, Peter C. *Renegade in Power: The Diefenbaker Years*. Toronto: McClelland and Stewart 1973

Newton, D. 'What Is Happening in Cape Breton?' *Canadian Geographical Journal* 87, no. 5 (November 1973): 24–31

Offe, Claus. 'The Attribution of Public Status to Interest Groups: Observations on the West German Case.' In *Organizing Interests in Western Europe*, ed. Suzanne Berger. Cambridge: Cambridge University Press 1981

– 'The Theory of the Capitalist State and the Problem of Policy Formation.' In *Stress and Contradiction in Modern Capitalism*, ed. L.N. Lindberg. London: Lexington Books 1975

Offe, Claus, and Volker Ronge. 'Theses on the Theory of the State.' In *Classes, Power and Conflict: Classical and Contemporary Debates*, ed. A. Giddens and D. Held. Berkeley: University of California Press 1982

Pal, Leslie A. 'Reply: Restraining Class in Policy Explanations.' *Canadian Journal of Political Science* 19, no. 1 (March 1986): 99–102

– 'Revision and Retreat: Canadian Unemployment Insurance.' In *Canadian Social Welfare Policy*, ed. J.S. Ismael. Montreal: McGill-Queen's University Press 1985

Paltiel, K.Z. 'The Changing Environment and Role of Special Interest Groups.' *Canadian Public Administration* 25, no. 2 (Summer 1982): 198–210

Panitch, L.V. 'Corporatism in Canada.' *Studies in Political Economy* 1 (Spring 1979)

– 'Dependency and Class in Canadian Political Economy.' *Studies in Political Economy* 6 (Autumn 1981): 11–12

– 'Elites, Classes and Power in Canada.' In *Canadian Politics in the 1980's*. 2nd ed., ed. M.S. Whittington and G. Williams. Toronto: Methuen 1984

– ed. *The Canadian State: Political Economy and Political Power*. Toronto: University of Toronto Press 1977

Parks, A.C. *The Economy of the Atlantic Provinces 1940–1958*. Halifax: Atlantic Provinces Economic Council 1960

Payn, E. 'An Industrial Revolution for Cape Breton.' *Atlantic Advocate*, September 1969

Penner, N. *The Canadian Left*. Scarborough, Ont.: Prentice-Hall 1977

Pepin, Pierre-Yves. *Life and Poverty in the Maritimes*. ARDA, 1968

Perlin, George. *The Tory Syndrome*. Montreal: McGill-Queen's University Press 1980

Phidd, R.A., and G.B. Doern. *The Politics and Management of Canadian Economic Policies*. Toronto: Macmillan 1978

Phillips, Paul. *Regional Disparities*. Toronto: James Lorimer and Co. 1978

Pickersgill, J.W. *My Years with Louis St. Laurent: A Political Memoir*. Toronto: University of Toronto Press 1975

– *The MacKenzie King Record*, Vol. 1. Toronto: University of Toronto Press 1960

Poetschke, L.E. 'ARDA and Poverty: Lessons in Regional Planning.' *Canadian Journal of Agricultural Economics* 16, no. 3 (1968): 38–47
– 'Regional Planning for Depressed Rural Areas: The Canadian Experience.' *Canadian Journal of Agricultural Economics* 16, no. 1 (1968): 8–20
Porter, John. *The Vertical Mosaic*. Toronto: University of Toronto Press 1965
Pratt, Larry. 'The State and Province-Building: Alberta's Development Strategy.' In *The Canadian State: Political Economy and Political Power*, ed. L.V. Panitch. Toronto: University of Toronto Press 1977
– 'Energy: Roots of National Policy.' *Studies in Political Economy* 7 (Winter 1982): 27–60
Pross, A. Paul. *Pressure Group Behaviour in Canadian Politics*. Toronto: McGraw-Hill 1975
– *Planning and Development: A Case of Two Nova Scotia Communities*. Halifax: Institute of Public Affairs 1975
– 'The Fishery: Ali vs. Frazier.' In *Governing Nova Scotia*, ed. B. Jamieson. Halifax: Dalhousie University School of Public Administration 1984
Przeworski, Adam. *Capitalism and Social Democracy*. Cambridge, Mass.: Harvard University Press 1986
Radice, Hugo, ed. *International Firms and Modern Imperialism*. New York: Penguin 1975
Radwanski, George. *Trudeau*. Toronto: Macmillan 1978
Rawlyk, G.A. 'The Farmer-Labour Movement and the Failure of Socialism in Nova Scotia.' In *Essays in the Left*, ed. L. Lapierre, J. MacLeod, C. Taylor, and W. Young. Toronto: McClelland and Stewart 1971
– 'The Maritimes and the Canadian Community.' In *Regionalism in the Canadian Community 1867–1967*, ed. Mason Wade. Toronto: University of Toronto Press 1969
Ray, D.M. 'Dimensions of Canadian Regionalism.' Dept. of Energy, Mines, Resources Geographical Paper no. 49. Ottawa 1971
– 'The Location of U.S. Manufacturing Subsidiaries in Canada.' *Canadian Economic Geography* 47 (1971): 389–400
Regenstreif, Peter. *The Diefenbaker Interlude: Parties and Voting in Canada*. Toronto: Longmans Canada 1965
Richards, J., and L. Pratt. *Prairie Capitalism: Power and Influence in the New West*. Toronto: McClelland and Stewart 1979
Sacouman, R.J. 'The "Peripheral" Maritimes and Canada-Wide Marxist Political Economy.' *Studies in Political Economy* 6 (Autumn 1981): 135–50
– 'Semi-Proletarianization and Rural Underdevelopment in the Maritimes.' *Canadian Review of Anthropology and Sociology* 17 (1980): 232–45
Saunders, S.A. *The Economic History of the Maritime Provinces*. A study prepared for the Royal Commission on Dominion-Provincial Relations. Ottawa: King's Printer 1939
– *Studies in the Economy of the Maritime Provinces*. Toronto: Macmillan 1939

Savoie, Donald. *Regional Economic Development: Canada's Search for Solutions*. Toronto: University of Toronto Press 1986
- 'Cooperative Federalism with Democracy.' *Policy Options* 3, no. 6 (November/December 1982): 54–8
- 'The Continuing Struggle for a Regional Development Policy.' In *Canada: The State of the Federation 1985*, ed. P.M. Leslie. Montreal: McGill-Queen's University Press 1985
- *Federal-Provincial Collaboration: The Canada–New Brunswick General Development Agreement*. Montreal: McGill-Queen's University Press 1981
Simeon, Richard. 'Studying Public Policy.' *Canadian Journal of Political Science* 11, no. 4 (December 1976): 548–80
Simeon, R. *Federalism and the Politics of a National Strategy*. Ottawa: Science Council of Canada 1979
Simeon, R., and D.J. Elkins. 'Regional Political Cultures in Canada.' *Canadian Journal of Political Science* 6, no. 3 (September 1974): 397–437
- eds. *Small Worlds: Provinces and Parties in Canadian Political Life*. Toronto: Methuen 1980
Simpson, Jeffrey. *Discipline of Power*. Toronto: Personal Library Publishers 1980
Skocpol, Theda. *States and Social Revolutions*. Cambridge: Cambridge University Press 1979
Skocpol, Theda, and J.J. Kenberg. 'The Political Formation of the American Welfare State in Historical and Comparative Perspective.' *Comparative Social Research* 6 (1983)
Skocpol, Theda, and M. Weir. 'State Structures and Social Keynesianism: Response to the Great Depression in Sweden and the United States.' *International Journal of Comparative Sociology* 24 (January/April 1983): 4–29
Smiley, D.V. 'Canada and the Quest for a National Policy.' *Canadian Journal of Political Science* 8, no. 1 (1975): 40–62
- 'The Federal Dimension of Canadian Economic Nationalism.' *Dalhousie Law Review* 1, no. 3 (October 1974): 541–79
- *Canada in Question: Federalism in the Eighties*. 3rd ed. Toronto: McGraw-Hill Ryerson 1980
Smith, David. *The Regional Decline of a National Party: Liberals on the Prairies*. Toronto: University of Toronto Press 1981
Smith, Denis. *Gentle Patriot: A Political Biography of Walter Gordon*. Edmonton: Hurtig 1973
Smith, W.Y. 'What Can Aid Maritimes?' *Financial Post,* 30 June 1962
Smitheram, V., D. Milne, and S. Dasgupta, eds. *The Garden Transformed: Prince Edward Island 1945–1980*. Charlottetown: Ragweed Press 1982
Springate, David. 'Difficulties Associated with DREE's Current Approach.' In *Canadian Economy: Problems and Policies*, ed. G.C. Ruggerie. Toronto: Gage 1981

- 'Regional Development Incentive Grants and Private Investment in Canada.'
  Ph D Thesis, Harvard Business School 1972
Stevens, Geoffrey. *Stanfield*. Toronto: McClelland and Stewart 1973
Stevenson, Garth. 'Continental Integration and Canadian Unity.' In *Continental Community? Independence and Integration in North America*, ed.
  A. Axline, J.E. Hyndman, P.V. Lyon, and M.A. Molot. Toronto: McClelland and Stewart 1974
- 'Canadian Regionalism in Continental Perspective.' *Journal of Canadian Studies* 15, no. 2 (Summer 1980): 16–27
- 'Federalism and the Political Economy of the Canadian State.' In *The Canadian State: Political Economy and Political Power*, ed. L.V. Panitch.
  Toronto: University of Toronto Press 1977
Strain, John Frank. 'Unemployment Insurance and the Maritime Economy.'
  MA Report, University of New Brunswick, 1980
Tarrow, Sidney. 'Regional Policy, Ideology and Peripheral Defence: The Fos-sur-mer.' In *Territorial Politics in Industrial Nations*, ed. S. Tarrow, P.J.
  Katzenstein, and L. Graziano. New York: Praeger 1978
- *Between Center and Periphery: Grassroots Politicians in Italy and France*.
  New York: Yale University Press 1977
- *Struggling to Reform: Social Movements and Policy Change during Cycles of Protest*. Western Societies Papers, Occasional Paper no. 15. Center for International Studies, Cornell University, 1983
Tarrow, Sidney, Peter J. Katzenstein, and Ruigi Graziano, eds. *Territorial Politics in Industrial Nations*. New York: Praeger 1978
Tennyson, Brian. 'Another Look at Confederation: A Case Study of Cape Breton.' *Acadiensis* 00, no. 0 (Autumn 1976):
Tomblin, Stephen G. 'The Council of Maritime Premiers: Is It Promoting the Integration of Government Services in the Maritimes?' MA Thesis, Dalhousie University 1979
Traves, Tom. *The State and Enterprise: Canadian Manufacturers and the Federal Government 1917–1931*. Toronto: University of Toronto Press 1979
Trudeau, P.E. 'The Expansion of the Atlantic Economy.' *Atlantic Advocate* 59, no. 7 (March 1969): 12–16
Tupper, Alan, 'Public Enterprise as Social Welfare: The Case of the Cape Breton Development Corporation.' *Canadian Public Policy* 4, no. 4 (Autumn 1978): 530–46
- 'The State in Business.' *Canadian Public Administration* 22, no. 1 (Spring 1979): 124–50
- *Public Money in the Private Sector*. Kingston Institute of Intergovernmental Relations, Queen's University 1982
United Nations. *Transnational Corporations in World Development: A Re-examination*. (1978)
Usher, D. 'Some Questions About the Regional Development Incentives Act.'

Canadian Public Policy 1 no. 4 (Autumn 1975): 557–75

Veltmeyer, Henry. 'The Underdevelopment of Atlantic Canada.' *Review of Radical Political Economics* 10, no. 3 (Fall 1978): 95–105

– 'A Central Issue in Dependency Theory.' *Canadian Review of Anthropology and Sociology* 17, no. 3 (August 1980): 198–213

Wallerstein, I. *The Origins of the Modern World System*. New York: Academic Press 1974

Walton, F.T. 'Atlantic Development: An Appraisal.' *Business Quarterly* 33, no. 2 (Summer 1968): 61–71

Wardell, M. 'Atlantic Premiers and APEC Meet at St. John's.' *Atlantic Advocate*, October 1958:

Watkins, Mel. 'A Staple Theory of Economic Growth.' In *Approaches to Canadian Economic History*, ed. W.T. Easterbrook and M. Watkins. Toronto: McClelland and Stewart 1967

Watson, M. 'The Regional Dimension of Planning.' In *Planning, Politics, and Public Policy*, ed. J. Haward and M. Watson. Cambridge: Cambridge University Press 1975

Watt, John. 'The Impact of a Growth Center on Labour Migration: The Strait of Canso, Nova Scotia.' MA Thesis, University of Waterloo 1977

Wearing, Joseph. *The L-Shaped Party: The Liberal Party of Canada, 1958–1980*. Toronto: McGraw-Hill Ryerson 1981

Weaver, C., and T.L. Gunton. 'From Drought Assistance to Mega-Projects: Fifty Years of Regional Theory and Policy in Canada.' *Canadian Journal of Regional Science* Vol. 5, no. 1 (1982): 5–37

Webb, J.T. 'The DOSCO Crisis: Some Political Aspects of a Regional Economic Problem.' MA Thesis, Carleton University 1973

Weeks, E.P. 'The Atlantic Provinces: A Case Study.' *Proceedings*, International Conference on Regional Development and Economic Change, Toronto 1965

Wenaas, C.J. 'Provincial Roles in Regional Development Programs.' In *Regional Poverty and Change*. Ottawa: Minister of Supply and Services 1976

Whelan, Hugh. 'Public Policy and Regional Development: The Experience of the Atlantic Provinces.' In *The Prospects of Change: Proposals for Canada's Future*, ed. A. Rotstein. Toronto: McGraw-Hill 1965

Whitaker, Reginald. *The Government Party: Organizing and Financing the Liberal Party of Canada, 1930–1958*. Toronto: University of Toronto Press 1977

– 'Federalism Democracy and the Canadian Political Community.' In *The Integration Question: Political Economy and Public Policy in North America*, ed. J.H. Pammett and B.W. Tomlin. Don Mills, Ont.: Addison-Wesley 1984

Wilbur, R. 'Maritimes: Planned Underdevelopment.' *Canadian Dimension* 7 (January–February 1971): 14–18

Williams, Glen. *Not for Export: Towards a Political Economy of Canada's*

Arrested Industrialization. Toronto: McClelland and Stewart 1983

Wilson, T. *Financial Assistance with Regional Development.* Report prepared for the Atlantic Provinces Research Board. Fredericton, NB: APRB 1964

Wolfe, D.A. 'The State and Economic Policy in Canada, 1968–75.' In *The Canadian State: Political Economy and Political Power*, ed. L.V. Panitch. Toronto: University of Toronto Press 1977

– 'Economic Growth and Foreign Investment: A Perspective on Canadian Economic Policy 1945–57.' *Journal of Canadian Studies* 13, no. 1 (Spring 1978): 3–20

Woodfine, William. 'Canada's Atlantic Provinces: A Study in Regional Economic Retardation.' In *Economics Canada*, ed. Mel Watkins and D.F. Foster. Toronto: McGraw-Hill 1964

Woodward, R.S. 'The Effectiveness of DREE's New Location Subsidies.' *Canadian Public Policy* 1, no. 2 (Spring 1975): 219–29

Young, R., P. Faucher, and A. Blais. 'The Concept of Province-Building: A Critique.' *Canadian Journal of Political Science*, 17 no. 4 (December 1984): 783–818

Young, R.A. 'Teaching and Research in Maritime Politics: Old Stereotypes and New Directions.' *Journal of Canadian Studies*, 22 (1986) and in *Teaching Maritime Studies*, ed. P.A. Buckner. Fredericton, NB: Acadiensis Press 1986

Government Documents

Canada

Atlantic Development Board. *Annual Report*, 1968–9

Cape Breton Development Corporation. *Annual Report 1982.*

– *13th Annual Report*, 1981

Constitutional Conference, February 1968, *Proceedings*

Debates and Proceedings, House of Commons. Vol. III, 27th Parliament 3157–8

Debates of the House of Commons, 20 March 1969, 6900

Department of Labour Employment and Manpower Utilization in Nova Scotia 1950–1960. Economic and Research Branch, Department of Labour, Ottawa 1964

Dominion Bureau of Statistics. *The Maritime Provinces Since Confederation.* Ottawa: 1926

Dominion-Provincial Conference, 1960. *Proceedings*, 25–27 July 1960

Dominion-Provincial Conference, 1946. Nova Scotia Submission and Plenary Discussion.

Dominion-Provincial Conference, 1935. *Proceedings.* DREE, *Development Agreements.* 1 April 1980

DREE. *Annual Report* 1980–81

- *Economic Development Prospects in Nova Scotia.* 1979
- *Departmental Profile.* September 1980
- 'Economic Development Prospects in Nova Scotia.' December 1979
- *Departmental Profile.* September 1980
- *Economic Development Prospects in Nova Scotia.* December 1979
- Discussion Paper. 'Canadian Manufacturing Prospects from a Regional Perspective.' 1978
- 'Summaries of Federal-Provincial General Development Agreements and Currently Active Subsidiary Agreements.' December 1977
- 'Strategic Regional Development Overview: Atlantic Region.' 1980
- 'Climate for Development: Atlantic Region.' Working paper prepared for submission to the Standing Committee on Regional Development, 1976
- *Annual Report* 1970–71. Ottawa 1972
Economic Development for Canada in the 1980's. November 1981
Federal-Provincial Conference, 1957. *Proceedings*
Federal-Provincial Conference, 1955. Preparatory Committee for the Federal-Provincial Conference, unpublished Minutes
House of Commons. Standing Committee on Regional Development. *Minutes and Proceedings* 1969–70, 15 April 1970
Major Projects Task Force Report, 23 June 1981
'Notes for an Address by the Rt. Hon. Jean Marchand, Minister of Regional Economic Expansion, at the Conference of the Community Planning Association, St. John's, Newfoundland,' 15 September 1969
'Notes for an Address by the Rt. Hon. Jean Marchand, Minister of Regional Economic Expansion at the Annual General Meeting of the Quebec Chamber of Commerce,' Sherbrooke, Quebec, 18 September 1970
Office of the Prime Minister. 'Reorganization for Economic Development,' Ottawa, 12 January 1982
Royal Commission on Canada's Economic Prospects (referred to hereafter as Gordon Commission). *Submission of the Government of Nova Scotia*, October 1955
- *Report.* Ottawa 1957
- *Final Report.* Ottawa 1957
Royal Commission on Coal (referred to hereafter as Rand Commission). *Report*, August 1960
Royal Commission on Dominion-Provincial Relations. *Report*
Royal Commission on Financial Arrangements between the Dominion and the Maritime Provinces. 1935
Royal Commission on Maritime Claims. 1926
Senate Committee on National Finance. *Government Policy and Regional Development.* Ottawa: Minister of Supply and Services 1982
Special Senate Committee on Land Use in Canada. *Proceedings*, 28 February 1957

Statements by the Rt. Hon. L.B. Pearson and Hon. Jean Marchand, Conference on Financing Higher Education, 24–26 October 1966
Statistics Canada. *The Labour Force*. Catalogue No. 71–001
Task Force on Atlantic Fisheries. *Navigating Troubled Waters: A New Policy for the Atlantic Fisheries*. Ottawa: Supply and Services 1982

Nova Scotia

Cansteel Corporation. *First Annual Report*, 1976; *Second Annual Report*, 1977
Department of Development. *Annual Report 1977*
– 'Problems Related to the Sydney Steel Corporation: Recommended Courses of Action.' Report of a Task Force for the Policy Board, 1979
– 'A Plan of Organization for the Strait of Canso Development Office,' January 1977
– *Building Competitiveness: A White Paper on Economic Development.* 1984
– *Strengths and Weaknesses of the Nova Scotia Economy.* April 1979
– *Sector Profiles.* 1979
– *Steel-Making Study.* 1973
– *Sector Profiles.* 1979
– *Towards an Economic Development Strategy for Nova Scotia.* 1980
– *Annual Reports*, 1972, 1977
Department of Lands and Forests. Ext. Note no. 66, 'Forestry Incentives for Increased Fibre Production in Nova Scotia,' March, 1970
Department of Mines and Energy. *Offshore Oil and Gas: A Chance for Nova Scotians*. July 1980
Department of Trade and Industry. *A Brief Review of the Fisheries of Nova Scotia* by J.W. Watt. May 1963
Fact-Finding Body on Labour Legislation. *Report* 1962
Province of Nova Scotia Voluntary Planning: A Review and Annual Report. 1975
Royal Commission on Provincial Development and Rehabilitation (referred to hereafter as Dawson Commission), *Report*. Halifax: King's Printer, 1944
Royal Commission of Provincial Economic Inquiry. *Report* and *Complementary Report.* Halifax: King's Printer 1934
– *Submission of the Government of Nova Scotia*. Halifax: King's Printer 1934
Voluntary Planning Board. *Annual Report.* 1967
– *Report on Progress.* 1965
– *A Review and Annual Report.* 1975

Papers

Liberal Party of Canada Papers (LPC Papers). National Archives

Angus L. Macdonald Papers (ALM Papers). Nova Scotia Public Archives
Provincial Secretary's Papers (PS Papers). Nova Scotia Public Archives

Personal Interview

Kent, Tom. Deputy minister, DREE, 1969–71; president, DEVCO, 1972–7; president, SYSCO, 1977–9. 23 September 1985

Newspapers and Magazines

Atlantic Advocate
Atlantic Insight
Canadian Business
Chronicle Herald (Halifax)
The Citizen (Ottawa)
Financial Post
Globe and Mail (Toronto)
Maclean's
Maritime Merchant
Monetary Times
Report on Business Magazine

Index

accumulation, process of, 5, 311–13
Acheson, T.W., on role of entrepreneurship in Maritime decline, 23
administrative recommodification, 313
agriculture: farm resettlement program, 65; inefficiency of Depression-era farming, 65; poor ranking of Nova Scotia in farm indices, 65; in the Maritimes in the 1960s, 172
Agriculture Rehabilitation and Development Act, establishment of, 162, 179
Agriculture Rehabilitation and Development Agency (ARDA): relationship with provinces, 187; program expenditures, 187; adjustment vs. welfare orientation of, 187–8; criticisms of, 191; changes under Trudeau, 213
Akerman, Jeremy, leader of Nova Scotia NDP, 233, 280
Alexander, David, 18
Americanization, of the Canadian economy, 6
Antigonish movement: Catholic leadership of, 71; limitations of, 71–4; philosophy and objectives of, 72–4

Anti-Inflation Board (AIB), 229
Appleyard, Major-General Kenelin, 147
Area Development Agency (ADA): criticisms of, 182–3; purpose and operation of, 183; reservations of Nova Scotia towards, 183; welfare orientation of, 183, 185, 186
Atlantic Development Board (ADB): creation and mandate of, 162–3, 179–81; composition and expenditures of, 181; criticisms of, 181–2; legacy of, 195
Atlantic Manifesto, 156, 158, 161
Atlantic Provinces Economic Council (APEC), 158, 222, 227; on process of development, 5; establishment and structure of, 144–5; criticism of ADB, 182, 183; development spending policy, 183–5; criticism of ADA, 183; on the restricted planning and programming focus of ARDA, 188; conflicts with Ottawa over spending policy, 185; 1980 analysis of DREE, 275–6
Atlantic Provinces Research Board (APRB), 145

Banting, Keith, 265–6
Barrett, Gene, 24–5, 27

involvement of in gypsum strike, 151; struggle for security of, 151

Lalonde, Marc, 215; as federal minister of energy in 1980, 270

Lamontagne, Maurice, 166, 178, 187

LeBlanc, Romeo, federal minister of fisheries, 242, 299–300, 302

Lessard, Marcel, minister responsible for regional development in 1974, 224, 264

Lewis, John L., international president of UMW, 56

Liberal party, federal: 1948 National Convention, 124; intra-party relations, 125–6; erosion of Maritime support for, 140; on 1957 and 1958 elections, 164; in the early 1960s, 164–5; the 1958 national leadership convention, 165; reconstruction of after 1958, 165–7; regional-development objectives of in early 1960s, 182–3; reaction of to DOSCO crisis in late 1960s, 199; in the mid-1960s and 1970s, 231–2; elimination of as a major party in Western Canada, 269, campaign platform of in 1980 general election, 269; regional and industrial development strategy of after 1980, 271

Liberal party of Nova Scotia: repudiation of past policies and advocacy of new social legislation by, 79; 1933 election platform of, 79–80; election victory of in 1970, 233

lumber industry, post-war decline of Maritime, 44

Lumley, Ed, minister responsible for DRIE in 1982, 293

McCurdy, F.B., attempts of to create an all-party union within Nova Scotia, 54

McCurdy faction, in Nova Scotia Conservative party, 76, 78

Macdonald, Angus L., premier of Nova Scotia: election as provincial leader, 79; limits of populism and reformism of, 85; social and economic conservatism of, 129–30; anti-bureaucratic and anti-planning philosophy of, 130–1; on provincial autonomy, 117–18; on centralism and bureaucracy, 117; position on 1948 federal leadership convention, 125; reaction of to Dawson Commission, 117; opposition of to post-war dominion-provincial fiscal proposals, 120–1

McDonough, Alexa, leader of Nova Scotia NDP, 281

MacEachen, Allan J., Nova Scotia MP and federal cabinet minister, 200–1, 302; as federal finance minister in 1980, 273

MacEwan, Paul, 280–1

McKinnon, Judge A.H., 151–2; 1962 report of, 152

Mackintosh, W.A., application of staples thesis of to Maritimes, 12–13

MacLaughlin, J.B., 56, 76

MacLean Commission, 63, 69; recommendations of, 58

McNair, John, premier of New Brunswick, response of to 1945 'Dominion Offer,' 121

MacPherson Commission, 158

Mahon, Rianne, 323

Manpower and Immigration, Department of: creation of, 191; programs of, 192

manufacturing: regional capacity of, 6; growth rate of in Maritimes after 1890, 37; Americanization of, 37–8; decline of regional capacity of, 43; in the Maritimes in the 1960s,

THE STATE AND ECONOMIC LIFE

Editors: Mel Watkins, University of Toronto; Leo Panitch, York University

This series, begun in 1978, includes original studies in the general area of
Canadian political economy and economic history, with particular emphasis on
the part played by the government in shaping the economy. Collections of
shorter studies, as well as theoretical or internationally comparative works,
may also be included.